Intercultural Communication
for Everyday Life

Intercultural Communication
for Everyday Life

John R. Baldwin, Robin R. Means Coleman,
Alberto González, and Suchitra Shenoy-Packer

WILEY Blackwell

This edition first published 2014
© 2014 John R. Baldwin, Robin R. Means Coleman, Alberto González, and Suchitra
Shenoy-Packer

Registered Office
John Wiley & Sons Ltd, The Atrium, Southern Gate, Chichester, West Sussex, PO19 8SQ, UK

Editorial Offices
350 Main Street, Malden, MA 02148–5020, USA
9600 Garsington Road, Oxford, OX4 2DQ, UK
The Atrium, Southern Gate, Chichester, West Sussex, PO19 8SQ, UK

For details of our global editorial offices, for customer services, and for information about
how to apply for permission to reuse the copyright material in this book please see our website at
www.wiley.com/wiley-blackwell.

Library of Congress Cataloging-in-Publication Data

Intercultural communication for everyday life / [edited by] John R. Baldwin, Robin R. Means
Coleman, Alberto González, and Suchitra Shenoy-Packer.
       pages   cm
   Includes bibliographical references and index.
   ISBN 978-1-4443-3236-0 (pbk.)
 1. Communication—Philosophy.   2. Intercultural communication.   I. Baldwin, John R., 1960–
   P90.I5545 2014
   302.23—dc23

                                        2013039721

A catalogue record for this book is available from the British Library.

Cover image: Paul Klee, *Individualized altimetry of stripes*, 1930. De Agostini Picture Library /
Bridgeman Art Library
Cover design by Simon Levy

Set in 10/12.5pt Minion by SPi Publisher Services, Pondicherry, India
Printed and bound in Singapore by Markono Print Media Pte Ltd

1   2014

Brief contents

Contents

Part two Elements 69

Part three Messages 135

Preface

Global needs meet an engaged community

There are increased interconnections in the world at large—from international business and education opportunities to domestic and international crises. There is open conflict in Syria, Burma, Somalia, and Colombia, and dormant conflicts, quiet but never quite resolved, in Palestine, Cyprus, Northern Ireland, and many other places. Recent natural disasters of cataclysmic proportions have struck Indonesia (2004), Japan (2011), and Haiti (2012), each demanding forces of collaborating international and domestic workers. Governments work across cultures and across nations (concepts we will treat separately in this book) to fight against the international flow of the drug trade, human trafficking, and other issues. And, at the same time, we have seen great changes within and across societies, from the "Arab Spring" and the overthrow of several totalitarian governments to the renewed debate over same-sex marriage in the United States in 2013.

Grand-scale problems require complex solutions; and these solutions require the synergy of efforts of people with different cultural perspectives. But even if we do not see the connection of global issues to our own lives or ever travel abroad, culture touches our lives. We live in a multicultural, global economy, where, to survive, most large businesses employ, buy, and sell across cultural and national lines. Many of us, regardless of our country of residence, have doctors, teachers, bosses, students, or employees from "cultures" besides our own. With new and interactive media, we might play online games, chat, or develop friendships or romances with people in other lands without leaving our own borders. Besides this, we each live within and are influenced and sometimes constrained by our own cultures. The more we know about our own culture, the more effective we will be where we live, the more we can engage in issues and problems within our own community (which have cultural elements), and the more we will see the strengths and limits of our own culture. As we see these strengths and limits, we will have more likelihood of being able to make choices and change those cultures.

Whether we are discussing world-level crises or community issues, there is a bright spot as we talk about social issues, and that is the rise of involvement of citizens in the public sphere—at least in some ways. Russell Dalton (2009) reports statistics showing that while the younger generation (Gen Y) has a decreased sense of citizen "duty" in terms of things such as following the law without thought, or voting, they have an increased sense of citizen "engagement", which includes seeking to understand opinions of others, "direct action, and elite-challenging activities" (p. 32). Engagement and duty are both impacted by things such as level of education, racial background, and religiosity. Increasingly, companies are encouraging their employees to participate in the community, and universities are promoting civic and political engagement.

There seems to be a fresh wind in the air as students in secondary schools, colleges, and universities seek to give back to the community. After a post-2005 decline, voluntarism increased to a high-point in 2011 ("Volunteering and Civic Life," 2012; Volunteering/Community Service, 2010), and service learning opportunities at universities abound. Some have said that one of the characteristics of the up-and-coming generation is a sense of social responsibility, though one study suggests that the Millennial Generation "may not be the caring, socially conscious environmentalists some have portrayed them to be" (Chau, 2012). Instead, they might be focusing more on "money, image, and fame". Statistics suggest that, at least in terms of volunteering, 16–18 year olds and those aged 25 and older historically volunteer more than the 18–25 set (Volunteering/Community Service, 2010). Students (especially in Western cultures like the United States, where "pragmatism" or "practicality" is a core value) have always wanted to study "what works"—what leads to better message production and consumption, better workplace practices, better relationships. But many students today often also seek ideas to help them engage better with the community. And knowledge of culture is central to such engagement.

Why another intercultural text? (Features of this book)

The need for solutions for community, as well as the growing interest in community engagement, is a driving force for the present book. We have three main goals in writing this text. First, we want to provide responsible knowledge of things cultural. Many introductory textbooks present simple explanations of things for the student new to cultural issues. We believe students are capable of deep thought, so, where possible, we introduce basic ideas, but then challenge students to critical thought about those ideas. Our second goal is for readers to be able to take something practical from the text for their own workplaces, relationships, and schooling, the traditional focus of intercultural studies. But the third goal is to bring an imagination of possibilities for community engagement—civic or political. We want to encourage readers, and ourselves as authors, to find ways to make the knowledge practical for making people's lives better, to address social issues, to meet the personal needs of people in our lives and in our classrooms. With this in mind, this book has several distinctive features:

- → The authors write for introductory readers, with clear definition of terms, but use original frameworks and introduce theories in a way that does not condescend to the reader.

- → We treat culture complexly. While we sometimes discuss national cultures, through most of the book we see cultures as distinct from national boundaries. Some cultures cross national boundaries, and a single city might have people of many different cultures within it. There are regional, urban–rural, or other cultural differences within nations; even organizations have cultures.

- → We construct a vision of culture that uses examples from around the world as much as possible, seeking to remove some of our own U.S.-centric bias as authors, and we use examples that relate to a variety of types of diversity, including age, sex, race, religion, and sexual orientation. While these, in and of themselves, do not constitute cultures, they often contain cultural elements, and there are cultural constructions of how a society treats different groups that deserve our attention as engaged citizens.

→ As authors with diverse backgrounds—rhetoric, media and African American studies, organizational communication, and intercultural/interpersonal communication— we (re)introduce notions to the study of intercultural communication not present in many books, including large sections on intercultural ethics and chapters on media, rhetoric, and globalization.

→ Throughout the book, we promote civic engagement with cues toward individual intercultural effectiveness and giving back to the community in socially relevant ways; we do this throughout the chapters and with discussion questions and engagement activities at the end of each chapter.

→ We weave pedagogy throughout the text with student-centered examples, thought (or "text") boxes, applications, critical thinking questions, a glossary of key terms, and online resources for students and instructors. These online resources include sample syllabi, test questions, glossary terms, power points, and class exercise options.

Focus and direction of this book

With these goals in mind, our text begins with a discussion of the foundations of intercultural communication. In chapter 1, we introduce several reasons why it is important to study intercultural communication, with updated situations and examples of world and community diversity. In chapter 2, we introduce our central concepts of political and civic engagement and discuss the importance and nature of ethical intercultural communication and cultural research. We then turn to different ways to define culture (chapter 3).

The second portion of the book focuses on elements that inform the intercultural communication process, starting with the foundation upon which all communication rests— values, beliefs, and world view (chapter 4). We consider the view we have of ourselves as that relates to the groups to which we belong—identity (chapter 5)—and then look at our attitudes towards those of other identities (chapter 6).

In the third part of our book, we look at the exchange of messages through different channels. We begin with verbal communication—that is, face-to-face communication as it relates to the use of words in interaction (chapter 7). We next consider the various channels of face-to-face communication that do not use words—nonverbal communication (chapter 8). This includes discussion of things such as space, time, touch, eye contact, and gesture. We examine messages given by speakers or in texts to persuade—rhetoric (chapter 9). Finally, we look at aspects of mediated communication, in terms of how we mediate identity and culture (chapter 10).

Our final section contains issues and contexts of intercultural communication, starting with the impacts of globalization, especially on media (chapter 11), then moving to cross-cultural adaptation and intercultural communication competence (chapter 12), intercultural relations, conflict, and negotiation (chapter 13), political communication (chapter 14), and finally the organizational context (chapter 15).

The order is intended to be flexible for the instructor. As we have used drafts of this text in our own teaching, we find that, after the foundational chapters, each chapter stands on its own; we can choose the chapters that best meet our needs, for example, with a special unit on media (or leaving media out), or skipping over the section on personal relationships. We encourage the student reading this preface to start each chapter you read by looking at the objectives at the top of each chapter—those are things that we, the authors, felt were most important as we wrote. Then read the discussion questions at the end. As you read, start with an understanding of the larger structure and bolded terms in the chapter, before you try to learn specific details.

In each area, there are areas for practical applications of culture to work and school, ways in which knowledge of culture will teach us about ourselves and give us more freedom over our choices, and aspects that will allow us to be more effective and engaged citizens in our communities.

References

Chau, J. (March 15, 2012). Millennials are more "Generation Me" than "Generation We," study finds. *The Chronicle of Higher Education*. Retrieved April 11, 2013, at http://chronicle.com/article/Millennials-Are-More/131175/.

Dalton, R. J. (2009). *The good citizen: How a younger generation is reshaping American politics* (rev. ed.). Washington, DC: CQ Press.

Volunteering/Community Service (2010). *CIRCLE: The Center for Information & Research on Civic Learning and Engagement*. Retrieved April 11, 2013, at http://www.civicyouth.org/quick-facts/volunteeringcommunity-service/.

Volunteering and civic life in America, 2012. (27 Nov, 2012). *The Federal Agency for Service and Volunteering*. Accessed January 31, 2013, at http://www.volunteeringinamerica.gov/index.cfm.

Acknowledgements

Each of the co-authors thanks the other authors for their contributions and feedback on chapters. But we are especially grateful to the people we have worked with at Wiley, especially Deirdre Ilkson, Elizabeth Swayze, Sarah Tracy, and Julia Kirk (our image wizard). We would also like to thank Jane Taylor (photos and permissions), Grace Fairley(website/instructor's manual), and Nora Naughton (final page proofs) for their countless hours of work on the project. These fine people have been a constant encouragement to us in the writing of this book, a process that, in the end, took four years. They believed in us and checked on us, sometimes with polite reminders to "get it in gear". We also thank the many anonymous reviewers that have provided comments on earlier versions of this text. You have made this a better text than it would have been with only our own efforts.

As it has come to revisions, we thank those who have helped us with different concepts. We appreciate the help of Professor Zhong Xin (professor of the School of Journalism and Communication, and Deputy Director of Public Communication Research Institute, Renmin University) and Professor Chen Xuan (School of Journalism, Journalism and Social Development Research Center, Renmin University) for their help understanding China's media policy, and to our colleagues Sandra Metts, Joe Blaney, Lance Lippert, and Steve Hunt for giving us insight on different aspects of the book, from face to media to civic engagement. A special thanks to Joe Zompetti, who has given us constant insight on everything semiotic, postmodern, postcolonial, and otherwise critical. And we thank our students, from whom we always learn so much, as we ourselves continue to be "students" of culture. Thanks especially to Liz Miller, graduate student at Illinois State, for giving a close read of much of the manuscript.

Finally, we thank our families and partners for putting up with the hours of work that the task has entailed, and for their support in the process. With family and connection in mind, John dedicates this book to his mom, Linda Jensen-Speight, who passed from this life quietly, during the final revisions of the text.

Robin wishes to thank Prof. William Laf Youmans, George Washington University, for his sage advice and contributions to the "globalization" chapter. She thanks John Baldwin for his vision and leadership on this project. And, a job well done to Alberto González and Suchitra Shenoy-Packer—"It was my pleasure working with you".

Al acknowledges the assistance of Eun Young Lee. He dedicates this book to the undergraduate and graduate student interculturalists at BGSU.

Suchitra dedicates this book to her students at Purdue University and DePaul University.

About the website

This text has a comprehensive companion website which features the following resources for instructors:

→ Powerpoint slides to accompany each chapter

→ Sample syllabi for both undergraduate and graduate courses

→ Testbank, containing problems for each chapter, along with answers

→ Glossary

→ Exercises for all chapters, along with a resource list and some general assignments.

Please visit www.wiley.com/go/baldwin to access the materials.

Walk through

Part opening page The book is divided into four parts. Each part opens with a list of the chapters it contains, followed by a short introduction summarizing the purposes of each chapter.

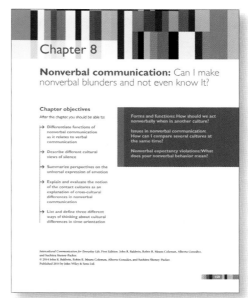

Chapter opening page Each chapter opens with a list of the main chapter objectives and the chapter table of contents.

End-of-chapter pedagogy Each chapter ends with a summary, a listing of the key terms in the chapter, discussion questions, action points, details of further resources under the heading "For More Information," and references.

Key terms and glossary Key terms are introduced in bold and clearly defined both in the text and in a complete glossary at the end of the book.

On the net This feature provides students with an activity based on visiting a website that ties into the text discussion.

Break it down These exercises encourage students to engage in civic action and apply their knowledge to the world at large.

music was that the lyrics centered on messages of anti-materialism, anarchy, freedom from conformity, and peace. The music launched a movement among young people who called themselves "Punks." Punks embodied the music through dress, speech, and lifestyle. It is a lifestyle, or scene, that has been particularly attractive to Whites, even promoting White identity through its representation of non-Whites (Duncombe & Tremblay, 2011). Though the punk scene has been understood to be predominately White, this cannot be further from the truth. James Spooner, in his 2003 documentary film *Afro-Punk*, chronicles a social movement within Black communities in the U.S. that led Black youths to the punk culture. You can even listen to "punk international" radio stations online. So, even though punk began as an expression of engagement among a particular youth identity in working class Britain, it continues to evolve, creating a connection that crosses national and race identities.

What do you think? View Afro-Punk artist James Spooner's film (http://www.afropunk.com/page/afropunk-the-movie). What are some of the reasons that Black youth would join a predominantly White movement (one that has even been understood at the margins to be exclusionary and racist)? What crises, contestations, and conflicts do Black youth encounter from Whites, Blacks, and society as a whole? How does their decision to lay claim to and proclaim their identity as punks reveal this to be an identity politics "move?" Overall, what are the identity experiences of Afro-Punks?

Figure 5.3 James Spooner, Toronto, September 10, 2007. Source: Scott Gries/Getty Images.

What do you think? These boxes ask the reader to think critically on an issue or examine their own opinions on a subject.

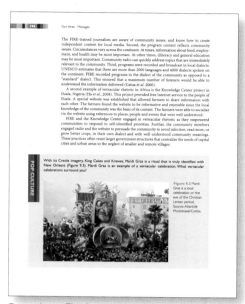

The FIRE-trained journalists are aware of community issues, and know how to create independent content for local media. Second, the program content reflects community issues. Circumstances vary across the continent. At times, information about food, employment, and health may be most important. At other times, illiteracy and general education may be most important. Community radio can quickly address topics that are immediately relevant to the community. Third, programs were recorded and broadcast in local dialects. UNESCO estimates that there are more than 2000 languages and 4000 dialects spoken on the continent. FIRE recorded programs in the dialect of the community as opposed to a "standard" dialect. This ensured that a maximum number of listeners would be able to understand the information delivered (Gatua *et al.* 2000).

A second example of vernacular rhetoric in Africa is the Knowledge Center project in Ihiala, Nigeria (Ha *et al.*, 2008). This project provided free Internet service to the people of Ihiala. A special website was established that allowed farmers to share information with each other. The farmers found the website to be informative and enjoyable since the local knowledge of the community was the basis of its content. The farmers were able to socialize via the website using references to places, people and events that were well understood.

FIRE and the Knowledge Center engaged in vernacular rhetoric as they empowered communities to respond to self-identified priorities. Further, the community members engaged radio and the website to persuade the community to avoid infection, read more, or grow better crops, in their own dialect and with well-understood community meanings. These practices often resist larger government structures that centralize the needs of capital cities and urban areas to the neglect of smaller and remote villages.

POP CULTURE

With its Creole imagery, King Cakes and Krewes, Mardi Gras is a ritual that is truly identified with New Orleans (Figure 9.3). Mardi Gras is an example of a vernacular celebration. What vernacular celebrations surround you?

Figure 9.3 Mardi Gras is a local celebration on the eve of the Christian Lenten period. Source: Atlantide Phototravel/Corbis.

Pop culture This feature uses examples from the media and pop culture as jumping off points for the reader to apply their knowledge.

Foundations

I f you try to build a structure of some sort, you know that you need certain materials to make it—bricks, wood, plastic, metal—and some plan for the structure—a blueprint. As you consider these things, you will need to think of how the building will be used. Will it be a restaurant? A bank? A hockey rink? But before you lay the first brick, you must make sure that your building is on firm footing: you need a good foundation.

In the same way, we will soon describe the things that make up intercultural communication (part two), the ways we use it (part three), and the different functions we can use it for (part four). We provided a general road map to the book at the end of the Preface. But before we do any of that, we need to lay a groundwork—a foundation—of some basic principles. That is the purpose of the first part of the book.

In chapter 1, we provide a rationale for studying intercultural communication. Many companies and students no longer require a reason for studying intercultural communication, as the need for skills in this area are part of conventional wisdom. Still, you may find the facts in the section interesting, and as you talk to future employers of your skills in intercultural communication, some of them may still need convincing of the need to consider culture. Even though there are many benefits of studying intercultural communication, there are also some limitations, which we also address. Finally, we speak briefly about the history of the study of intercultural communication. We speak of it because it gives us context for what we study, and context is important to understanding what we do and why we do it. We treat it briefly, as we want to keep our focus primarily practical.

Chapter 2 introduces what we feel are the most important principles for practicing and researching intercultural communication. We could, here, discuss what it means to be a

Intercultural Communication for Everyday Life, First Edition. John R. Baldwin, Robin R. Means Coleman, Alberto González, and Suchitra Shenoy-Packer.
© 2014 John R. Baldwin, Robin R. Means Coleman, Alberto González, and Suchitra Shenoy-Packer.
Published 2014 by John Wiley & Sons Ltd.

"competent" communicator across cultures, but we need to know more about sending and receiving messages first. It is important that we be aware of what it means to be ethical in our communication, so we discuss different ethical approaches in depth. It is an ethical position by the authors that leads us to feel that communication—and intercultural communication especially—should be related to civic and political action, so we introduce these terms and their relationship to intercultural communication. Finally, as much of what we understand about culture involves research of some sort, we introduce different ways of seeing the world as they relate to studying culture and communication.

Finally, in chapter 3, we are ready to introduce a definition of culture; but we notice that defining culture is not that easy, because people from different disciplines often see culture in different and opposing ways. We discuss some of these ways and provide our own tentative definition. We describe some of the key components of culture, such as values, norms, and beliefs, and then provide a model to help explain the influences that might be present, to greater or lesser degrees, in any communication, but especially in intercultural or intergroup communication.

With these foundations—a reason to study culture and communication, an understanding of ethical communication and civic engagement, and an view of the nature of culture—we will be able to look more closely at the components that impact the creation and interpretation of messages between and within cultures.

Chapter 1

A rationale for studying intercultural communication: Why should we know about other cultures?

Chapter objectives

After this chapter, you should be able to:

→ **Provide several reasons, with evidence, as to why it is important to study intercultural communication**

→ **Describe possible limitations of studying intercultural communication**

→ **Summarize briefly the history of intercultural communication as a field of research**

Building a rationale: Why do we need to know about intercultural communication?

The history and focus of intercultural communication: Where did we come from?

Intercultural Communication for Everyday Life, First Edition. John R. Baldwin, Robin R. Means Coleman, Alberto González, and Suchitra Shenoy-Packer.
© 2014 John R. Baldwin, Robin R. Means Coleman, Alberto González, and Suchitra Shenoy-Packer.
Published 2014 by John Wiley & Sons Ltd.

n 1994, a tsunami hit countries in the Indian Ocean, triggered by an earthquake measuring 9.1 on the Richter scale—the power of about 23,000 atomic bombs (*National Geographic News*, 2005). The tsunami destroyed whole cities and vast tracts of farmland and made many formerly occupied islands uninhabitable. It killed more than 225,000 people in countries including Indonesia, India, Sri Lanka, Thailand, and the Maldives (Brunner, 2007). The World Bank Fact Sheet (Tsunami recovery in Indonesia, Dec, 2006) listed the need for 80–100,000 homes and noted the destruction of more than 2000 schools and 100 health facilities. The World Bank enlisted the help of 15 nations and international agencies (the World Bank, the Asian Development Bank, and the European Commission) to help with the repair and restoration of the region (Aceh Post-Tsunami Reconstruction, 2006). Many such disasters have occurred since, including the 2011 earthquake and resulting tsunami in Japan (see Figure 1.1).

In this story, we see a major international crisis that required multicultural and multinational cooperation. While this case reflects an obvious need for intercultural communication, individuals can also benefit from such an education, even if they never travel outside of their hometown. Many students around the world today are re-investing in their community, with a sense of social responsibility that surpasses that of their parents. Many readers of this book are members of that generation, but even those of different ages may find themselves increasingly aware of the world around them. In this chapter, we highlight the importance of understanding intercultural communication. We then turn our attention to the reasons that we should bring that understanding back to the communities—local, regional, and world—in which we live.

Figure 1.1 International workers cooperate after the Japanese Tsunami of 2011. What role could you have in international cooperation to solve world problems?
Source: YONHAP/EPA.

Building a rationale: Why do we need to know about intercultural communication?

Many university researchers, journalists, business leaders, civic leaders, and bloggers around the world have begun to call our attention to the need to understand cultures and intercultural communication. Whereas at one time, one had to justify the need for an organization or individual to study other cultures, in today's globalized world such a need seems simply to be assumed. The reasons and benefits of studying intercultural communication are broad, from personal growth to community investment to financial incentives. We review these and other motives here.

But before we begin, we should probably define some key terms. Each of these is complex, and we will discuss them in more detail in chapter 3. We will define **culture** simply as the way of life of a group of people, including symbols, values, behaviors, artifacts, and other shared aspects. Culture continually evolves as people share messages, and, often, it is the result of struggle between different groups who share different perspectives, interests, and power relationships (Hecht *et al.*, 2006). For our purposes, **communication** is the process of creating and sending symbolic behavior, and the interpretation of behavior between people. And **intercultural communication** occurs when culture impacts the communication between two or more people enough to make a difference. This differs from **international communication**, which focuses on media systems. Communication between diplomats and international politicians is intercultural, but this is a special type of communication as the communicators represent not only their own interests, but also those of larger organizations or nations. This last form of communication might take place for economic advancement or for the addressing of world problems. UNESCO, in its 2009 World Report executive summary, highlights the need for dialogue across many areas of social and global development. In its closing recommendations, it advocates the development of guidelines for cross-cultural dialogue, the creation and distribution of audio-visual (mediated) materials that are culturally sensitive, the promotion of (cross-cultural) media literacy, the development of minority–majority member dialogues within national cultures, and the creation of "real and virtual forums" for the development of "cultural intelligence" in the business and marketing world (UNESCO, 2009, p. 35). In fact, the name of the UNESCO report involves "cultural diversity" and "intercultural dialogue." But as we shall see, addressing global problems is only one reason to study intercultural communication.

The personal growth motive

Many students live in the here and now—the world of room- or apartment-mates, school or sports organizations, and jobs. Our first motive has to do with the benefit to you, as a person, of learning about other cultures. While there are many personal benefits in learning about other cultures, we will focus on three: worldmindedness, self-awareness, and personal empowerment.

First, learning about cultures and intercultural communication can simply help us better understand others in the world. Bradford 'J' Hall (2003) lists "freedom from ignorance" as one of the benefits of studying intercultural communication (p. 22). Knowing about other cultures helps us to be more responsible employees, travelers, consumers and producers of media, and world citizens, bringing to each interaction an increased awareness of others and competence. Hall states, "As we are freed from ignorance and negative attributions, we are able to build better relationships. . . with a wide variety of people" (p. 22). Communication and contact over time can bring us, in both our face-to-face and socially mediated interactions, from a state of ethnocentrism, where we feel that our way is best, to a state where we see the value in the perspectives and ways of living of others. The greatest benefit will come from both education and contact, as these can help us to appreciate cultural difference within our own nation and across borders (see chapter 5).

As we learn more about other cultures, we also learn more about our own cultures and about ourselves. The more people study other languages, the more they learn about their own language; much the same is true when studying cultures. If you grow up in a culture that makes arguments through deductive, linear logic ("If A is true, and B is true, then C must be true"), you may never be aware of that approach to argumentation until you study or live in a culture in which one makes an argument through an extended, even circular story.

Finally, knowledge of and extended experience with other cultures make us more flexible as individuals. Young Yun Kim and Brent Ruben (1988) suggest that learning new cultures gives us new ways to think, feel, and act. We might, over time, become "intercultural persons," able to move freely between cultures, or at least understand different cultural perspectives more easily. This knowledge makes us aware that the things that we always took for granted as simply fact, or "natural," are, in fact, cultural. We realize that what we always thought was friendship, success, beauty, family, or democracy is in fact something that our culture has defined for us, and often such forces are not simply the neutral flowing of culture from one construction of beauty to another, but are manipulated by corporations, advertisers, politicians, and citizens who benefit from particular views of the world. Knowledge of cultures gives us the agency to choose between different ways of being a friend or being successful. It "gives us a broader view of our own lives and the problems we face" (Hall, 2003, p. 22), even if our choices are constrained by social, political, and economic circumstances.

The social responsibility motive

We are not simply isolated individuals—we live in contact with others, and we have responsibility to live together peaceably and ethically (see chapter 2). But, as Marshall McLuhan's (1962) metaphor of the Global Village illustrates, our communities become more interconnected because of increased technology, media, and ease of travel. In addition, more and more people share this planet with its limited space and resources. As well, a complex web of changing labor relations, social policies, tribal and international conflicts, religious fervor, and other things lead to an increase in social problems. Some of these come from the growing stress on the environment brought about by an increase both of people and of industry. As we face global environmental change (and debate the causes of that change), there is an increased need for global discussion among leaders for policies that are equitable to nations and that can seek to preserve and improve the environment. One such effort was the Kyoto Protocol (2012), an initiative by the United Nations Framework Convention on Climate Change, aimed at encouraging 37 industrialized nations to work more actively to reduce greenhouse gases.

ON THE NET

The **UN Framework Convention on Climate Change** lists 191 nations that have ratified the **Kyoto Protocol**, established in 1997 to reduce greenhouse emissions: http://unfccc.int/kyoto_protocol/status_of_ratification/items/2613.php. Is your nation among those that have ratified it? Go onto websites such as http://www.guardian.co.uk/news/datablog/2011/jan/31/world-carbon-dioxide-emissions-country-data-co2 or http://www.carbonplanet.com/country_emissions to see where your country ranks in total and per capita emissions. What are some of the reasons that some of the countries with the highest production of greenhouse gases might not ratify an agreement such as the **Kyoto Protocol**? What are the implications for such choices for citizens of the countries involved?

Of course, the environment is only one of the issues that demand global cooperation. A global population clock (Current world population, n.d.) gives the population of the world, at the writing of this paragraph, as 7,109,925,897. According to the World Bank (2013), about 20% of those live in poverty (defined here as less than $U.S. 1.25 income per person per day), or 1.22 billion in 2010. Although it is good news that poverty is down from 43% of the earth's population in 1990, poverty still remains a pressing problem. But how we address it requires a "dialogic" approach (Martin, *et al.*, 2002), in which we talk with people within the situation to understand their own view of poverty and how to address it (see chapter 2). A UNESCO World Report (2009) advises, "Cultural perspectives shape how poverty is understood and experienced" (p. 25). Developmental approaches must take into account local cultural perspectives to be successful. This holds true for issues such as human trafficking, drug trafficking, child soldiers, violence against women, and the search for cures for illnesses such as HIV/AIDS, cancer, or heart disease.

In addition to social issues, wars and armed conflicts are occurring throughout the world. One website, Wars in the World (2012) outlines "hotspots" involving 61 different nations and 313 militias and separatist groups. In many cases, struggles are not armed, but are battled over prestige, social status, and social capital within nations, as groups strive to gain recognition and equal opportunity within their own countries, from the Roma in Hungary and other European nations to the Ainu of Japan. This includes struggles for equality for groups of different races, sexes, sexual orientations, and religious affiliations. Some might include within this discussion social class inequalities. For example, Global Finance's online magazine (Global Finance, n.d.) ranks counties based on how great the difference is between poorest and richest families, with Chile, Turkey, Mexico, and the United States being at the unequal end of the spectrum, and Slovenia, Denmark, and Norway having the most equality in incomes. Difference in worker pay may be another indicator of inequality. A popular Internet image (see Figure 1.2) points out supposed disparity among CEOs and average employees in certain countries. However, a *Tampa Bay Times* online news article links to reports that show that the U.S. figure has no basis in research (*Tampa Bay Times*, 2012). The article cites several reputable organizations like the Institute for Policy Studies and the Economic Policy Institute to note that the current ratio is probably only somewhere between 185 to 1 and 325 to 1. Such discrepancies led to the 2011 Occupy Wall Street movement and the protest for economic justice for the "99%." U.S. American CEOs don't consider the contrast to worker pay or even to their cross-national peers, to be important. Rather, they consider their pay comparable to peers in other high-producing industries.

Figure 1.2 This Internet image suggests a greater disparity in pay between senior employees and average workers in some nations than others. However, some research suggests the figures may be exaggerated. What are the benefits or issues of having extremely highly paid CEOs? Source: *Tampa Bay Times*, 2012.

Country	Ratio of pay CEO : Average worker
Japan	11.1
Germany	12.1
France	15.1
Italy	20.1
Canada	20.1
South Africa	21.1
Britain	22.1
Mexico	47.1
Venezuela	50.1
United States	475.1

The economic motive

Even though movements like Occupy Wall Street claim economic injustice, in part, at the hands of big business, we could not exist without corporations, and they have made contributions to societies worldwide. Most students work for some organization at some point in their lives, and it is the business context that provides our next motive for the study of intercultural communication. An E-How Money Internet site (Nelson, n.d.) suggests corporate profitability as the first motive for knowing how to communicate well across cultures. The article cites Wal-Mart's failed $US 1 billion expansion to Germany, led by an American manager who sought to import American practices and clerk–customer relations that just did not make sense in Germany. The company eventually withdrew from Germany.

It should come as no surprise to us that such difficulties would occur, with an ever-expanding and ever-more-interconnected international economy. Multinational corporations continue to grow, constituting an ever-increasing piece of the world economy. Several writers have argued that some multinational corporations (MNCs), such as Wal-Mart, Exxon Mobil, General Motors, and British Petroleum (BP), surpass many nations when comparing company revenues to gross domestic product (de Grauwe & Camerman, 2002). The International Trade Administration, in the United States, reports that manufactured exports support six million jobs, or nearly one out of five manufacturing jobs in the United States (Ward, 2009). Such statistics represent trends around the world. A joint study by the International Labour Office and the World Trade Organization reports that in the mid-1980s, 30% of world GDP was related to global trade; that figure had risen to 60% of world GDP by 2007.

Both the OECD and current CEOs (in an interview study of 1500 CEOs worldwide by an IBM "CEO Study") see a coming shift in global economic power from developed nations to developing nations (Radjou & Kalpa, 6 Aug, 2010). This is evidenced by world events, such as when the nation island of Samoa changed time zones from one side of the dateline to the other, skipping Friday, December 30, 2011, altogether. This changed its alignment from the United

States to its current most important trading partners, according to Prime Minister Tuilaepa Sailele Malielegaoi (ABC News, 2011). Such a shift in world economics drives a need for what Navi Radjou and Prassad Kalpa (6 Aug, 2010) call "polycentric" organizations—those that leverage potential of new employees both from the Millennial generation and from around the world. Still, only 23% of the CEOs interviewed felt that globalization would have a major impact on their organization in the next five years. And, while Western CEOs see more than 50% of their future growth as coming from world markets like India and China, only 2% have senior leadership from those areas. Statistics such as these, as well as the growing involvement with major corporations in world politics, has led Thomas McPhail (2010) to suggest that large and powerful nations have ceded their leadership of the world to the new giants—multinational corporations.

Although we see the benefit in local jobs and economies of world trade and globalization (something we will talk more about in chapter 11), we realize that these are not neutral forces. One such example is the tension between two world forums: the World Economic Forum and the World Social Forum. The World Economic Forum is "an independent international organization committed to improving the state of the world by engaging business, political, academic and other leaders of society to shape global, regional and industry agendas" (World Economic Forum, n.d.). The forum, held each year in Davos, Switzerland, is composed of leaders from 1000 organization "members" from many sectors—such as construction, engineering, food and beverage, financial services. One stipulation for membership is that the corporation members must be leaders in their sectors, often with at least $US 5 billion in turnover. Forbes rates Klaus Schwab, the leader of the forum, as number 66 among the world's most powerful people (Forbes.com, 2009).

In open opposition of the World Economic Forum, a group of people began the World Social Forum in Porto Alegre, Brazil in 2001. According to a website comparing the two forums:

> The first World Social Forum was held in Porto Alegre, Brazil in January 2001, and was conceived of by the Worker's Party of Brazil and other Brazilian civil society organizations as a counter gathering to the World Economic Forum held for decades in Davos, Switzerland. The Social Forum stands for the ideals of people-centered globalization, with "Another World is Possible!" as its battle cry. (Washington Peace Center, 2013)

The initial forum had 20,000 participants, with delegates from 117 nations. It has fought to develop local policies to resist both the cultural and economic influences of globalization, especially as such forces, according to the forum, tend to benefit the interests of more powerful economic nations and, particularly, big business. While the themes of the WSF change from year to year, common themes are democratic development, human rights, equality and non-discrimination (e.g., sexism, racism, religious sectarianism), the fight against militarization, the environment, and imperialist globalization. Members of the 2012 conference included some from the Occupy Wall Street movement in the United States and the Indignant movement in Spain. The conference had the theme "Capitalist Crisis, Social and Environmental Justice" (Utopia, 25 Jan, 2012).

Before we assume that the battle between the forums is cut and dried and without debate, we should note that the stated purpose of the World Economic Forum is "improving the state of the world" (Forbes.com, 2009). To that end, leaders are concerned with world crises and situations, but see the response as being in global economic development. So, for example, one frequent participant, Bill Gates, founder of Microsoft, pledged $US 750 million to the Global Fund, which focuses on world solutions for fighting malaria, tuberculosis, and AIDS/HIV (Treinor, 26 Jan, 2012).

The cross-cultural travel motive

In addition to the number of workers traveling abroad and the economic motive, we see, with modern technology, an increased number of international travelers for different reasons. We have noted above the high rates of international workers. However, we also see high numbers of cross-cultural travelers in three other groups—tourists, students, and refugees.

Regarding tourism, the United Nations World Tourism Organization (UNWTO) anticipated one billion tourists, either domestic or international, globally in the year 2012. The Secretary General of the UNWTO, Taleb Rifai, echoes the perspective of the UNWTO, that increased tourism can create jobs and lead to sustainable world development in an environmentally conscious manner (World Tourism Organization, 2012). Tourism, of course, has a larger impact on some countries than others. Nationmaster.com (2009a) notes that the country with the highest number of tourists (again, counting both local and international tourists) is Turkey, with the Caicos Islands (with over 12,000 tourists for each 1000 inhabitants). Other top ratios of tourist to population include places we might expect—Monaco, Caribbean and Pacific Island nations, and so on—but also Bahrain, Iceland, Cyprus, and Austria. Other countries that still thrive on tourism rate much lower in the ratio of tourist to inhabitant, such as the United States (number 105 on the list), Japan (132), and Brazil (152). While tourism is important for these locations, the impact of tourism may be on local cultures and communication. Tourism grows and falls by region and with the economy. For example, tourism in the Asia-Pacific region grew by 13% between 2009 and 2010, with the Middle East showing the highest increase in tourism (14.1%) that year (United Nations ESCAP, 2011). France was first as a destination for international travel (in contrast to the Nationmaster statistics), but third in revenue, with the United States being third on the list for arrivals, but first in terms of revenue generated, with tourists spending an average of $1616 each within the United States. To consider the impact of tourism on culture, we should consider both the number of tourists per size of population, but also the economic impact on the country (Tourism Intelligence Network, n.d.).

What do you think? What are the positive and negative aspects of a high degree of tourism on a local culture? What are some of the ways that people within a culture might receive the benefits of cross-cultural tourism while minimizing the negative impacts?

Chapter I   A rationale for studying intercultural communication: Why should we know about other cultures?

II

Figure 1.3 The number of students traveling internationally is growing by an average of 12% per year. What do you think are the reasons that drive this increase? Undergraduate international students outnumbered graduate international students in 2011/12, the first time since 2000/01. Source: Open Doors® Report on International Educational Exchange, 2012.

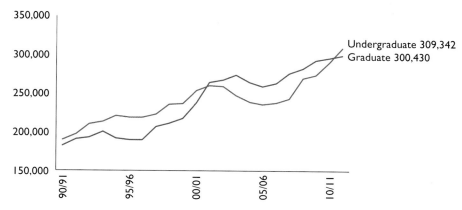

Another major source of international travel is international education. Very likely, many readers of this book are reading it in a country outside of their own. The Institute of International Education, based in the United States, reported a 5% increase in international students studying in the U.S. from the 2009/10 year to the 2010/11 year, with students from China, India, and South Korea constituting nearly 50% of the students. There were nearly 300,000 each of undergraduate and graduate students studying abroad in the United States (Institute of International Education: Open Doors, 2012). BBC News, reporting statistics from UNESCO, suggests that the increase in students crossing national borders is an international phenomenon, with a "sharp increase" of 12% of students studying internationally around the world (see Figure 1.3). China, alone, had 440,000 students abroad in 2011 (Coughlan, 9 Mar, 2011). The growth of international study has economic impacts both for host countries and for universities, but for our purposes, the greater impacts are on the students who travel abroad and on the students and teachers with whom they work.

One group of people travels not by choice but to escape hostile situations. This group consists of refugees and asylum seekers. The United Nations Refugee Agency (United Nations High Commissioner for Refugees; UNHCR, 2012–2013) defines a **refugee** as someone who has traveled outside of her or his country because of a fear of threat to freedom or life based on reasons of group belonging (e.g., race, sex, ethnicity, political affiliation, tribal group). The **asylum seeker** differs slightly in that she or he is seeking legal protection from the new state, rather than simply moving there because of conditions of strife. Some flee not from threat of a government or ruling party, but from threat of famine.

Like the groups above, these travelers do not always cross national borders. As we will see when we discuss the nature of culture in chapter 3, rarely do cultural borders coincide with national borders. Thus, an internal migration of refugees might provide just as "intercultural" an experience as the crossing of refugees from one country to another. The United Nations Refugee Agency fact sheet (*Guardian*, 2011) lists 10.5 million refugees and people in "refugee-like conditions," as well as 14.7 million internally displaced persons as of January, 2011 (see Figure 1.4). Adding these to those recently returned "stateless people" (those who do not belong to any nation state), and others, amounts to a total population of

Figure 1.4 Are there refugees or displaced persons in your country? What sort of help or support do they need? What policies and conditions lead to refugees in your nation or those that your nation is involved with? Is there anything you can do to aid refugees in your area?

Source: http://www.guardian.co.uk/news/datablog/interactive/2011/jun/20/refugee-statistics-mapped

© 2011 Guardian News & Media Ltd, reproduced with permission.

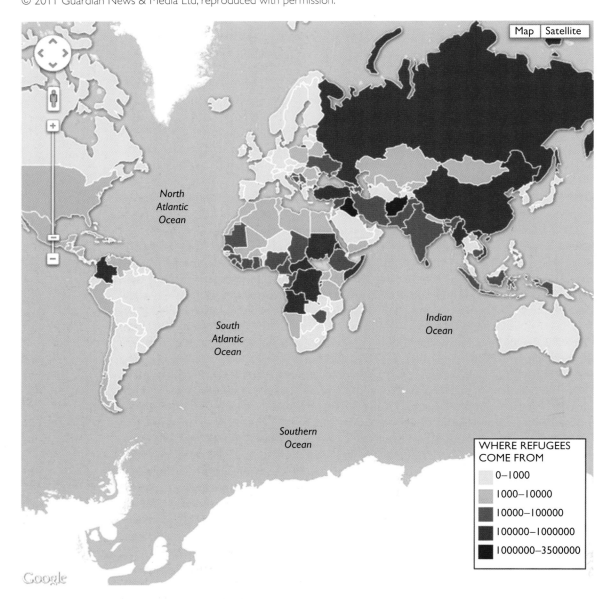

concern of 33.9 million people (Populations of concern, n.d.). Other statistics rate the number of refugees at nearly 16 million (Nationmaster.com, 2009b), with a total of 43.7 million forcibly displaced persons. Contrary to the belief of many that the majority of cross-border refugees go to the so-called "wealthy nations," four out of five of these refugees are currently housed in the developing world (UNHCR 2011 refugee statistics: *Guardian*, 2011).

The media motive

Another reason to know more about culture in general and intercultural communication specifically is that we are consumers and producers of mediated messages that travel across cultural borders. As in our discussion of cross-cultural travelers above, we should think of such cross-cultural media usage both in terms of national cultures and cultures within national boundaries. First, in terms of national cultures, new technology has drastically changed the ways in which we see the world. McPhail (2010) notes how Turner Broadcasting Company's Cable News Network (CNN) changed the way we did news, with coverage of international events in the 1980s and early 1990s, such as Tiananmen Square and the Gulf War. Like other major networks, such as the British Broadcasting Company (BBC) or Al Jazeera, CNN had international partners all over the world, in places such as Angola, Belize, Greece, and Venezuela. But the coverage made news coverage both more immediate—often with live coverage of events—and more internationally focused, something more relevant in the United States perhaps than other countries, as national network news tended to give only brief coverage of international events. In addition, the Turner Network began the rise of global media conglomerates, as Turner sought to increase cable sales with the creation of Nickelodeon, Arts & Entertainment (A&E), USA, Disney, Showtime, HBO, ESPN, and C-Span. McPhail covers giants in several industries—advertising, news services, and the international music industry. International news giants include Deutsche Welle (Germany), Channel News Asia, and Euronews. Music industry giants include Vivendi-Universal (France), Sony (Japan), EMI Group (United Kingdom), Warner (United States), and BMG (Germany).

At any one moment, depending on where we live, we see products advertised by companies in other countries, listen to music made in other countries, see adverts for products made in other countries, or watch news about what has happened in other countries. Especially in the last instance, it is helpful for us to understand the cultures involved to be able to understand what is happening in a particular location. For example, in 2011 National Geographic filmed a special on the troubling conflict between Turkish- and Greek-descended inhabitants of Cyprus, noting the division that resulted from a 1974 conflict. However, Benjamin Broome (2002) notes that Turkish and Greek Cypriots see different major turning points for the centuries-old tensions in Cyprus. The latter date, 1974, is the date of a Greek coup and, more importantly, of the arrival of Turkish troops that led to the current division of the island. This is the date the Greek Cypriots tend to label as the start of the current conflict. Turkish Cypriots, however, trace the conflicts back to the 1960s and Greek Cypriot efforts to join the island (which is off the coast of Turkey) to Greece. In this case, there are two totally opposing perspectives of the history, and, while the National Geographic programme seeks to be balanced, it takes one of the perspectives more prominently. With this in mind, we must realize that any news source or even information source we read, such as Wikipedia.com, is written from a cultural perspective.

. . . .

ON THE NET

A great deal of controversy surrounded the release and content of a video documentary, *Kony 2012*, produced by a group called Invisible Children (http://invisiblechildren.com/kony/), an advocacy and development group working with children in the war-torn areas of Uganda and its African neighbors ("Programs," n.d.)—including child soldiers (Figure 1.5a). The video is about Joseph Kony, of the Lord's Resistance Army in Uganda (Figure 1.5b), which the video names as one of the world's worst war criminals. Do some Internet research on the video. What are some different perspectives about its merits? How would a deeper understanding of Ugandan culture(s) inform you of the meanings in the video?

. . . .

Figure 1.5b Joseph Kony, of the Lord's Resistance Army in Uganda, answers journalists' questions.
Source: Stuart Price/AP/Press.

Figure 1.5a Child soldier, Uganda 1996.
Source: Lars Astrom/AP/Press Association Images.

The very presence of sources like Wikipedia and YouTube alert us to another key aspect of media, and that is the rise of computer-mediated and social media. There is no doubt that the Internet has changed our lives and, in some ways, connected us to the world. In 1995, only 0.4% of the world, or 16 million users, were on the Internet. By December, 2011, the figure had reached 2,267 million, or 32.7% of the world population (Internet growth statistics, n.d.). Sifry's Alerts (Sifry, 22 Sep, 2008) reports that Technorati, a website that tracks blog posts, was tracking 133 million blogs as of September, 2008, with about 10.4 new blog posts posted every second. *How Much Information?*, a report out of University of California, Berkeley (2003), notes the difficulty of imagining or quantifying how much "information" there is. However, based on size of information produced (e.g., five exabytes in 2002 alone, or the equivalent of 37,000 libraries the size of the Library of Congress in the United States), the amount of recorded information per person in the world (about 800 megabytes), new information via emails (400,000 terabytes/year), and so on, suggests that the amount of "new information" in the world might be doubling every three years (University of California, Berkeley, 2003).

Two things are apparent with this explosion of new information. First, if we are on the Internet, we will have contact with people from other cultures. We might play *Left for Dead* to kill off the zombies, meeting players from other cultures, then browse online news from Al Jazeera or the BBC, then video-chat with or email friends or family in another part of the world. Social networking gives us MySpace, Friendster, Google Plus, Orkut (popular in Brazil), Mixi (Japan), Renren (China), Cyworld (South Korea), and Facebook. The latter, founded in 2004, now has more than 3000 employees and 845 million users (Newsroom: Factsheet, 2012). Many of us use Twitter, possibly with worldwide feeds. Or we might engage in friendship networks or online random chats like Omegle or Chatroulette.

Break it down

Go on to a chat site with a positive reputation—preferably one that is international, such as Omegle.com or Chatroulette (chat safely!). Chat with people from your own country or others, and see what you can find out about their culture and current issues within that culture, from the other person's perspective. (If you are speaking to an individual, don't expect her or him to be able to speak for the whole culture!) What are some strengths and limitations of this exercise?

But such cross-cultural social networking also interacts with culture. Cultures shape how people use social networking sites, with research just now being published in this area. For example, a 2010 study found that Chinese and U.S. American students presented themselves differently on social networking sites, with the Chinese presenting themselves as competent or using supplication more than the U.S. Americans, and the latter using more ingratiation than the former (Chu & Choi, 2010). Another study found ethnic differences between African, Asian, and Caucasian U.S. Americans in aspects of Facebook usage, such as references to family in the "About Me" section, the number of self-descriptions, the number of groups to which they belonged and the presence of another person in their profile picture (DeAndrea *et al.*, 2010). The interconnectedness we have through the Internet and social media also has the potential to impact culture, either positively or negatively, something we will return to in our discussion of globalization (see chapter 11). Some, for example, have credited the use of cell phones and Twitter with having a major role in Middle Eastern struggles for democracy in the late 2000s.

What do you think? Having considered some of the reasons for studying culture and communication, which do you feel are the most important reasons, and why? How might some of the purposes that people study intercultural communication compete against each other? For example, could studying intercultural communication to promote national and business interests indirectly contribute to situations where one needs to study intercultural communication to help refugees or address the needs of the poor? Is there a way to reconcile such difficulties?

Challenges of studying intercultural communication

Even though there are many benefits of studying intercultural communication, Bradford "J" Hall (2003) summarizes some things to watch out for. One of these is the danger of oversimplifying our understanding of cultures. The UNESCO World Report (2009) advises, for example, against reducing our understanding of culture to national identities and to resist the danger of seeing cultures as stagnant and unchanging. There are many cultural identities within national cultures and that cross national boundaries, such as the Ewe tribe in Africa, which can be found in Ghana, Togo, and Benin, or the Basque people, who are found in Spain and France. Some cultures, such as Celtic culture, have left remnants in many nations, and other groups, such as the Roma in Europe, continue to exist in many places, with similarities among all Roma, yet many differences even within the group. We understand, by not simplifying, that cultures are fluid and constantly changing. Hall warns us against overgeneralizing—that is, while individuals are influenced by their cultures, they are not their cultures and have unique aspects and experiences that distinguish them in some ways from all other members of their culture. Finally, Hall notes, there is a tendency to exaggerate differences. This happens first of all because difference simply draws our attention more than similarity. It is much more interesting to think of how Swiss and Germans may be different than how they are alike (Kopper, 1993). But the film industry and television often magnify the differences. For instance, the 1986 Hollywood movie, *Gung Ho* (Blum & Howard, 1986), about a U.S. American factory bought and run by a Japanese company, makes Japanese and American business styles seem more different than they probably are. Finally, even research supports difference: it is much harder to publish research that highlights similarity than research that finds differences.

The history and focus of intercultural communication: Where did we come from?

With an increase of intercultural interaction and recognition of cultural groups within national boundaries, it is no surprise that scholars from the late 20th century onward have dedicated increasing time and effort to the understanding of intercultural communication. But as a field of study, intercultural communication is relatively new. Some writers look to the roots of this field of study in writers such as Charles Darwin and Sigmund Freud (Rogers & Hart, 2002). However, most see the beginning of the modern study of intercultural communication in the works of Edward T. Hall (Figure 1.6) and his colleagues at the Foreign Service institute in the 1940s and 1950s. Wendy Leeds-Hurwitz (1990) outlines how the focus of the early anthropologists and linguists set the stage for how our discipline first conceived of culture and how it would do research (See chapter 2). Hall and his colleagues saw culture as patterned and predictable. Beginning with his book *The Silent Language* (1959), Hall provided a great contribution to the study of intercultural communication. He shifted research focus from specific cultures to an examination of interaction between people from different cultures. He developed many frameworks, for space usage (**proxemics**), for time (**chronemics**), and so on, giving us many terms we still use in the discipline of intercultural communication today.

We see two important aspects for our beginnings in terms of focus and rationale for the study of intercultural communication. The first is that the study of intercultural communication began with the Foreign Service Institute, a branch of the United States government, to help its diplomats be more effective in meeting state goals (Leeds-Hurwitz, 1990). Some might argue that the very discipline was born in relations of power. But clearly, we also see an organizational focus that continues today. This relates to the second aspect: Hall's pragmatic focus. Much of the previous sociological and anthropological study of culture had been broad, looking at religious, leisure, family, education, labor, and other systems. But Hall found that his trainees most needed to know how to communicate effectively. So he and his colleagues really focused on practical

Figure 1.6 Edward T. Hall, who wrote a number of books between the 1950s and the 1970s, including *The Silent Language, The Hidden Dimension,* and *Beyond Culture,* that form a foundation for the modern study of intercultural communication.
Source: Karin B Hall/Photo © 2004 Warren Martin Hern, reproduced with permission.

aspects—how close to stand, how much to touch, how to think of time. Hall produced training methods and extended the study of intercultural communication to business workers, missionaries, and students.

Leeds-Hurwitz (1990) notes that the field of anthropology was not interested in this narrow focus on communication, so the new field of study found itself "homeless." Guo-Ming Chen and William Starosta (1998), provide an excellent, concise summary of what happened over the next few years. Our coverage will be still more concise. There was brief coverage of culture and communication in the 1960s, but the 1970s saw a great growth in the field. Many new college texts, associations, and publications began in that decade, including *The International Journal of Intercultural Relations* (a cross-disciplinary, international journal put out by SIETAR), *The Handbook of Intercultural Communication,* and the first issue of *The International and Intercultural Communication Annual.*

We call the 1970s the decade of research, as many scholars were researching a variety of topics. Young Yun Kim (1984) summarizes much research of that time, noting there was a lot of research in the fields of cross-cultural transitions (e.g., culture shock), international business, cross-cultural counseling, and technology transfer.

We call the 1980s the decade of theory; where scholars were looking at the connection between many variables in the 1970s, in 1983, the first major theory book came out,

Intercultural Communication Theory: Current Perspectives, an issue of *The International and Intercultural Communication Annual* edited by William Gudykunst. In 1988, Kim and Gudykunst published a second volume of the annual on current theories, *Theories in Intercultural Communication*. Richard Wiseman, a colleague of Gudykunst's, published a third issue of the annual, *Intercultural Communication Theory*, in 1995. Many, but not all, of the theories in these books sought to find the variables that predicted certain aspects of intercultural communication, such as conflict outcomes, adjustment, cross-cultural relational development, or effectiveness. Many theories are from a similar perspective, treating communication research as social science and seeking causes and effects of culture and communication or trying to predict differences between cultural communication styles.

Even as early as 1987, scholars were beginning to attempt to "de-Westernize" communication theory. Thus, Daniel Kincaid (1987) edited a book compiling writings of different authors from different nations on notions such as Chinese rhetoric. New currents were swirling in the discipline. Ethnography of communication—a study of specific cultures largely using observation—had been growing out of sociology into communication during the 1980s, and scholars were clearly seeing the relevance to culture studies; however, this approach treated culture differently (see chapter 3)—as more fluid and local, for example, the culture of Grateful Dead fans or of a specific Chicago motorcycle gang. At the same time, informed by Marxist studies, came a new approach that looked specifically at power relations in society, such as **patriarchy** and **racism**, or the way some definitions (such as of success, democracy, freedom, or family) gain power over other ideas. This approach questioned the very content of the intercultural communication field. Theory books and journals, some claimed, kept a particular academic view of what "theory" and "culture" were, excluding other views. Other writers have also challenged Western ideas of theory. Molefi Kete Asante (1980) promotes an Afrocentric perspective, challenging the ability of Western theory to describe the realities of African and African-descended peoples. More recently, Yoshitaka Miike (2007, 2010) argues that Western theories tend to speak in "totalizing" terms, as if European reality reflects that of all cultures. Western theory "disregards, downplays, or overshadows certain values and elements that have been historically embraced in non-Western cultures" (2010, p. 3). Miike (2007) feels that Western theories often ignore cultural contexts and tend to privilege notions such as individuality and independence, self-enhancement, reason, rights and freedom, and pragmatism and materialism.

The 1990s became a decade of controversy. For example, previous handbooks of intercultural communication (e.g., Asante & Gudykunst, 1989; Gudykunst & Mody, 2002) contained some, but little ethnographic work and almost no critical approaches. But a 2010 handbook (Nakayama & Halualani) focuses exclusively on newer approaches to culture and intercultural communication that frequently deal with dominant and subordinate cultures, mistreating or misrepresenting people from other cultures, and social inequality. If your library has access to *The International and Intercultural Communication Annual*, you will see that it is always rich, each issue focusing on a specific topic (organizations, identity, relationships, etc.), but with a clear shift in the 1990s to also include issues of empowerment and resistance.

Parallel to the changes in content in the field, there has been an increasing growth in the internationalization of researchers. We see three major changes in the last 15 years: a tremendous increase of qualitative and critical research; a great influx of mediated and social media communication; and a rise of international scholars. In fact, a great many of the authors currently publishing in the journals that are focused on intercultural communication come from all over the world. And their focus is on much more than business and foreign travel and culture shock. It includes issues of rhetoric (e.g., public speech), advertising, and small group communication, but also protest and the ways dominant, powerful nations negatively impact nations with growing media economies in terms of cultural flow. The growth of diversity in researchers has also led to new theoretical directions. If anything, the 2000s have become an era of collaboration and division. If you went to a communication conference today, you would find a wide variety of research with many different methods and cultures represented.

Summary

There was a time many years ago when, if you wanted to talk to an organization about the need to train for cultural diversity or world diversity, you had to convince them of why this was necessary. As we have seen in this chapter, there are still some organizational leaders who feel that globalization will not have a major impact on their organization. But most people in organizations, at universities, and even in our everyday lives, probably see an awareness of how to communicate with others who are different from us as a central skill. We have seen in this chapter that, although studying culture poses certain risks of overgeneralization, over-simplification, and exaggeration of cultures, it also has many benefits. Some of these benefits are practical: studying culture will help us understand the multicultural workplace. It will aid us as we travel abroad or work with others who travel voluntarily or by force. It will help us to understand the media we see that cover stories from around the world or come from different countries or different cultural groups within our own country.

Each motive has a practical side. How will knowledge of culture help me to have better outcomes? But a newer generation is seeking more than simply knowing how to make more money by knowledge of culture, turning such knowledge into yet another commodity in a capitalist system. Rather, people today, young and old, are turning their eyes toward the needs of others—in their community and in the world at large. For example, volunteerism in the United States reached its highest point in five years in 2011, with 64.3 million U.S. Americans volunteering (Volunteering and Civic Life in America, 2012). The World Volunteer Web (Volunteerism worldwide, n. d.) provides reports and resources on volunteering around the world. We see that knowledge of culture and intercultural communication can help us be better world citizens, better able to engage in the sorts of dialogues the United Nations Global Report urges for a better world for tomorrow. And part of that better world is us, as individuals, as we gain the empowerment that knowledge of culture gives us over some of our own choices.

KEY TERMS

culture, 5	proxemics, 16
communication, 5	chronemics, 16
intercultural communication, 5	patriarchy, 18
international communication, 5	racism, 18
refugee, 11	sweatshops, 20
asylum seeker, 11	

Discussion questions

1   Think about the people around you at your school, in your workplace, or in your neighborhood. How would you describe their level of awareness of domestic and international cultures and identities? How about your own? What are some specific areas in which you would like to develop in terms of your cultural knowledge and skills during this course?

2   In what ways, if any, do you think globalization of media, especially social media like Facebook, is influencing your culture? Does it influence all cultures equally? Why or why not?

3   There are many possible issues in the world to be concerned about. Alone or in groups, come up with a list of what you think are the top five issues that demand global cooperation. What are the top five issues in your own community?

4   The use of international "**sweatshops**"—factories in developing nations with an inexpensive labor force, or using child labor, is controversial. Some feel that it is abusing people, especially children, in those cultures. Others feel it provides wages that the people might not have otherwise. What do you think are the benefits and disadvantages of sweatshops? Why do they exist? Should we fight to stop them, and if so, what steps would we take?

5   The sweatshop issue (question 4) and others presented in this chapter raise a difficult question. Each issue seems to have two—or several—sides. How can we maintain hope to seek solutions without falling into a despair of not knowing what the action is?

Action points

1   Perform an Internet or library search to understand diversity in your area. What kinds of diversity are there? What are some things that the different groups hold in common? What are some points of difference? Are there particular issues that require dialogue? Brainstorm ways with your friends to start such a dialogue or to join one, if it is already in progress.

2   The Internet joins us in many ways to people from different cultures. Join Yahoo.groups (http://groups.yahoo.com/) or some other chat or listserv. Join a group specifically related to a specific culture or global issue. See what you can learn about the culture or issue, especially from people within the culture or who have experience with the issue. Share what you find with your classmates or friends.

3   Join a group at your school or in your community that is dedicated toward alleviating some sort of social distress. This might be a known group, like Amnesty International, or it might be a group in your community, for example, to help repair cars for people who do not have money.

For more information

Hofstede, G.J., Pedersen, P.B., & Hofstede, G. (2002). *Exploring culture: Exercises, stories, and synthetic cultures*. Yarmouth, ME: Intercultural Press.

Kulich, S.J. (2012). Reconstructing the histories and influences of 1970s intercultural leaders: Prelude to biographies, *International Journal of Intercultural Relations*, 36(6), 744–759. Entire issue provides profiles of early writers in the field of intercultural communication.

Malewski, M. (2011). *GenXPat: The young professional's guide to making a successful life abroad.* Yarmouth, ME: Intercultural Press. (e-book)

OECD (2012). *OECD Factbook 2011–2012: Economic, environmental, and social statistics.* OECD Publishing.

Storti, C. (1994). *Cross-cultural dialogues: 74 brief encounters with cultural difference.* Yarmouth, ME: Intercultural Press.

References

ABC News. (2011). *Samoa skips Friday in time zone change*, 31 December. Accessed March 14, 2012, at http://www.abc.net.au/news/2011-12-30/samoa-skips-friday-in-time-zone-change/3753350

Aceh post-tsunami reconstruction: Lessons learned two years on. (2006). *The World Bank: News & Broadcast*, December 21. Accessed August 20, 2013, at http://web.worldbank.org/WBSITE/EXTERNAL/NEWS/0,,contentMDK:21164835~pagePK:64257043~piPK:437376~theSitePK:4607,00.html

Asante, M.K. (1980). *Afrocentricity: The theory of social change.* Buffalo, NY: Amulefi Publishing.

Asante, M.K., & Gudykunst, W.B. (Eds.). (1989). *Handbook of international and intercultural communication.* Newbury Park: Sage.

Blum, D. (Producer), & Howard, R. (Director). (1986). *Gung ho* [Motion picture]. USA: Paramount Pictures.

Broome, B. (2002). Views from the other side: Perspectives on the Cyprus conflict. In J.N. Martin, T.K. Nakayama, & L.A. Flores (Eds.), *Readings in intercultural communication* (pp. 101–112). Boston: McGraw-Hill.

Brunner, B. (2007). Tsunami factfile. *Infoplease.* Accessed February 14, 2013, at http://www.infoplease.com/spot/tsunami.html

Chen, G.-M., & Starosta, W.J. (1998). *Foundations of intercultural communication.* Boston: Allyn & Bacon.

Chu, S.-C., & Choi, S.M. (2010). Social capital and self-presentation on social networking sites: A comparative study of Chinese and American young generations. *Chinese Journal of Communication, 3,* 402–420. doi:10.1080/17544750.2010.516575.

Coughlan, S. (9 Mar, 2011). Record numbers of international students. *BBC News.* Accessed March 12, 2012, at http://www.bbc.co.uk/news/business-12671198

Current world population. (n.d.). *Worldometers: Real time world statistics.* Accessed April 12, 2013, 11:40 a.m., at http://www.worldometers.info/world-population/

DeAndrea, D.C., Shaw, A.S., & Levine, T.R. (2010). Online language: The role of culture in self-expression and self-construal on Facebook. *Journal of Language and Social Psychology, 29,* 425–442. doi:10.1177/0261927X10377989.

de Grauwe, P.D., & Camerman, F. (2002). How big are the big multinational companies? *Tijdschrift voor Economie en Management, 17* (3), 311–326. Accessed March 8, 2012, at https://lirias.kuleuven.be/bitstream/123456789/266744/1/2002-3_311-326p.pdf

Forbes.com (2009). World's most powerful people: #66 Klaus Schwab. Accessed March 12, 2012, at http://www.forbes.com/lists/2009/20/power-09_Klaus-Schwab_OTWW.html

Global Finance (n.d.). *Wealth distribution and income inequality by country.* Accessed January 31, 2013, at http://www.gfmag.com/tools/global-database/economic-data/11944-wealth-distribution-income-inequality.html

The Guardian (2011) *UNHCR 2011 Refugee statistics: full data.* 20 June. Accessed March 12, 2012, at http://www.guardian.co.uk/news/datablog/2011/jun/20/refugee-statistics-unhcr-data

Gudykunst, W.B. (Ed.). (1983). *Intercultural communication theory: current perspectives* (published as *The international and intercultural communication annual*). Beverly Hills: Sage.

Gudykunst, W.B., & Mody B. (Eds.). (2002). *Handbook of international and intercultural communication.* Thousand Oaks, CA: Sage.

Hall, B.'J.' (2003). *Among Cultures: The challenge of communication* (2nd ed.). Belmont, CA: Wadsworth.

Hall, E.T. (1959). *The silent language.* Garden City, N.Y.: Doubleday.

Hecht, M.L., Baldwin, J.R., & Faulkner, S.L. (2006). The (in)conclusion of the matter: Shifting signs and models of culture. In J.R. Baldwin, S.L. Faulkner, M.L. Hecht, & S.L. Lindsley (Eds.), *Redefining culture: Perspectives across the disciplines* (pp. 53–73). Mahwah, NJ: Lawrence Erlbaum Associates.

Institute of International Education: Open Doors. (2012). *International student enrollment increased by 5% in 2010/2011, led by strong increase in students from China.* Accessed March 14, 2012, at http://www.iie.org/en/Who-We-Are/News-and-Events/Press-

Center/Press-Releases/2011/2011-11-14-Open-Doors-International-Students

Internet growth statistics. (n.d.). *Internet world stats: Usage and population statistics.* Accessed March 13, 2012b, at http://www.internetworldstats.com/emarketing.htm

Kim, Y.Y. (1984). Searching for creative integration. In W.B. Gudykunst & Y.Y. Kim (Eds.), *Methods for intercultural communication research* (pp. 13–30). Beverly Hills: Sage.

Kim, Y.Y., & Gudykunst, W.B. (Eds.). (1988). *Theories in intercultural communication* (published as *The international and intercultural Communication Annual).* Beverly Hills: Sage.

Kim, Y.Y., & Ruben, B. (1988). Intercultural transformation: A systems theory. In Y.Y. Kim & W.B. Gudykunst (Eds.), *Theories in intercultural communication,* (pp. 299–321). Newbury Park, CA: Sage.

Kincaid, D.L. (Ed.). (1987). *Communication theory: Eastern and Western perspectives.* San Diego: Academic Press.

Kopper, E. (1993). Swiss and Germans: Similarities and differences in work-related values, attitudes, and behavior. *International Journal of Intercultural Relations, 17,* 167–184.

Kyoto Protocol. (2012). United Nations Framework Convention on Climate Change. Accessed March 14, 2012, at http://unfccc.int/kyoto_protocol/items/2830.php

Leeds-Hurwitz, W. (1990). Notes in the history of intercultural communication: The Foreign Service Institute and the mandate for intercultural training. *Quarterly Journal of Speech, 76,* 262–281.

Martin, J.N., Flores, L.A., & Nakayama, T.K. (2002). Ethical issues in intercultural communication. In J.N. Martin, T.K. Nakayama, & L.A. Flores (Eds.), *Readings in intercultural communication* (pp. 363–371). Boston: McGraw-Hill.

McLuhan, M. (1962). *The Gutenberg galaxy: The making of typographic man.* Toronto, Canada: University of Toronto Press.

McPhail, T.L. (2010). *Global Communication: Theories, stakeholders, and trends.* Boston: Allyn & Bacon.

Miike, Y. (2007). An Asiacentric reflection on Eurocentric bias in communication theory. *Communication Monographs, 74,* 272–278.

Miike, Y. (2010). An anatomy of Eurocentrism in communication scholarship: The role of Asiacentricity in de-Westernizing theory and research. *China Media Research, 6*(1), 1–11.

Nakayama, T.K., & Halualani, R.T. (Eds.). (2010). *The handbook of critical intercultural communication.* Malden, MA: Wiley-Blackwell.

National Geographic News (2005). *Deadliest tsunami in history,* 7 January. Accessed February 14, 2013, at http://news.nationalgeographic.com/news/2004/12/1227_041226_tsunami.html

Nationmaster.com (2009a). *Economy statistics—tourist arrivals (per capita) (most recent) by country.* Accessed March 12, 2012, at http://www.nationmaster.com/graph/eco_tou_arr_percap-economy-tourist-arrivals-per-capita

Nationmaster.com. (2009b). *Immigration statistics—refugees.* Accessed March 14, 2012, at http://www.nationmaster.com/graph/imm_ref-immigration-refugees

Nelson, L. (n.d.). The importance of effective cross-cultural communication in international business. *E-How: Money.* Accessed March 6, 2012, at http://www.ehow.com/about_6472127_importance-cultural-communication-international-business.html

Newsroom: Factsheet (2012). *Facebook.* Accessed March 14, 2012, at http://newsroom.fb.com/content/default.aspx?NewsAreaId=22

Populations of concern. (n.d.). *UNHCR-Global Appeal 2012–2013* (pp. 108–109). Accessed March 12, 2012, at http://www.unhcr.org/4ec230f516.html

Programs. (n.d.). *Invisible children.* Accessed March 13, 2012, at http://invisiblechildren.com/media/videos/program-media/kony-2012/

Radjou, N., & Kalpa, P. (6 Aug, 2010). Do multinationals really understand globalization? The ability of global companies to leverage global opportunities is surprisingly shallow. *Bloomberg Businessweek.* Accessed March 14, 2012, at http://www.businessweek.com/globalbiz/content/aug2010/gb2010086_282527.htm

Rogers, E.M., & Hart, W.B. (2002). The histories of intercultural, international, and development communication. In W.B. Gudykunst & B. Mody (Eds.). *Handbook of international and intercultural communication* (2nd ed., pp. 1–18). Thousand Oaks, CA: Sage.

Sifry, D. (22 Sep, 2008). Technorati's state of the blogosphere, September, 2008. Available at http://www.sifry.com/alerts/2008/09/technoratis-state-of-the-blogosphere-september-2008/

Tampa Bay Times. (2012). Viral Facebook post on CEO-worker pay ratio has obscure past. Politifact.com. Accessed March 15, 2012, at http://www.politifact.com/truth-o-meter/statements/2011/oct/10/facebook-posts/viral-facebook-post-ceo-worker-pay-ratio-has-obscu/

Tourism Intelligence Network (n.d.). *Number of tourists or tourism revenues?* Accessed February 14, 2013, at http://tourismintelligence.ca/2006/05/16/number-of-tourists-or-tourism-revenues/

Treinor, J. (26 Jan, 2012). Bill Gates tells Davos, "Economic crisis is not an excuse for cutting aid". *The Guardian: World Development.* Accessed

March 12, 2012, at http://www.guardian.co.uk/world/2012/jan/26/bill-gates-davos-aid

UNESCO (2009) *UNESCO World Report: Investing in cultural diversity and intercultural dialogue: Executive summary*. Accessed August 5, 2013, at http://unesdoc.unesco.org/images/0018/001847/184755e.pdf

UNHCR. (2012–2013). *UNHCR-Global Appeal 2012–2013*. Accessed February 14, 2013, at http://www.unhcr.org/4ec230f6b.html

United Nations ESCAP. (2011). *Statistical yearbook for Asia and the Pacific, 2011*. Accessed August 22, 2013, at http://www.unescap.org/stat/data/syb2011/iv-connectivity/tourism.asp

University of California, Berkeley. (2003). *How Much information? 2003: Executive summary*. Accessed March 14, 2012, at http://www2.sims.berkeley.edu/research/projects/how-much-info-2003/printable_report.pdf

Utopia (25 Jan, 2012) Social Forum declares, "Together we are the 99%". Thematic social forum 2012: Capitalist crisis: Social and environmental justice. *Common dreams: building progressive community*. Accessed March 12, 2012, at http://www.commondreams.org/headline/2012/01/25-0

Volunteering and civic life in America, 2012. (27 Nov, 2012). *The federal agency for service and volunteering*. Accessed January 31, 2013, at http://www.volunteeringinamerica.gov/index.cfm

Volunteerism worldwide. (n.d.). *World volunteer web*. Accessed January 31, 2013, at http://www.worldvolunteerweb.org/resources/research-reports/national.html

Ward, J. (2009). Importance of trade to U.S. economy highlighted in world trade week events. *International Trade Association*, Accessed March 8, 2012, at http://trade.gov/press/publications/newsletters/ita_0509/wtw_0509.asp

Wars in the World (2012). *List of ongoing conflicts*, 7 March. Accessed March 14, 2012, at http://www.warsintheworld.com/?page=static1258254223

Washington Peace Center. (2013). *The world social forum and world economic forum*. Accessed August 20, 2013, at http://washingtonpeacecenter.net/pla_theworldsocialforum

Wiseman, R. (Ed.). (1995). *Intercultural communication Theory* (published as *The international and intercultural communication annual*). Thousand Oaks: Sage.

World Bank. (2013). *Poverty & Equity Data*. Accessed August 20, 2013, at http://povertydata.worldbank.org/poverty/home/

World Economic Forum. (n.d.) Accessed March 8, 2012, at http://www.weforum.org/

World Tourism Organization (2012) One billion tourists key to creating jobs and stimulating the economy. Accessed March 12, 2012, at http://media.unwto.org/en/press-release/2012-03-05/one-billion-tourists-key-creating-jobs-and-stimulating-economy-unwto-secret

Chapter 2

Action, ethics, and research:
How can I make a difference?

Chapter objectives

After this chapter, you should be able to:

→ Define ethics and morality

→ Describe and evaluate universal ethical approaches and ethical relativism

→ Differentiate between civic and political engagement and relate them to culture

→ Outline three approaches (paradigms) to cultural research in communication

→ Distinguish between various research focuses in intercultural communication

Muslim veils in French schools: How can we determine right from wrong in intercultural situations?

"Not in our town:" What is the role of intercultural communication in civic engagement?

How can we do responsible cultural research?

Intercultural Communication for Everyday Life, First Edition. John R. Baldwin, Robin R. Means Coleman, Alberto González, and Suchitra Shenoy-Packer.
© 2014 John R. Baldwin, Robin R. Means Coleman, Alberto González, and Suchitra Shenoy-Packer.
Published 2014 by John Wiley & Sons Ltd.

Every year more college students, secondary-school students, and working citizens commit themselves to helping others. This help might take the form of "alternative" breaks, in which college students go in groups to cities or regions of their country that need more development or a special service boost, such as a clean-up after a hurricane (Figure 2.1). According to Break Away, a website describing such opportunities, alternative spring breaks began in the United States in the late 1980s and early 1990s (Break Away, n.d.). They began "as part of an overall surge of interest in institutionalizing community service on college campuses," rather than the typical break in which university students went to a "party" location. In 2010, more than 72,000 U.S. students participated in such breaks. In 2011, 64 million U.S. Americans volunteered as part of some organization (Federal Agency for Service and Volunteering, 27 Nov, 2012). Many Christians do short-term group service projects within and outside of the United States, to address situations of poverty or disaster. The numbers doing such trips have increased from 120,000 in 1989 to 2,200,000 in 2006, with travelers spending a total of $1.6 billion U.S. dollars (Corbett & Fikkert, 2009).

However, Steve Corbett and Brian Fikkert (2009) charge that, often, civic engagement to help the poor does more harm than good. The best-intentioned effort at injecting aid or bringing money into a community can increase dependence, reduce the dignity of local individuals, and harm those who are giving. The givers can be paternalistic and can stereotype the poor. Such a charge raises difficult questions. When we are interacting with people from other cultures within and outside of our nation, what guidelines, if any, can direct our actions and communication? Should we, as citizens, be involved in addressing needs in other cultures? What is our role in the politics or the world around us? Some of us might want to get involved in or give to causes such as

Figure 2.1 Students often do service projects as part of alternate spring breaks, mission trips, or other group efforts. Many times, these works provide wonderful service for communities, but they can also have unforeseen ethical implications. Source: Edwin Remsberg/Alamy.

Habitat for Humanity, Save the Children, or Amnesty International. Others of us might ask, "Is that really my responsibility?" or tell ourselves, "Maybe that's something I'll do when I'm older." If we want to do such service projects, how can we best understand local communities and their needs? These questions lead us to three issues that we will consider in this chapter: intercultural communication ethics; civic engagement; and cultural research.

Muslim veils in French schools: How can we determine right from wrong in intercultural situations?

An issue that is dividing much of Europe, and especially France, at the time of writing of this text, is the cultural and religious multiculturalism of Europe. One case study from the cultural debate serves to introduce our discussion of ethics: whether the French government should be able to outlaw religious imagery, such as large crosses, yarmulkes, or, perhaps the most controversial, veils for Muslim women (Figure 2.2). On one side of the debate, the French government is concerned with religious division and violence in the schools as well as traditional fears of loss of cultural prestige, as Muslim culture exerts a stronger influence across Europe. On the other side are notions of modesty and decorum held by Muslim women, many people feel that it is against their religious practices not to cover their heads or portions of their faces. The issue relates to similar questions: Does one nation have the right to tell another nation how to handle its human rights? Should the global feminist movement seek to change

Figure 2.2 The issue of wearing visual markers of religion, such as the veil, has become a topic of hot political debate in France. In the mid-1990s, these students at Saint-Exupery Secondary School, in France, could still wear veils. Source: Jean-Pierre Rey/ Gamma Rapho/Getty Images.

the status of women in places where such changes grate against the grain of the culture? Should one offer a "bribe" to a public official to avoid a minor charge or to ensure that some legal process happens in a timely manner? Or, within a specific culture, is it ethical for a university or business to restrict freedom of speech by limiting "hate speech?" If we remain silent when we see intolerance, such as someone telling a joke that puts down a culture or group of people, is that silence wrong? All of these deal with the notion of ethics.

Ethics and morality

Ethics and morality are linked to notions of right and wrong; while **morality** deals with any behavior that might be considered right or wrong, **ethics** deals specifically with the rightness or wrongness of our interactions with others, that is, the application of moral principles to behavior with others (Wines & Napier, 1992). In some cultures, taking drugs might be considered immoral, but stealing or lying—as they involve others more directly—are questions of ethics. It is often easier to determine what is morally or ethically acceptable within a culture. It is more difficult to compare the systems of right and wrong between two cultures or when people from two cultures are interacting, following different moral systems.

We all follow some form of guidelines as we interact with others. Let us imagine that you wish to download your favorite reggae music, illegally, from the Internet. Some common ethical approaches might lead you to different decisions. **Utilitarianism**, or determining the greatest benefit for the greatest number of people, would lead you to ask who might be helped or hurt by illegal downloading of media content. The **categorical imperative**, which uses logical questions like, "What if everyone did this?" would lead you to think about what would happen, economically, if everyone only downloaded music illegally. The **golden mean**, which involves avoiding extremes in decision-making, might suggest that if the music is not obtainable for purchase or if you just want to try it out before you buy, you might download, but not make a steady practice of it. **Ethical egoism** refers to making choices based simply on what seems good or beneficial to us, without a regard for others—you download the music because you want it and can get away with it (Griffin, 2009).

Ethical discussions in intercultural communication often lead to one of four approaches. First, writers often skirt discussing ethics altogether. For example, one book might spend 600 pages discussing how to spread new ideas, artifacts, or behaviors into a culture (such as teaching people to have protected sex), but contain no reference to ethical implications of cultural change; while another spends hundreds of pages talking about how to blend international business styles, but mentions ethics only briefly, in a one-page discussion of whether we should give bribes. A second approach is to present practical checklists of ethical guidelines for intercultural communicators, such as learning from others or knowing ourselves. Such lists promote respectful intercultural communication, but these may overlook deeper complexities of ethics or rely on a single ethical system for their formulation. This leads to the last two approaches, which struggle against each other in the field of intercultural communication: some seek a universal or cross-cultural guideline for ethical behavior; and others argue that each culture should determine its own set of ethics.

What do you think? In many nations, today, college students find the things they need a major chain store. Imagine that you shop at such a store, because it is convenient, and the prices are the lowest in town. But you find out that the organization engages in unfair labor practices. It hires most employees part-time, to avoid paying for health insurance. It discriminates against women or minority members by not giving them promotions. Employees are underpaid and easily fired, but the CEOs and owners are very rich. What are the ethical implications of you shopping or not shopping at such a store?

Determining a universal ethical stance

Many intercultural teachers and writers look for a **meta-ethic**, an overarching guideline of behavior toward other people that either can or should be applied to people in all cultures. But determining what that ethic should be is difficult. It would not be fair, for example, to apply a Judeo-Christian ethic to people who do not follow that religious system. Utilitarian, golden mean, and other ethical stances described earlier can inform intercultural communication (Hall, 2003), though each has limitations in actual application. Stella Ting-Toomey (1999) recommends a "derived" ethical universal approach: we look across cultures to see if they hold ethical principles in common. Once we find ethical stances that overlap, we can combine these for an approach that applies to interaction in any culture (Wines & Napier, 1992). For example, the United Nations Charter on Human Rights puts forth a series of rights agreed upon by people of many nations, such as the "right to life, liberty, and security of person" (United Nations, n.d.). The Charter advocates against all slavery or degrading punishments, and for representation before the law.

Other writers offer universal ethical principles such as the **humanistic principle**, which states that we should not harm others and should treat them well (Hatch, 1994). This is similar to the **peace principle**, which centers the notion of human spirit as the basis for universal ethics: "The guiding principle of any universal code of intercultural communication should be to protect the worth and dignity of the human spirit" (Kale, 2000, p. 452). These principles state that we should not engage in any behavior that has a negative impact on the welfare of others. With this in mind, racism, poverty, and creating human suffering are unethical, and so is ignoring such injustices. This principle forms the first major component of Judith Martin and Thomas Nakayama's (2002) approach, which proposes that any ethic that we apply across cultures, whether for everyday intercultural communication or scholarly research into other cultures, should involve treating and representing others with dignity and respect. With this in mind, it becomes ethical for college students or

ON THE NET 🖱

Ethics matters: Find an ethical case study in the list of business ethics case studies at http://ethics.sandiego.edu/resources. How might different cultures approach the same case differently? What behavior might be appropriate if people in the case took some of the different universal ethical approaches? How might the humanistic or peace principles be useful in the situation?

workers first to treat their colleagues with dignity, but also to be aware of and not ignore larger social issues, such as human trafficking.

A second principle that Martin and Nakayama (2002) describe, the **dialogic ethic**, states that as we determine ethics across cultures, we should discuss with the parties involved what sorts of ethical guidelines should be in effect. It is sometimes hard to determine what is right and wrong based on the humanistic principle, especially when behaviors in question do not seem harmful, or when what is helpful to one party acts against the wellbeing of another. This is in line with Mikhail Bakhtin's (1981) idea of a dialogic imperative, in which there is no monologue, but a comparison of competing perspectives—or Jürgen Habermas' (1998) notion of "communicative freedom" (p. 119), which states that ethical discussion occurs when everyone has the ability to engage in discussion, without coercion or constraint by others, such as through unequal power relations (Niemi, 2008).

For example, an ethical question that has influenced international politics is the degree to which there should be a free flow of media between cultures. Allowing unrestricted importation of international media often harms local artists, musicians, and media systems in developing countries. But restricting its importation limits the advancement of media systems in media-dominant nations, impacting jobs and economies in those nations. Most ethical differences are not central to issues of dignity, and intercultural communicators can overlook them (Hatch, 1994). But some differences are important enough to address— questions of human rights, slavery, and genocide (United Nations, n.d.). Before either side agrees to ethical guidelines, they should talk to each other to negotiate an ethical approach that works for both parties. The dialogic ethic is based on building relationships with people before we make ethical decisions about their behavior, and requires understanding, empathy, and caring.

Ethical relativism

Other writers advocate **cultural relativism**, the idea that people in each culture create their own accepted norms about what is right or wrong, with each ethical system being equally as acceptable as any other system. One possible issue with cultural relativism is that all members of a culture could accept a practice that by most standards (e.g., the United Nations Universal Declaration of Human Rights) would be harmful for some members. For example, if most members of a culture believe in bride burning, slavery, torture, or human sacrifice, cultural relativism dictates that those outside the culture should say nothing about it. Ethical relativism has strong implications for human rights activists (e.g., Amnesty International) and initiatives by some national governments to impose a view of human rights on others.

In sum, we see that ethics are an important part of intercultural communication. It is important to be aware of our own ethical approach. But as we interact with people from other cultures, there are often differences in how we are expected to treat others. People offer a variety of universal ethical approaches (meta-ethics) to guide our behavior, including the humanistic and dialogic principles, developed specifically for intercultural communication. Others believe that we can only understand the ethics of each culture uniquely. In most ethical, moral, and religious systems, however, considering the good of others—and working toward that good—seems to be a worthwhile ethical goal.

"Not in our town:" What is the role of intercultural communication in civic engagement?

With a broader conception of culture—viewing culture as ever-negotiated and distinct ways of life, rather than simply as national or ethnic groups—we can see that cultural differences exist in many of the dilemmas that face us in the cities and towns where we live and study. In a world of increasing diversity, we are faced with intolerance toward those of other races, countries, or social class backgrounds. There are individuals in our communities who may not have access to the same resources as others. There may be a gap in levels of achievement our local schools, due in part to a chasm between the culture of the children and the culture of the educational system (García & Guerra, 2006). People on many college campuses call our attention to social issues that often have a cultural component, such as the status of refugees from different countries, or political and religious division in places such as Northern Ireland. And agencies for civil and human rights around the world organize activities that relate to awareness and tolerance. Around the world, citizens strive, often in protest, for human and civil rights (Figure 2.3).

As one example, the United States values **altruism**, the notion of doing good to someone, even a stranger and **voluntarism**, the idea of giving one's own time, for no apparent benefit to oneself (Althen *et al.*, 2003). People in the United States give time or money to help tsunami victims or AIDS orphans. They volunteer in organizations like Habitat for Humanity or the American Cancer Foundation (even if they do not know someone with cancer personally). Some sources say that as many as 26% of U.S. Americans volunteer for some charitable organization each year (Bureau of Labor Statistics, 2008). They give money and time for complete strangers, leading some Koreans to think that U.S. Americans treat strangers like friends and friends like strangers (Kohls, 2001).

Figure 2.3 Unemployed citizens demand new workers' rights in front of the Macedonian Parliament in Skopje, November 27, 2007. Source: Ognen Teofilovski/ Reuters.

Many U.S. Americans stand up to prejudice through efforts such as the "Not in Our Town" campaigns that began after intolerance toward Jewish people in Billings, Montana (Not in Our Town, n.d.). At the same time, in response to many efforts toward social change, we say "Not in My Back Yard," a statement so common people refer to it by the acronym NIMBY. For example, many U.S. Americans who disagree with the detainment of Iraq refugees in Guantanamo Bay during the Iraq War, might oppose a facility housing those same refugees in their own community.

Political and civic engagement

There are different ways to get involved in the community. Some involvement has a political motive, and some does not. Involvement that includes participation in the political system is referred to as **political engagement**. Political engagement includes working on community problems, serving in organizations with a "stake in political policies or outcomes," supporting or talking to others about political causes, writing letters or blogging about political or social issues, working on campaigns, signing petitions, raising public awareness (e.g., through rallies, street theater, or boycotts), and voting (Colby *et al.*, 2007, pp. 30–31). Such efforts need not be connected to a specific political party, but rather regard issues that involve public policy, spending, and socio-political attention. For example, students in nations with a large foreign worker population, such as Germany or Malaysia, might host a public debate on immigration issues. Students might study and inform politicians or the public of the cultural needs, perceptions, or conditions of the local homeless community. Efforts at political engagement often cross cultural lines. For example, a discussion of Haitian workers in the Dominican Republic requires knowledge about Haitian and Dominican cultural differences, Dominican nationalization policy, prejudices between groups, and the intersection of international politics and economies.

At the same time, many are less concerned about public policy than they are about the everyday wellbeing of others, for example, people who need homes, children who need mentoring, or immigrants and travelers who need to learn the host language. College students might be involved in local children's or history museums, efforts to renovate a downtown or campus area, no-kill animal shelters, and so on. Involvement in the community, regardless of politics, is referred to as **civic engagement**. Civic engagement often leads those involved to feel a sense of responsibility to their community, engaging in civil society, and helping the common good, with activities including learning about diversity, engaging in public problem solving, or assuming leadership roles in organizations (Jacoby, 2009). For example, a recent news report suggests that, although volunteering is a new concept in Russia, 160,000 people have applied to volunteer time at the 2014 Sochi Olympics (Itasaka, 2013).

Once civic engagement turns to social issues, promoting local and global justice, or taking an active role in the political process, it becomes political engagement. To distinguish civic from political engagement, for example, if a student group raises awareness about the homeless or immigrants, it is political engagement; if the students simply donate time working in a homeless culture or teaching immigrants the host language, it is civic engagement.

People and groups have long promoted voluntarism. One of the founding principles of Harvard College in 1636 was preparing students to engage actively with community life.

Social leaders like educator and philosopher John Dewey and U.S. President Franklin Roosevelt promoted connections between universities and the social problems of the day. U.S. President George H. W. Bush passed the National and Community Service Act in 1990 (Jacoby, 2009). Now, many universities focus students' attention on civic and political engagement. Organizations such as the American Democracy Project and the American Association of State Colleges and Universities (Jacoby, 2009), as well as specific institutions, such as Georgetown University and University of Wisconsin-Madison, support programs to get students involved with the community in some way (Welch, 2009).

Defending civic and political engagement among college students

In college, we might be politically involved or see the need to volunteer. However, there are practical and ideological reasons why we may choose not to become engaged or even avoid the discussion of civic or political engagement in the university setting. Practical reasons—those most often in the forefront of students' minds—include logistical issues: "I barely have time to work and do my studies," "I don't know how to get involved," "I'd rather spend my spare time with friends." There are several responses to these issues. First, in a way, the patterns we establish in college often guide us as we enter the so-called "real world" after college. We are busy with classes, exams, and jobs—but often no busier than when we graduate and have full-time jobs, children, or other commitments. Second, there is a need for someone to reach out and help others—if we do not, who will? Third, there are personal benefits for helping others. If you are from a "collective" culture (see chapter 4), you might find reward in contributing not only to your family or work-group, but to the community at large, forging a new, broader sense of group identity. If you are an "individualist," you may find personal reward, a sense of feeling good about yourself, from helping others (Bellah *et al.*, 1996). University life gives us many rewards—friendship, career development, networking opportunities. But involvement in the lives of others gives us a different reward.

POP CULTURE

Consider the song, *Solo le Pido a Dios*, by Argentine singer, Leon Gieco. How might this song impact its audience in its context? (You may have to do some Internet research to answer this.) What songs have impacted your life as regards to helping others or thinking about your social world?

Solo le Pido a Dios (Leon Gieco)

I only ask of God
That I will not be indifferent to the pain
That the dry death will not find me
Empty and alone, without having done enough

I only ask of God
That I will not be indifferent to the justice
That they will not strike my other cheek
After a talon has scratched my destiny

I only ask of God
That I will not be indifferent to war
It is a great monster and steps mightily
Upon all the poor innocence of the people
                                    [Trans. J. Baldwin]

Some people have ideological reasons against teaching civic and political engagement in the classroom. Some claim such teaching indoctrinates students with a specific (supposedly liberal) ideology—it leads them to the left of politics. However, a detailed study of more than 20 courses and programs incorporating Political Engagement Projects (PEPs) at a variety of universities discovered that teaching exercises that created civic and political engagement among students increased their likelihood of being involved in their communities as adults, but did not change their political ideology. If they were conservative going into the class, they became involved as conservatives. If they were politically liberal, they engaged in the community in ways true to that political approach (Colby *et al.*, 2007).

POP CULTURE

Some popular music groups, like Rage Against The Machine Gogol Bordello (a Gypsy punk band, Figure 2.4), U2, or Green Day, make political activism a large part of their musical focus. What popular artists do you know that include social themes in their music? What are some of the issues and values they promote? What are some strengths and limitations of using popular music for social change?

Figure 2.4 Yuri Lemeshev, of Gogol Bordello, a Gypsy punk band from New York, U.S.A., performs in Moscow, Russia, July 23, 2010. Source: Will Ireland/Metal Hammer Magazine/Rex Features.

Another concern critics raise is that the purpose of the college classroom is to teach skills and ideas that help one's career, rather than instilling students with values of civic engagement (Fish, 2008). People with this view often feel that the family should be the ones to instill values of civic or political engagement in children. Colby *et al.* (2007) respond that "reasonably well-informed, capable, engaged, and public-spirited citizens are essential if a democracy is to flourish" (p. 26). Civic engagement, they argue, leads to citizen participation and to a more informed public, as those who become civically engaged often see more of the complexities of society and learn more about the social problems on which they focus. While students have agency to be civic and politically engaged, there are often constraints—political, economic, or cultural—that act upon their ability to be engaged. For example, the political system in Myanmar prohibited the unregistered congregating of more than five people, but allowed foreign non-governmental organizations (NGOs) to enter with humanitarian aid.

Finally, some people with a liberal perspective criticize political and civic engagement efforts for not going far enough. In some cases, we might become engaged in a project, like feeding hungry children, because we see ourselves as a cultural (or even racial) savior. Some approaches to civic engagement could disempower those receiving the supposed help, leading to dependence on those providing the help. Such efforts could hide the unequal access that some groups have to resources and power. John Eby (1998) suggests that most civic engagement ignores larger structural issues, diverts attention from social policy to voluntarism, and leads students to a limited concept of real human needs and how to address them. Colby *et al.* (2007) respond that civic engagement gives at least some sense of the choices that are possible and may instill a sense of **efficacy** among people—that is, the sense that, with their own work or combined with others, they can accomplish a task to which they set themselves. In this way, students will not wait for cultural or political elites to make decisions for them, but will personally influence the contexts and structures that impact their lives.

Doing civic engagement

Getting involved matters. The humanitarian ethic noted earlier states that if people are suffering and we do nothing, we are contributing to their suffering. At the same time, Martin and Nakayama's (2002) dialogic ethic suggests that as we become engaged we must participate with those influenced by our actions to determine the goals and the outcomes in a way that empowers them and creates culturally responsible engagement.

The question remains: what would this skeleton of civic engagement that we have provided look like with "flesh and bones" on it? We present here three different cases of civic engagement that pertain to culture in some way, based on real exercises used by instructors.

Case 1 One of the priorities of the National Organization of Women (NOW) is promoting a national amendment to the U.S. Constitution that ensures the rights and safety of women, including statements regarding women's rights to abortion (National Organization for Women (NOW), n.d.). An intercultural specialist or group of students could investigate the organization and its objectives and how it relates to local cultures, politics, and civic attitudes for and against the organization. People might investigate organizational or community members' views of the organization's mission and effectiveness, to promote local strategies for more effective outreach to the community. Or they might do an experiment on student groups on a college campus, seeing what effect different types of awareness messages from NOW have on students.

Case 2 In Israel, there is long-standing tension between Jewish and Palestinian Israelis. Students and civic workers could investigate the roots of this tension, including historical hatreds, social inequalities, and attitudes. They could study issues of prejudice and locate points of similarity between the groups. Then they could develop an awareness campaign, stage unity marches, or build programs that promote helpful contact (see chapter 6) between children and adolescents of the two groups.

Break it down

Look in your local phonebook and newspaper, or on the Internet, or, if there is a volunteer agency or network at your school, talk to that office. Make a list of the possible areas of civic or political engagement in your community or at your school that might have some connection to culture.

Case 3   An instructor teaching how to give a persuasive speech to his students pointed out that part of understanding persuasion is to understand the diversity of audiences. Some of his students resisted, echoing a common stance that the standard public speaking class-room is not a place to focus on race or class, and that in fact, many college classes simply spend too much time on these "trite" topics. One student, "Henry," held such an opinion, until the instructor gave the students an assignment to interview someone of a different racial, sexual, and social class background. Henry described "Sara," a middle-aged African American and her perception of her treatment in public places. Joseph Zompetti (2006, para 32) summarizes Henry's speech to the class:

> As Henry told us the story of Sara, he became impassioned with empathy and concern. At times, his eyes clouded up, but his voice remained stern and assertive. Henry sincerely appeared to be moved by his interview with Sara. Given his earlier dislike for discussing identity, the audience, too, was enwrapped in Henry's speech. They seemed amazed at his transformation and appreciated his sincerity. When he concluded his speech, Henry declared, "I've learned that society does treat people differently, and that people have predispositions toward other people . . . and I've learned it all from Sara." At that moment in time, it seemed as if everyone in the class, particularly Henry, understood the importance of identity and public speaking.

There is both benefit and need for us to look beyond our own desires and careers. We live in a social world, and as such, must be concerned with the needs of the people around us. We can get involved in the lives of others for the sake of making the world a better place; or we can do so at a level that involves public policy and spending.

How can we do responsible cultural research?

Part of being culturally ethical is providing accurate representations of others and of cultural concepts. One way we may choose to be involved, especially as we gain the skills a college education provides, is by doing research for civic groups. At a minimum, organizations or groups might expect us to understand research. But how can we do or read research effectively? The final section of the chapter introduces approaches to research, and then closes with one last look at ethics as they relate to cultural, cross-cultural, and intercultural research.

Assumptions that guide cultural research

As we look at journal articles in the area of intercultural and cross-cultural communication, one might be full of statistics; another, observational notes or example quotations from only a few participants; another, an in-depth rhetorical analysis of a text (such as a Nelson Mandela speech or a Norah Jones music video). People look at both culture and civic engagement differently. One way to understand the variety of intercultural research is to explore the types of underlying assumptions researchers might have. These assumptions tend to revolve around issues of what is real (at least, what is the reality that we should be considering), what counts as knowledge, and what the role of the researchers' values should be in conducting research. These apply to how scholars do research, but here we will apply them to our own understandings of the world.

Ontology refers to assumptions about the nature of reality. We often take our way of seeing the social world as natural. But in fact, there are several ways to see reality, especially social reality (Miller, 2005, and Potter, 1996, outline some of these differences). For example, when we think of how men and women communicate in a college setting, we might think of sex as something that leads men to communicate one way and women another, even if we recognize that social upbringing, along with or instead of physical differences, is what influences behavior. That is, we think of behavior in terms of external and internal causes and effects. If this is the case, then if we can change causes in a social situation, the outcomes will change (like changing seating in a classroom to influence the development of interracial friendships). Or we might believe fundamentally that people have free will. So, regardless of any cultural patterns, each woman or man makes unique choices about how to behave. Or you might think that gender is always changing and that we "create" gender by the way we talk, the jokes we tell, and the images we make.

How we see the world is related to our **epistemology**, or assumptions about knowledge. If we believe that each person has her or his own reality (e.g., "beauty is in the eye of the beholder"), we will not make or believe in statements that describe how people are alike. If we do research, we will want to talk to individuals to find their own perspectives of reality, or perhaps we might describe the understandings of a single group of people. But if we believe in internal and external causes for behavior, we will likely read and trust research that uses methods that filter out researcher opinion, like experiments or closed-ended surveys, and we might prefer to make claims only after we have done research on a large group of people, even using statistics.

In addition to our views of reality and knowledge, each of us has assumptions regarding the role of our values as we do research on culture and communication, which is our **axiology**. We might think that research can or should be value-free, especially if we believe in cultural relativism, noted before. Or we might think that we really cannot see anything, including research, apart from our own opinions and biases. We could even believe that in a world with social inequalities, we would be wrong not to bring our values to our research, doing research and taking action to address such inequalities.

Approaches to studying culture and communication

With these definitions in mind, we can better understand the notion of "paradigms" in the communication field. The three **paradigms**—ways of seeing the (social or scientific) world—most common in communication research are the scientific, humanistic, and critical paradigms, though some consider postmodernism to be a fourth paradigm. Different approaches to the world are often connected to preferred ways of doing research (Figure 2.5). If you do **scientific** research, you will hold many of these assumptions: (1) Social behavior

Figure 2.5 Methods and examples of cultural, cross-cultural, and intercultural research

Method	Characteristics	Example
Experiment	There are typically two or more conditions with different treatment (or a "control" group with no treatment). Researchers observe behavior or give a survey after the treatment to see if the treatment led to any differences.	Aubrey *et al.* (2009) found that women who viewed sexualized images (i.e., with high skin exposure) rate their perceptions of their own bodies as more negative than those who see images with less exposure.
Survey (closed-ended)	Researchers give a list of items to which participants respond. The survey is often, but not always, created from previous literature or pre-existing measures.	Kim *et al.* (2009) gave surveys measuring several cultural and individual variables among groups of different ethnic backgrounds in the United States. The more individuals saw themselves in terms of their connection to others, the more they were concerned with threats to self and other's image in attempts to persuade.
Survey (open-ended)	Researchers give open-ended questions to participants, either in a list or as a diary. Then, the researchers group responses into themes, either interpreting them (themes with discussion) or turning them into numbers to look for group differences.	Imahori & Cupach (1994) analyzed open-ended questionnaires to determine differences in communicative and emotional responses to embarrassing predicaments between Japanese and U. S. Americans.
Interviews and focus groups	Researchers talk with participants, following a strict interview format (standardized), or a more flexible format (semi-structured). Standardized interviews are more easily turned into categories that can be analyzed with statistics. Semi-structured interviews usually lead to themes with quotations. A focus group is an interview done with a group of people.	Graham, Moeiai, & Shizuru (1985) used standardized interviews and statistics to determine differences in problems perceived by intercultural and same-culture married couples. Cheong & Poon (2009) used focus groups to uncover meanings and usages of Protestant Chinese immigrants to Canada, providing quotations from participants.

(Continued)

Figure 2.5 (*Continued*)

Method	Characteristics	Example
Observation	Researchers go into a culture and watch behavior. They can participate to different degrees and might also do interviews, analyze documents, and so on. This can be either in the realm of *interpreting* a behavior in context, or *counting frequencies* of the occurrence of a behavior.	Carbaugh *et al.* (2006) did fieldwork and observed interaction to discover (and interpret) Finnish understandings of silence. Remland *et al.* (1995) used systematic observation to determine cultural differences between several European countries regarding use of touch, distance, and body angle in conversation.
Language analysis	Researchers record naturally occurring language and use either previous theory and terms to analyze the language, or look at the turn-taking and other features of language to understand culture.	Hei (2009) used discourse analysis and face management theory (see Ch. 7) to categorize, from taped everyday conversation, ways Malaysians use direct and indirect ways to refuse requests or offers.
Textual analysis	Researchers interpret a text, such as a website or speech, often using the approach of a particular theory as a lens through which to look at the text.	Endres & Gould (2009) analyzed student essays from an intercultural communication class to see how students "perpetuate White privilege" by confusing being White with the notion of Whiteness and by seeing their whiteness as grounds for charity to other groups.
Media content analysis	Researchers develop a coding scheme to look at specific aspects of a text. The analysis is often quantifiable and can be submitted to statistics.	Glascock & Ruggiero (2004) analyzed six telenovelas and one drama to find that women were portrayed as more domestic with lower status and more focus on attractiveness than men, and that lighter-skinned Latinas/Latinos were more likely to have lead roles than those with darker skin.
Media criticism	Researchers apply an interpretive lens from previous theory to understand a media text.	Stijn (2009) used concepts of group power and hierarchy to examine how Western news media create a global (and Euro-centered) "center" in the way they report about domestic and international disasters, that is, making Western suffering more understandable and substantively different than suffering of global "Others."

Note: This list is intended as a list of many of the methods used for research on culture and communication. It is not intended to be exhaustive.

is predictable because people act based on internal and external causes. (2) Researchers should be systematic and remove personal biases, to understand the universal laws that govern communication behavior. (3) Research might be quantitative, using statistics, but researchers could also use observation or other methods and still believe that they are "uncovering" a world external to themselves. (4) Research is often done to test the relationship between variables in a theory, with a goal to provide better predictions of communication outcomes. We should note that scholars do not believe humans are totally predictable—just similar enough in many ways to make "probable" predictions (Metts, 2004). As an example, you might study whether international travel leads college students or business people to have less ethnocentrism or reduced racism.

The second paradigm is often called **humanistic** or **interpretive**. "Humanistic" implies that humans are unique from other aspects of nature, based on their ability to use symbols or some other aspect of their human essence (Potter, 1996). Research is "interpretive" in that you might try to understand (or interpret) individual texts or small groups of individuals or instances. As you research, you might admit your own values as influencing how you see the reality of the people you study. Common assumptions of this view include: (1) People are not (or are less) predictable because they make choices. (2) Researchers should provide an interpretation of a group's reality or of an isolated media text. (3) Research should consider behavior or texts holistically and within larger social contexts. (4) Research should provide an explanation of a specific phenomenon in a culture from that culture's perspective, or an analysis of a speech or media text through application of a set of terms. In this perspective, you might investigate how people on a soccer team create a sense of belonging through joke telling and insults. Or you might investigate metaphors in a speech by Kenyan environmental activist Wangari Maathai.

We can see a difference between social scientific and interpretive views of culture in a common distinction some have made between approaches to understanding culture. On one hand, in an **etic approach**, researchers develop some framework of terms or dimensions, such as cultures where people focus more on the individual and those where people focus more on the group, or those where people touch more and stand closer and those where they touch less and stand further apart. Researchers then apply the framework or theory to compare cultures in their behavior, according to terms the researcher has developed. Researchers using an **emic approach** will not want to impose their understandings of meanings or behaviors on a culture, but will seek to set aside their own understandings. Often using observation or talking to people, they try to discover the categories and meanings people in their own cultures give to their behavior and social reality (Gudykunst & Nishida, 1989)

The third paradigm, **critical** research, seeks to address social injustice in the world or explain how groups with different ideologies about the world struggle with each other to make their views dominant. Unlike the first two paradigms, in critical research, authors deliberately take their values into research. If you take this approach to doing research, you might analyze music videos quantitatively to see if the portrayal of women gives them the same choices and status as men. Or you might study how different groups within your culture or university struggle to make a particular definition of "education" dominant, excluding or putting down other views. Much of critical theory is about ideology and hegemony. **Ideology** here refers to a set of assumptions that we use to interpret the world around us (van Dijk, 1998)—it is different from a paradigm in that it often deals with social structures and power. **Hegemony** is defined as some form or level of control over another group, such as political, cultural, or economic power (Zompetti, 2012). Critical researchers, including most feminists, would now look at gender differences in communication in terms of possible oppression or marginalization of women's communicative styles (Kramarae, 1980), either through media texts or in face-to-face communication, such as through interruptions, topic choice, or slurs people use for men or women.

One new branch of critical theory involves **postcolonialism**—a field of study that looks worldwide at problems created by colonization, seeking to bring awareness to these problems and provide empowerment to those harmed by colonial relations (Shome & Hedge, 2002). We can see the imposition of one cultural system from cases as distinct as European colonization of Africa and Asia to more modern forms of economic colonization, with one-way media flows that lead strong media cultures to receive little outside influence, while influencing other cultures greatly. Key notions of postcolonialism include notions of **diaspora**, where people from one culture spread out across many different cultures, and **hybdridity**, where cultural elements blend within a culture (we will say more on these in chapter 3). The dominant group represents diverse groups within its society in different, usually unequal and unfair ways, and there are impacts of postcolonial relations within a society on how subordinate (and dominant) groups see their identity and **agency**, the choices one feels one has. Often, people in subordinated groups, although still having agency, are constrained by the power relations of the dominant group (Shome & Hedge, 2002). At the same time, some writers argue that these power relations are more complicated than they seem at first: the subordinate do have some agency, can represent the dominant group, and have their own bases of power within hybrid relations (Garcia Canclini, 1995).

> ***What do you think?*** Are there "real" differences between men and women and the way they communicate (and what are they)? Or are these differences socially constructed through communication? If they are socially constructed, are they done in a way that disadvantages women and privileges men (give examples)? Or even in ways that are inconsistent and contradictory?

From critical theory grew an approach called **postmodernism**. Postmodernism involves not a single construction of some aspect of culture, but several. These social constructions place notions, such as "womanhood" or "manhood", together with different concepts. Men are told to be "sensitive new age guys", to be good fathers or boyfriends, but are also told they should be over-focused on women's body parts and see women as something to be "conquered." That is, there are contradictory discourses, or presentations of ideas, about things such as what it means to be a man or to be truly Japanese, or what counts as success, constitutes "disease," or merits "punishment" in a given culture (Foucault, 1995). Postmodernism rejects much of what modernistic research, including humanistic research stood for, such as linearity, reason, hierarchy of structure, and the search for given meanings or single explanations. Postmodernists often feel that things such as modern specialization, industrialization, urbanization, and rationalization (focus on reason) serve to sustain systems of domination and control (Best & Kellner, 1991). Meaning, they suggest, is not linear or rational; rather it jumps and leaps, the lines between disciplines (and even between work and play, research and art) should be blurred, and we should bring what has been left out—emotion, spirituality, rurality, and so on—back into academic thought (Rosenau, 1992). The value of analyzing different discourses about things such as illness, crime, masculinity, or democracy, is that it shows us how power works through and between these discourses. If you take a postmodern view as you do research, you would be less likely to make any claim about how a particular group, like Apache U.S. Indians, Japanese *burakumin*, or Black Hondurans, are alike, but would expect there to be different ways of living out each identity. Or you might study how different groups in your culture seek to define notions like "family" or "success" in different ways that would provide power or cultural prominence to one group or another.

Research can, but does not have to be linked to social action (political and civic engagement). There is much research needed to make our communities and our world a better place. But many people do research for practical means, such as to improve intercultural business or education, or because of personal interest in some aspect of communication (e.g., do people in southern France use nonverbal communication differently than those in the north of the country?).

But all research has ethical implications. Aside from standard research ethics of being confidential, not manipulating our participants, and so on, in intercultural research, we must be responsible in how we describe other cultures, making sure that our accounts are true to how people in those cultures will see them. We should be careful not to look at other cultures as strange, quaint, or folkloric (there are power relations involved even when we do research). If we make a claim about a culture or about intercultural communication processes, it should be based on sound research, and not just opinion. And we should consider the consequences of anything we present from our research on those we research. As an example, one researcher at a national conference presented a study on the values of Mexican workers in *maquildadoras*—foreign-owned and -run factories in Mexico. The research was funded by the company, with a report of Mexican values given to the foreign owners. In this case, the owners could feasibly use the report to control the workers or get them to work for cheaper wages. Research can have consequences, so it inherently involves ethics.

Differences of focus in culture-and-communication studies

Using the methods mentioned, we might look at different aspects of culture and communication. We often use "intercultural communication" as a broad name for all of these, but there are different types of research and communication that involve culture:

Cultural communication research commonly refers to the study or practice of communication in a single culture. Ethnographers in anthropology have taken such an approach for many years. We might study how people in the context of a sports bar use banter with strangers about the game. **Cross-cultural communication** is a term that never describes interaction—only research, as it applies to studies that compare two or more cultures. We might compare how members of different national cultural, ethnic, or age groups demonstrate public displays of affection. That is, we would consider how Turks and Thais differ in displays of affection, but not how they communicate with each other. This last idea more appropriately describes what we can most precisely call **intercultural communication**—defined in chapter 1 as communication between people of two different cultures, when the culture impacts the communication enough to make a difference. For example, we might consider interaction between Indian and Arab residents of Dubai in the hotel industry. **Co-cultural communication** refers to communication between people of different groups within a larger, dominant culture (what we used to call subcultures). There is a limitation in the notion of co-culture, however, as often the differences between groups within a nation (say, the Hmong community and White young professionals in the northwestern United States) may be more different than differences between different nations (say, Australia and New Zealand). Finally, we will use **intergroup communication** to refer to those instances where group perception and processes (e.g., prejudices, stereotypes) impact communication, even if there are not real cultural differences (Baldwin & Hunt, 2002).

Some scholars look at culture as it relates to communication that is not exclusively face-to-face, but also mediated. **Developmental communication** refers to communicative efforts to bring more development (e.g., water, farming resources, family planning, economic advancement) to communities (though some prefer to call this **communication for social change** because of the condescending implications of the notion of "development"). **International communication** is a vague term. Some use it interchangeably with intercultural communication, though only when referring to cultures as nations. Others use it to refer to national media systems, and finally, others use the term to refer to those situations in which one is speaking for a nation, such as diplomats. In these cases, cultural and personal factors influence the communication process (see chapter 3), but so does the fact that the person is representing the interests of a larger group.

Summary

In this chapter, we looked at three separate but related issues. We considered ethics, looking at the tension between ethical relativism and the idea of a meta-ethic, a single ethic used to guide behavior regardless of cultures. While we framed our discussion in terms of interpersonal ethical choices, the field of international media entails similar ethical decisions. The ethical stance people take will influence the way they do research. For example, someone might believe that to do research that does not address or highlight social injustice is to be unethical. Another researcher might believe that if one seeks to uncover the social reality of a group, and that group does not believe that its gender relations are oppressive, then to impose this view on the research is unethical.

Related to ethics, we introduced the notions of civic and political engagement. We saw that individuals can be politically or civically engaged regardless of political stance. There is a growing need for colleges and universities, in the development of complete citizens, regardless of the country of the student, to promote civic action in a way appropriate to students' culture, and, in some cases, to encourage both students and faculty to strive for cultural change. But we also saw that even an open embracing in the college classroom of civic and political engagement does not have to influence the student's particular political world view.

Finally, we saw that both ethics and engagement relate to research. As intercultural thinkers, we will gain knowledge and skills that lead us to understand both our own culture and the cultures of others around us better. This knowledge gives us agency and power, within the constraints of our own cultural, political, and social situations. A growing knowledge of culture may equip us more to make a positive influence on the world in a way that is culturally sensitive. And one way that many may choose to do this (or may be forced to, in the context of an intercultural class) is through conducting cultural, cross-cultural, or intercultural research. Hopefully the ideas here will help us to be better local and global citizens, wherever we find ourselves.

KEY TERMS

morality, 27	humanistic, 39
ethics, 27	interpretive, 39
utilitarianism, 27	etic approach, 39
categorical imperative, 27	emic approach, 39
golden mean, 27	critical, 39
ethical egoism, 27	ideology, 39
meta-ethic, 28	hegemony, 39
humanistic principle, 28	postcolonialism, 40
peace principle, 28	diaspora, 40
dialogic ethic, 29	hybridity, 40
cultural relativism, 29	agency, 40
altruism, 30	postmodernism, 40
voluntarism, 30	cultural communication, 41
political engagement, 31	cross-cultural communication, 41
civic engagement, 31	intercultural communication, 41
efficacy, 34	co-cultural communication, 41
ontology, 36	intergroup communication, 42
epistemology, 36	developmental communication, 42
axiology, 36	communication for social change, 42
paradigms, 36	international communication, 42
scientific, 36	

Discussion questions

1 Some people grow discouraged realizing that there are multiple approaches to ethics and morality and find it easier to give up, choosing simply not to think about it. What are some problems with ignoring or giving up on understanding ethics?

2 Many modern media sources use parody and humor to highlight social problems and issues (from parody newspapers (*The Onion*, http://www.theonion.com) to faux-news shows (*The Daily Show with John Stewart, The Colbert Report*) to movies (*Wag the Dog*). What do you think are the strengths and limitations of using parody and humor to address social issues?

3 Writers have tried to make a distinction between civic and political engagement. To what degree do you feel these two can be treated separately? What are the implications, strengths, and limitations of university classes that include a civic or political engagement focus?

4 Imagine a topic for a specific cultural, cross-cultural, or intercultural communication study. What would you want to know? Which method might you choose, and why would it be appropriate for your topic and study goals?

5 Read through the United Nations Universal Declaration of Human Rights (http://www.un.org/en/documents/udhr/). What are the challenges for creating such a document? In what ways do the rights proclaimed reflect or contradict practices in your culture?

Action Points

1   Look through your local newspaper. Find coverage of a political or social issue. If the article discusses the perspectives of people or organizations involved, see if you can guess what ethical perspective they might be taking. How might a clearer understanding of ethical stances help us as we read about it, or the people in the story as they interact with one another?

2   Consider socially motivated music groups or artists (Woodie Guthrie, Bob Dylan, Greenday, U2, Sting, Nas) or genres (some rap music). What potential, if any, do you feel this work has for social change?

3   Go to your college's website or visit its student services office. Make a list of all student organizations that are focused in some way on helping others (service organizations) or working for social causes. Which do you find most interesting? Visit a meeting and see what it is about.

4   In groups or pairs, with your instructor's supervision, conduct a small research project in which you either interview or survey people in a group that is involved in the community or about such a group (e.g., you might ask about motivations or the activities of group members, or perceptions of the group by community members). Discuss your findings with the class. What type of knowledge does your study give you? What are some types of knowledge or claims that you could not make from your study?

For more information

Dalton, R.J. (2009). *The good citizen: How a younger generation is reshaping American politics* (rev. ed.). Washington, DC: CQ Press.

Fish, S. (2008). *Save the world on your own time.* New York: Oxford University Press.

Fitch, P. (2004). Effects of intercultural service learning on intellectual development and intercultural sensitivity. In M. Welch & S.H. Billig (Eds.), *New approaches to service learning: Research to advance the field* (pp. 107–126). Greenwich, CT: Information Age.

Jacoby, B. (2009). Civic engagement in today's higher education : An overview. In B. Jacoby & Associates (Eds.), *Civic engagement in higher education: Concepts and practices* (pp. 5–30). San Francisco: Jossey-Bass.

Putnam, R. (2000). *Bowling alone: The collapse and revival of American community.* New York: Simon & Schuster.

References

Althen, G., with Doran A.R., & Szmania, S.J. (2003). *American Ways: A guide for foreigners in the United States* (2nd ed.). Yarmouth, ME: Intercultural Press.

Aubrey, J.S., Henson, J.R., Hopper, K.M., & Smigh, S.E. (2009). A picture is worth twenty words (about the self): Testing the priming influence of visual sexual objectification on women's self-objectification. *Communication Research Reports, 26,* 271–284.

Bakhtin, M. (1981). *The dialogic imagination: Four essays by M. M. Bakhtin* (Ed. M. Holquist, Trans. C. Emerson & M. Holquist). Austin: University of Texas Press.

Baldwin, J.R., & Hunt, S.K. (2002). Information seeking behavior in intercultural and intergroup communication. *Human Communication Research, 28,* 272–286.

Bellah, R.N., Madsen, R., Sullivan, W.M., Swidler, A., & Tipton, S. (1996). *Habits of the heart: Individualism and commitment in American life* (updated ed.). Berkeley: University of California Press.

Best, S., & Kellner, D. (1991). *Postmodern Theory: Critical interrogations.* New York: Guilford.

Break Away (n.d.). *Frequently asked questions* Accessed February 5, 2013, at http://www.alternativebreaks2013.org/faq/

Bureau of Labor Statistics. (2008). *Volunteering in the United States, 2008.* Accessed September 3, 2009, at http://www.bls.gov/news.release/volun.nr0.htm

Carbaugh, D., Berry, M., & Nurmikari-Berry, M. (2006). Coding personhood through cultural terms and practices : Silence and quietude as a Finnish "natural way of being." *Journal of Language and Social Psychology, 25,* 203–220. DOI: 10.1177/0261927X06289422

Cheong, P. H., & Poon, J.P.H. (2009). Weaving webs of faith: Examining Internet use and religious communication among Chinese Protestant transmigrants. *Journal of International and Intercultural Communication, 2,* 189–207.

Colby, A., Beaumont, E., Ehrlich, T., & Corngold, J. (2007). *Educating for democracy: Preparing undergraduates for responsible political engagement.* Stanford, CA: Jossey-Bass.

Corbett, S., & Fikkert, B. (2009). *When helping hurts: How to alleviate poverty without hurting the poor and yourself.* Chicago: Moody Press.

Eby, J.W. (1998). *Why service-learning is bad.* Accessed September 3, 2009, at http://glennblalock.org/~gblalock/glennblalock/wiki/uploads/ACSM1110f09/whySLbad.pdf

Endres, D., & Gould, M. (2009). "I am also in the position to use my Whiteness to help them out": The communication of Whiteness in service learning. *Western Journal of Communication, 73,* 418–436.

Federal Agency for Service and Volunteering. (27 Nov, 2012). *Volunteering and Civic Live in America.* Accessed February 5, 2013, at http://www.volunteeringinamerica.gov/

Fish, S. (2008). *Save the world on your own time.* New York: Oxford University Press.

Foucault, M. (1995). *Discipline and punish: The birth of the prison.* (Trans. A. Sheridan). New York: Vintage.

García, S.B., & Guerra, P.L. (2006). Conceptualizing culture in education: Implications for schooling in a culturally diverse society. In J.R. Baldwin, S.L. Faulkner, M.L. Hecht, & S.L. Lindsley (Eds.), *Redefining culture: Perspectives across the disciplines* (pp. 103–115). Mahwah, NJ: Lawrence Erlbaum Associates.

García Canclini, N. (1995). *Hybrid cultures: Strategies for entering and leaving modernity.* (Trans. C.L. Chiappari & S.L. López). Minneapolis: University of Minnesota Press.

Glascock, J., & Ruggiero, T. (2004). Representations of class and gender on primetime Spanish-language television in the United States. *Communication Quarterly, 52,* 390–402.

Graham, M.A., Moeiai, J., & Shizuru, L.S. (1985). Intercultural marriages: An intrareligious perspective. *International Journal of Intercultural Relations, 9,* 427–434.

Griffin, E. (2009). *A first look at communication theories* (7th ed.). Boston: McGraw-Hill.

Gudykunst, W.B., & Nishida, T. (1989). Theoretical perspectives for studying intercultural communication. In M.K. Asante & W.B. Gudykunst (Eds.) *Handbook of international and intercultural communication* (pp. 17–46). Newbury Park: Sage.

Habermas, J. (1998). *Between facts and norms.* (Trans. W. Rehg). Cambridge, MA: MIT Press.

Hall, B."J." (2003). *Among cultures: The challenge of communication* (2nd ed.). Belmont, CA: Wadsworth.

Hatch, E. (1994). The evaluation of culture. In L.A. Samovar & R.E. Porter (Eds.), *Intercultural communication: A reader* (7th ed., pp. 408–414). Belmont, CA: Wadsworth.

Hei, K.C. (2009). Moves in refusal: How Malaysians say "no". *Chinese Media Research, 5*(3), 31–44.

Imahori, T.T., & Cupach, W.R. (1994). A cross-cultural comparison of the interpretation and management of face: U.S. American and Japanese responses to embarrassing predicaments. *International Journal of Intercultural Relations, 18,* 193–219.

Itasaka, K. (6 Feb, 2013). How do you say "volunteer" in Russian? Sochi 2014 Olympics introduces a new concept. *NBC.com.* Accessed February 7, 2013, at http://worldnews.nbcnews.com/_news/2013/02/06/16852233-how-do-you-say-volunteer-in-russian-sochi-2014-olympics-introduces-a-new-concept?lite

Jacoby, B. (2009). Civic engagement in today's higher education. In B. Jacoby & Associates (Eds.), *Civic engagement in higher education: Concepts and practices* (pp. 5–30). San Francisco: Jossey-Bass.

Kale, D.W. (2000). Peace as an ethic for intercultural communication. In L.A. Samovar & R.E. Porter (Eds.), *Intercultural communication: A reader* (9th ed., pp. 450–455). Belmont, CA: Wadsworth.

Kim, M.-S., Wilson, S.R., Anastasiou, C.A., Oetzel, J., & Lee, H-R. (2009). The relationship between self-construals, perceived face threats, and facework during the pursuit of influence goals. *Journal of International and Intercultural Communication, 2,* 318–343.

Kohls, L.R. (2001). *Learning to think Korean: A guide to living and working in Korea.* Yarmouth, ME: Intercultural Press.

Kramarae, C. (1980). *Women and men speaking: Frameworks for analysis.* Rowley, MA: Newbury House.

Martin, J.N., & Nakayama, T.K. (2002). Ethical issues in intercultural communication. In J.N. Martin, T.K.

Nakayama, & L.A. Flores (Eds.), *Readings in intercultural communication* (2nd ed., pp. 363–371). Boston: McGraw-Hill.

Metts, S. (2004). Introduction to communication theory. In J.R. Baldwin, S.D. Perry, & M.A. Moffitt (Eds.), *Communication theories for everyday life* (pp. 55–73). Boston: Allyn & Bacon.

Miller, K. (2005). *Communication theories: Perspectives, processes, and contexts* (2nd ed.). Boston, MA: McGraw-Hill.

National Organization for Women (NOW) (n.d) *Who we are*. Accessed Aug. 23, 2013, at http://www.now.org/history/history.html

Niemi, J.I. (2008). The foundations of Jürgen Habermas's discourse ethics. *The Journal of Value Inquiry, 42*, 255–268. doi:10.1007/s10790-008-9119-7.

Not in our town. (n.d.). *Public Broadcasting System*. Accessed September 3, 2009, at http://www.pbs.org/niot/about/index.html

Potter, W.J. (1996). *An analysis of thinking and research about qualitative methods*. Mahwah, NJ: Lawrence Erlbaum Associates.

Remland, M.S., Jones, T.S., & Brinkman, H. (1995). Interpersonal distance, body orientation, and touch: Effects of culture, gender, and age. *The Journal of Social Psychology, 135*, 281–297.

Rosenau, P.M. (1992). *Post-modernism and the social sciences: Insights, inroads, and intrusions*. Princeton, NJ: Princeton University Press.

Shome, R., & Hedge, R.S. (2002). Postcolonial approaches to communication: Charting the terrain, engaging the intersections. *Communication Theory, 12*, 249–270.

Stijn, J. (2009). The hierarchy of global suffering: A critical discourse analysis of television news reporting on foreign natural disasters. *Journal of International Communication, 15*(2), 45–61.

Ting-Toomey, S. (1999). *Communicating across cultures*. New York: Guilford.

United Nations. (n.d.). *Universal Declaration of Human Rights*, Article 1. Accessed February 14, 2013, at http://www.un.org/en/documents/udhr/

van Dijk, T.A. (1998). *Ideology: A multidisciplinary approach*. London: Sage.

Welch, M. (2009). Moving from service-learning to civic engagement. In B. Jacoby (Ed.), *Civic engagement in higher education: Concepts and practices*. San Francisco: Jossey-Bass.

Wines, W.A., & Napier, N.K. (1992). Toward an understanding of cross-cultural ethics: A tentative model. *Journal of Business Ethics, 11*, 831–841.

Zompetti, J.P. (2006). Embracing a critical communication pedagogy: A radical examination of the common communication course. *Radical Pedagogy, 8*, Accessed February 14, 2013, at http://radicalpedagogy.icaap.org/content/issue8_2/

Zompetti, J.P. (2012). The cultural and communicative dynamics of capital: Gramsci and the impetus for social action. *Culture, Theory and Critique, 53*, 365–382.

Chapter 3

Origins: Where does our "culture" come from?

Chapter objectives

After this chapter, you should be able to:

→ **Compare two different models for how to understand communication and meaning**

→ **Explain some of the debates concerning the definition of communication**

→ **Describe different views of the relationship between culture and communication**

→ **Provide three competing views of how one could define culture**

→ **List some of the elements that might influence an interaction with someone from another culture or group, applying the model of communication provided in this chapter**

The relationship between communication and culture: How do they inform each other?

Defining culture: How can we define culture—and what are the implications of our definition?

Aspects and elements of culture: What is culture like?

A model of interaction: How can we best understand intercultural and intergroup communication?

Intercultural Communication for Everyday Life, First Edition. John R. Baldwin, Robin R. Means Coleman, Alberto González, and Suchitra Shenoy-Packer.
© 2014 John R. Baldwin, Robin R. Means Coleman, Alberto González, and Suchitra Shenoy-Packer.
Published 2014 by John Wiley & Sons Ltd.

People from one culture or nation sometimes call another group "uncultured." Professors and concerned citizens raise concerns about a "culture war." Organizations give training in "cultural sensitivity". Travelers abroad might suffer "culture shock", and some people say there is a "culture clash" between the younger and older generations (Figure 3.1). We see the word "culture" used in many different and sometimes contradictory ways by people in their everyday lives and by researchers from different fields.

These uses of the term culture highlight several issues that are central to our study of culture and communication. First, we must consider what culture even means. In the 19th century, authors like Matthew Arnold (1882/1971, p. 36) defined culture as "a study in perfection", leading to a clear distinction between **high culture**, referring to activities and expressions that represented what people believed to be moral and intellectual refinement (opera, theater, museums), as opposed to **low, or popular culture**, which included the everyday activities and expressions of people. But few scholars today hold such a definition. Another issue is whether, just by belonging to a particular racial, age, sex, national or other group, one can be said to have the "culture" of that group. Even if nations should not be considered as cultures, as we stated in chapter 1, people debate how large or small a group can be considered a culture—from a couple to an organization to a region of the world.

This chapter introduces possible ways to define culture, some of the building blocks and aspects of culture, and, finally, a model to help us understand intercultural or intergroup communication. But in order even to get to this point, we should first pause to consider the nature of communication itself.

Figure 3.1 Intergenerational communication. Does just being in a different age bracket or cohort (Generation Y, Baby Boomer, etc.) automatically mean that we speak from different "cultures"?
Source: Anna Peisl/Corbis.

The relationship between communication and culture: How do they inform each other?

Edward T. Hall (1959, p. 191) said, "Culture is communication, and communication is culture." That is not to say the two are equal, but rather that there is a close connection between communication and culture. If you are studying intercultural communication as part of a degree in some area of communication, you may already have encountered some sort of definition of communication, such as that communication is the transfer of meaning between a sender and a receiver. However, there is much debate as to whether something is or is not communication.

Defining communication

Katherine Miller (2005) summarizes the debate surrounding the notion of communication. She says most scholars agree that we should refer to communication as a process, rather than simply as a single message. We can think of a **message** as a set of symbols—words, sounds, or images—placed together to represent some meaning. While a message might transfer an idea from one person to another, that transfer exists in an ongoing set of messages and ongoing relationships. The concept of **process** refers not just to the message itself, but how it is intended, sent, received, and interpreted. For example, one standard model of communication (Shannon & Weaver, 1949/1964) describes communication as a message produced intentionally by a source and encoded by a **transmitter**; this made sense as one of the originators of the model was in telecommunications and imagined signals going through wires. The encoded message, now a signal, traveled through a **channel** and was decoded by a **receiver**, so that a message would arrive at a destination. **Noise** can interfere with the passing of the message through the channel (see Figure 3.2)

Such a model applies, for example, to a video-chat discussion between Christelle, a French student, and Guillermo, a friend she has made in Argentina. The Argentinian does not really hear her voice, but sound waves coming through cyberspace, and "noise" can be interference in the transmission, a poor Internet connection, or laughter in the Internet café where she is typing. In face-to-face communication, Christelle's voice and gestures become the transmitter, as she translates her ideas into a message. The channel is airwaves and the receiver, her friends'

Figure 3.2 Shannon and Weaver's model of communication is commonly used to explain the communication process.
Source: © Shannon, C., & Weaver, W. 1949/1964. The Mathematical Theory of Communication. Reproduced with permission of the University of Illinois Press.

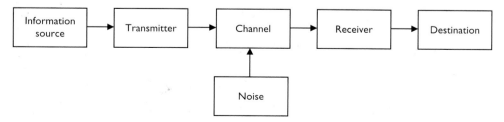

ears and eyes. In modern application, noise can be physical, such as whether the room is too cold, or it can be psychological. In this case, cultural and language differences are a type of noise. If Christelle wants her message to be better understood, she could do things to overcome "noise," such as giving the message at a different time, building some (but not too much) repetition into her message, or using more than one channel, like verbal and visual symbols.

Some suggest that this model is too linear and that, especially in face-to-face communication, both parties send and receive messages at the same time. The idea of **feedback** in the model addresses this criticism to some degree. That is, the receiver later, or even at the same time, gives some verbal or nonverbal response to the sender. Here, we find a second area of agreement, that communication is **transactional**. Communication involves give and take between two or more people, not just of message exchange, but of mutual influence: communicators influence each other, even if they are not aware of the influences. A third area of agreement is that communication is **symbolic**—communicators use words (verbal or printed); images such as photographs or emoticons; sounds such as sighs, grunts or laughter; and nonverbal behaviors such as a wave of the hand or a wink, to represent something else.

The fact that communication is symbolic is important for the study of culture, as it deals with the meaning of words. The symbolic nature of communication shows us that breakdowns in communication are based not only on psychological or physical noise, but also on meaning. The Ogden-Richards Triangle of Meaning (Ogden & Richards, 1923/1969) (Figure 3.3) suggests that we connect the words of people in our environment with the reality we experience. For example, we see a little furry animal, and someone says "guinea pig." This links the **reality**, the actual object in our environment, with a **symbol**, a sound or visual representation of the reality. Later, when someone uses the word or image, we sort through the **references**, or thought images in our mind, for the one that links to the symbol we originally heard in regard to that object or action. This is important in cultural communication. First, we realize that the same symbol—"guinea pig"—can be associated with different cultural realities. In each culture, if someone uses the symbol, it links directly to the thought, and if someone sees the object, it links to the thought. But the link between the

Figure 3.3 Ogden & Richards' Triangle of Meaning: People from different cultures—or even the same family—will have differences in meaning for a word, due to different experiences with the word. Source: adapted from Ogden & Richards (1923/1969).

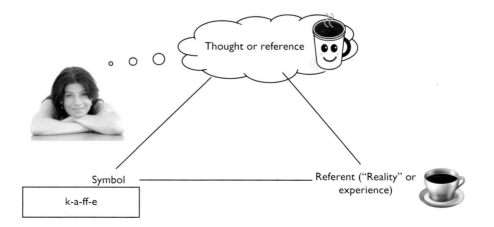

symbol and what it represents is not exact. A symbol means something different to each person, as no two people have the same experience with an object or with the symbol. One reader might think of a "guinea pig" as a furry pet she had as a child, but a reader in a different culture might think of an animal used in healing rituals or as a tasty snack. We see the cultural power of symbols in globalization: Starbucks, a coffee shop corporation with outlets around the world, has decided to drop the word "Starbucks" from the logo, similar to the wordless Nike "swoosh." The idea is that the image itself will link in consumers' minds, not only to coffee, but to a whole set of ideas associated with the identity of the Starbucks shops.

At the same time, scholars in the field of communication disagree on some points, such as whether or not one can communicate with oneself. As you wonder what you should wear, are you "communicating?" Some say call this "cognition," or thought, and consider it the realm of psychology research. Others call it **intrapersonal communication**, when one creates messages for oneself, within the mind. Another debate is whether communication must be intentional. Paul Watzlawick and his colleagues (1967, p. 51) suggested that "one cannot not communicate." As long as we are in the presence of others, if we do something, like dozing off in class, and someone else attributes meaning to the behavior, it is communication. Some people consider unintentional "symptomatic" nonverbal behaviors like yawns to be communication, stating that as long as another person gives meaning to the behavior, it is communicative (Andersen, 1991). Others argue that giving meaning to another's behavior is a psychological process, and say communication only occurs if someone intentionally sends a message and it is received (Motley, 1990).

What do you think? When people from different cultures work together, there are often different time expectations. One person might want to follow "clock time;" another might want to work out an argument until it is completed, even if it means running late for another appointment. To what degree do you think organizations should make clear expectations for things like time orientations, on which multicultural employees differ?

This debate is important in the study of intercultural communication, as in nonverbal communication. While we may want to study how people from different cultural groups create messages intentionally, it is also important to consider the unintentional effects of our messages. For that reason, the authors of this book consider **communication** to be the process of behaving and interpreting behavior (verbal, nonverbal, mediated) between people.

The relationship between communication and culture

The notion that communication is transactional, which includes the idea that communicators affect each other, lead us to a final consideration regarding communication, and that is its relationship to culture. One possible relationship is that culture is a variable that influences communication. In this view, "culture" or some aspect of identity (such as biological sex, age, or ethnicity) characterizes a group. If this is true, then we will make predictions about people based on culture. For example, Austria values equality and minimizes status (Hofstede, 2009), whereas people in Singapore see status differences as important for society (see chapter 4). In the same respect, many writers have done studies on how men or women, Blacks or Whites in the United States, or older and younger people might differ in terms of communication, treating sex, race, or age as a variable. A different view of culture states that people of a particular culture or identity group create values, beliefs, and norms of behavior through communication. This **constitutive approach** says that we socially create meanings and culture (Berger & Luckmann, 1966): Mahatma Gandhi and those who struggled with him reconstructed not only the politics but the self-definition of India. Sandra Metts (2004) suggests that communication both represents and constitutes reality. That is, we can use communication to describe things, much like the semantic triangle in Figure 3.3. But at the same time, cultures are in a constant process of change, some deliberate and some accidental, through the transactional communication of their members.

Break it down

The idea that that cultures continue to change and evolve through their communication is useful for civic engagement. We can see how organizational, family, or religious cultures change through time. While outside influences such as natural disasters or epidemics may constrain this change, ultimately, it is how people communicate about these things that leads to change. Think about a culture or identity group to which you belong. Think about the strengths and limitations of some aspect of that group. Make a list of potential actions that individuals or groups could pursue to bring a cultural shift in a direction that is more wholesome or effective for a greater number of members of the culture.

It might be that a view that culture and communication change each other through time is too simple. So there is a third approach—that the social construction of culture is an active process in which groups, with more or less awareness, struggle with one another. Culture change or stability is not simply a process of communication, but of intergroup striving—sometimes deliberate and sometimes not—through communication, law, policy, and other efforts, to make a particular cultural view dominant. In sum, the three views of relationship between communication and culture—culture as variable predicting communication; culture as created through ongoing communication; and culture and its creation serving certain power interests—correspond to the scientific, humanistic, and critical views of research (see chapter 2).

Defining culture: How can we define culture—and what are the implications of our definition?

The competing views of the relationship between culture and communication suggest that any single definition of culture will probably represent only certain research and theoretical perspectives. Researchers at different times have analyzed the variety of definitions of culture (Baldwin et al., 2006; Kroeber & Kluckhohn, 1952). In contrast to the early definition of culture as moral or intellectual evidence, noted at the beginning of this chapter, today we often treat culture as a group of people. We might talk about the Inuit culture of Canada and the United States, or the Ainu of Hokkaido, Japan, thinking not of beliefs or values, but of "the people who share culture" (Winkelman, 1993, p. 86). Others treat culture as a set of things that exist in a system, pattern, or structure, related to each other. This might be a system of meanings—values, norms, and beliefs (e.g., Keesing, 1981) or a whole "way of life" (Williams, 1981, p. 43). Others place meanings, behaviors, artifacts, and social systems all within the system of what they call culture. Culture for these writers is:

> The deposit of knowledge, experience, beliefs, values, attitudes, meanings, hierarchies, religion, notions of time, roles, spatial relations, concepts of the universe, and material objects and possessions acquired by a group of people in the course of generations through individual and group striving. (Samovar & Porter, 2003, p. 8)

Often, these writers not only focus on the structure of culture, but also on what it does; that is, on its function. It solves some problem for people or helps a group adjust to the stimuli in its environment. We might call these last approaches to culture the "suitcase" model of culture, as it treats culture like something that a family, organization, or other group has and passes on to others.

Some recent writers treat culture with the constitutive view described above, seeing cultures as "variable, open, and dynamic systems, and not as uniform, total, or totalizing entities" (Markus *et al.*, 1996, p. 863). Culture is like a "verb" (Street, 1993)—active and always changing. It both changes and is changed by the messages we create (Figure 3.4). And still others describe culture as a "contested zone in which different groups struggle to define issues in their own interests," with different groups having unequal access to the

Figure 3.4 Some views of culture focus on how ongoing communication is constantly creating and recreating your organizational culture.
Source: Dream Pictures/Blend Images/Corbis.

resources to get their message out to public forums (Moon, 2002, p. 16). In any culture there is a way of thinking or acting held by most people, but there are also other groups who hold and promote different ways of thinking or acting. Finally, other writers take a more post-modern view, not looking for what makes a group homogenous; instead they analyze how different sets of ideas compete for attention, such as how different groups in U.S. American society vie to define the meaning of "family" or how there are different ideologies of what it means to be "Black" in the United States.

What do you think? Think about the culture of your own group (from organization to nation—you decide!), especially if there is some conflict going on in the culture (e.g., new views of how the organization should operate; struggles around new views of the role of men and women in a religious organization). What are some of the dominant cultural premises, ways of action, or meanings? What are some that are "residual" or emerging? In changing cultures, which type or types of definition do you find most helpful and why?

It is important how we think and talk about culture or other identities such as sex/gender, race sexual orientation, or age. Much traditional intercultural research has treated and sometimes still treats cultures, sexes, or racial groups as "variables" and tries to describe or predict differences between these groups. This research is useful, as it does provide some general guidelines for us as we travel across national boundaries; but it hides the fact that even within the city of Athens, Greece, for example, we should expect to find several or many different cultures. Definitions that focus on the dynamic nature of culture are helpful for they slow down our tendency to think of cultures as unchanging. We often read books or see movies that describe a particular culture, but people from that culture might tell us that it really doesn't represent what their culture is like today. Church cultures, organizational cultures, and neighborhood cultures are always changing. More critical perspectives help us to understand that forces actively seek to change culture, sometimes through things such as political lobbying, or grassroots campaigns for social change, as we see in the growing environmental focus in many nations. But as we know, other forces give different understandings of things such as global climate change, and environmental issues frequently get mired down in political debates. In a similar way, if we look at growing individualism in Western (and other) cultures, we see that advertisers seek to promote and define that individualism in such a way that we define ourselves by purchasing consumer goods. Cultural notions of beauty support a multi-billion dollar cosmetic industry, and so on.

Each view of culture has its merits. We do believe that there are regularities, as shown through research, that, on the average, Russians will likely treat humor differently than Australian Aboriginals. Thus, social scientific research to understand cultures has an important place, especially as we develop organizational, local, and national policy. But we need a view of culture that both sees culture beyond national boundaries and admits its shifting nature. The politics of cultural change are important to admit, and people who hold the more political definitions of culture usually do not accept the traditional notions of culture. With a critical view of culture, for example, we see how different groups try to influence the assumptions about what education should be in our universities or national cultures. But we should not think that all such efforts are deliberate. Sometimes we tell jokes, make videos, or use communication patterns that simply pass on ways of thinking. Not all of these will be about one group or idea dominating another.

In the end, it is hard to find a definition of culture that covers all perspectives. We define **culture** in this book as the way of life of a group of people, including symbols, values, behaviors, artifacts, and other shared aspects, that continually evolves as people share messages and is often the result of struggle between different groups who share different perspectives, interests, and power relationships.

Aspects and elements of culture: What is culture like?

Cultures, whether we think of them as a system of elements or as a process of struggle between groups, are made up of certain components and act in certain ways. If someone asked us simply to "describe our culture," we might have difficulty, as culture seems formless and hard to get a hold of. It would be like trying to carry all of our books, pens, and papers to school, but without having a bag of some sort to carry them in! However, a list of aspects of culture gives us a way to organize our thoughts about culture. In this section, we describe elements of culture and then describe what it is like. The elements constitute or make up a culture—its parts, and the characteristics are how it operates, much like the wheels, frame, and cables are parts of a bicycle, but the way they work together to take us from one place to another describe how the bicycle functions.

Aspects of culture

Culture consists of a variety of concepts, behaviors, artifacts, and systems. The concepts include things like **values** (ideals or priorities a culture holds to be important), **beliefs** (ideas about the nature of things, with **world view** pertaining to beliefs specifically about humans and their role or place in the cosmos), and **rules**, **norms**, and **mores** (expectations for how one should act in certain situations, with the norms pertaining to whether those expectations have beliefs about the morality of an action and mores being strong enough to bring some social sanction if one does not follow them) (see chapter 4). In Brazil, family and time with friends are especially important, and it is important to show hospitality to them (values); and people speak of the future in a way that suggests a belief in God that may permeate everyday thinking more than in many Western cultures (world view).

The rules, norms, and mores are the mental patterns for behavior, with actual behaviors following these to a greater or lesser degree. Behaviors may be work-related (functional), have no apparent symbolic meaning (such as taking the bus in the big city, simply because it is the only transportation one might have available), or have symbolic meaning. A complicated class of behaviors and meanings is the **communication system** of a culture—the set of signs and symbols one uses to transfer ideas, emotions, or impressions to others. These include verbal behaviors, such as the carrying on of conversation; nonverbal behaviors, including everything from how close one stands to whether one has tattoos and facial piercings; paraverbal behaviors, which include sounds (laughter, sighs), and sounds of speech that are not words themselves (rate of speech, accent/pronunciation, pauses, intonation); and mediated messages, including those created through art, mass media, or other mediated forms. (We talk about messages in chapters 7–10). Language brings together elements of both thought and behavior. Concepts, behavior, and artifacts usually work together, such as the example of money. Money is an artifact with meaning, but we also have cultural ideas about how it should be used, which lead to different spending and saving behaviors in different cultures.

In the Brazilian example, there are many functional behaviors that are just the carrying on of life. In the Amazon city of Manaus, most people take two or three showers a day. However, actions reflect cultural concepts, such as values. It is also polite to offer guests a brief shower before visiting or eating. When eating at someone's house, the host may put a lot of food on the guest's plate, with the idea that it should be more than enough. The guest should show that it is more than enough by leaving some on the plate (behavior reflecting hospitality and connection). People use the *jeito brasileiro*—the "Brazilian Way"—building interpersonal connections to cut through the bureaucracy of systems. And, to reflect a view of the divine in everyday life, many people still say, "*se Deus quiser*" (God willing), when talking about plans for the future.

All of these aspects fit within various **social systems** of culture. Sociologists and anthropologists describe a variety of such systems—economic, educational, family, legal, political, leisure, and so on. To these, we add media systems. These systems provide a context within which cultural and intercultural communication occurs. Context is also a major influence on communication. For example, William Gudykunst and Young Yun Kim (2003) consider the physical setting (are we communicating in a tavern or in an office?), the climate, the potential of the context for interaction (are we at a movie or in a meeting?), and even the furnishings, as these impact the communication event. However, if we look at communication between Greek and Turkish Cypriots, Palestinian and Jewish residents of Israel, or Blacks and Whites in the United States, we must consider historical tensions as well as social, political, and economic contexts. Both views of context—environmental and social— are important, because relational, historical, and economical contexts, including contexts of warmth or hostility, advantage or disadvantage, influence our communication.

Characteristics of culture

Several authors have outlined some of the ways culture functions and some of the main characteristics of culture (e.g., Brislin, 2006; Samovar & Porter, 2004). These authors make important points about what culture is like that can guide our thinking as we look later at specific aspects of culture. We will summarize these, with some points of our own.

· ·

ON THE NET

Larry Samovar and Richard Porter (2004) suggest that one of the ways we learn our culture as we grow up is through proverbs. Here are a few examples:

- "Be not afraid of growing slowly. Be afraid only of standing still." – Chinese proverb
- "If you wish good advice, ask an old man" – Romanian proverb
- "This world is a harsh place, this world" – Zulu proverb

Find several proverbs from a particular culture (e.g., Romania, Italy) on the Internet. What can you find out about the culture from its proverbs?

· ·

Culture is learned and transmitted As we noted earlier, culture is learned and passed on, either through the generations, or, in younger organizational cultures, through the years. People who study culture note how we learn culture—it is not something that we are born with. We might mistakenly think that because someone is from such-and-such culture, she is naturally aggressive, or she should be able to hold her alcohol. Even if there is a genetic component to many such traits, actual behaviors are learned culturally. Samovar and Porter (2004) note how we learn culture through things such as cultural sayings or proverbs (see "On the Net," earlier), art, and mass media. We also learn culture from our family, friends, schools, churches, and other social institutions. The process of learning one's own culture is **enculturation**, with this referring to the people or processes that teach one the culture. If someone travels to another culture, that person goes through **acculturation**, the process of learning another culture, and **deculturation**, the unlearning of one's own culture. But we also learn culture through other means, as we will see below under culture change.

Culture is closely related to symbolic behavior (communication) As we noted before, culture is intricately tied to communication. First, communication is the primary means one learns culture. One might also learn through observation. But if culture is the human-made part of our environment (Brislin, 2000), then we would not have any culture if people did not communicate to create it. Thus, culture is created (and changed) through communication.

Cultures change… and stay the same Samovar and Porter (2004) note that all cultures are dynamic; that is, they are always changing. They outline three means of change: **invention** or **innovation**, where someone within a culture derives or creates a new artifact (like a cell phone), a new behavioral practice (like text-messaging someone), or a new idea (like communism), which, in turn, changes that culture. Cultures also change through **diffusion**, or the spread of artifacts, behaviors, and ideas across a group or culture or between groups or cultures. Thus, as communism spreads from its early roots (Marx) in Germany to Russia, China, Cuba, and other countries, it is "diffusing." In the same way, environmentalism, feminism, and ideas of civic engagement, have spread from culture to culture. Scholars study the spread of the cell phone through Amazonian or desert cultures, and study ways to get a culture with a high HIV + population, as a culture, to adopt safer sex. Finally, cultures can change through **acculturation**. Different from our first use of the word, which refers to individuals adapting their behaviors to a new culture, in this sense, acculturation refers to extensive contact between two groups, for example, that share the same space (for example, Black, White, Korean, and Latino cultures in a Los Angeles, USA, neighborhood). **Hybridity** is a notion that describes cultural blending between two cultures in contact. This can be in the form of a language that combines elements of two languages (see chapter 7), new art or music styles (K-pop, or Korean-pop music), or behaviors (using traditional medicine while one also sees a doctor) (Ashcroft et al., 2007). Postcolonial writers such as Jolanta Drzewiecka and Rona Halualani (2002) argue that in hybridity, elements are not blended evenly, but through power struggles and inequalities between groups. Some authors study the struggles within cultures between the tensions of change and stability, with different cultures (nations, organizations, churches, etc.) valuing change or stability to different degrees, and even different individuals within those groups having competing needs for change and stability (Martin et al., 2002).

What do you think? Consider a major city near you. Many cities have groups that have moved in large numbers from a single homeland to a variety of locations (a **diaspora**). There might be a blend of cultural practices, values, or world views as the two groups live side by side (**hybridity**). Consider the particular blend of peoples (e.g., Filipinos in Hong Kong; Indians in Caribbean nations; Chinese in Singapore). Describe the elements of each culture that are adopted or considered valid by the other culture. Is the cultural trade balanced? What factors do you think might influence whether either group adopts cultural traits of the other? In these cases, is a "melting pot" possible or beneficial? Why or why not?

Culture exists at different, interlocking levels We can also think of culture as existing at different levels. Young Yun Kim (1984) outlines several such levels (Figure 3.5). At the largest level are macroregional regions, large areas of the world that share cultural similarities, such as Southeast Asia, Latin America, or the Middle East. At the next level, we find regional or national cultures, such as the Australian Outback, or Chinese culture. Many authors in intercultural communication have studied differences between different national groups. Increasingly, however, researchers are thinking in terms of **co-cultural groups** as cultures as well. These are groups that share a space together, sharing some aspects of a dominant culture, and mixing or blending their cultures to a greater or lesser degree. Smaller cultural groups are organizational cultures, where even the company one works for, like Caterpillar or the Catholic Church, might have its own corporate values (influenced from location to location by regional/national cultures). Kim's smallest level of culture is "individual" culture; but since we believe culture is something that must be shared at some level, we do not see this as a culture. We do believe that there can be family or relational cultures. Carley Dodd and John Baldwin (2002), borrowing from Julia Wood's (1996) idea of relational cultures, suggest that, at a "microcultural" level, even families can have their own expectations, norms, and so on.

Figure 3.5 Levels of Culture. Young Yun Kim describes several levels at which culture might exist. We have modified her figure to include family cultures, but deleted individual culture, as we feel culture is shared.
Source: Kim, 1984, p. 18. Reproduced with permission.

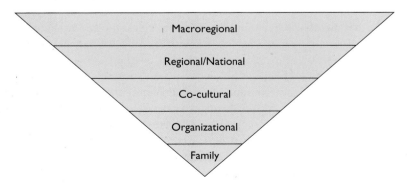

Certainly, these levels inform each other, and some may impact communication. Often co-cultural differences may be greater than national differences. Similar groups, such as farmers in China and in the Pantanal of South America might have more in common which each other than either group has with big-city dwellers in those two regions. The larger group we get, the more cautious we should be with claims. For example, China contains many cultural regions, which, while largely similar, will also pose some differences, and the "Middle East" consists of at least 18 distinct nations, each with various "cultures" within it, and characterized by a variety of languages, religions, and ethnic backgrounds.

Culture is mostly invisible to its members Brislin (2000) notes that most cultural members might have difficulty explaining their culture to others. As we will see in chapter 4, this is because so much of what is actually cultural is beyond our awareness. Our life within our culture is like a fish swimming in water, unaware of what makes up its environment.

Culture changes and is changed by its environment We've noticed that cultures are always changing (and staying the same), and we see above that communication works as a major force in both cultural change and stability. But social, political, and even physical environments impact culture. Andean native tribes, like the Aymara, will have cultural aspects that fit the mountain climate, while Western Samoa residents will select behavior suitable to an island culture and a tropical climate. Catastrophes such as the HIV-AIDS virus or the sudden rise of a hard-line military dictatorship can impact cultures. Still, even among mountain indigenous peoples or Sub-Saharan tribal cultures, there will be differences, as each group uses communication to make sense of its environment.

Birth and demographics are not culture Although culture has different definitions and exists at many levels, one thing that holds all definitions together is that culture is shared. Because of that, we suggest that there are differences between terms such as race, ethnicity, and culture, between sex and gender, and so on. **Race** refers to supposed biological differences between groups. We say supposed because even scientists who study people groups cannot agree on how many "races" there are, and the biological make-up of people of different racial groups is much more similar than it is different. In fact, race is as much (or more) political and social as it is biological. For example, the United States at one time determined that "one drop" (legally 1/16) of so-called Black blood made one White. The fact that the government did not define it the other way around highlights the racist assumptions of such a law.

Ethnicity is not race or culture; rather, it refers to a sense of shared history and geographical ancestry, usually along with other markers, such as culture, language, or religion (Herbst, 1997). We see that a single race can have people of many different ethnicities, but just because someone in the United States shares Native ancestry (ethnicity), they may not hold any elements of Native culture. Notably, most of these ethnicities refer to regions that only made sense after the rise of the nation state. Ethnicity is usually understood to relate to one's heritage both in terms of culture and location of ancestry, though many people think in terms of ancestry, even if they do not celebrate the culture of that ancestral group. Herbert Gans (1979) describes what he calls **symbolic ethnicity**, often held by the third and later generations of an ethnic group in a culture, where rather than engaging in ethnic cultures or organizations, people assimilate to the dominant culture but still use symbols, such as the

Jewish star, to represent their identity of ancestry. In sum, ethnicity is not equal to race, nor is either equal to culture. Two people of the same race can be of totally different cultures. Beyond this, we argue that being female, gay, or over 35 does not make one part of a culture unless the person shares communicative meaning with others from that same group.

The aspects of culture are interrelated
Samovar and Porter (2004, p. 44) suggest that "culture is an integrated system." In other words, if one aspect of a culture changes, that will impact other aspects of the culture. We can see this in the United States after World War II. Many African Americans moved to northern cities to take jobs while White men were at war (though, of course, many African Americans also took part in the war). Aside from the range of new technology that the war inspired, when the soldiers came home, they took their jobs back. There was a rise in union participation (to remove the Blacks from the jobs so the Whites could have them back), and the women who had also taken jobs were sent back home to take care of children. Black joblessness grew, as did segregation in the urban centers; there was a post-war rise of both Black consciousness and women's rights, and so on.

People may act differently from culture, but that does not mean that culture is not there
Gerry Philipsen and his colleagues (2005) point out that every group that has a language "code" also has a unique culture. They suggest that as long as people follow the norms, rules, and premises of their cultures, we can predict their behavior. But these codes of culture are only guidelines, and people have the agency to follow or not follow them. Brislin (2006) states that even though we can think of cultural mistakes cultural members make—exceptions to the cultural rules—the very fact that we realize they are exceptions proves that there is an overall cultural preference for certain **attitudes** or behaviors. We would go a step further to note that these are not always "mistakes and errors," but that many of us seek deliberately to overturn, transgress, or disrupt culture. We saw this in Britain and the United States from the 1970s onward with the Punk Rock movement.

ON THE NET

Mark Rosenfelder, a "con-langer" (creator of constructed languages and worlds)—"mostly after midnight, with a touch of lime"—has created an extensive web page on aspects of language and culture (http://www.zompist.com). This includes contributed pages on "How to tell if you're American" (or Quebequois, Colombian, Swedish, Greek, or Texan). See if it describes your culture. Think about ways that you are like or not like your culture. If you are different from your culture in some ways, what does that mean for you as you communicate with other people from other places?

People in all cultures are ethnocentric
Finally, one thing that all cultures seem to have in common is that they are ethnocentric. **Ethnocentrism** refers to the belief that our culture or group is better than others. We may not feel this way intentionally, but because of the invisible nature of culture, we fall into the second definition of ethnocentrism: using our cultural framework as a tool with which to guide people from other cultures. We see ethnocentrism in the names we often use for ourselves—Jew and Gentile, Greek and Barbarian. Even many names of people groups are translated, literally, "the people" (e.g., Inuit), the "civilized people" (Titska Watich), or the "original people" (Sahnish) (Original Tribal Names of Native North American People, 2007). Each country's map seems to highlight or center

Figure 3.6 The meaning of a name. Zhong-guo is the Chinese name for China (the English name refers back to a specific dynasty of about 2000 years ago). It is comprised of two symbols, meaning "center country." While other countries may not show this centering of themselves in their name, all cultures are to some degree ethnocentric.

that country, and in some cases, even the name of the country, like China's (Figure 3.6) reflects a sense of that country's location in its own esteem of the world. However, we feel that it is not useful for intercultural effectiveness or for moving and adjusting to other cultures and that it is something that we can learn to recognize and even reduce in ourselves and others.

A model of interaction: How can we best understand intercultural and intergroup communication?

As we have noted, the face-to-face and mediated sharing of messages between people of different cultures is a process of exchange (a transactional process) in which parties bring something to the exchange as producers and consumers of messages. Our question in this section is, with all there is to consider in an intercultural interaction, can we simplify it in such a way that will help us be better communicators? We present here a model of intercultural/intergroup communication that we hope you will find practical. A model of communication is much like a diagram or model of a Vespa, for example, for someone who works on motor scooters. The model should serve to help us make sense of the interaction, but it should also be useful if there is some breakdown in communication to help communicators troubleshoot what has happened in the interaction.

As we have seen above, race and ethnicity are not culture, just as age is not culture. But sometimes, these things impact our communication, even if culture is not present. In this case, we want to begin our model by discussing the first axis, **intergroup communication**. Henri Tajfel and John Turner (1986), in their social identity theory, suggest that we always perceive others on some continuum from interpersonal to intergroup. They argue that we always see people, at least in part, in terms of the groups to which they belong (see chapter 6). In the case of war or intergroup conflict, we often see members of the other group only as group members. If we have a spouse or lover, we probably see that person mostly in terms of interpersonal aspects—we interact with them and have expectations of their behavior in terms of our personal knowledge of them. As we get to know people, we move from seeing them only as group members to knowing them more and more as individuals (**interpersonal communication**). Still, at some point, the groups to which we and the others belong are probably still in the back of our minds.

William Gudykunst and Tae-Sop Lim (1986) modified this original model to account for things such as intercultural romantic relationships, by treating interpersonal and intergroup as two separate dimensions (two axes of our model), with both ranging from low to

Figure 3.7 A three-axis model of communication. Communication with anyone will have three aspects that become more or less important in interaction: perception of the other as an individual, perception of the other as a group member, and real cultural differences.

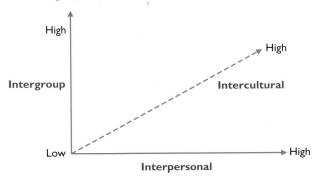

high. Communicators could perceive a given interaction as high in both intercultural and intergroup aspects, such as when two people from different ethnic groups are close friends and both understand each other in terms of individual characteristics and validate the groups to which the other belongs. One could be high in intergroup perception but low in interpersonal perception (seeing the person only as a group member), or high only on interpersonal (interacting with the other primarily as an individual). But one could also be low on both factors. This might happen in a culture that treats people primarily in terms of role relationships. We might interact with the cashier at the pharmacy or the person who cleans our building as a "non-person," acting as if they are not even there except to meet functional needs. Here, both group identification and interpersonal perception are low.

Although Gudykunst and Lim's (1986) revision is good, it treats intercultural and intergroup communication the same. In our model, we separate these to create a third axis—intercultural communication. If cultures exist, as we suggest above, from very large to very small—such as organizational cultures, classroom cultures, and so on—then we could easily say that all communication is inherently intercultural, and the term ceases to have any meaning. We define **intercultural communication**, then, as communication in which cultural differences are large enough to impact the production or consumption of messages. But more realistically, communication can range from very low on the intercultural aspect to extremely high.

Thus, we present a model with three axes (Figure 3.7), with three dimensions that can exist from low to high. The three dimensions are unrelated, so we have to imagine the model in three-dimensional space. The interpersonal axis reflects the degree to which we see and treat the person as an individual. This axis is important because it reminds us that, even if we are speaking with members of other groups or cultures, we are ultimately speaking to or listening to media created by individuals, who will both reflect and differ from their cultures. The intergroup axis deals with our perception of the other as a group member. Thus, it deals with our perceptions of and feelings toward the other group, and includes things such as stereotypes and prejudice (see chapter 6). We might interact with someone in our neighborhood who looks different from us and act assuming the person is different—even if we are culturally the same. The third axis, intercultural communication, deals with real differences in everything from values and world view to verbal and nonverbal communication, to cultural perceptions of roles and how people should act in those roles (e.g., as teachers and students). If this dimension is high but the intergroup dimension is low, we might talk with someone who looks like us and think that they are from "our" group, but without our awareness, cultural differences may impact the conversation. In media and rhetorical communication, the interpersonal dimension will likely be low (unless an audience member knows the speaker or media producer), but the cultural dimension may be important, and, on the intergroup dimension, someone might discount a speaker or media message simply because of the group that she, he, or it represents.

All interactions can be thought of in terms of these three dimensions. If Helena, a Chilean manager, is talking to Carlos, a representative from his culture in Colombia, cultural differences may be present, but not as large as if he were from The Philippines. When they first work together, the interpersonal element will be low, but will increase the more direct contact they have. But if Claudio is Afro-Colombian, each may come to the interaction with stereotypes about the other race (or the other sex, or the fact that Francisca does not speak the Colombian variety of Spanish or that Claudio grew up in a small town, unlike Francisca's big city). In this case, the problem will not be cultural differences—these, in fact, might be minimal—but rather perceived differences. Their interaction would be high in intergroup communication. Likely, all three elements may shift in importance between and even within interactions between the two of them.

Summary

In this chapter we considered the nature of communication and culture and their relationship to each other. Some feel that culture should best be treated as a variable that predicts communication; others see communication as a process that is continually shaping culture. These two views seem to oppose each other, though they do not need to. A constitutive view of communication allows us to consider that communication shapes culture, which in turn shapes communication, and so on. Definitions of culture and communication reflect the same ways of thinking (**paradigms**) that have influenced the fields that look at culture and communication, especially scientific, humanistic, and critical ways of thinking (see chapter 2). We might think of culture like a suitcase of things (values, beliefs, artifacts, norms) that we pass on to the next generation, as a never-ending process, or as a struggle between groups for power for power or prestige.

Finally, we presented a model of communication that considers three dimensions—individual, intergroup, and intercultural. This model shows us that we are always communicating with individuals from cultures and groups, not the groups themselves. But it also shows us that as we communicate with someone in another culture, like a United States person talking with someone from France, stereotypes and prejudice, and not only cultural difference, may be present. So also, two people in the same culture might think that there are differences just because the other person looks different or wears a different political or religious name, but in terms of real differences in values, beliefs, and behaviors, the two could be very much the same.

How we think about culture is important for civic and political engagement. If we are engaged, our action shapes the cultures with which we interact, or our own culture. Our action or inaction, at a minimum, reproduces and shapes our culture. But some causes in which we are involved also involve us in ideology struggles within our culture. Gun control is currently a controversial issue in the United States. The right to own guns to protect oneself against a tyrannical government is written into the U.S. constitution. But as we get involved to address bullying in schools, to provide support to those who have been at schools where there are shootings, or to advocate for the continued right to own guns in the face of increasing government restrictions on gun ownership, we engage in a debate that shapes culture. After one recent school shooting, there were calls not to make the issue political, though even silence in the face of such issues provides support for whatever the status quo way of thinking is. The way we think about culture and cultures will shape the way we describe other cultures and work and interact with people from those cultures, in and out of civic engagement efforts. Hopefully, a more complex view of culture and its components will help us to interact with people as individuals informed by their cultures, and see their cultures as complex and dynamic.

KEY TERMS

high culture, 48	more, 55
low/popular culture, 48	communication system, 55
message, 49	social systems, 56
process, 49	enculturation, 57
transmitter, 49	acculturation, 57
channel, 49	deculturation, 57
receiver, 49	invention, 57
noise, 49	innovation, 57
feedback, 50	diffusion, 57
transactional, 50	acculturation, 57
symbolic, 50	hybridity, 57
reality, 50	diaspora, 58
symbol, 50	co-cultural groups, 58
references, 50	race, 59
intrapersonal communication, 51	ethnicity, 59
communication, 51	symbolic ethnicity, 59
constitutive approach, 52	attitude, 60
culture, 55	ethnocentrism, 60
value, 55	intergroup communication, 61
belief, 55	interpersonal communication, 61
world view, 55	intercultural communication, 62
rule, 55	paradigms, 63
norm, 55	

Discussion questions

1 Describe a traditional fairy tale in your culture. What values, beliefs, or behaviors does it promote? If you could write a new ending to the tale to reflect cultural change, what would you write?

2 Think about an interaction you have recently had with someone from a different group (in terms of age, culture, ethnicity, etc.). Look at it using the model of culture. Which

aspects of communication were most relevant in the interaction (personal, cultural, intergroup) and why?

3 Do you feel that different genres of music in your culture reflect different "cultures?" Find a video (on YouTube, if it is available in your culture) or a song from the type of music you like. Analyze the lyrics and style of music to see if you can determine some things about culture at different levels (national, ethnic, music genre).

4 Do you feel that "race" is biological, or socially and politically created? Give evidence for your opinion. What are the implications of either approach to "race?"

Action points

1 Find a copy of your local school or community paper and read through the editorial section (paper editorial and letters to the editors). What are the key issues of the day? What conflict or struggle over cultural meanings, values, or practices do these reflect? Which do you feel are the most important, and why?

2 Volunteer to work in a homeless shelter or soup kitchen, hopefully more than once. Before you go, look up the "culture of poverty" on the Internet—don't forget also to look up criticisms of the idea that there is a culture of poverty. Serve, but also observe people around you. Talk to them if you can, and get to know them. How are they similar, but also different from one another? Does simply being poor give one certain cultural characteristics, or vice versa?

3 Interview a politician in your city or an administrator in your school about current issues or debates in your community. Write a short paper or blog post summarizing the issue—what are the sides? How does the notion of culture (or competing cultures) inform your understanding of the debate?

For more information

Abu-Lughod, L. (1991). Writing against culture. In R.G. Fox (Ed.), *Recapturing anthropology: Working in the present* (pp. 137–162). Santa Fe, NM: School of American Research Press.
Baldwin, J.R., Faulkner, S.L., Hecht, M.L., & Lindsley, S.L. (Eds.). (2006). *Redefining culture: Perspectives across the disciplines*. Mahwah, NJ: Lawrence Erlbaum.
Kroeber, A.L., & Kluckhohn, C. (1952). *Culture: A critical view of concepts and definitions*. Cambridge: Harvard University Press.
Moon, D.G. (2008). Concepts of "culture:" Implications for intercultural communication research. In M. K. Asante, Y. Miike, & J. Yin (Eds.), *The global intercultural communication reader* (pp. 11–26). New York: Routledge.
Shuter, R. (2000). Revisiting the centrality of culture. In J.N. Martin, T.K. Nakayama, & L.A. Flores (Eds.), *Readings in cultural contexts* (pp. 38–48). Mountain View, CA: Mayfield.

References

Andersen, P.A. (1991). When one cannot not communicate: A challenge to Motley's traditional communication postulates. *Communication Studies, 42*, 309–325.

Arnold, M. (1882/1971). Culture and anarchy: An essay in political and social criticism. In I. Gregor (Ed.), *Culture and anarchy: An essay in political and social criticism* (pp. 1–176). Indianapolis: Bobbs-Merril.

[Reprint of London: Smith, Elder, & Co., 1882 version]

Ashcroft, B., Griffiths, G., & Tiffin, H. (2007). *Postcolonial studies: The key concepts* (2nd ed.). London: Routledge.

Baldwin, J.R., Faulkner, S.L., Hecht, M.L., & Lindsley, S.L. (Eds.). (2006). *Redefining culture: Perspectives across the disciplines*. Mahwah, NJ: Lawrence Erlbaum.

Berger, P.L., & Luckmann, T. (1966). *The Social construction of reality: A treatise in the sociology of knowledge*. New York: Doubleday.

Brislin, R.W. (2000). *Understanding culture's Influence on Behavior* (2nd ed.). Ft. Worth: Harcourt.

Brislin, R.W. (2006). Culture and behavior: An approach taken in psychology and international business. In J.R. Baldwin, S.L. Faulkner, M.L. Hecht, & S.L. Lindsley (Eds.), *Redefining culture: Perspectives across the disciplines* (pp. 83–90). Mahwah, NJ: Lawrence Erlbaum Associates.

Dodd, C.H., & Baldwin, J.R. (2002). The role of family and macrocultures in intercultural relationships. In J.N. Martin, T.K. Nakayama, & L.A. Flores (Eds.), *Readings in intercultural communication: Experiences and contexts* (2nd ed., pp. 279–288). Boston: McGraw Hill.

Drzewiecka, J.A., & Halualani, R.T. (2002). The structural-cultural dialectic of diasporic politics. *Communication Theory, 12*, 340–366.

Gans, H.J. (1979): Symbolic ethnicity: The future of ethnic groups and cultures in America. *Ethnic and Racial Studies, 2*(1), 1–20.

Gudykunst, W.B., & Kim, Y.Y. (2003). *Communicating with strangers: An approach to intercultural communication* (4th ed.). Boston: McGraw Hill.

Gudykunst, W.B., & Lim, T.S. (1986). A perspective for the study of intergroup communication. In W. B. Gudykunst (Ed.), *Intergroup communication* (pp. 1–9). London: Edward Arnold.

Hall, E.T. (1959). *The silent language*. New York: Doubleday.

Herbst, P. (1997). *The color of words: An encyclopedia of ethnic bias in the United States*. Yarmouth, ME: Intercultural Press.

Hofstede, G. (2009) Cultural dimensions. *Itim International*. Accessed March 2, 2011, at http://www.geert-hofstede.com

Keesing, R.M. (1981). Theories of culture. In R.W. Casson (Ed.), *Language, culture, and cognition* (pp. 42–67). New York: Macmillan.

Kim, Y.Y. (1984). Searching for creative integration. In W.B. Gudykunst & Y.Y. Kim (Eds.), *Methods for intercultural communication research* (pp. 13–30). Beverly Hills: Sage.

Kroeber, A.L., & Kluckhohn, C. (1952). *Culture: A critical view of concepts and definitions*. Cambridge: Harvard University Press.

Markus, H.R., Kitayama, S., & Heiman, R.J. (1996). Culture and "basic" psychological principles. In E.T. Higgins & A.W. Kruglanski (Eds.), *Social psychology: handbook of basic principles* (pp. 857–913). New York: Guilford.

Martin, J.N., Nakayama, T.K., & Flores, L.A. (2002). A dialectical approach to intercultural communication. In J.N. Martin, T.K. Nakayama, & L.A. Flores (Eds.), *Readings in intercultural communication* (pp. 3–13). Boston: McGraw-Hill.

Metts, S.M. (2004). Introduction to communication theory. In J.R. Baldwin, S.D. Perry, & M.A. Moffitt (Eds.), *Communication theories for everyday life* (pp. 3–20). Boston: Allyn & Bacon.

Miller, K. (2005). *Communication theories: Perspectives, processes, and contexts* (2nd ed.). Boston: McGraw Hill.

Moon, D.G. (2002). Thinking about 'culture' in intercultural communication. In J.N. Martin, T.K. Nakayama, & L.A. Flores (Eds.), *Readings in intercultural communication: Experiences and contexts* (2nd ed., pp. 13–21). Boston: McGraw Hill.

Motley, M.T. (1990). On whether one can(not) not communicate: An examination via traditional communication postulates. *Western Journal of Speech Communication, 54*, 1–20.

Ogden, C.K., & Richards, I.A. (1923/1969*). The meaning of meaning; A study of the influence of language upon thought and of the science of symbolism*. London: Routledge.

Original tribal names of Native North American people. (2007). *Native Languages of the Americas*. Accessed March 2, 2011, at http://www.native-languages.org/original.htm

Philipsen, G., Couto, L.M., & Covarrubias, P. (2005). Speech codes theory: Restatement, revisions, and response to criticisms. In W.B. Gudykunst (Ed.), *Theorizing about intercultural communication* (pp. 55–68). Thousand Oaks: Sage.

Samovar, L., & Porter, R.E. (2003). Understanding intercultural communication: An introduction and overview. In L.A. Samovar & R.E. Porter (Eds.), *intercultural communication: A reader* (10th ed., pp. 6–17). Belmont, CA: Wadsworth.

Samovar, L., & Porter, R.E. (2004). *Communication between cultures* (5th ed.). Belmont, CA: Thompson-Wadsworth.

Shannon, C., & Weaver, W. (1949/1998). *The mathematical theory of communication*. Urbana: University of Illinois Press.

Street, B.V. (1993). Culture is a verb. In D. Graddol,
L. Thompson, & M. Byram (Eds.), *Language and
culture* (pp. 23–43). Clevedon: BAAL in association
with Multilingual Matters.

Tajfel, H., & Turner, J.C. (1986). The social identity
theory of intergroup behavior. In S. Worchel & W.G.
Austin (Eds.), *Psychology of intergroup relationships*
(2nd ed., pp. 7–24). Chicago: Nelson-Hall.

Watzlawick, P., Beavin, J.H., & Jackson, D.D. (1967).
*Pragmatics of human communication: A study
of interactional patterns, pathologies, and paradoxes.*
New York: Norton

Williams, R. (1981). The analysis of culture.
In T. Bennett, G. Martin, C. Mercer, & J. Woollacott
(Eds.), *Culture, ideology and social process: A reader*
(pp. 43–52). London: Open University.

Winkelman, M. (1993). *Ethnic Relations in the U.S.*
St. Paul, MN: West.

Wood, J. T. (1996). Communication and relational
culture. In K. M. Galvin & P. Cooper (Eds.),
Making connections (pp. 11–15). Los Angeles:
Roxbury.

Elements

Part two

In the first section of the book, we looked at the foundation of what culture is, why we should study it, and at least one aspect of what should guide all cultural communication—ethics. In this section, we break down three main aspects that impact how we produce and consume messages: the "ideas" prominent within a culture, our view of ourselves (identity), and our attitudes toward people of other groups. William Gudykunst and Young Yun Kim (2003) argue that these three aspects influence all messages we send and receive, as these, in turn, are influenced by the contexts of the communication.

While some see culture as the whole "way of life" of a group of people (Williams 1981, p. 43), others feel that culture is really a set of beliefs, values, and expectations for behavior—but not the behaviors or artifacts themselves. Regardless of how we define culture, it makes sense that the ideas of culture—beliefs, values, and norms—are what drive behavior and the creation of texts and artifacts (which, in turn, produce and reproduce the cultural ideas). In chapter 4, we review these different components and outline some approaches that scholars have used to try to understand specific cultures and to compare cultures with one another.

Chapter 5 turns to issues of identity. We discuss how we see ourselves as individuals and in terms of the groups to which we belong. We outline some approaches to how we develop identity, then move to how we experience different identities daily, specifically, through the politics of identity. That is, we talk about how identities within a culture exist in power relationships, often with the dominant culture media tending to misrepresent (or not represent at all) people of particular identities. We present some specific examples of identity politics, such as Orientalism—a Western way of thinking about and describing Middle Eastern and other cultures.

Intercultural Communication for Everyday Life, First Edition. John R. Baldwin, Robin R. Means Coleman, Alberto González, and Suchitra Shenoy-Packer.
© 2014 John R. Baldwin, Robin R. Means Coleman, Alberto González, and Suchitra Shenoy-Packer.
Published 2014 by John Wiley & Sons Ltd.

How we think about ourselves and our groups is closely tied to how we see others' groups, so in chapter 6, we address issues of prejudice, tolerance, and appreciation. We introduce a variety of terms related to prejudice, such as ethnocentrism, xenophobia, and heterosexism. Further, we discuss where types of intolerance such as "racism" lie, that is, whether we should think of them only in individual terms of personal attitude or see them in social structures as well. This discussion is important, because if, as the goal of civic engagement of this book implies, we seek to redress or reduce intolerance and act toward appreciation, we need a better understanding of the problem of intolerance. In that way, our solutions will more effectively address the specific forms of intolerance within our societies.

References

Gudykunst, W. B., & Kim, Y. Y. (2003). *Communicating with strangers: An approach to intercultural communication* (4th ed.). Boston: McGraw Hill.

Williams, R. (1981). The analysis of culture. In T. Bennett, G. Martin, C. Mercer, & J. Woollacott (Eds.), *Culture, ideology and social process: A reader* (pp. 43–52). London: Open University.

Chapter 4

Subjective culture: What is the base upon which cultural communication is built?

Chapter objectives

After this chapter, you should be able to:

→ Explain the difference between subjective and objective aspects of culture

→ Differentiate between norms, rules, values, beliefs, mores, taboos, and laws

→ Produce examples of primary dimensions of culture

→ Compare the emic and etic approaches to understanding subjective culture

→ List some strengths and limitations to each approach to understanding culture

Basic building blocks of culture: What are the most important things to know?

Cultural values: What are some useful frameworks for understanding culture?

World view: What are the beliefs at the center of our "world?"

Intercultural Communication for Everyday Life, First Edition. John R. Baldwin, Robin R. Means Coleman, Alberto González, and Suchitra Shenoy-Packer.
© 2014 John R. Baldwin, Robin R. Means Coleman, Alberto González, and Suchitra Shenoy-Packer.
Published 2014 by John Wiley & Sons Ltd.

The Peace Corps, an agency known around the world for sending workers across borders to help other communities, has produced a video of 15 top cultural mistakes that cross-cultural travelers can commit (Peace Corps, n.d.). For example, in Denmark, if you are squeezing past people in a row to find a seat, you should face the people you are passing instead of having your back toward them, in contrast to the practice of facing away from people as you step in front of them, as is the case in many cultures. In Colombia, you should not indicate someone's height by showing your hand at a certain level, as this gesture is only used to describe animals. In Romania and other parts of Eastern Europe, it is great to give flowers to a friend—but hand them with the blossoms down and not up, and be sure to give an odd number of flowers on a happy occasion as even numbers are for funerals. And in Sierra Leone, you cannot just say goodbye to your guest at your door. To be culturally appropriate, you should walk your guest part of the way home, "at least to the first bridge."

The Peace Corps video gives useful hints: learn about the culture from books or natives of the culture before traveling; observe other people in the culture; watch for awkward silences; be direct in addressing misunderstandings and polite in asking questions or making apologies for misbehaviors; inform others helpfully if they make a mistake in your culture; laugh about it, if the blunder is not serious. Even though the behaviors listed in the video are about specific cultures, they teach us about behaviors common in other places. Romanian flower rules help us realize that cultures have intricate gift-giving rules. When do you give gifts? Do you open them in front of the giver? How do you wrap or package them? The Sierra Leone practice of walking to the first bridge is similar to customs in other cultures, such as China. If you are traveling abroad, it is helpful to learn about the details of that culture—etiquette, manners, things that might be offensive. But there are many things we might not be aware of, things that the guidebooks miss.

Each gaffe mentioned above is based on a deeper foundation of meanings. This aspect of meaning and thought that distinguishes culture is what Harry Triandis (2002) refers to as **subjective culture**. He distinguishes this from **objective culture**, which refers to the artifacts that a culture produces. Aspects of culture defined in chapter 3—values, beliefs, and world views—form the deep structure of a culture. Although it is important to understand aspects of verbal and nonverbal communication, organizational etiquette, and, beyond communication, social, political, and religious organizations, one thing that helps us best understand other societies is their subjective culture. This forms the foundation upon which all other elements of communication and society are built.

Basic building blocks of culture: What are the most important things to know?

Many cross-cultural trainers have described culture as an "iceberg," as evidenced by the many examples of the iceberg model of culture that can be found on the Internet. Figure 4.1 provides one such representation. The idea of the metaphor is that what one sees on the surface of culture are things such as literature, music, food, dance, art, and architecture. In cultural celebrations, these are often the main things we represent—a cultural diversity fair might include music or food from different ethnic or cultural groups. But there is an invisible part of culture that includes things such as how we raise our children, how we make a

Figure 4.1 The iceberg model of culture shows that much of our culture—and that of others—is beyond our awareness.
Source: *AFS Orientation Handbook* Vol. 4, p. 41. New York: AFS Intercultural Programs Inc., 1984.

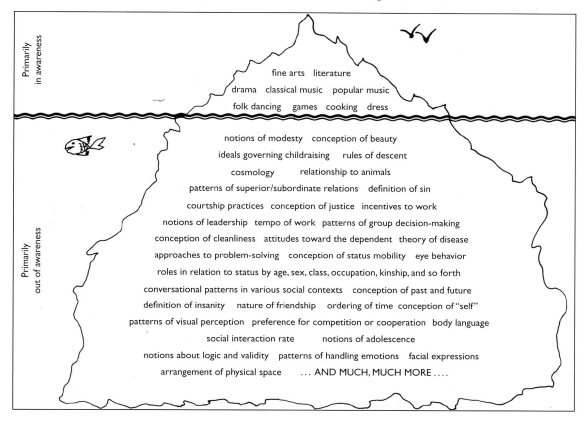

logical argument, how and to whom we show status, and what the pace of life is. These are hidden from view, so we often assume them to be natural, rather than cultural. We assume that everyone knows how to raise children or be a friend, that everyone else's way will be the same as our way. If culture impacts our relationship or communication, it is much more likely to be over things such as the rules for when to express emotion or what constitutes modesty, rather than whether one of us likes post-punk music and the other cool jazz. Because we are not aware that these things change from culture to culture, we are likely to judge one another negatively when someone does them differently.

Different types of belief form the deep structure of culture. **Beliefs** are assumptions about the nature of something, a thought about the connection between two or more concepts. For example, a belief that the Earth is round is a thought that connects the notion of the Earth with the notion of roundness. If you believe that China had printed periodicals and books before 900 C.E., several hundred years before the Gutenberg Press, you would have a belief about printing presses, China, and time periods. Beliefs are interwoven with other beliefs of different types into **belief systems**. Islam, Buddhism, or animism represent such sets of interrelated beliefs. There are more specific types of beliefs within each belief system. For example, religious belief systems contain a **world view**, or beliefs about the connections between humans and the larger elements of the universe. Each system is a set of assumptions or cognitions about things such as the purpose of humans, the nature of deity, and the relative position of humans to nature and the rest of the cosmos.

A **value** is a type of a belief that a thing, idea, or activity is important and should serve as a guide for behavior. For example, the reason for walking a guest part of the way home is so the guest does not have to leave alone. But more than that, the act reflects what is important to the culture: hospitality and connection. Often, we can express values with single words or phrases, such as honesty, freedom, success, or family. Values are enduring—that is, they do not change easily; and they influence behavior (Rokeach, 1973). Even if surface features of a culture change, values will be much slower to change, like the deep currents of the ocean that sit beneath the changing surface waves. We will be concerned here with **cultural values**, held by the majority of members of a cultural group, rather than individual values. Finally, **attitudes** describe the way we relate to things, actions, or people. They are more of an emotional (or "affective") reaction to things, influenced by and influencing beliefs, values, and norms.

What do you think? Think about two cultures or co-cultures of which you are a member. For example, if you are a typical college-age student, you might be a member of a late adolescent or young adult culture, but also of a particular national, ethnic, or other culture (e.g., Korean, Latino/a, or Deaf). What are some ways in which the values, world view, beliefs, and attitudes of these two groups are similar or different? How do you find resolution when the values and beliefs of the groups you belong to collide?

Other types of cultural belief involve behavior more directly. **Rules** are prescriptions for behavior—cultural beliefs about which behaviors are appropriate in certain situations. These refer to things that we can or cannot, should or should not do. For example, in U.S. culture, if professors ramble without a point during their lectures, they might be weird or out of place, but not necessarily bad people. William Gudykunst and Young Yun Kim (2003) define **norms** as expectations for behavior with a moral component. If someone violates a norm, the person is seen as a bad or immoral person. Thus, if a teacher lies to give one student privilege over another in grading, the teacher would be seen as violating a norm. If the norm is very strong, with negative social results for violating it, it becomes a **more**. A **taboo** is a cultural more so strong people do not normally even mention it. If a government legalizes what one can or cannot do in terms of behavior, it becomes a **law**. Rules, norms, mores and laws are also linked to values, beliefs, and world views.

Values and world views are the bedrock upon which norms and rules, and, in turn, communicative behavior, are built, so we will devote the rest of this chapter to more detailed consideration of these. Values and world view drive our communication behavior. At the same time, individuals cannot always act upon their values, beliefs, or world view. Very often, social and structural constraints are present in people's lives that work against their agency, and people have unequal access to the ability to enact cultural values or express their beliefs. A fuller understanding of the foundations we present in this chapter would include the situation of people within their social class, ethnic, religious, political and relational group, and other contexts.

Figure 4.2 Tattoos reveal both personal beliefs and values, as well as cultural norms. Chelsea and DE'votion at X Factor audition, Birmingham 2011.
Source: John Robertson/Alamy.

We can understand the way the different types of belief relate to each other by considering the cultural notion of beauty. Cultures have different beliefs about what is beautiful. For example, one culture may value multiple lip plates (Mursi women of Ethiopia; Kayopo men of the Amazon), or body painting (Australian Aborigines), or detailed and extensive tattoos. What is considered beautiful in terms of weight, the number and location of body piercings, hair styles, and clothing changes through time in a given culture. We have beliefs about what tattoos mean and what types of people wear them. A belief that tattoos are "cool" indicates an attitude to either like or admire them, or even to get one. Forces work to change values, beliefs, norms, and attitudes, such as climate change, contact with other cultures, and, perhaps especially, the media. Whether we get tattoos, work out to build our bodies, or cover our skin to keep it pale, however, our choices will reflect deeper cultural values, like the need to stand out or the need to conform, the need to show social status, or the value of friends (Figure 4.2).

Cultural values: What are some useful frameworks for understanding culture?

Shalom Schwartz (1992), researching values in 20 countries, derived a list of 11 values seen to be represented in some way in all cultures. These **universal values** are: self-direction (independent thought and action); stimulation (activity, variety); hedonism (pleasure); achievement (success, prestige); power (social status); security (safety, stability); conformity (restraint of action); tradition (passed-on behaviors); spirituality (personal meaning in life); benevolence (positive interaction with and influence on others); and universalism (understanding and appreciating all people). Schwartz contends that these same values exist in all cultures, but that each culture will place higher priority on some over others.

Milton Rokeach (1973) provides a different approach to values. He determined two lists of values. **Terminal values** represent the end states or desired outcomes of action for individuals. These include things such as a comfortable life, salvation, true friendship, freedom, pleasure, mature love, and self-respect. **Instrumental values** are those characteristics, traits, or "modes of conduct" (p. 7) that people in a culture hold to be important for reaching societal goals—the "means" to the end. They include things such as being polite, cheerful, honest, or courageous. Values do not operate in isolation, but work together with other values in "value systems." Barbara Reynolds (1984) used this approach to find that both Germans and Americans value true friendship and democracy, but that, in 1984, Germans were more concerned with a world at peace than Americans were (terminal values), which Reynolds attributed to the geographic closeness of Germany's neighbors. For instrumental values, Americans ranked ambition fourth, whereas it was near the bottom of the list for Germans. One limitation of the approach is that words have different nuances in translation. In some cultures, someone who is "ambitious" is grasping and greedy, whereas in U.S. culture the person has initiative and is a "go-getter." Both Germans and Americans may value democracy and true friendship, but it is likely that these concepts have quite different meanings in the two cultures.

High- and low-context cultures

Edward Hall (1997), a pioneer author in intercultural communication, suggested high and low context as one dimension by which we can understand cultures. This framework answers the question, "Where does meaning lie?" In a high-context message, meaning is in the situation and the background, roles, and relationships of the speakers. Low-context communicators embed meaning in the actual words—that is, the words of a message can be taken more at their more obvious value. The lower the context, the more direct one might expect messages to be, even down to including direct, rather than implied, criticism. The higher the context, the more meaning will be hidden in nuances of word meaning and nonverbal behavior, often with high(er) context individuals and communicators being more in tune with nonverbal behavior. High and low context do not describe values, specifically, but cultures that value discreet behavior or preserving harmony in one's group tend to be more high context; those that value honesty and independence of thought are more low context.

High-context cultures, then, are cultures in which meaning tends to be implicit, that is, inside of the communicators, because they know what to expect based on the circumstance and on role and status relationships. **Low-context cultures** tend to place more meaning in the "explicit code," that is, in the words themselves. In this type of culture, people might assume that if a guest needs something, the guest will ask for it (Hall, 1997). People in high-context cultures might seek different sorts of information than low-context cultures when they want to understand someone, and might be more likely to ask about your family, university, or home town (your "context"), where someone from a low-context culture might ask about your personal opinions (Gudykunst & Nishida, 1986). As an example, South Korean culture has the concept of *nunch'i* (Robinson, 2000), in which a host must anticipate the needs of the guest. This reflects a notion common to many high-context cultures, in which the guest need not (or should not) voice a request for something

("Hey, can I get a drink of water?") because this would tell the host that she or he had not met the guest's needs.

While researchers or organizational trainers often speak of low- and high-context cultures, some see cultures on a continuum from very low to very high context. Co-cultures, organizations, or families may also differ in the general level of context people rely on. Some churches might state everything clearly for visitors—now we stand, now we sit, let's say this together; while in others, everyone is just expected to know what to do, with no explicit directions. All cultures have high- and low-context situations, though there may be cultural preferences toward one mode or the other.

What do you think? Some training organizations use high and low context to describe female-male communication differences in the workplace. In your culture, do you feel that females and males differ in the "context" of their communication? Specifically, do you think males and females differ in how much they look to words and to other aspects for information in interaction? If there are differences, what might be some reasons for those differences?

Hofstede's cultural dimensions

One of the most commonly used frameworks of values across academic disciplines is that developed by Geert Hofstede (1980; 1986), an organizational psychologist from The Netherlands. Hofstede defines a value as a "broad tendency to prefer certain states of affairs over others" (p. 19). In 1980, he published a now-classic work in which he studied employees working from 1967 to 1973 for a large multinational corporation he called HERMES (actually IBM Corporation), collecting initially over 117,000 surveys from 66 nations. Through his survey study, he developed four value dimensions, with each country receiving a score on each dimension; scores are available at his website (Hofstede, 2009).

The dimensions The first dimension, **power distance**, refers to whether people in a culture tend to value status difference and see it as appropriate. Essentially, as power distance increases, people in a culture—including those of lower status—are more likely to think that it is acceptable that people of different social status (however that is determined) be treated differently (Hofstede & Bond, 1984). Hofstede sees impacts of power distance, like all of the dimensions, on "general norm[s], family, school, and workplace" (Hofstede & Bond, p. 37), and "politics and ideas" (Hofstede, 1997, pp. 37; 43). In a higher power distance culture, students are more likely to see teachers as experts; there will be a clear hierarchy with deference to superiors in organizations; managers and status elites will expect preferential treatment and the lower status individuals will feel that this is just and right; governments will more likely be autocratic (e.g., dictatorships, strong central government); the middle class will be smaller. In low power distance cultures, parents and children are more likely to interact like equals (e.g., there will be no "yes, ma'am" or "yes, sir"); bosses will work together with employees to set goals; democracy and majority vote will be common in organizations and society; people will expect equal rights and equal treatment of everyone.

Hofstede (2001) defines the second dimension, **masculinity/femininity**, as related to male and female emotional rules. In work goals, masculine cultures privilege directness, efficiency, competition, and goal (outcome) orientation; and feminine cultures privilege service, cooperation, modesty, and caring for others. But also, in feminine cultures, there is less sex differentiation in tasks—a role fluidity in which men and women share more tasks. In masculine cultures, roles are more rigid, with men and women doing separate tasks. A limitation of this dimension is that, since it contains different aspects—directness, task-focus, role overlap—a country might seem to be "masculine" in one dimension, but "feminine" on another. Workers in Britain and Italy score considerably higher in masculinity in Sweden, but they score close to each other. But it is likely that Britain and Italy differ in important ways in gender roles and directness of communication.

The third dimension, **uncertainty avoidance**, pertains to the overall desire for structure and predictability in a culture. In higher uncertainty avoidance cultures, people tend to distrust things or people that violate expectations—what is strange is seen as bad. Countries with lower avoidance of uncertainty, such as Scandinavian countries, are often more flexible in terms of violation of expectations. Strangers might be more welcome, and what is different might actually be seen as good. Uncertainty avoidance (UA) might play out in the classroom in that, in a lower UA culture, a teacher is more likely to say "I don't know," teachers may seek opinions from parents, and classroom learning may be open-ended. In higher UA cultures or situations, students will want more structured learning. Teachers and students may see "truth" as absolute. And children may report lower belief in their ability to accomplish tasks independently (self-efficacy, Hofstede, 2001). For example, in Greece, the country where people scored the highest on UA, it is generally expected that citizens will hold to the Greek Orthodox religion, and strangers and unusual behavior are less welcome—even our word for fear of strangers (see chapter 6), xenophobia, comes from Greek.

The last dimension, **individualism-collectivism (I/C)**, refers to the links between the person and her or his social network. In more collective societies, people rely more upon social networks, such as extended family or workplace, to set goals. Decisions will be made with the group in mind. For example, individuals from The Philippines may feel a strong obligation not only to nuclear family (father, mother, and children), but to the success of nieces and nephews, even donating family funds to the education of these individuals. In more individualistic cultures, people tend to make decisions based upon personal interest and advancement or on the nuclear, rather than extended family. In terms of organizations, a more individualistic culture will probably have more people who change jobs frequently, in terms of how the change addresses personal or nuclear family goals, as opposed to long-term employment (Germany) or even lifetime employment (Japan). Even emotional displays work to preserve connections with others, rather than people valuing open expression of what they are feeling (Matsumoto, 1991). Figure 4.3 illustrates where Hofstede's research located several cultures on two of his dimensions. Many researchers see individualism-collectivism as the most important dimension for understanding cultural differences in communication, with some authors, such as cross-cultural psychologist Harry Triandis and his colleagues giving it extensive attention and research (Kim *et al.*, 1994; Triandis, 1995).

Figure 4.3 A comparison of some countries on Hofstede's individualistic/collectivistic and power distance dimensions.
Source: © Geert Hofstede B.V., quoted with permission.

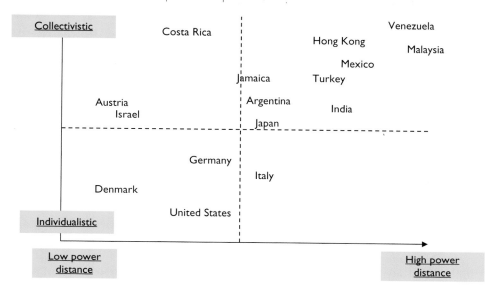

ON THE NET

Describe a culture that you have visited (or your own), or do a comparison of two cultures in terms of Hofstede's four dimensions. What behaviors lead you to place the cultures on different places on the dimensions? After you are done, go to Hofstede's website at http://geert-hofstede.com **and see how his research places them! (You can compare two specific cultures at** http://geert-hofstede.com/ hofstede_dimensions.php) **Do you agree or disagree with his classification? Why or why not?**

Critiquing Hofstede's dimensions Hofstede's value dimensions have received much critical attention in and outside of the communication discipline (Courtright *et al.*, 2011). Cheryl Nakata (2009, p. 3) calls this framework "the dominant cultural paradigm in business studies," with Hofstede among the top-three authors cited in international business. An Internet search of business articles reveals thousands of studies motivated by or using the framework. The framework lists among its strengths the vast database of participants from now over 100 countries and cultures (Hofstede, 2009); the statistical strength of the measure; the simplicity of the framework (Nakata, 2009); and the ability we have, with participants from different cultures taking the same measure, to compare cultures on a specific set of dimensions. The tool is a favorite among those who do organizational training.

Hofstede (1980), himself, emphasized two important caveats. First, like low and high context, cultures range in a continuum on any single dimension. If we consider Figure 4.3, we will see that Japan is on the collective side of the average for *all* countries, but is much more individualistic than many other collectivistic nations. Second, Hofstede suggested that national scores on the dimensions are only average scores. When we speak of cultural differences, say, between Pakistan and Australia, we should recognize that many Pakistanis

some countries   *others*   *countries*

will score more "individualistic" than some Australians, and many Australians will be more "collectivistic" than most Pakistanis. Unfortunately, people often simply group people into nations and nations into dichotomies like individualistic and collectivistic.

Several authors have raised criticisms beyond the misapplication of the original dimensions. In international business, Nakata (2009), summarizing the work of authors contributing to her book, lists several theoretical challenges that require going "beyond" Hofstede and other simple classification schemes. First, our assumptions about larger areas (such as the "Middle East" or "Northern Europe") mislead us in assumptions about a culture's individualism, or the level of individualism practiced within a specific context of life (say, organizational life as opposed to family life). Hofstede's (2009) data might lead us to assume most Sub-Saharan African nations are collectivistic and high power distance. However, one study of managers among the Nnewi people of Nigeria suggests that participants felt that Nnewi entrepreneurs needed honesty, confidence, and "individual self help"—that is, individualism (Madichie *et al.*, 2008, p. 292).

Second, organizational culture (and national culture in general) is more complex than Hofstede treats it. Multinationalism leads to increasingly fluid boundaries between cultures, with many subgroups in each culture. This suggests that any strict application of a Hofstede score to a culture will hide the many co-cultural differences within that culture. For example, younger nationals from the United Arab Emirates are more individualistic than those that are older, though they still value the Islamic work ethic and the use of *wasta*, or interpersonal connection, in the workplace (Whiteoak, *et al.*, 2006). Qin Zhang (2007) discusses that Chinese families are evolving and are now just as focused on expressive conversation as American families.

Third, Nakata (2009) argues that we need a dynamic view of the very nature of culture. She suggests that Hofstede "maintained that culture undergoes barely perceptible change" (p. 13). Nakata and her colleagues argue that cultures develop and evolve over time, even if underlying values are slower to change. Finally, Nakata suggests that we need to look at culture from different methodological windows (e.g., surveys as well as open-ended data collection, ethnography).

From these criticisms, we can summarize three new directions of value research. First, scholars add new dimensions to the original four. For example, Michael Bond and his colleagues with the Chinese Culture Connection (1987) introduced **Confucian work dynamism**, which involves respect for tradition, thrift, persistence, and personal steadiness—in essence, a long-term pragmatism that values education and hard work. On Hofstede's (2009) website, China and other East Asian cultures score high on the dimension he calls long-term orientation, where many Western cultures score quite low. This is especially surprising, in that the United States, which some authors state places practicality—or pragmatism—among its highest values, leading to a focus on "achievement, action, work, and materialism" (Althen *et al.*, 2003), actually scores quite low on a longer-term pragmatism. This suggests that mainstream U.S. culture, while being practical, prefers short-term solutions, or even "quick fixes."

A second approach is to recognize that the values were originally meant to apply to *cultures* and not to *individuals*. Thus, Min-Sum Kim (2005) compares **self-construal**, a psychological notion of how strongly one sees oneself independent from others or connected to others (independent and interdependent self-construals, respectively) to individualism-collectivism. This echoes what scholars and teachers have long said—that *individuals are not cultures.* Thus, just because Socorro is from Guatemala, the country with the lowest individualism score on Hofstede's (2009) website, this does not mean she, herself, will reflect collective values. In fact, if she has an "independent" self-construal, she might make quite independent choices. Timothy Levine and his colleagues (2003) in turn critique the general understanding of self-construal. It may not be only about inter- and independence, but also about autonomy and agency, or even about different types of interdependence. The very division of inter/independent construals may be based on a Western idea of self and ignore other views of the self.

A third approach to the critiques is to complicate the dimensions. All scholars have always said that all dimensions exist in all cultures. But intercultural scholars are trying more and more to avoid the sort of generalization that says, "Sri Lanka is collectivistic, The Netherlands is individualistic." Instead, different co-cultures within a given nation, like France, are more individualistic, and other co-cultures are more collectivistic. These can be ethnic groups, rural versus urban groups, age groups, and so on. The dimensions may exist in tension within cultures, with cultural members constantly negotiating tensions between role flexibility and role fluidity, between need for structure and need for flexibility, and so on. A fourth solution, to which we will turn in just a moment, is not to use the dimensions at all.

Other dimensions and frameworks Before we move on to approaches that abandon this sort of framework, we should note that there are, in fact, other frameworks that authors have used to characterize cultures. Gudykunst and Kim (2003) outline two other major approaches. One of these comes from anthropology—the value orientations of anthropologists Florence Kluckhohn and Fred Strodtbeck (1973). The focus of this list deals more both with world view—our specific beliefs and values about the connections between humans and the elements (another, nature, time) and with general value orientations (activity). We will talk about this more later. Another set of dimensions, by sociologist Talcott Parsons (1951), has strongly informed some approaches to intercultural business communication, so we will consider it more in chapter 15.

Culture-specific (emic) approaches

All of the frameworks we discuss above reflect what we call in chapter 2 an **etic approach**— a set of terms or a theory that researchers develop from outside of any one cultural system, allowing them to compare cultures using the approach. An **emic approach** is quite different, even opposed to, the idea of cultural dimensions—it favors understanding each culture in its own terms (Gudykunst & Nishida, 1989). The first is more preferred by researchers in what we call in chapter 2 the social scientific approach, and the latter, by those in the humanistic approach. Scholars from an emic approach often think that terms universally applied to all cultures may hide the nuances and unique elements of each culture with frameworks that were developed by scholars outside of those cultures. Instead, these authors seek to explain communication behaviors in specific cultures. Clifford Geertz (1973), for example, argues for an "interpretive theory" of culture (p. 3), in which anthropologists travel to cultures and provide rich descriptions of single cultures. The various aspects of a culture—sacred symbols, values, the notions of morality and aesthetics ("ethos"), and the use of symbols, are all intertwined in "webs of meaning," which the researcher unravels. The explanations are not meant to predict anyone's behavior, though the norms, world views, and values *guide* behavior in that cultural members usually tend to follow them.

Robert Bellah and his colleagues (1996) conduct such an analysis of the United States from a sociological perspective. Based on five years of research in four different projects and multiple interviews with more than 200 people across the United States, the authors provide a book-length investigation of individualism in the United States as it relates to American culture. They see everything from governmental systems to romantic feelings and behavior as infused with individualism. This underlying value, they argue, is leading to some crises in contemporary culture, such as the "failure of community" (p. xxiii, a theme echoed by Robert Putnam in his analysis, *Bowling Alone*, 2000), and a decline of public involvement and trust, as well as in family values and civility. Increasing individualism, they argue, is leading to a decline in **social capital**—the sense of involvement in one's community, including social organization, trust, networks, a sense of citizenship, and norms. Hofstede (1980) listed the United States as the most individualistic of the nations studied; Bellah *et al.* (1996), in the preface to their revision of their original 1985 study, state boldly: "The consequences of radical individualism are more strikingly evident today than they were even a decade ago" (p. xi), leading, they contend, to increased alienation from others and a growing loss of "civic membership" in America. Such loss in social capital in a country has the possibility to limit students' engagement in civic or political engagement (though, as we saw in chapter 1, there may be some evidence of reinvestment in community).

Many studies of culture use *ethnography*. This method involves detailed observing, usually involving interaction with people, to understand their lives. Gerry Philipsen and others applied this approach specifically to communication, calling it **ethnography of communication**. Philipsen and his colleagues (2005) outline a theoretical perspective that relies on this approach, **speech codes theory**. In this theory, a **speech code** is the system of symbols, meanings, assumptions, and norms for communication adopted by a group of people. That group of people, a **speech community**, is rarely as big as a nation, but is likely a specific group of people, such as a Harley Davidson motorcycle gang, parents at a Taekwondo studio, or theater majors at a particular university. The theory is "grounded in the observation of communication conduct in particular times and places" (Philipsen *et al.*, 2005, p. 56). The theory proposes that, in any speech community, there are multiple speech codes from which people can choose. For example, someone might use one code (variety of speech, norms for speaking, and so on), with friends on the cricket pitch or volleyball court, and quite a different code with instructors. The codes tell us how to act as a "real" member of the community and also who has status and who does not. The codes guide our behavior, but they do not cause us to behave a certain way. Most importantly, the theory argues that each speech community has a way of communicating that is distinct. The theory does not make predictions about how people will communicate in a culture or across cultures. Rather, it provides a framework for analysis that allows us to interpret and gain an understanding of specific types of communication behavior in any culture.

Recognizing the existence of codes and knowing how to interpret them can also help us to be better communicators. If we are aware that there may be a different order of actions and different behaviors depending on who the participants are in the situation, we can be better observers and learners. For example, we see someone enter an informal close group in Mexico and see that the person greets everyone present, rather than giving a general "hello" to the room. We can determine who does what, in which order, and what the norms of behavior are, to learn the behavior ourselves. But we can also use the framework for social change. For example, if we see that communication in the classroom is structured to give central power to an instructor, so that students do not have the resources (training, authority) to raise questions, we can work to change the situation to give students more power.

What do you think? A Jewish Passover Seder has its own set of rules (participants, norms, act sequence), although these will change from one community to another (Figure 4.4). But even our everyday meals have rituals, often unspoken. Watch the dinner table conversation with your family or friends. Identify a specific genre of behavior (like retelling the day's events, bragging rituals, joke sequences, children asking parents' permission to do something). How might an ethnographic approach make sense of your "speech code?" Is your code unique, or does it borrow from larger cultural codes?

Figure 4.4 As U.S. President, Barack Obama, hosts a traditional Jewish Passover Seder at the White House (2009), he must be aware of the proper rules for communication in such an event.
Source: The Image Works/ TopFoto.

Studies using ethnography in general, or specifically, "ethnography of communication," demonstrate the diversity of cultures people have analyzed. Donal Carbaugh (2005), in his book *Cultures in Conversation*, summarizes his analysis of specific behaviors in different cultures, such as the use of small talk and "friendliness" behaviors in America and Sweden, the use of silence and the reluctance to be a polished speaker among Blackfoot Indians, and the negative responses of a public television audience in Russia to Phil Donohue attempting to get them to talk about the assumed problem of teen sex and pregnancy. David Poveda and Beatriz Martín (2004) studied stories told by two small groups of Roma (Gypsy, or *Gitano*) children in Spain, analyzing the communicative gaps between these children, educated first in their home, and the teachers of the Spanish schools they began to attend.

Whereas ethnography has a central focus on observation of some sort, other researchers use methods such as interviews, which also allow in-depth understandings from the perspectives of cultural members. Stephen Croucher (2009) did in-depth interviews with

42 Muslims in France to understand their perceptions and experiences regarding cultural adjustment and assimilation. And Mark Ward, Sr. (2010), after attending 250 worship services in 17 U.S. states, analyzed forms of speech in Fundamentalist Christian churches in the United States. Rona Halualani and Jolanta Drzewiecka (2008) study Polish and Hawaiian diasporic groups. A **diaspora** is a large group of people that have spread outside of their country or territory of origin, usually maintaining some notion of identity to the homeland. Based on 300 interviews and narratives from Hawaiians compared to an understanding of Polish people living abroad, Halualani and Drzewiecka study the tensions of identity, such as "sameness" and "unity" with the culture of origin and issues of descent, faced by these groups.

World view: What are the beliefs at the center of our "world?"

All of what we have said so far regarding values applies to other aspects of culture—norms, beliefs, and world view. World view is a key aspect of culture. As we said above, this is a specific set of beliefs about the relationship of humans to one another and to greater elements in the cosmos. Geertz (1973, p.127) calls the world view of a people "their picture of the way things in sheer actuality are, their concept of nature, of self, of society. It contains their most comprehensive ideas of order." As we noted above, Geertz sees all aspects of culture as interrelated. As he studies the people of Bali, an island in the Pacific, he notes that world view plays out in Balinese notions of time, in the complex set of names, nicknames, family, and status names people have for one another, and in ceremony, such as the Balinese cockfight, in which men, through their roosters, enact a particular notion of what it means to be a "man" in Bali. World view is connected to communication and ritual, and each of these to our notions of "personhood" and how we enact the different identities that we hold.

Kluckhohn and Strodtbeck (1973), psychological anthropologists, published an analysis of five communities within a 40-mile area in the southwestern United States—a Mormon community, a Texas homestead, a Spanish-American village, and two Native American villages—showing how they differed on several dimensions. Many authors have reproduced this framework, and, while scholars often refer to it as dealing with "value orientations," it really pertains more to world view. The authors suggest that "there is a limited number of common human problems for which all peoples at all times must find some solution" (Kluckhohn & Strodtbeck, 1973, p. 10). Value orientations combine cognitive (thought), affective (feelings) and directive (behavioral) elements to direct human behavior. The values guide us beyond our mere choice, especially since we may often not be aware of them or be able to articulate them. Kluckhohn and Strodtbeck (1973, p. 11) list five basic questions that humans are trying to answer:

1 What is the character of innate human nature?
2 What is the relation of man to nature (and supernature)?
3 What is the temporal focus of human life?
4 What is the modality of human activity?
5 What is the modality of man's relationship to other men?

Figure 4.5 Kluckhohn and Strodtbeck's value orientations.
Source: Adapted from Kluckhohn & Strodtbeck, 1973.

Orientation	Postulated Range of Variations		
Human Nature	Evil	Neutral/Good + Evil	Good
Human-(Super) Nature	Subjugation to nature	Harmony with nature	Mastery over nature
Time	Past	Present	Future
Activity	Being	Being-in-becoming	Doing
Relational	LIneality	Collaterality	Individualism

They pose a framework of different orientations in response to these (Figure 4.5), noting that all value orientations exist in all cultures, but that each culture will rank them differently. Space constraints here do not allow us a full exploration of these, but we can see how they might distinguish cultures in terms of world view in a couple of the dimensions. Some do seem more like values, such as the relational orientation, which includes individualism and two forms of collectivism: lineal, in which the collective might be a tribe or extended family (many African cultures); and collateral, in which the important group would be a work-group (Japan).

We especially see world view in three of the dimensions, though it is related to all of them. In terms of humans' relation to deity (or the supernatural, God, the elements), people in some cultures privilege the idea that we are subject to nature, a sort of fatalism that suggests that humans are at the whims of the gods ("The Devil made me do it!"). In some Latin American cultures, a common saying is "*Así soy yo*"—that's just how I am. Traditionally, a common view was that nature would just "take over" when men and women were alone, which led to very strict supervision of young dating couples. In Brazil, when young men wanted to talk with young women, they used to have to do so through the bars on the front windows, leading to the courtship expression, *comendo grade* (eating grate). People in other cultures see humans as being more in control of nature—they seed the clouds to make it rain and seek to analyze and even control the human genome. And people in yet other cultures tend to seek harmony with nature, seeing themselves working together with the elements ("We eat the buffalo, but then when we die, we feed the grass that feeds the buffalo"). Related to our view of the relationship between humans and the supernatural are our views of human nature (are humans evil, good, or a combination of the two?) and of our activity orientation.

The *doing* orientation, specifically, reflects a culture where the focus is on activity that is often measurable in external accomplishments, a characteristic of U.S. culture, where there seems to be a flurry of activity, with even things like eating ("fast food") geared toward moving us to the next activity. The *being* orientation is characterized by spontaneous expression and living for the impulses of the moment. This represents, perhaps, cultures where "hanging out" or just spending time together, for the sake of the time and not for some observable purpose, are important. In such a culture, such as many Latin American cultures or African American culture within the United States, the person you are with may be more important than the schedule on a clock. In *being-in-becoming* cultures, there is a goal, but it is not measurable (as are awards or status or money), but is instead internal. It is the development of the whole person, such as is achieved through some forms of Eastern meditation.

It is easy to want to classify cultures. Scholars say the United States values a future, progress, pragmatism, and a view of nature that sees it as something to meet human needs (mastery over nature). Asian Indian culture is framed as more fatalistic, with the traditional caste system, a view that humans are subject to the divine; U.S. Indian (Native American) tribes are seen to live in harmony with nature. But each of these borders on cultural stereotypes. A closer analysis of any culture, as Kluckhohn and Strodtbeck (1973) themselves said, will reveal elements of all of the dimensions, though there may be preferences for some. Thus, a deeper understanding of the fabric of Indian culture would, no doubt, reveal themes of fatalism, but with complicated threads of the person impacting her or his own destiny.

We should also note that this is only one framework and that other dimensions or aspects are possible. Carley Dodd (1998), for example, speaks of **guilt cultures**, in which people are motivated by a sense of remorse when they engage in bad behaviors, based on a sense of personal responsibility more common in individualistic cultures. On the other hand, in **shame cultures**, people are motivated by a sense of social obligation, and are more likely to act in a way to protect the honor or "face" of their group than out of a sense of personal responsibility. In **spirit(ual) (or sacred) cultures**, there is a sense of presence of the spiritual or divine in everyday life, and in **secular cultures**, life problems and solutions are seen in terms of science and human ideas. Often, these do not correspond to religious attendance. In many Spanish-speaking South American cultures, if one is planning for the future, one might say, "*Si Dios quiere*"—if God wills, similar to the "*In sh'Allah*" of Arabic-speaking cultures. But in the United States, where church attendance is often higher, people relegate God to certain spheres of life, but do not perceive the divine in the day-to-day workings of life or nature. And cultures that are still traditionally Christian, such as much of Europe, have entered what some have called a post-Christian age, in which atheism is as likely or more likely than faith in a deity.

Break it down

World views and value systems have things that help us progress as a society and things that work against healthy society. Sometimes, even good values, taken to an extreme, can impede progress, community, or other aspects of a culture. With your friends or in a group of classmates, engage in a discussion that considers both the strengths and limitations of the values and/or world view of your culture (national, organizational, university, co-culture, etc.). What changes could be made in your culture to help it meet multiple goals that are beneficial for the citizens of the culture? What are some concrete things you as a group or individual could do toward bringing about these changes?

Summary

This chapter has been about what we consider to be the deepest foundations of culture—values, beliefs, and world view. These constitute the bedrock upon which behavioral rules and norms—expectations for appropriate behavior in situations, sometimes with implications for morality—are built. Norms and rules, in turn, guide our verbal, nonverbal, and mediated behavior. It is certainly good to learn the etiquette when we travel to other cultures, and there are many good sources that present this sort of information (see the suggested readings in the "For more information" section below). But if we know the underlying structure of a culture—the part that usually lies beneath the surface in the iceberg model of culture—then the rest of the parts of culture may make more sense, and we may be able to act appropriately even in those areas where we do not yet know the specific rules and norms.

We defined key terms regarding the mental frameworks that form the basis upon which cultural and intercultural communication is built. These include values, beliefs, world view, norms, and rules. One approach to understanding these is to develop a single set of terms that can apply to all cultures, such as Hofstede's dimensions or E.T. Hall's notion of high- and low-context cultures. Other scholars believe that any use of such frameworks forces us to think of cultures in terms that scholars have created and instead seek to understand each culture from the perspective of the people of that culture. Each approach has strengths and limitations. The first allows for cross-cultural comparisons, as long as we are aware of the limitations of such frameworks. The second allows us to understand cultural behavior in terms of unique cultural histories and contexts. Use of either approach, without care, could lead us to think of cultures as overly uniform and stagnant, as well as to ignore the role of social, economic, and political systems that might work against people's ability to live out their values within a given culture.

As we turn our attention to communication and to political and civic engagement, we must keep in mind that any geographic space has a variety of cultures and co-cultures sharing that space, with fluid and overlapping boundaries, and that cultures are constantly changing through ongoing communication, political, and social, and even geographic and climactic forces. As we engage in civic or political projects, we realize that these always exist within value frameworks, sometimes of cultural values, and sometimes of values of the organization. In some cases, cultural values (like exaggerated individualism) might work against civic engagement—or we might use appeals to personal growth and fulfillment, in such cultures, to motivate participation in engagement, since even the reasons for participating in civic engagement will be influenced by our cultural values and world views. And finally, we may see that in any culture, we may need to strive to change behaviors and messages to bring them more in line with values, or, a much harder task, seek to change values to be more wholesome and inclusive for all. Regardless of our engagement goals, we recognize that an understanding both of the underlying structure of culture and of its ability to change should help us to be better intercultural communicators.

KEY TERMS

subjective culture, 72

objective culture, 72

belief, 73

belief system, 73

world view, 73

value, 74

Discussion questions

1   What do you think are the disadvantages and advantages of each of the two approaches to understanding cultural communication, etic and emic?

2   Martin *et al.* (2002), suggest that change and stability exist in all cultures in tension with each other. Think of your own culture. What are some things that you see changing, and what are some things that seem to stay the same? Are the things that remain the same on the top or the bottom of the "iceberg" model of culture? Think of how the things that change more or less quickly in a culture relate to each other.

3   As we note in this chapter, some scholars claim that there is a decline of "civility" and social capital in America. If you are in an American classroom, discuss whether you agree or disagree with this notion. If you are not in an American classroom, think of a particular cultural value or ritual that seems to be in transition, and discuss why you think that it is or is not changing—and whether such change is beneficial (or not) to your culture.

4   What seem to be the dominant concepts of world view in your culture? Don't just answer in terms of overall religious belief, but with a deeper discussion of what you think under-lying views of reality, knowledge, or the purpose of life are in your culture.

5   Are there different cultural groups within your community? If so, discuss how these groups might be alike and different in terms of some of the concepts in this chapter.

Action points

1   Find a current political issue in a country besides your own. For example, at the writing of this chapter, people are wondering whether Julian Assange should be allowed to keep a website called Wikileaks, which leaks information from government documents; and Spain is contemplating banning smoking in bars and restaurants. Discuss this issue with your class or with friends, talking about the underlying value, more/normative, or world view of the culture as these relate to the issue.

2 Go online and view the 20-minute video, "The Story of Stuff" (http://www.storyofstuff. com). Think about your own use of goods and resources. How does this use reflect or contradict your own culture's values? How does your usage impact people in other cultures for good or bad? What changes could you make in your life to use less "stuff?" Also, what are your agreements or disagreements with the idea in the video?

3 The International Youth Foundation (http://www.iyfnet.org) describes stories of young people—teens and young adults changing their world in different ways. Go to the "success stories" link (http://www.iyfnet.org/success-stories) and locate a particular success story to read. In your journal, write about what the young person has done: What is the location of social change? What cultural values or world view aspects might help or get in the way of the young person's efforts (you may have to do additional Internet research to know more about the culture)? How might such an effort translate to your own community, if someone wanted to do something similar?

For more information

Althen, G., & Bennett, J. (2011). *American ways: A cultural guide to the United States*. Yarmouth, ME: Intercultural Press.

Hofstede, G., Hofstede, G.J., & Minkov, M. (2010). *Cultures and organizations: Software of the mind: Intercultural communication and its importance for survival* (3rd ed.). New York: McGraw Hill.

Martin, J.N., Nakayama, T.K., & Flores, L.A. (2002). A dialectical approach to intercultural communication. In J.N. Martin, T.K. Nakayama, & L.A. Flores (Eds.), *Readings in intercultural communication: Experiences and contexts* (pp. 3–13). Boston: McGraw Hill.

McSweeney, B. (2002). Hofstede's model of national cultural differences and their consequences: A triumph of faith—a failure of analysis. *Human Relations, 55*, 89–118.

Morrison, T., Conaway, W.A., & Borden, G.A. (1994). *Kiss, bow, or shake hands: How to do business in sixty countries*. Holbrook, MA: B. Adams.

References

Althen, G., with Doran, A.R, & Szmania, S.J. (2003). *American ways: A guide for foreigners in the United States* (2nd ed.). Yarmouth, ME: Intercultural Press.

Bellah, R.N., Madsen, R., Sullivan, W.M., Swidler, A., & Tipton, S.M. (1996). *Habits of the heart: Individualism and commitment in American life* (updated ed.). Berkeley, CA: University of California Press.

Carbaugh, D. (2005). *Cultures in conversation*. Mahwah, NJ: Lawrence Erlbaum Associates.

Chinese Culture Connection (1987). Chinese values and the search for culture-free dimensions of culture. *Journal of Cross-Cultural Psychology, 18*, 143–164. Doi:10.1177/0022002187018002002.

Courtright, J.L., Wolfe, R., & Baldwin, J.R. (2011): Intercultural typologies and public relations research: A critique of Hofstede's dimensions. In N. Bardhan (Ed.), *Public relations in global and cultural contexts* (pp. 108–139). Mahwah, NJ: Lawrence Erlbaum Associates.

Croucher, S.M. (2009). *Looking beyond the hijab*. Creskill, NJ: Hampton.

Dodd, C.H. (1998). *Dynamics of intercultural communication* (5th ed.). Boston, MA: McGraw-Hill.

Geertz, C. (1973). *The interpretation of cultures*. New York: Basic Books.

Gudykunst, W.B., & Kim, Y.Y. (2003). *Communicating with strangers: An approach to intercultural communication* (4th ed.). Boston: McGraw Hill.

Gudykunst, W.B., & Nishida, T. (1986). The influence of cultural variability on perceptions of communication behavior associated with relational terms. *Human Communication Research, 13*, 147–166.

Gudykunst, W.B., & Nishida, T. (1989). Theoretical perspectives for studying intercultural communication. In M.K. Asante & W.B. Gudykunst (Eds.), *Handbook of international and intercultural communication* (pp. 17–46). Newbury Park: Sage.

Hall, E.T. (1997). Context and meaning. In L.A. Samovar & R.E. Porter (Eds.), *Intercultural communication: A reader* (8th ed., pp. 45–54). Belmont, CA: Wadsworth.

Halualani, R.T., & Drzewiecka, J. (2008). Deploying "descent": The politics of diasporic belonging and intercultural communication. *International and Intercultural Communication Annual, 31,* 59–90.

Hofstede, G. (1980). *Culture's consequences: International differences in work-related values.* Beverly Hills, CA: Sage.

Hofstede, G. (1986). *Culture's consequences: Comparing values, behavior, institutions, and organizations across cultures* (2nd ed.). Thousand Oaks, CA: Sage.

Hofstede, G. (1997). *Cultures and organizations: The software of the mind.* New York: McGraw-Hill.

Hofstede, G. (2001). *Culture's consequences: Comparing values, behaviors, institutions, and organizations across nations.* Thousand Oaks: Sage.

Hofstede, G. (2009). Cultural dimensions. *ITIM International.* Retrieved on March 28, 2011 from http://geert-hofstede.com

Hofstede, G., & Bond, M.H. (1984). Hofstede's cultural dimensions: An independent validation using Rokeach's Value Survey. *Journal of Cross-Cultural Psychology, 15,* 417–433. doi:10.1177/0022002184015004003.

Kim, M.-S. (2005). Culture-based conversational constraints theory. In W.B. Gudykunst (Ed.), *Theorizing Intercultural Communication* (pp. 93–117). Thousand Oaks: Sage.

Kim, U., Triandis, H.C., Kâĝitçibaşi, C., Choi, S.-C., & Yoon, G. (Eds.). (1994). *Individualism and collectivism: Theory, method and implications.* Thousand Oaks, CA: Sage.

Kluckhohn, F.R., & Strodtbeck, F.L. (1973). *Variations in value orientations* (2nd ed.). Westport, CT: Greenwood.

Levine, T.R., Bresnahan, M.J., Park, H.S., Lapinski, M.K. Wittenbaum, G.M., Shearman, S.M., Lee, S.Y., Chung, D., & Ohashi, R. (2003). Self-construal scales lack validity. *Human Communication Research, 29,* 210–252.

Madichie, N.O., Nkamnebe, A.D., & Idemobi, E.I. (2008). Cultural determinants of enterpreneurial emergence in a typical sub-Sahara African context. *Journal of Enterprising Communities, 2,* 285–299.

Martin, J.N., Nakayama, T.K., & Flores, L.A. (2002). A dialectical approach to intercultural communication. In J.N. Martin, T.K. Nakayama, & L.A. Flores (Eds.), *Readings in intercultural communication: Experiences and contexts* (pp. 3–13). Boston: McGraw Hill.

Matsumoto, D. (1991). Cultural influences on facial expressions of emotion. *Southern Communication Journal, 56,* 128–137.

Nakata, C. (2009). Going beyond Hofstede: Why we need to and how. In C. Nakata (Ed.). *Beyond Hofstede: Culture frameworks for global marketing and*

management (pp. 3–15). New York: Palgrave-Macmillan.

Parsons, T. (1951). *The social system.* Glencoe, IL: Free Press.

Peace Corps (n.d.). *Cultural gaffes at home and abroad.* Paul D. Coverdell—Worldwise Schools. Accessed July 26, 2012, at http://wws.peacecorps.gov/wws/multimedia/videos/culturalgaffes2/

Philipsen, G., Coutu, L.M., & Covarrubias, P. (2005). Speech codes theory: Restatement, revisions, and response to criticisms. In W.B. Gudykunst (Ed.), *Theorizing about intercultural communication* (pp. 55–68). Thousand Oaks, CA: Sage.

Poveda, D., & Martín, B. (2004). Looking for cultural congruence in the education of *gitano* children. *Language in Education, 18,* 413–434.

Putnam, R.D. (2000). *Bowling alone: The collapse and revival of American community.* New York: Simon & Schuster.

Reynolds, B.K. (1984). A cross-cultural study of values of Germans and Americans. *International Journal of Intercultural Relations, 8,* 269–278.

Robinson, J. (2000). Communication in Korea: Playing things by eye. In L.A. Samovar & R.E. Porter (Eds.), *Intercultural communication: A reader* (9th ed., pp. 74–81). Belmont, CA: Wadsworth.

Rokeach, M. (1973). *The nature of human values.* New York: Free Press.

Schwartz, S. (1992). Universals in the content and structure of values: Theory and empirical tests in 20 countries. In M. Zanna (Ed.), *Advances in experimental social psychology* (Vol. 25, pp. 1–65). New York: Academic Press.

Triandis, H.C. (1995). *Individualism and collectivism.* Boulder, CO: Westview.

Triandis, H.C. (2002). Subjective culture. *Online Readings in Psychology and Culture.* Accessed April 13, 2013, at http://dx.doi.org/10.9707/2307-0919.1021.

Ward, M., Sr. (2010). "I was saved at an early age": An ethnography of fundamentalist speech and cultural performance. *Journal of Communication and Religion, 33,* 108–144.

Whiteoak, J.W., Crawford, N.G., & Mapstone, R.H. (2006). Differences of gender and generational differences in work values and attitudes in an Arab culture. *Thunderbird International Business Review, 48*(1), 77–91.

Zhang, Q. (2007). Family communication patterns and conflict styles in Chinese parent-child relationships. *Communication Quarterly, 55,* 113–128.

Chapter 5

Identity: Struggle, resistance, and solidarity: How can I think about my identity and that of others?

Chapter objectives

After this chapter, you should be able to:

→ Describe sources of your identity

→ Differentiate between personal and social identities

→ Apply the notion that identities are a social construction by giving examples of messages or communication that produce and reproduce (that is, communicate) your identities

→ Illustrate identity politics—that is, how power defines our own and others' identities

→ Integrate the notions of ideology and hegemony as these apply to identities, and how they play out through face-to-face and mediated communication practices of Othering and the symbolic annihilation of race

An introduction to identity: Who am I, really?

Identity and communication: How do we communicate our identities?

Identity and politics: How can our identities be political?

Identity in intercultural communication: What are some problematic ways to think about the identities of other groups?

Identity, solidarity, and civic action: Can I make a difference?

Intercultural Communication for Everyday Life, First Edition. John R. Baldwin, Robin R. Means Coleman, Alberto González, and Suchitra Shenoy-Packer.
Published 2014 by John Wiley & Sons Ltd.

Barack Hussein Obama II became the 44th President of the United States on January 20, 2009. With a Kenyan father, an Indonesian stepfather, and a mother from Kansas, U.S.A., Obama was born in Hawaii, but spent four years of his childhood in Indonesia, and is conversational in Indonesian. He is a graduate of Columbia University and has a degree from Harvard Law School. Shortly after his election, Obama met King Abdullah of Saudi Arabia during a presidential visit, and inclined slightly in his direction. The White House hastened to deny that Obama's gesture was a bow (he was just taller than the King and had to bend to shake hands), although Saudis saw it as a bow and appreciated it. Obama commented that we needed to show more respect to others in culturally appropriate ways; however, a *Washington Times* editorial (2009) suggested the act was "a shocking display of fealty to a foreign potentate," and that by it, Obama was showing great respect not only to King Abdullah, but to Islam.

This incident illustrates the many debates Obama's identity has raised. Many feel he is not qualified to be President of the United States, simply because a Black man cannot represent the U.S. Most people are not this callous but, still, other questions swirl around Obama: Is he really American, or is his Hawaiian birth certificate a forgery? Is he really a Muslim disguised as a Christian, and can a Muslim represent the United States? (A similar question haunted John F. Kennedy's bid for presidency as the first Catholic U.S. President.) Is Obama a hyper-liberal, even a socialist, in his economic and political policy? (This question is asked despite the fact that many Europeans might consider his policies more conservative than even conservative European governments.) Can he even represent Blacks well, given his Ivy League degree and the fact that he was not brought up within the U.S. Civil Rights Movement? All of these questions involve identity, in one way or another.

Each of us has different "identities"—student, Black, Italian, Socialist, Christian, and so on—and some of these identities may be more important than others to how we see ourselves. Some writers (Tajfel & Turner, 1979) state that we really cannot think of ourselves apart from groups to which we belong. But thinking of ourselves in terms of identity may not be a bad thing. In 1996, cultural theorist Stuart Hall challenged scholars to answer what, on its surface, appeared to be a rather simple question: "Who needs identity?" Hall readily shared his belief that we *all* need to have some identity. However, in asking the question, Hall was asking us to revisit and offer a refreshed interrogation of identity as a concept. Indeed, Hall's request for a renewal of our understanding of identity remains timely, as making sense of who we are, and understanding our similarities and differences, is always important to making sense of our intercultural relationships. More important for our purposes here, our identities are tightly wrapped up with our communication. Our identities inform us how we should communicate in certain situations, and in turn, we create those identities through communication.

An introduction to identity: Who am I, really?

Let us begin by teasing out Hall's assertion that we all need identity by considering how identity serves us. When we ask ourselves, "Who am I?", "How do I sustain my 'self'?", and "Who am I in relationship to others?", we are asking questions of identity. The answers we come up with in response to these queries provide a roll call of identity considerations. If we ask, "Who am I?" one response might be based on **classification**, or how we are understood by some social category such as White, male, or gay. In asking the second question, "How is my identity formed and maintained?" our answers might draw on essentialist and seemingly fixed sources, such as nature and biology, or on non-essentialist and variable sources, for instance, nurture and social constructions. For example, take Jenna, a young female professor with "natural" blonde hair. If she identifies as a blonde, as young, or as a woman, her identity is based on some biological trait. It is possible that Jenna also identifies as a scholar, which implies a particular line of work and way of thinking about the world. This is neither biologically determined nor part of a human nature, but reflects a socially constructed position, one that may have been nurtured through years of schooling.

Often, stereotypical thinking involves the social construction of meaning that gets attributed to identities that appear fixed. When Jenna encounters people who, as a result of the "dumb blonde" stereotype, incorrectly presume she is not very bright, their presumption is evidence that "blonde" has been made to mean something in certain social contexts that has nothing to do with nature or biology. Notably, the blonde stereotype applies mostly or exclusively to women and not to men. A **stereotype** is an oversimplified, often unvarying attribute assigned to a group, or to a person because that person is a member of a group. There is no real connection between hair color genes and level of intelligence, but one has been imagined socially and given expression in blonde jokes. The lesson is that we derive our identities and their meanings from different types of attribute—from nature to nurture—and others do the same for themselves, but also for other people.

Finally, the question, "Who am I in relationship to others?" leads us to think about group identities, or membership in a particular group of people who share similar identities. Group identity can be formed around material or economic conditions. For example, we might be members of a rural community, while others are members of a suburban community. Our living conditions might be characterized by significant wealth, while others might be experiencing abject poverty. Membership in one group could mean little interaction with members of another; it could also frame our preconceptions and understandings when we do interact with members of other identity groups. These various understandings of "who we are" and "who we are in relationship to others" help us to make sense of one another within intercultural encounters.

Identity, then, is defined by our "knowing" of ourselves. This knowing means taking an inventory of who we are. Part of that inventory involves our concepts of ourselves as unique individuals; whether, for example, we are shy, athletic, or interested in soccer—our **personal identities**. Part of the inventory involves our role identities (for example, work or professional roles), relational identities (for example, enemies, family members, lovers), and our membership in groups (such as national, religious or political groups, social organizations, or regional identities). These latter, group-based aspects of identity make up our **social identity**. Social identity is where the individual meets larger collective bodies, or groups of affiliation. This can raise many interesting issues as people struggle to define groups and groups impact individuals.

Woodward (1997) in her book *Identity and Difference* suggests that one way to recognize who we are is by considering how we are different from others. We know who or what we are, based on who or what we are not. How do you really know that you are a college student? One answer is that you know you are a college student because you are not, at this time, enrolled full-time in a trade school or you are not serving on active duty in the

What do you think? The character Kelly Bundy from the television situation comedy *Married, With Children* (1987–97) was depicted as blonde, sexy, sex-crazed, and far from bright. By contrast, the character Elle Woods, played by Reese Witherspoon in the film *Legally Blonde* (2001) discovers she is more than merely blonde and sexy; she also has brains. How is "blondeness" defined in media? How do these representations move blondes from having a physical trait to being linked to a kind of identity? *Legally Blonde* seems like an improvement over the representations in *Married, With Children*, but how might the film actually be reinforcing the same stereotypes?

Figure 5.1a Elle Woods from the film *Legally Blonde* (2001).
Source: Topham/Picturepoint/TopFoto.

Figure 5.1b Kelly Bundy from the television situation comedy *Married, With Children* (1987–97).
Source: UPPA/TopFoto.

military. That is, identities involve **categorization**, a mental process of grouping things, attributes, behaviors, and people into like clusters. Specifically, we group people into **in-groups**, those groups to which we see ourselves belonging, **out-groups**—groups with which we do not associate or cooperate, and **reference groups**, groups that we value and look to for guidance (Gudykunst & Kim, 2003). Identities become complex when someone holds a group as a reference group, looking to it for guidance, while people in the reference group exclude the individual as an out-group member, and members of the in-group mock the person for identifying with the reference group.

Identity and communication: How do we communicate our identities?

Social identity theory and stages of identity development

Identities cannot exist without communication. Identity is conveyed through languages, or those things that we use to communicate. We can think of identities as a sense of belonging to a group that affects our communication (social scientific approach). If we see identity like this, we might look for differences in communication between men and women, Chinese- and Malay-descended Malays, or Afrikaner and Black South Africans. One prominent theory that has considered identity is social identity theory (Tajfel & Turner, 1979). This theory suggests that: (1) How we see ourselves is closely tied to how we see the groups to which we belong. (2) When we interact with others, we see them in some combination of personal terms and expectations and their membership in groups. (3) When we place people in groups, we tend to compare those groups against our own, usually in a way that makes our groups look better to us. Writers have applied this theory to a wide variety of identities, including sex, sexual orientation, social class, race, ethnicity, physical ability/disability, and national identity (e.g., Harwood & Giles, 2005), and particularly to how perception of group identities impacts communication (Ng *et al.*, 2004).

Another line of research on identity considers how children grow up to see themselves within a particular identity. Derald Wing Sue and David Sue (2008) outline several models of Black and White identity development, which might transfer in some ways to minority and majority identity development in countries outside of the United States. For example, William Cross (1991) describes the minority development stages of pre-encounter (marked by a desire to assimilate to dominant culture and devalue one's own group), encounter (the person begins to challenge the old way of thinking and reconsider her or his identity), immersion-emersion (the person engages fully in the minority culture, separating from the dominant culture), internalization (the person resolves insecurities between old and new identities), and internalization-commitment (the person makes a decision for social change and civil rights). Janet Helms (1995) outlines a similar model for White (or majority) development that begins with initial contact, a phase in which the majority member is unaware of intolerance, believes in equality of opportunity, and so on; the person then confronts and understands intolerance, perhaps passing through a stage of White (or dominant-group) guilt, and moving to a stage that values diversity and encounters it without intimidation or discomfort. Teresa Nance and Anita Foeman (2002) apply these to suggest positive messages that parents can share with biracial children to help them build a wholesome, positive identity.

Identity is created through communication

Some frame identity as something that is constantly changing, because we are always creating and shaping our identities through communication, a view that is more "humanistic;" that is, identities are a **social construction**. They are created through communication in the context of our social world, histories, and relationships. As such, identities are inherently political, with our identity claims and investments not only naming us, but at times also affording us more or less power given the context (e.g., "stay-at-home soccer mom" vs. "welfare mother" vs. "career mother"). Michael Hecht and his colleagues (2005) state the complexities of identity well. They argue that identities are not fixed; rather they are dynamic and multiple (see also Woodward, 1997). Even in a given conversation, some of our identities fade into the background, but then someone might say something or do something that makes us think about a particular identity (or makes it "salient") to us—that is, identities are emergent in conversation. Identities are always changing in some ways and remaining the same in others, again through communication. In sum, identities are heterogeneous, classified and made sense of in all sorts of ways; that is, they represent a process of understanding.

When we talk of language or that which communicates, we are not simply referring to oral, written, or even electronic communication. Rather, it is important to understand that all things "speak" or communicate, and therefore those things challenge us to make sense of them and to assign them meaning. Even the most mundane things "mean" something. The style of cell phone we use, the way we cut or style our hair, the type of (un)bottled water we drink, the leisure activities in which we engage, and the clothes that we wear reflect our personal and group identities in different ways.

You are what you eat: Food as an example of identity

Consider how the food you eat (or don't eat) is a symbol of your cultural identities. Ask yourself:

→ What foods do I cook and what foods do I eat raw? What does this say about my relationship to nature?

→ What cultural practices do I draw upon to transform nature from one state to another?

→ How do the foods I eat reveal my relationship to other cultures and parts of the world?

→ How do I classify my food, and what does it mean? For example, what counts as an entrée or dessert? How do individual food items become an "Italian" dinner or a "soul food" dinner?

→ When do I consume food? What are my mealtimes? Do I engage in fasting? What are "diet" foods, and what does it mean when I go "off" a diet? How might diet foods be different from "good" foods?

→ What are good foods? What are children's foods? What are ordinary foods versus foods reserved for celebrations?

The lesson here is that foods are not merely sustenance, but are intimately linked to our political, social, moral, ecological, religious, and communal identities (Benson, 1997). The same might be said of smells. For example, Jim Drobnik (2006) has edited an entire book on smell culture around the world. As an example, one essay notes that smell in early New York City was a code for "class, racial, and ethnic differences and antagonisms" (Manalansan, 2006, p. 45). Smell bias continues today; one woman was voted into the New York city council based on her platform, part of which complained about those "foreign" Asian smells in the neighborhood.

Identity and politics: How can our identities be political?

Not only do we construct the identities of our own groups, but we also construct the identities of other groups through communication, such as through the stereotypes of blonde women mentioned earlier. The words we choose as we talk to others, our turn-taking and interruption patterns, even our nonverbal stances, work to construct the identities of others in interaction.

POP CULTURE

The 2007 Rutgers University women's basketball team comprised eight Black and two White players. Based on this information alone, we can come up with a fairly lengthy list of group identity categories: college student, basketball player, female, Black or White, east coast residents, and so on.

In April 2007, on his MSNBC show *Imus in the Morning*, talk show host Don Imus called these women "nappy-headed hos." Bernard McGuirk, the *Imus* show's executive producer, followed up by calling the team "hard-core hos." Through racial insults and sexist slurs, the two men revealed their views on the social identities—the role, relationship, and group identities—of these women. How did Imus and McGuirk reclassify the members of the Rutgers' University basketball team? How did the host and producer's comments serve to empower these men while disempowering the women? In short, how might these remarks be interpreted as political? How might comments such as these lead to a crisis of identity—a disruption of relatively stable understandings of the self—for these women?

Figure 5.2a Don Imus appearing on Al Sharpton's radio show.
Source: Spencer Platt/Getty Images.

Figure 5.2b Kia Vaughn, Scarlet Knights v LSU semi-final, April 1, 2007.
Source: Raleigh News/MCT/Getty Images.

Sometimes we even battle within our own groups to define identities certain ways. If someone does not hold to our vision of what our identity should be, we say things like, "You're just not Black enough" or call them traitors to their identity. One way of being a competent communicator is to ascribe, or give to others, the identity that they choose in an interaction setting. For example, if a woman wants to interact as a business professional or an athlete, we should treat her in terms of that identity, and not first as a "woman" (Collier & Thomas, 1988). As we discuss the politics of identity, we are taking a more "critical" approach to identity (see chapter 2). Here we will consider several aspects of the politics of representation.

Identity politics

How we are identified is often outside of our control. Skin color, gender, role expectations, nationality, social class, and body size all "classify" us. In other instances, we voluntarily claim—and even proclaim—membership in an identity. Bumper stickers, t-shirts, and other paraphernalia reveal how we celebrate who we are: "Proud to be Italian American;" "Viet Nam War Veteran"; "Anarchist;" "100% Cruelty Free;" or "I'm Here, and I'm Queer." But why overtly invest in an identity when it can mark you and others as different, or to put it another way, you as a member of an in-group, and others as part of an out-group? **Identity politics** describes the practice of laying claim to an identity in order to help ourselves integrate into our communities and fit into parts of our social world. Holding membership can mean belonging, and can reveal the relationship between your subjective position—who you feel you are—and social situations—how you interact with and relate to the world.

Though these identifications may spark what Woodward (1997) characterizes as crisis, contestation, conflict, or some other kind of resistance, they also make you part of a collective or even a movement, which can be understood as a political point of departure for celebration and activism. That is, identity politics refers not only to how we see ourselves as part of a community, but how these communities or identity groups vie for various types of power—social status, economic power, the power to define social norms, and so on. Groups are actively in the process not only of defining themselves, but also of defining other groups, through images, media, interpersonal messages, rhetoric, and, if a group can do so, even legislation. Such self- and other-defining works to position groups in power relations to one another.

We can see the politics of identity as dominant groups within a given culture frame depicting members of other groups. Much research investigates how Blacks, Latinas/Latinos, lesbians and gays, or women are portrayed in mainstream American culture. Some investigate how American writers—even journalists who claim to be objective—describe other cultures, like Central America, in ways that support U.S. intervention in those countries (Lule, 2003). And a part of the ethnic conflict in Rwanda that resulted in nearly 800,000 deaths in a period of 100 days in 1994 was the radio propaganda description of the Tutsi tribe by broadcasters from the Hutu tribe (BBC, 2008). We will deal more with prejudice and media later (see chapters 6 and 10).

Punk rock and identity politics: A case study in brief

Punk rock began in Britain in the mid-1970s and was immediately political, engaging youth and working class culture politics, through rage and violations of social and musical convention (Dunn, 2008). It took hold in the U.S. later in the 1970s. A key characteristic of the music was that the lyrics centered on messages of anti-materialism, anarchy, freedom from conformity, and peace. The music launched a movement among young people who called themselves "Punks." Punks embodied the music through dress, speech, and lifestyle. It is a lifestyle, or scene, that has been particularly attractive to Whites, even promoting White identity through its representation of non-Whites (Duncombe & Tremblay, 2011). Though the punk scene has been understood to be predominately White, this cannot be further from the truth. James Spooner, in his 2003 documentary film *Afro-Punk*, chronicles a social movement within Black communities in the U.S. that led Black youths to the punk culture. You can even listen to "punk international" radio stations online. So, even though punk began as an expression of engagement among a particular youth identity in working class Britain, it continues to evolve, creating a connection that crosses national and race identities.

What do you think? View Afro-Punk artist James Spooner's film (http://www. afropunk.com/page/afropunk-the-movie). What are some of the reasons that Black youth would join a predominantly White movement (one that has even been understood at the margins to be exclusionary and racist)? What crises, contestations, and conflicts do Black youth encounter from Whites, Blacks, and society as a whole? How does their decision to lay claim to and proclaim their identity as punks reveal this to be an identity politics "move?" Overall, what are the identity experiences of Afro-Punks?

Figure 5.3 James Spooner, Toronto, September 10, 2007. Source: Scott Gries/Getty Images.

As another example of identity politics and representation, in March 2006, rap artist and movie star Ice Cube's co-created reality television show *Black.White.* premiered on the FX network (USA). The premise of *Black.White.* was provocative. A Black family, the Sparks from Atlanta, Georgia, and a White family, the Wurgels from Santa Monica, California, move in to a Los Angeles home together, for six weeks. They are encouraged to explore race relationships, specifically prejudice and stereotypes, through very close interactions. The show did not stop there. Each family was prompted to live like the opposite race, interacting with the social world, by changing their "race," or, more accurately, by changing their physical appearance thanks to the wonders of Hollywood make-up. The Sparks family adopted fairly realistic "White face," while the Wurgels assumed "Black face." In some of the show's more charged moments, Brian Sparks gets to experience life as a White male. He is privy to the race talk of some Whites he encounters, and is intrigued by some of the assumptions and misconceptions they hold about Black people and Black culture. Specifically, Brian is taken aback when a White male shares with him that there is a nearby all-White neighborhood that is good and "safe" because it lacks diversity. At the same time, Bruno Wurgel, living as a "Black" man, comes to believe that racism may not be as prevalent, or as much of a hindrance, as the Sparks believe. Bruno comes to this conclusion when he is able to get through his day without being called "nigger" and when he receives attentive service by a car salesperson at a car dealership.

Black.White. is worth interrogating. Its premise is simultaneously overly simplistic in its exploration of race relations, but it is also intriguing, perhaps because there are some who think that the complexities of race can be explored in this way. The series raises some interesting questions that merit our attention. For example, what norms, values, and beliefs about race does this series present? To what extent does the series suggest racial identity is the product of nature/biology or nurture/social construction? How we present, or even represent, our values provides us with crucial insight into our beliefs and how we view our social world. In other words, it gives us insight into our ideologies.

Ideology, the KKK, and subtle White power

But what is ideology? **Ideology** is a *system* of meanings. It is a system because it draws upon a range of perspectives that each of us holds to assist us in making meanings, or sense, of the social world as well as our role and function in that world. That system of meanings, very often, includes our personal identities, which work to help us figure out how we should engage with the world. David Croteau and William Hoynes (2003), in their book *Media/Society*, provide a clear and accessible definition for this particularly complex term. Ideology, they write, is "related to concepts such as *worldview*, *belief system*, and *values*." They want us to understand that ideology as a concept is even broader as it refers "not only to the beliefs held about the world, but also about the basic ways in which the world is defined" (p. 160).

While we are using media examples to talk about ideology, ideology is not necessarily limited to media. Instead, we circulate and display our ideologies in a number of ways, such as through our behaviors, practices, beliefs, and other (non-mediated) communication—through the jokes we tell, through verbal and nonverbal interaction patterns, through the terms we use to talk about others, such as calling women "girls" or "babes," and so on.

For example, Kathleen Blee (2002), in her book *Inside Organized Racism: Women in the Hate Movement*, reveals how women who hold membership in Ku Klux Klan, based on their system of identity investments, beliefs, and values, can come to view a racist rally as nothing more than a "community social gathering" or even like "summer camp." Blee helps us to understand how the women make sense of their participation in racist gatherings, as well as their place in the world. The women noted that the gatherings they attended focused on family, complete with games for children and children's books for story time. The gatherings featured food, much like a block party or religious meeting, often in the form of picnics where participants each brought a dish. Recipes were exchanged. Hymns were sung. The women's relationship to the "racialist movement" was so normal and mundane that they could relate their activities to other common social gatherings and rituals in the social world. Blee writes that this world appeared so normal for the women that they did not deem it necessary to note that the children's books housed stories of racism, the recipes were "White power" recipes, or the hymns were anthems of racial supremacy. In short, the women's ideologies worked to define their world, and their relationship to it, as racist, anti-Semitic, and xenophobic.

John Warren (2001) looked at racialized identities from quite a different group—everyday college students in a performance class. The students doing performances about identity sometimes complained about those of other races, and sometimes about racism. Interestingly, when one student performed the role of a "racist," he referred only to KKK members, and, when enacting one, he "stupefied" his language, slumped his posture, and added a southern drawl (p. 99). Warren argued that, by marking racists as "Other", the White students were able to ignore or absolve themselves from the daily, more subtle expressions of race, racism, and identity in their own communication. Notions of "marking" racists as people besides themselves and of seeing themselves as "color blind," Warren contends, allow Whites to distance themselves from the racial power that they hold, probably without being aware of it.

What do you think? If, at times, ideologies appear commonplace, mundane, natural, and obvious, how are they also powerful? Moreover, how do ideologies secure power for some, while rendering others less powerful? What are some ways that an identity group to which *you* belong (racial, ethnic, religious, sexual, sexual orientation, political, etc.) strives to gain more power or works to maintain the power that it currently holds? Consider how your answers can reveal the presence of "dominant" ideologies—ideologies that privilege the powerful.

Our considerations of women in the hate movement and Whites discussing race in the classroom help us to better understand two things about ideology. First, ideology often orders how we think about our world without us even realizing it. Second, ideology works to define and explain our social world, and aids us in making value judgments about that world. It is important to note that ideology need not be tied to the negative or the controversial. For example, what does it mean that sports are featured, with their own section or segment, as "news" in media, but religion is not? Or, additionally, as Croteau and Hoynes (2003) note, what does it mean to have a "business" section in newspapers, but not a "labor" section?

Hegemony: National-regional and sexual orientation power plays

Hegemony is another complex, but interrelated concept. It describes how the powerful keep their power in a society, largely by making their (dominant) ideologies seem common-sense, taken-for-granted and not worthy of questioning. However, what is so clever about hegemony as a process is that if we move to challenge that power, the powerful do not necessarily respond in repressive ways, but through system-maintaining acts of cooptation, or borrowing from resistance, to give the appearance of change. We can see both overt and subtle moves at identity repression in the case of Catalonia, Spain. Through a long and complex history, this large region in the northeast of Spain has resisted cultural dominance by the capital. The dictator Francisco Franco, in the 1930s, outlawed the regional language, Catalan. But more subtly, elements of Spanish (specifically, Castilian) identity abounded in the region, from bullfights to movie posters in Spanish.

In a similar way, we see both overt, political resistance and subtle, everyday resistances among Catalonians today. The region outlawed bullfighting, in large part because it represented Madrid, and not Catalonian culture. There is a national (Catalonian) opera house and a national (Catalonian) art museum in Barcelona. As one gets off the plane at the international airport, all directions are in large Catalan writing, with mid-sized English translation, and a small Spanish translation at the bottom. On the subways, local residents graffiti the movie posters, writing Catalan spellings and word endings on top of the

Figure 5.4 Characters from *The L Word* bring a particular representation of lesbianism to mainstream American media.
Source: Showtime/The Kobal Collection/Segal, Carole.

Spanish. And at a protest to mark and mourn the "siege" of Barcelona by Spain, nearly 300 years ago, 1.5 million people marched in protest on September 11, 2012 (BBC, 2012). Still, whenever the CBS show, *The Amazing Race*, has gone to Barcelona and the island of Mallorca, greeters salute the contestants in Spanish, not in Catalan or in *Mallorquí*, the Mallorcan dialect of Catalan. In the 2008 season of the programme, participants were pelted with tomatoes, representing a festival in Valencia, a region that is "more" Spanish, though still fighting to keep its own cultural identity and language strong in the face of national Spanish influence.

Catherine Hammond (2006), an instructor at the University of Michigan, who researches the representations of lesbians in entertainment television, has this to say about the way hegemony accommodates resistant ideas while maintaining dominance (Figure 5.4):

> Okay, so hegemony makes sense right? We'll [the television networks] throw lesbians a bone and give them their own show, to give them something to shout about. But, we are going to make sure all of the women on the show are conventionally feminine. So, some differences in group representation are happening. But, there are also some resistant ideologies being appropriated. More, any major differences in the representation of women which could shift relative distributions of power remain unrepresented.

Identity in intercultural communication: What are some problematic ways to think about the identities of other groups?

Thinking about identity, as well as ideology and hegemony, is useful as we consider those things that work to facilitate, as well as impede, intercultural communication. We can understand identity as presentations and representations of the self. When our identities are familiar to, interesting to, or valued by another, the possibilities of open, productive communication are possible. However, in understanding that who we are is based on who we are not, we also run the great risk of "**Othering**" those who are among the "not's," thereby excluding and rendering them as inferior or alien to us.

Orientalism

Cultural theorist Edward Said (1978) talks about how, historically, the powers of the "West"—through the thinking, learning, and consciousness that drove the formation of Western empires—relied on a process of Othering. That is, they know they are "Western" based on who they are not, which, in Said's theory of **Orientalism**, was the "Oriental." The Orient becomes a mirror image of what is inferior and alien to the West. This was used to justify and advance Western colonization in other parts of the world. The term the "Orient" has been associated, often pejoratively, with Asia; however, Said does not map the Orient in this way. Rather, he argues that the Orient can be understood as sweeping generalizations and stereotypes crossing all sorts of cultural and national boundaries. It is about the practice of power, how domination of other people involves developing simplistic and often derogatory understandings of them.

According to Said (1978), an Oriental male is often understood or even depicted as feminine, weak, and yet dangerous because he poses a (sexual) threat to White, Western women. The Western, White male is a masculine savior keeping threat at bay. The Western woman is poised and the center of normalcy. By contrast, the Oriental woman is alluringly exotic, but can be dominated. The Oriental can be simultaneously sensual (women) and hypersexual (men and women); passive (men and women) and aggressive (men and women). Additionally, the Oriental is eccentric, backward (lacking in civility and progress), and stands apart from Western values, which include mythical notions of enlightened superiority, control, and refinement.

To disabuse ourselves that this notion of Orientalism is stereotypically confined to the East, let us consider how the African American male can be "Oriental" by turning to representation. In the 1997 futuristic science fiction movie *The Fifth Element*, the African American actor Chris Tucker plays a hyper-effeminate DJ/radio personality named Ruby Rhod (Figure 5.5). In the movie, Ruby is adorned in various provocatively revealing, figure-hugging, off-the-shoulder costumes that sexily reveal his cleavage while accentuating his slender frame. He frequently changes wigs, sometimes going brunette, and other times platinum blond. His favorite shade of lipstick is red. His voice is high, his manner, like his name, is stereotypically feminine. Ruby trembles with fear, screaming and hiding, when danger is encountered, and he turns to the White, rugged, hyper-masculine Korben, played by Bruce Willis, for protection and reassurance. Ruby, to apply Said's concept, is understood and depicted as a feminine and weak Other, thereby rendering him less powerful than, and dependent on, Korben.

However, Ruby has another side to him, which is represented in the double entendre of his last name, "Rhod." In the movie, Ruby's hypersexuality and virility are on display as he flirts and has sex with a variety of women. In one scene, Ruby reveals that he has even slept with the (White) Emperor's daughter. Thus, Ruby Rhod is presented as a corrupting threat to White womanhood. Taken together, his femininity, his blackness, his passivity in the face

Figure 5.5 Ruby Rhod (played by Chris Tucker), in *The Fifth Element* (1997) shows how Edward Said's notion of Orientalism can apply to African American males.
Source: Columbia/Tri-Star/ The Kobal Collection/ English, Jack.

Chapter 5   Identity: Struggle, resistance, and solidarity: How can I think about my identity and that of others?

105

of danger, and his aggressive sexuality not only mark him as "Oriental", but also subtly work to provoke a loathing/Othering of those he may be viewed as representing. The sexuality of Black men in popular culture is often depicted as non-masculine, ambiguous—such as cross-dressed characters—or aggressively lustful/polygamous/hyper-masculine. This is the result of the exotification that is central to Othering. This example shows that belief systems reaffirm the particular social orders in which they function and that they manifest in inter-cultural exchanges. This means they play out in the development of our identities as well as in the representation of others' identities—but not always in ways that are obvious to us on first glance.

The symbolic annihilation of race

Threats to identity through representations are often subtle, rather than overt (e.g., the dumb blonde stereotype). The concept of the **symbolic annihilation of race** is able to address concerns about representation that go beyond issues of stereotyping. It gives a name to covert representational problems, specifically a group's absence from, or trivi-alization or condemnation in, representations, such as those in media (Tuchman, 1978). Symbolic annihilation also calls our attention to the notion that those racial groups who are not presented as fully developed in media may also see their social status diminished.

Very often, we see criticisms of representations center on how groups and cultures are distorted or on how those representations are damaging, both to those represented and to the understanding and experience of dominant groups (Hunt, 2005). These concerns often surface in response to stereotypes. For example, one stereotype assigned to men of a more petite stature is that they must possess a "Napoleon complex." This offensively describes an inferiority complex that is purportedly often seen in men who are short; these men seek to overcome their "shortcomings" by overcompensating through extreme displays of machismo, bravado, and a bullying attitude. "Positive" rep-resentations may initially slip under our radar because their danger is not so readily apparent, but they are also harmful. For example, stereotypes of Asians as the smart, model-minority group or of Blacks as excellent athletes and dancers are troublesome because they confine our perceptions of these groups to a very limited and unrealistic expectation. In addition, there is the problem that some groups face in that they are invisible or excluded from representations. This issue was considered earlier in this chapter regarding the representation of lesbians on television.

What do you think? Consider the racial implications of this "positive" state-ment: "Barack Obama is articulate." Does it suggest indirectly that Black people are generally incompetent, or is it a normal, insignificant observation? How might the description of a gay male as "articulate," on the other hand, highlight stereotypes in a different way?

Where the term "stereotype" falls short in helping us to understand representations is that it does not function well in capturing the connotations associated with absence, omission, or even an inclusion that is not so obviously problematic (or negative). To fill this gap, the related, yet distinct concept of the "symbolic annihilation of race" becomes useful (Coleman & Chivers Yochim, 2008). Scholars have made the devaluation of group members' competence, achievement, and humanity, part of the definition of stereotype. When members of marginalized groups do appear, it is in a way that reinforces the dominant ideology, making such domination appear natural and acceptable. For example, there are the frequent stereotypes of Chinese-American men as members of violent triads (gangs), nerdy, or essentially foreign. These images can be seen in the film *The Departed* (2006), which presents an Asian gang, the 2009 Intel TV commercial depicting Ajay Bhatt, the inventor of the USB drive, as an untraditional rock star, and in the TV situation comedy *In The House* (2008), which portrays an Asian woman as a housekeeper clad in a 1960s Cultural Revolution uniform. These are only half of what diminishes their social status. The other part is absence—there are currently no representations in U.S. media that center on a nuclear Asian or Asian American family in a prime-time television drama.

Symbolic annihilation also helps us to see when groups have been subtly trivialized or condemned in media. Tierney (2006), in his study "Themes of Whiteness in *Bulletproof Monk*, *Kill Bill*, and *The Last Samurai*," illustrates how some racial groups are victimized through such representations, as well as how the treatment of these groups works to reaffirm the power of other groups. Each of these films features a helpful and generous Asian who gives all of himself (yes, it is men who are depicted as especially giving) and his culture in support of Whiteness. *Kill Bill* provides an interesting example of this giving. In the film, a Chinese craftsman of Hong Kong's most valuable, precise, and deadly swords has retired, thereby depriving future generations of Chinese of the benefit of learning the craft of swordmaking and denying martial artists' the ownership of skillfully crafted weapons. However, the craftsman affably agrees to turn over his most prized possession—the last of his swords—to a White American woman who has come to Hong Kong, ultimately, to kill dozens of Chinese people. Tierney observes that in films such as *Kill Bill*, as well as *Monk* and *Samurai*, Whiteness becomes reaffirmed as a site of racial advantage and privilege. In each of these films, Whites are able to enter into cultures that are foreign to them, and not only quickly adapt but also excel. Indeed, they often take on some part of Asian culture and perform it better than the indigenous people who have been born into it. This has the effect of trivializing and even condemning the racial Other. The greater impact is that such representation erases or "writes out the history, politics, struggles, and conditions that produced these specific cultural practices" (Tierney, 2006, p. 609).

Symbolic annihilation is not confined to entertainment media. Rather, cultural trivialization can rear its head among more serious discussions. For example, around the world, news reporters have ignored the effects of (neo)colonialism—the domination of a country and/or its corporations over another country—by describing non-Western countries as "third world" and "underdeveloped," rather than "overly exploited" and "colonized," while the United States and Western Europe have been referred to as "first world" and "superpowers" (Moore, 1992). In sum, the term "symbolic annihilation" is especially useful when describing non-representations as well as the destructive consequences of poor or absent—but not obviously stereotypical—media depictions of groups and cultures.

POP CULTURE

A recent, popular trend in U.S. film is for African American men to portray African American women. For example, Eddie Murphy, Martin Lawrence, and Tyler Perry have all portrayed Black women. These portrayals are seemingly "positive," as the men often depict the women as mature, doting, kind, loyal, and family-centered (Figure 5.6).

Discuss how these portrayals might represent both stereotypes *and* symbolic annihilation. Now, focus on the notion of "annihilation." Does annihilation have to be final? What is its opposite? Can you begin to theorize about moving from annihilation to symbolic reclamation?

(a)

Figure 5.6 In recent films, African American males have portrayed seemingly positive impressions of African American females; however, these portrayals have problems of their own.
Sources: (a) Dreamworks/The Kobal Collection/McBroom, Bruce; (b) 20th Century Fox/The Kobal Collection; (c) Tyler Perry Company/The Kobal Collection.

(b)

(c)

Identity, solidarity, and civic action: Can I make a difference?

Our discussion about identity need not be all doom and gloom. In fact, perhaps one of most intriguing aspects about identity is its potential to invite interest across cultures, and to spark action as a result of that interest. When we think of the Civil Rights Movement in America, some of the images that immediately come to mind are those of Dr. Martin Luther King, Jr. in the 1960s, joined by a largely Black citizenry united in a call for equality. However, the quest for civil rights was neither a predominantly Black nor a predominantly Southern one. Rather, racial groups of all backgrounds united toward common goals of change. Perhaps it is unknown to some that Blacks, Asians, and Mexicans (a great many from the U.S. west coast) came together to secure equal rights and improved resources in their communities. Their efforts focused on community organizing to bring about improvements in the education and health systems, to end police brutality, and to build socio-economic power. These groups came to be known as the Black Panther Party, the Red Guard, and the Brown Berets, respectively. The Black Panther Party served as a template for these groups' public presentation (e.g., the groups' uniforms) as well as for their action plan (e.g., uniting their communities through social action programs and challenging discrimination in the legal system). They were collectively mobilized by imposed identities in America that marked them as minorities and second-class citizens. They fought anti-Black, Brown, and Asian stereotypes that led to practices such as racial profiling or the denial of equal employment and pay. While each worked to assert their unique racial, ethnic, and cultural identities (an identity politics move), they also sought to remind the populace that they were, indeed, Americans, and should be treated accordingly. As such, their unity, or interracial/interethnic solidarity, was centered around the political, and less around the cultural.

Political solidarity often led to very personal bonds. For example, Yuri Kochiyama, a Japanese American, united with civil rights leader and activist El-Hajj Malik El-Shabazz (also known as Malcolm X), joining his Organization for Afro-American Unity. It was Kochiyama who was present when El-Shabazz was assassinated in Harlem in 1965, and it was she who cradled him in her arms as he died. Over her lifetime, Kochiyama has been front and center in the fight for human and civil rights for Japanese Americans, Puerto Ricans, and African Americans. In 2005, she was nominated for the Nobel Peace Prize.

In sum, while much of what we have said focuses on negative constructions people from one group place upon other groups, these last examples demonstrate our power of choice. As an example of this, modern feminists note that the construction of patriarchy, or masculine power, is not simply something that men create, but something that many women consent to. However, women and men can resist patriarchal notions of sex and gender identity, and members of ethnic minorities (and dominant cultures) can resist stereotypes and can promote new constructions of identity. Victor Frankl (1962/1985), an Austrian psychiatrist and Holocaust survivor, argues that the one thing others cannot take away from us is "the last of the human freedoms—to choose one's attitude in any given set of circumstances, to choose one's own way" (p. 65). Our identities are often

Break it down

Analyze the comics section of the newspaper in your local town in terms of representation of ethnic, sex, and/or other forms of diversity. To what degree does it numerically represent the demographics of your community? Are ethnic minority members represented in a wide array of roles (e.g., lead roles) or are they presented stereotypically? Write a letter to the editor about your findings—or, if the representations call for change, work even more actively by meeting with the features editor of the paper.

constrained by dominant media representations, by ways of speaking, by laws and policies, and by historical, economic, and social structures. Our freedom in our identities is bound, but within those bounds, we still have freedom to respond in some way. Further, to echo the ideas of the communication theory of identity, noted earlier, people within a single group can work together to respect one another's own constructions of a single identity, to give those, even within our own identity group, the freedom to frame their identity as they choose (Hecht *et al.*, 2005).

Summary

In this chapter, we introduced how we can better make sense of who we are and how we view others by understanding identities. Asking difficult questions about our identity claims, either those we form or that others form for us, helps us to better understand the ideologies, beliefs, and assumptions that we hold. We have learned that identity is understood through communication or language, and language constructs identities and their significance. Moreover, it is through language that we are able see or mark identity as difference; that is, we know who we are based on who we are not. Defining who we are is not as simple as "I am this one thing because I am not that one thing." We also know that our identities are numerous and come from a multiplicity of sources.

We also learned that, because identity is often understood through difference, it can lead to intercultural conflicts fueled by struggles over power. Examples are as numerous as they are disheartening, and include intergroup relationship challenges between Blacks and Hispanics in the United States, between ethnic groups in China, between sedentary farmers and nomadic groups backed by the government in Darfur, and between Muslims, Serbs, and Croats in the Balkans.

Identity claims carry with them expectations about how to behave, and tastes; however, they do not always follow simply from identity. For example, we know that Black youth are not a monolithic group, and that some invest in hip-hop culture, some in pop culture, and still others in punk culture—to provide just a few examples. Still, expectations of identity performance are often introduced and reinforced through media stereotypes. For example, masculinity is defined for much of the world as rugged, powerful, heterosexual, and in control (such as films like *Iron Man*, *Quantum of Solace*, or *The Dark Knight*). Media can also be used by some to change or exploit identities. Marketers have tried to redefine people's identity as "activists" as being tied to consumption. One example would be an advert inviting people to shop at Macy's department store, promising that if you use your Macy's interest-bearing credit card the company will make a small donation to a charity.

Perhaps one of the most useful things to remember about our identities is that our differences can become the source of new similarities as we forge new identities and coalitions between identity groups. And at the same time, there is often considerable diversity within our identity groups. With this in mind, one way to foster cultural communication (as well as political and social communication) is to consider ways to unite "within" as well as "across." There are impediments to achieving improved communication (e.g., stereotypes or symbolic annihilation), but we also believe that awareness and information dissemination are a very important part of activism. Helping others to identify the roadblocks to cultural communication is a key first step toward developing strategies to breaking those roadblocks. Instead, reaching for some level of "knowing"—making sense of who we are, how we are the same, and how we are different—is always important to making sense of our intercultural relationships.

KEY TERMS

classification, 92

stereotype, 93

personal identity, 93

social identity, 93

categorization, 94

in-groups, 94

out-groups, 94

reference groups, 94

social construction, 95

identity politics, 98

ideology, 100

hegemony, 102

Othering, 103

Orientalism, 103

symbolic annihilation of race, 105

Discussion questions

1 Either in a group or on your own, come up with as many advantages you can think of, of being in the dominant ethnic or racial group in your country. For example, in the United States, what are the advantages of being White? How do majority Blacks' advantages compare in a different country, such as South Africa or Jamaica? Follow up your work by reading Peggy McIntosh's famous essay, "Unpacking the White Knapsack" (1988), available on the Internet. What invisible advantages do other dominant groups (males, middle class, heterosexuals) have, if any?

2 Why would a person emulate or appropriate the practices of someone ethnoculturally different from themselves? How might reasons be similar or different between someone from a dominant group emulating a minority group and vice versa?

3 Given the power of media's influence on identities, in what ways can identities be linked to resistance?

4 On the Internet, locate a list of "ethnic identity markers." Think of an ethnic identity that you hold. How does it represent each of the different markers? How might another identity community, such as the Deaf community, be similar to or different from an ethnic identity? (See http://deafculture.com/ethnic_culture or a similar website for discussion.)

5 Think about one or more of the identities that you hold. In what ways are these identities changing, and in what way are they remaining the same? What types of messages work to change or maintain the identities (media, computer, face-to-face, rituals, etc.)?

Action points

I Look again at the analysis of the comics section of your local newspaper in the "Break it down" textbox. Conduct a similar analysis of your favorite television show (e.g., *Smallville*, *Grey's Anatomy*), or magazine (e.g., *Sports Illustrated*). For example, analyze how *Sports Illustrated* represents women's versus men's sports. Send a letter to the editor about your findings.

2 Look through newspaper archives or public records of your local community. See if you can locate whether minority groups are treated equally to dominant groups in terms of public policy, such as police stops or arrests, housing availability, public school funding, marriage or insurance laws, or some other indicator. Write a letter to your public officials, either praising them for steps toward equality or urging them to specific action.

3 Make a list of public service organizations in your area that work for equality of (identity) opportunity, such as teaching immigrants the dominant language in your country, tutoring children in lower socio-economic neighborhoods, or providing more equality in housing. Choose one and donate your time one weekend to the agency of your choice.

For more information

Exploring America's *"National Identity"*, Accessed August 15, 2013, at http://www.npr.org/templates/story/story.php?storyId=4074849

James and Grace Lee Boggs Center to Nurture Community Leadership, Accessed August 15, 2013, at http://boggscenter.org

Merskin, D. (1998). Sending up signals: A survey of Native American media use and representation in the mass media. *The Howard Journal of Communication*, 9, 333–345.

Newport, F. (2009). *Religious identity: States differ widely*. Accessed August 15, 2013, at http://www.gallup.com/poll/122075/Religious-Identity-States-Differ-Widely.aspx

Shaheen, J. (2001). *Reel bad Arabs: How Hollywood vilifies a people*. New York: Olive Branch Press.

Tuchman, G. (1978). Introduction: The symbolic annihilation of women by the mass media. In Tuchman, G., Daniels, A.K., & Benét, J. (Eds.), *Hearth and home: Images of women in the mass media* (pp. 3–38). New York: Oxford University Press.

References

BBC. (2008). Rwanda: How the genocide happened. *BBC News*, December 18. Accessed Oct. 31, 2013, at http://www.bbc.co.uk/news/world-africa-13431486

BBC. (2012). Huge turnout for Catalan independence rally. *BBC News Europe*, September 11. Accessed February 25, 2013 at http://www.bbc.co.uk/news/world-europe-19564640

Benson, S. (1997). The body, health and eating disorders. In K. Woodward (Ed.), *Identity and difference* (pp. 121–166). Thousand Oaks, CA: Sage.

Blee, K. (2002). *Inside organized racism: Women in the hate movement.* Berkeley, CA: University of California Press.

Coleman, R.M., & Chivers Yochim, E. (2008). The symbolic annihilation of race: A review of the "Blackness" literature. *African American Research Perspectives, 12*, 1–10.

Collier, M.H., & Thomas, M. (1988). Cultural identity: An interpretive perspective. In Y.Y. Kim & W.B. Gudykunst (Eds.), *Theories in intercultural communication* (pp. 99–122). Beverly Hills: Sage.

Cross, W.E. (1995). *Shades of black: Diversity in African American identity.* Philadelphia: Temple University Press.

Croteau, D., & Hoynes, W. (2003). *Media/society: Industries, images, and audiences* (3rd ed.). Thousand Oaks, CA: Pine Forge.

Drobnik, J. (Ed.). (2006). *The smell culture reader.* Oxford: Berg.

Duncombe, S., & Tremblay, M. (Eds.). (2011). *White riot: Punk rock and the politics of race.* London: Verso.

Dunn, K.C. (2008). Never mind the bollocks: The punk rock politics of global communication. *Review of International Studies, 34,* 193–210.

Frankl, V. (1962/1985). *Man's search for meaning: An introduction to logotherapy.* (Trans. I. Lasch). New York: Simon & Schuster.

Gudykunst, W.B., & Kim, Y.Y. (2003). *Communicating with strangers: An approach to intercultural communication* (3rd ed.). Boston: McGraw Hill.

Hall, S. (1996). Introduction: Who needs identity? In S. Hall & P. DuGay (Eds.). *Questions of Cultural Identity* (pp. 1–17). London: Sage.

Hammond, C. (2006). Lecture, "Media and identity," University of Michigan, October 19.

Harwood, J., & Giles, H. (Eds.), (2005). *Intergroup communication: Multiple perspectives.* New York: Peter Lang.

Hecht, M.L., Warren, J.R., Jung, E., & Krieger, J. (2005). The communication theory of identity: Development, theoretical perspective, and future directions. In W.B. Gudykunst (Ed.), *Theorizing intercultural communication* (pp. 257–278). Thousand Oaks, CA: Sage.

Helms, J.E. (1995). An update of Helms's white and people of color racial identity models. In J.G. Ponterotto, J.M. Casas, L.A. Suzuki, & C.M. Alexander (Eds.), *Handbook of multicultural counselling* (pp. 181–198). Thousand Oaks, CA: Sage.

Hunt, D. (2005). Making sense of blackness on television. In D. Hunt (Ed.), *Channeling blackness: Studies on television and race in America* (pp. 1–24). New York: Oxford University Press.

Lule, J. (2003). Waters of death in Central America. In K. Anokwa, C.A. Lin & M. B. Salwen (Eds.), *International communication: Concepts and cases* (pp. 91–110). Belmont, CA: Thomson/Wadsworth.

Manalansan, M.F., IV. (2006). Immigrant lives and the politics of olfaction in the global city. In J. Drobnik (Ed.), *The smell culture reader* (pp. 41–52). Oxford: Berg.

McIntosh, P. (1988) White privilege: Unpacking the invisible knapsack. Excerpted from P. McIntosh, "*White privilege and male privilege: A personal account of coming to see correspondences through work in women's studies,* Working Paper 189. Wellesley MA: Wellesley College Center for Research on Women. Accessed August 20, 2013 at http://www.amptoons.com/blog/files/mcintosh.html

Moore, R. (1992). Racist stereotyping in the English language. In M. Anderson, & P. Hill Collins, (Eds.), *Race, class, and gender: An anthology* (pp. 317–329). Belmont, CA: Wadsworth.

Nance, T.A., & Foeman, A.K. (2002). On being biracial in the United States. In J.N. Martin, T.K. Nakayama, & L.A. Flores (Eds.), *Readings in intercultural communication: Experiences and contexts* (pp. 35–44). Boston: McGraw-Hill.

Ng, S.H., Candlin, C.N., & Chiu, C.Y. (Eds.). (2004). *Language matters: Communication, culture, and identity.* Hong Kong: City University of Hong Kong Press.

Said, E. (1978) *Orientalism.* New York: Vintage.

Sue, D.W., & Sue, D. (2008). *Counseling the culturally diverse: Theory and practice* (5th ed.). Hoboken, NJ: Wiley.

Tajfel, H., & Turner, J. (1979). An integrative theory of intergroup conflict. In W. Austin & S. Worchel

(Eds.), *The Social Psychology of Intergroup Relations* (pp. 33–47). Monterey, CA: Brooks-Cole.

Tierney, S. (2006). Themes of Whiteness in *Bulletproof Monk*, *Kill Bill*, and *The Last Samurai*. *Journal of Communication*, 56, 607–624.

Tuchman, G. (1978). Introduction: The symbolic annihilation of women by the mass media. In G. Tuchman, A.K. Daniels, & J. Benét (Eds.), *Hearth and Home: Images of women in the mass media* (pp. 3–38). New York: Oxford University Press.

Warren, J.T. (2001). Doing Whiteness: On the performative dimensions of race in the classroom. *Communication Education*, *50*(2), 91–108.

Washington Times. (2009). Editorial: Barack takes a bow, 7 April. Accessed July 27, 2012, at http://www.washingtontimes.com/news/2009/apr/07/barack-takes-a-bow/

Woodward, K. (1997). Concepts of identity and difference. In K. Woodward (Ed.), *Identity and Difference* (pp. 8–50). Thousand Oaks, CA: Sage.

Chapter 6

Intolerance–acceptance–appreciation:
How can we make the world
a more tolerant place?

Chapter objectives

After this chapter, you should be able to:

→ **Define key terms relating to prejudice and intolerance**

→ **Distinguish between different aspects of perception as they relate to intolerance**

→ **Compare and contrast what may or may not be intolerance, based on several tensions from literature and popular discussion**

→ **Outline causes of intolerance at individual, societal, and other levels**

→ **Develop a platform of solutions for a particular intolerance that recognizes the complexity and cultural specificity of the problem**

Framing the problem: Where can we recognize intolerance?

Looking to a better future: What are some causes of and solutions for intolerance?

Intercultural Communication for Everyday Life, First Edition. John R. Baldwin, Robin R. Means Coleman, Alberto González, and Suchitra Shenoy-Packer.
© 2014 John R. Baldwin, Robin R. Means Coleman, Alberto González, and Suchitra Shenoy-Packer.
Published 2014 by John Wiley & Sons Ltd.

On July 22, 2011, a Norwegian, Anders Behring Breivik, set off a number of bombs in Oslo as a diversionary tactic and then stormed a youth camp on the picturesque island of Utøya. He killed almost 70 people, mostly teens and young adults. In trial hearings, Breivik showed no remorse. In fact, he said he wished he had been able to kill more people (*New York Times*, 2012), and he thought it odd that the victims, so unaccustomed to violence, seemed unable to run. But he shot them anyway (Cowell, 2012). At his hearings, Breivik rejected the authority of the court, claiming he killed in self-defense, fighting against the Islamic incursion into Norway. The victims, however, were not Islamic; rather, they were members of the youth division of the Norwegian Labour Party, the liberal party in power in Norway, whom Breivik claimed were supporters of "Muslim colonization."

The case is informative regarding the culturally specific and transnational character of intolerance. Locally, the massacre has its roots in the rise in the number of immigrants into Europe from Islamic nations. Abraham Foxman (2011, para 5), National Director of the Anti-Defamation League, argues:

> The attacks in Norway seem to stem from a different source. They are the first to emerge from a relatively new, specifically anti-Islamic ideology that moves beyond religious or racial intolerances to incorporate anti-Islamic sentiment as the focal point of a larger worldview.

Anti-Islamic sentiment in Norway reflects a larger anti-Islamic sentiment in other cultures that shows the complexity of this specific intolerance—one that combines intolerance based on religion and race, as well as a concern in many Western nations about preserving national cultures. And it illustrates a specific intolerance that is embedded not only in individual intolerance, but in the material social conditions of immigrants from Islamic nations throughout Europe—conditions that often include segregation, joblessness, differential opportunities, police violence, and so on, and that, for example, gave rise to a series of riots involving North Africans in France in 2005.

At the same time, there is a universal component to the violence. Hate crime reports remain steady toward ethnic groups, the homeless, religious groups, or others. And such violence has a context in the many *non*-violent ways people express intolerance every day, as we often unintentionally create breeding grounds of ideas that allow such intolerances to be born and flourish. Finally, we see intolerance as key to intercultural communication. As we saw in our model of communication (see chapter 3), all communication involves not only real cultural differences, but also the perception of self and others in terms of groups. Because of group-based perception and treatment, intolerance or appreciation of other groups is a central part of intercultural communication. But what types of intolerance exist? Where do these begin and what contributes to them? And how can we seek to reduce intolerance? These are the topics of the current chapter.

ON THE NET

Recent Internet news gives reports of statistics and stories on hate crimes from Chile to Canada, from Russia to Rwanda, from Germany to Ghana (see, e.g., Glet, 2009; Spagnoli, 2008). Locate information on hate crimes in your own area. Think about some of the possible reasons such hate crimes occur. What is it about the person, the culture, the economic or political environment, the media and entertainment systems, or other factors, that may frame a context for such violence?

Framing the problem: Where can we recognize intolerance?

In this chapter, we explain a variety of forms of intolerance in a world that seems not to be growing any more tolerant with the passage of time. In 1992, there were 4558 hate crimes in the United States and 2000 in Germany (*Tempe Daily News Tribune*, 1993). The Federal Bureau of Investigation of the United States noted, in more recent statistics, 6604 hate crimes in 2009, down from 2008 (Federal Bureau of Investigation, 2010). Traditionally, it has been said that there is an average of 40 armed conflicts in the world at any point in time, a figure supported by a 1988 *U.S. News and World Report* article (Barnes *et al.*, 1988; see Wars in the World, 2012). We see ongoing strife that includes both attitudes and social policy in Ireland, Israel, Cyprus, and Columbia. At the same time, we see progress, such as laws against untouchability in India, the banning of sodomy laws and increased acceptance of homosexuality in China (Lau, 2010), and the rise of intercultural and interracial marriages in the United States. Our eventual purpose in this chapter is to propose some solutions for intolerance; however, an effective solution to any problem requires thoughtful consideration of the nature of the problem.

In this section, we outline some of the potential forms of intolerance, and then end with some debates about "where the problem lies," with **racism** as an example. But before we begin, we need to define some terms. **Intolerance** refers to any thought, behavior, policy, or social structure that treats people unequally based on group terms. By contrast, **tolerance** is "the application of the same moral principles and rules, caring and empathy, and feeling of connection to human beings of other perceived groups" (Hecht & Baldwin, 1998, pp. 66–67). We might think that tolerance is the opposite of intolerance, and that tolerance should be our goal. But increasingly, scholars have lamented the half-hearted feeling associated with tolerance. To "tolerate" someone implies merely putting up with them. So, many authors suggest an even greater acceptance than tolerance: appreciation. **Appreciation** refers to the attitude and action of not only accepting a group's behaviors, but also seeing the good in them, even adopting them, and actively including the individuals of a group. Appreciation involves such things as "respect, sensitivity, engagement, recognition, and solidarity" (Hecht & Baldwin, 1998, p. 67).

Terms: What are some different types of intolerance?

Intolerance or appreciation can exist at many different levels that all inform one another. They exist in our thoughts and attitudes, relationships, rituals, social and organizational policies. They are inherently communicative, as we create, spread, and resist intolerance through face-to-face and mediated communication. In this section, we consider several types of intolerance.

Cognition   Our minds and senses, like a computer, are constantly gathering data from what goes on around us. It is impossible to notice everything, so we make choices in what we see or hear. **Selective attention** is the idea that we only pay attention to certain things, impacted by what we hold to be important and our negative or positive expectations. If we expect male athletes to perform more poorly in a classroom, we might not notice the soccer player or weightlifter who participates in class frequently or see the intellectual strength in his essays. Once we see something, **selective perception** shapes how we interpret it. In the current example, if we have negative expectations of the male athlete, then when Gerhard, a soccer player, writes an essay, we might perceive his arguments to be weak. Finally, as we go to retrieve the "data" from the computer-that-is-our-brain, we only remember certain things (**selective recall**). If we are trying to remember what Gerhard said or did in class, we might only remember the things that confirm our pre-existing ideas (Baldwin & Hunt, 2002).

Gordon Allport (1979) gives an example of how this works, as he describes U.S. American attitudes. He notes that a Jewish person and the famous President, Abraham Lincoln, might engage in the same behaviors in terms of spending money wisely. Americans might perceive President Lincoln as "thrifty"—a word with very positive connotations—but the Jewish person as "stingy"—a word with connotations that the person is money-grabbing and unwilling to help others. Psychological research introduces the notion of **attribution**, a process by which we give meanings to our own behavior and the behavior of others. Attributions are important in all communication, because when we interact with others, we do not respond to what they do or why they do it, but to why we think they did it. We make a variety of mistakes when we give meaning to behavior, because we often do not see our own motivations (or those of others) objectively. In the **fundamental attribution error**, we overestimate the role of personal characteristics in someone's behavior and do not place as much weight on context. In personal relationships, if an acquaintance shows up late, we think it is because she is careless, or lazy, or does not value the relationship, rather than that it might be because of a difficult bus schedule (Ross, 1977). The **self-serving (or egocentric) attribution bias** leads us to give attributions that frame our behavior as normal and appropriate and give meanings to others' behavior that make us look better—at least in our own minds (Kelley, 1967). The **ultimate attribution error** combines the last two errors: If people we do not like have a success, we attribute it to the context (they were lucky, the coaches were on their side), but if they fail, we blame personal characteristics (they are incompetent; Pettigrew, 1979). But we blame our own failures, and those of people or groups we like, on context, and attribute success to character (Figure 6.1). Miles Hewstone and Colleen Ward (1985) demonstrate this effect by looking at what they call "ethnocentric attribution." They found that in both Malaysia and Singapore, Malays give their own group members more positive attributions (e.g., character attributions for positive behavior) than they did the Chinese, though the Chinese did not differ in the attributions they gave in either location.

Figure 6.1 We give meaning differently to our own behaviors and those of our group than we do to that of others or other groups, especially if they are groups that we do not like.

	Something good happens	Something bad happens
Out-group member	**External**: Attribute it to context: She got the job because the boss plays favorites	**Internal** (personal characteristics): He lost the business deal because he's lazy and a sloppy worker
In-group member	**Internal**: Attribute it to personal characteristics: She got the job because she's a hard worker	**External** (context): He lost the business deal because he wasn't given enough time to prepare

ON THE NET 🖱️

Do some Internet research on global attitudes toward your country (try search words "perceptions of X" or "stereotypes of X"). For example, "perceptions of United States" leads to articles that suggest that Muslims elsewhere in the world feel that the United States acts "unilaterally," or without considering the needs and interests of others (even allies) on the world stage (Kohut, 2005). What are the perceptions others have of your country? What historical or social backgrounds might be behind the perceptions? How do you feel about them?

Stereotypes   One of the primary cognitions researchers have considered is **stereotypes**—oversimplified attitudes we have toward others because we assume they hold the characteristics of a certain group, or "a generalization about what people are like; an exaggerated image of their characteristics, without regard to individual attributes" (Herbst, 1997, p. 212). Research suggests that:

1   Stereotypes function to help people make sense of the world. They are related to **categorization**, the mental process of grouping things, attributes, behaviors, and people into like clusters. Categorization is necessary; without it, we would have to make sense of each new object, action, and person anew. According to social identity theory (see chapter 5), when we see others, we automatically put them into groups (student/teacher, man/woman, my group/not my group), and then evaluate them. Stereotypes are not the categories we have, but the thoughts or attributes we associate with groups of people.

2   People have stereotypes of other groups and of their own group. A study of the stereotypes Aboriginal and Anglo Australian high school students had of their own and the other group showed that Anglo Australians' stereotypes of Aboriginals were fairly negative, intense, and consistent, while their stereotype of their own group was quite favorable. In one study, Aboriginals felt positively toward Anglo Australians, and only moderately positively toward their own group (Marjoribanks & Jordan, 1986). In many of the stereotypes (e.g., good parents, strong sense of right, reliable), the most positive scores were Anglos of themselves, and the lowest, Anglos of the Aboriginals.

3   Stereotypes are often based on a "kernel of truth" (Allport, 1979). For example, North Americans often stereotype Latin Americans has having a "lax" view of time—"*mañana* time", in which people are always late. There is a truth that in many Latin American co-cultures, the present relationship one is in might be more important than the time on the clock; however, Latino punctuality may depend on the type of appointment (e.g., a business meeting versus a party), co-cultural differences based on social class, urban versus rural cultures, and individual preferences in time orientation.

4   All people have the tendency to rely on stereotypes. Patricia Devine has led a line of research that demonstrates that when people are able to focus on it, they can use their emotional energy to override their stereotypes and to **individuate** or personalize the other—to see the person as an individual, rather than as a group member. But when we are busy thinking about something else, we tend to resort to the stereotypes we

learn in our culture about other groups; that is, while we can control stereotypes, they are, in part, automatic (Devine & Sharp, 2009).

5   We may stereotype people differently depending on the group in which we mentally place them. If we have stereotypes toward people who are blind but also toward people who smoke, if we see a blind person smoking a cigarette, it will likely trigger stereotypes about smokers; but if she is using a cane, it will more likely trigger stereotypes about blind people.

Prejudice   As we note earlier, there is a thin line between types of cognition and intolerance. Most of the cognitive processes we note here are a necessary part of making sense of our world. However, often, these cognitive processes are tinged with and shaped by intolerance. Perhaps the main distinction between an intolerant and tolerant cognitive process is the affect, or emotion, that accompanies it. Gordon Allport (1979) defines **prejudice** as "an attitude in which we are hostile towards or avoid another person because of the group to which that person belongs" (p. 7). Many are able to distinguish dislike of individuals from that of governments. Saied Reza Ameli (2007) looked at anti-American attitudes of British Muslims after September 11, 2001. Interview participants differentiated the acts of the U.S. Government and media, which they perceived to be anti-Muslim, from everyday citizens, whom they felt, at worst, might just be misguided, blind to government involvement, or brainwashed.

It is important to recognize prejudice as an attitude or feeling, because if we focus only on reducing stereotypes or changing other thoughts, but do not change feelings, the prejudiced person may just find another reason to dislike the members of the target group. Realistically, however, changing attitudes will impact feelings, and altering feelings will lead to more appreciative expectations, perceptions, and attributions.

A specific type of prejudice is ethnocentrism. William Sumner (1940) describes **ethnocentrism** as a perception in which "one's own group is the center of everything, and all others are scaled with reference to it" (p. 13). Some distinguish between ethnocentrism as a belief in the goodness of one's own group, a feeling that may actually serve some positive functions for group survival and the efficacy of a group (Rosenblatt, 1964), and a more negative ethnocentrism, in which one sees other groups negatively. It may be that ethnocentrism is "a belief in the inferiority of other groups" (Herbst, 1997, p. 80), or we might even inadvertently judge others (that is, make attributions of behavior) based on our own culture's standards. As we see, ethnocentrism involves both a perception, for example, of the right or natural way to do things, and an attitude of evaluation, in which we see our way as better.

We see ethnocentrism in a wide range of behaviors—like names that groups call themselves (Greeks versus Barbarians, Jews versus Gentiles, Japanese versus *gaijin*). Many indigenous tribes in the United States had names that meant some version of *the people, the original people, the best people*, or *the real people* (*National Relief Charities Blog*, n.d.). Most countries make maps with their own culture at the center. Indeed, the Mercator Projection, a map used by much of the Western world, created in 1569 by Gerardus Mercator, distorts the world, making the northern hemispheric continents look much larger than the southern continents (Figure 6.2). (Most scholars now use more accurate maps; Ríos, n.d.) As noted in chapter 3, ethnocentrism may be one of the few traits that may be universal to all cultures (Herbst, 1997), and it relevant to intercultural communication. In one study (Neuliep *et al.*, 2005), Americans higher in ethnocentrism, when watching a video of an

Figure 6.2 Compare the Mercator standard map, used for centuries in the Western world, in which Greenland (0.8 million square miles) takes up about the same amount of space as Africa (11.6 million square miles), with the Peters projection.

World mercator projection map with country outlines

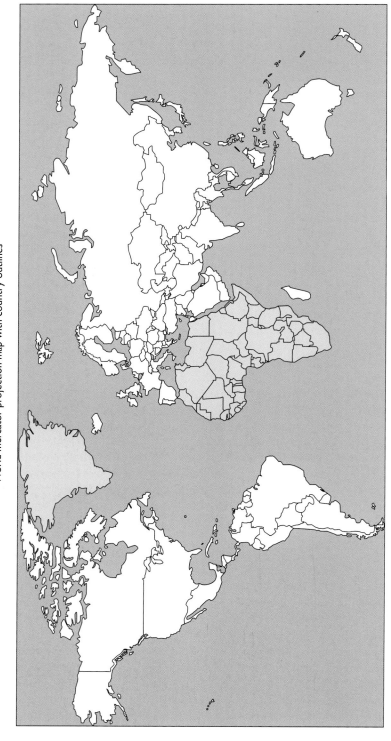

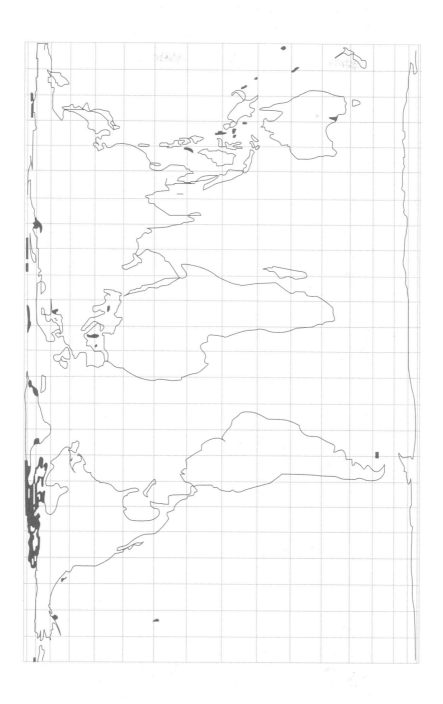

Asian manager reprimanding an American employee, rated the manager as less attractive and competent than those lower in ethnocentrism; they also reported they would be less likely to hire such a manager.

What do you think? Often, we hear calls for **nationalism**, a sense of pride in and loyalty to our nation. This pride can serve many functions, such as allowing us to protect our families and way of life. Some people call us to be economically loyal to our country (e.g., "Buy American"). What are the strengths and limitations of such loyalty? Some suggest that nationalism is linked to ethnocentrism. What do you think? Can one be loyal to one's nation without placing it above or as superior to others? Why or why not?

Related to but distinct from ethnocentrism, **xenophobia** is the fear of people who are different from oneself. It means, literally, a fear of foreigners. Fear of people who are different might be a natural human response, though our societies tell us whom we should fear and why. For example, politicians in Britain and other countries have hidden racism behind the supposedly natural desire to protect national culture. Sometimes, "xenophobia" hides other forms of intolerance. Marvin Barker (1990), for example, argues that Tory politics of the 1980s framed racism and ultra-nationalism as simple expressions of tribal belonging or a natural favoring of one's own group. Paul Gilroy (1987), in a well-known book called *There Ain't no Black in the Union Jack*, describes how British racism is wrapped up in defining its national identity as something that is White and Christian. Teun van Dijk (1993) argues that in Central European countries such as Holland, Germany, and Austria, "racism" is often associated in the collective mind with the Holocaust. Instead, people do not like to think in terms of racism, but rather in terms of *Ausländerfeindlichkeit—* fear of foreigners (xenophobia). He contends that this fear is not directed at all foreigners, but only those perceived to be racially different. Ruth Mandel (2008) supports this, noting that Turkish descendants are not integrated into Germany, in part due to Turkish immigrants' desire to maintain their own religion while living in what she calls the "Christian Club" of Europe (p. 11).

Behavior There is a wide variety of behaviors that might be called intolerant, from very subtle to very overt. One study shows how men tend to interrupt women differently than women do men, often taking the speech turn from them (Zimmerman & West, 1975). Another demonstrates that men and women use more "visual dominance" (more eye contact while listening then speaking) when assigned to a high-power/ expertise role in an interaction, but when status is not involved, women use eye contact with men as if they were in a lower power position, and men, as if in a higher power position (Dovidio *et al.*, 1988).

We might simply avoid people from certain groups. Cross-cultural psychologist Richard Brislin (1991) discusses what he calls **arms-length racism**, in which one might even be openly friendly toward people of another group, but prefer to keep them at "arm's length" (p. 368). We often allow people from other groups varying degrees of social closeness. A particular South African White might be comfortable working side by side with a Black, but may not want the Black to move into the neighborhood. Or she might be okay with the Black living in the neighborhood, but would not consider being close friends. Or she might even be friends, but not want to have the Black person marry her brother or sister.

Brislin (1991) also lists more overt types of intolerance. **Redneck racism** is a blatant intolerance we see when someone speaks openly and negatively about other groups. If we are speaking of racial intolerance, this might include racist jokes or statements with an intent to hurt or put down members of the other group, racial slurs or **ethnophaulisms** (names that we call other groups), or even open discrimination, vandalism, physical or sexual abuse, or other harmful behavior (including "flaming" behaviors on Internet video and news sites). If these are based on group belonging, we call them **hate crimes**. At an even more severe and societal level are slavery and **ethnic cleansing** (the attempt to remove a population by murder or forced deportation from a country or area of a country; Herbst, 1997), such as the Holocaust or the genocides of Rwanda, Darfur, or Bosnia.

Policy and social structure   Finally, some people look at intolerance woven into social structures. For example, we might see social policies such as unequal punishments for crimes more frequently committed by Blacks or Whites in a given society, funding structures for public education that propagate class and racial inequalities (Kozol, 1991), organizational and legal policies that "blame the victim" in cases of rape or sexual harassment, national language policies that work against the pride and identity of certain language groups, and so on. For example, **redlining** is a practice in which U.S. banks avoid giving mortgages to people wanting to purchase in certain neighborhoods or to people of different ethnic or racial groups. Real estate agents may prefer not to show families of color homes in predominantly White affluent neighborhoods, because they do not want to lose the business of White owners in the neighborhood. The Immigration Service might be more likely to stop and ask for identification from someone who supposedly looks like a foreigner (different color skin); airport security might "profile" to search people who appear to have certain ethnic or national backgrounds, and the shopping mall security might be more likely to follow and observe people of certain ethnic groups. Unequal policing, housing, education, medical treatment, and life expectancies reflect intolerance that is built into the very social structure of society.

Debates: Where does racism lie, and who can be racist?

With a better understanding of the thoughts, feelings, behaviors, and policies that can be either intolerant or appreciative, we can now turn to some difficult questions about certain forms of intolerance. This is an important discussion, because sometimes we engage in discussions with others about who can be racist or sexist. (Can Blacks be racist? Can women be sexist?) Sometimes people debate whether an act is indeed racist or not. For example, are racist jokes racist if we tell them among our friends, some of whom are members of the target group? Is ethnic humor acceptable when told by members of the targeted group? We will use racism as a specific example; however, the location and definition of "racism" has parallel application for terms like sexism, classism, and homophobia.

Is racism an attitude or a behavior? As we've seen earlier, intolerance exists within the minds of individuals, in behavior—including communication behavior—and in policies and social structures. Some feel that an attitude, for example, that one racial group is superior to another, is "racist," whereas others feel that racism must include behavior or even social policy (as we shall see below).

How overt does it have to be to be "racist"? A second question that arises as we think about intolerance is how visible (or "overt") something must be to be considered intolerance. Since the 1970s, authors in the United States and Europe have noted a change in intolerance, especially sexism and racism: it is now politically incorrect to show racism or sexism openly. Instead, people hide attitudes in subtle wording or nonverbal behaviors. Writers have called this by a variety of names: covert racism (or sexism), everyday racism, **subtle racism**, modern racism, and others. These terms refer to an intolerance that one still holds toward another person because of the group to which the person belongs, but that is expressed in difficult-to-notice ways. People might, without their own awareness, hide racism in political attitudes, where one holds conservative attitudes regarding social justice toward those who are different (McConahay, 1986). Such attitudes might be that racial intolerance no longer exists, that minority members are getting more than they deserve and are pushing too hard for change, and that failure to advance economically is due strictly to group members' own lack of motivation (Sears & Henry, 2003). Conservative attitudes are often linked to racial dislike. Sometimes, we express racial and other intolerances by hiding them "symbolically" in discussion of issues, such as welfare, gang violence, or joblessness. Scholars have referred to this as **symbolic racism**.

Should racism be determined by intent or result? In many cultures, organizations or individuals engage in practices for what seem to be economic reasons—policies noted earlier, such as redlining, racial profiling at the airport, or clerks following Blacks through stores. In each case, the apparent reason for the behavior might be financial—the banker (real estate agent, immigration agent, mall security) might not perceive any personal prejudice. In the same way, media makers may simply want to sell a product. Often, the defense for such actions is based on intent: "I'm not trying to hurt Blacks…" (or women, gays, lesbians, Turks, Haoles, *gaijin*, Gentiles, Palestinians, Greek Cypriots, Roma, etc.); "I'm just protecting my business" (or culture, or homeland, etc.).

However, recent authors have redefined racism not in terms of what one intends to do, but by "exclusionary practices"—practices that treat people differently because of supposed racial differences. These practices refer "to both intentional actions and unintended consequences which create patterns of inequality" (Miles, 1989, p. 78). We pass on sets of ideas that oppress others not because we want to, but simply because these are the ideas with which we were brought up. One such idea is the **rape myth**, which suggests that, even if women say no to men's sexual advances they still want sex, or if they are drunk and not clearly in control, sex is okay. This idea is reproduced in many advertisements and shows, from the more tame to the more provocative; however, some organizations, such as Where is Your Line? (2010) challenge these myths.

Is racism individual, institutional, or societal? Core to the question of who can be racist (sexist, etc.) is whether racism is strictly based on individual thought or behavior. In much general thought today, racism is personal avoidance, dislike, or mistreatment of a group coupled with societal power. **Sexism** is defined as a system of ideas, images, laws, beliefs, and practices that work against women in the favor of **patriarchy** (a system of male-based power), and **heterosexism** as a system of images, policies, and collective thought that privileges heterosexual relationships and marginalizes or disenfranchises those in homosexual relationships. (This last concept is quite different from **homophobia**, an irrational fear of someone who is lesbian or gay, as homophobia really describes a problem in the individual mind, while heterosexism describes organizational policy.) In each of these cases—racism, sexism, and heterosexism—societal power combines with group-based negative attitude. By this logic, in Western Europe, for example, Blacks cannot be racist, and women cannot be sexist. The Black person might have "racial prejudice," but it would not be called racism. Others feel that each of these words should be able to refer to an individual's thought or action regardless of her or his group belonging. To return to Miles' (1989) definition earlier, if a Black person engages in a behavior that excludes or treats Whites differently based on race, it would be racist.

It seems useful to be able to call any behavior (or thought) that excludes based on race "racist". At the same time, we realize that there is an experiential difference between a White person who experiences a racially intolerant act, probably as a surprise to everyday expectations, and the person of color who experiences the same act as part of a history and social system that supports such acts. For the person of color, the experience of such an act may not be a violation of expectations, but just another in a long line of frequent **microaggressions**—everyday expressions of intolerance that people of non-dominant racial, sex, gender orientation, and other groups must live with that are often too subtle even to notice, but that become part of the fabric of one's life (DeAngelis, 2009; The Microaggressions project, 2012).

POP CULTURE

Intolerance is held in place by those in power—not always deliberately—but also by systems of laws, ideas, and images. People in the empowered group are often unaware that their practices support those systems, and those disadvantaged by the systems also unintentionally consent to the control. A recent fictional book series, *The Hunger Games*, by Suzanne Collins (http://www.scholastic.com/thehungergames/) tells the story of oppression by one group, the Capitol, over all of the districts. For many years, the districts have consented to the oppression, through media manipulation and threat of violence and death. But Katniss Everdeen, the heroine, begins accidentally to bring the oppression to people's awareness. Readers are left wondering at each stage if the districts will continue to yield to the Capitol or stand up to the oppression. The first book was the source for a popular movie in 2012.

Looking to a better future: What are some causes of and solutions for intolerance?

As we consider possible responses to intolerance, it is easy to think of education as a solution. Many organizations, universities, and community programs make education about differences a primary part of their platform for change. This solution ignores that intolerance exists beyond the individual. We see an example of this limitation in the debate among educational authors between "multicultural education" and "anti-racist" education. The first takes a well-intentioned and honest attempt to reduce intolerance by letting students know more about different groups. But those who support anti-racist education feel that the multiculturalists focus social change at the level of the individual student's mind: if the student has more tolerant ideas, that should reduce intolerance. This ignores intolerance built into laws, organizational policies, and media systems (Rattansi, 1992). If social system factors impact intolerance, solutions must also include those factors. Education by itself is a relatively simple solution to a complicated problem—we might miss the chance for more effective change. Addressing a complex problem requires a complex understanding of that problem.

Understanding the problem: Possible causes of intolerance

The best understanding of any complex problem, including intolerance, requires understanding from different perspectives, and, to use the language from chapter 2, from different types of research perspectives (e.g., scientific, humanistic, critical). In other places, we have outlined many of the aspects that might contribute to intolerance (Baldwin & Hecht, 2003; Baldwin, 1998), and in some ways, these echo the "locations" where intolerance can exist. Briefly, these include:

→ *Biological and instinctual influences*: Some authors suggest that prejudice might come from instincts, such as the desire to preserve one's one gene pool or one's own biological line (thus, we have cultural preferences for marrying within the group). Or it might simply be an instinct to fear what is different (e.g., xenophobia). Two dilemmas with this approach are that politicians have sometimes used it to support the idea that prejudice is natural to humans (which we do not deny), but then to use this as a reason not to fight against it but to use it to build policy. Another dilemma is that, even if prejudice has some basis in instinct, we still need words and language to tell us which groups we should fear, why we should fear them, and what we should or should not do about it.

→ *Individual-level influences*: We discussed earlier, the role of cognition in intolerance, including stereotypical beliefs about others or the belief that our group is superior (ethnocentrism). Such perceptions include categorizing people into in- and out-groups, as well as stereotypes and feelings of group superiority. Allport (1979) introduces many psychological reasons, in what he calls a psychodynamic approach, for not liking people from other groups. These include things such as a personality structure that is rigid or likes authority and predictability; feelings of inferiority (or feelings of our group's inferiority); or a need to blame others for faults that we (or our group) might have. If intolerance serves psychological needs for people, education will be a limited solution. We see this in cases of group-based bullying, which meets psychological functions for the bully, though in an inappropriate and ineffective way. Many researchers study the impact of personality structure on prejudicial communication (often from a social-scientific approach), or, more recently, the subjective experiences of those who are targets of intolerance (often researched humanistically).

→ *Group-level influences*: Even if someone feels negatively toward other groups, certain social structures are more likely to instigate intolerance. These social structures can also impact how we categorize and stereotype out-group members. Group-based factors include immigration patterns, comparative social status of groups, permeability of group boundaries, and labor force problems like joblessness. Research in this area borrows from sociological ideas of authors like Max Weber, who looks at how groups seek to obtain and maintain privilege, or Karl Marx, who focused on the ownership of business and industry. Some writers believe that the elite promote intolerance among workers to keep them divided; but most writers today see group-based power in more complex ways, including the keeping of certain groups as the "center"—the standard by which other groups are measured. Many critical writers focus on group-based ideas (ideologies) and how these work to give groups power or fight for power (see, e.g., essays in Nakayama & Halualani, 2010).

→ *Legal-policy influences*: Other writers focus on legal issues, such as feminist legal studies or the critical race theory movement, which suggest that legal policies that claim to be color- or sex-blind are unequal and promote existing sexual and racial hierarchies. Sometimes organizational policies are informal, such as a "good old boys' network," in which one gains opportunities for advancement based on whom one knows—with such positions often going to those who look, act, or believe like those already in power. Social and legal policy often promotes or battles against group-based inequality (Brzuzy, 1998). The case of law and policy is difficult, because supporters suggest that there are non-race-based reasons for the laws, so cases of legal and policy discrimination are harder to prove and create fiery debate.

→ *Rhetorical and media influences*: Finally, we recreate intolerance in language and rhetoric, as well as media. Even verbal and nonverbal behavior, such as eye contact and word choice, might create group-based mistreatment, often without us knowing it. For example, some argue that there are many negative names to call women in U.S. American society, most of which have some sexual connotation, but much fewer such terms for men. Rhetorically, speakers create visions of "us" and "them," much as early U.S. Americans did of Irish immigrants, and as Adolf Hitler did through his propaganda machine in 1930s Germany, making the Jewish people a scapegoat for Germany's economic and social problems, and thus providing a justification for his "final solution." And a great many scholars have turned their attention to look at media representation around the world, how the media systematically either ignore or under-represent a group or present the group in a limited or stereotypical way (see chapter 10).

The various influences of intolerance are interconnected. For example, the thoughts we have about a group may be influenced in part by our interpersonal experiences, but are largely shaped by the rhetoric we hear (see chapter 9) and the media imagery to which we are exposed. There may be real differences in groups, for example, in crime rates; but these are often shaped by other social forces, such as differences in educational spending and job opportunity. Laws and polices sometimes hold intolerance in place, but this is at least in part because people with intolerant ideas penned the laws, or because people who are unaware of the effects of exclusion sit by and say nothing about them. For example, if we treat it as an overarching system of inequality, sexism includes unequal treatment of women (often built into policies and opportunities)—but those inequalities are based on stereotypes of women, which are reproduced through jokes and media imagery.

What do you think? Is it a compliment or is it sexist? In many Latin American countries, men engage in the practice of *piropos*—compliments (usually) to a pretty woman, who is a stranger walking by. The *piropo* can be poetic, romantic, or crude (http://www.piroposcortos.com). Elizabeth Kissling and Cheris Kramarae (1991) argue that such compliments build a hostile and threatening environment for women or, at a minimum, maintain sexual hierarchies, though in some cultures, they are very common. Do you feel such street comments are sexist and promote inequality, or are they compliments to be appreciated? What would happen if women said them to men, or men to other men?

Addressing the problem: Possible solutions to intolerance

As we have seen, intolerance is a complex problem that requires complex solutions. A true platform of change should address solutions at the levels of the individual, interpersonal communication, mediated communication, social structure, and law and policy.

Individual-focused initiatives It would be easy to find exercises—or whole books of exercises—on the Internet for changing the way people think. Many use education, especially in the workplace. Strategies for education or training include everything from just becoming more aware of difference (such as a "diversity bingo" icebreaker), to interactive games such as Barnga or BaFa BaFa, to role plays, to group problem-solving games (see Fowler & Blohm, 2004, for an analysis of the strengths and limitations of various methods). Many organizations have time periods (days or months), publications, and events dedicated to learning more about the major cultures that make up the organization or community. Schools might have a month to focus on "women's history," or the contributions of various groups. We feel that these solutions provide a fair start, but such events usually leave many groups out, and they do much less good than adopting diversity as a mindset that rides throughout the curriculum or throughout the organization, rather than limiting focus to a month or day.

Contact theory One theoretical approach, from a social scientific perspective, that has received much research support is called the **contact hypothesis**, a theoretical statement that suggests that the more time people from groups that do not like each other spend with each other, the better group relations will become. Years of research have demonstrated that this statement is too simple. Groups can live side by side for years and only seem to grow to hate each other more with the passing of time. Still, many have developed "contact events" that, with the right elements, seem to reduce intolerance between groups. Research has continued to add the conditions required for such events to be the most effective, to the extent that now "contact" is not merely a hypothesis, but a "theory," sometimes called intergroup contact theory. Contact works the best if members in the contact event (a) have equal status, (b) work together on a task rather than competing against each other, (c) have a shared goal, (c) have communication with each other, (d) have the opportunity to develop ongoing friendships, and (e) have the support of an overseeing group, such as a school administration (Dovidio *et al.*, 2003).

Such events can work to change both thought (cognition) and feeling (affect). One way these work is that they allow us to see others not simply as group members, but as individuals. We see a good example of contact at work in the 2000 U.S. movie, *Remember the Titans*, based on a real story, in which coach Herman Boone (played by Denzel Washington) works through Black–White prejudices to create an integrated and successful American football team in 1971. Of course, contact situations only work if members apply their liking for members of the event to others in the group after they leave the event, and research is still trying to determine if such events have long-lasting effects.

One individual-level solution is to make people aware of the privilege that they might have, based on their social status, sex, racial, or other positions. For example, at the writing of this textbook, the full-page comics of the newspaper in the moderately racially diverse town of the author of this chapter has no comic characters who are not White. In essence, animals, such as Garfield, have more of a speaking voice in the comics than anyone of any ethnic or racial group that is not White. If one worships in a male-dominated church or temple that is trying to encourage wider roles for women, it will likely be much easier for women to be aware of the issues other women face in assuming the risky roles of new positions of leadership than it is for men, for whom such issues are invisible. Peggy McIntosh, in a famous essay entitled *White Privilege: Unpacking the Invisible Knapsack* (1988) discusses the many privileges she has every day as a White person in the United States, mostly beyond her awareness. The idea is that making those with power aware of such privilege might make them less resistant to change. Problems of the approach could be that it places responsibility for change on higher-power groups, ignoring intolerance held by those with less social power. This could also lead to patronizing, in which those in high-power groups seek to "help" those with less power, even telling them what to do or taking over change efforts.

Before leaving individual-level solutions, we should note that that **color blindness** (and, by extension other types of blindness, such as gender blindness), attempting to ignore "race" or ethnicity in social interaction, is not a goal that most trainers or researchers promote. Although some people of different races may prefer this, many do not. If I am African American, I may value that identity, and someone trying to be blind to it denies that important part of who I am. Since all policies and values reflect some cultural orientation, an approach that claims to be culturally blind will probably reflect the dominant culture, erasing or silencing minority cultural voices. Further, in each culture, there are aspects of difference that we simply cannot ignore. For example, some writers have argued that the United States is divided to its very core by both race and sex. Even if we are trying to be blind, some argue, we cannot not think terms of race and sex difference.

Communicative solutions Communicative solutions focus on interpersonal or mediated communication. We can be more aware of the words we use, the jokes we tell, the things we say. Directly and verbally addressing intolerance is a useful solution, though it may be best to focus on why behaviors or policies exclude groups, rather than calling them "racist," or "sexist," as these words often make people focus more on defending themselves against a charge than addressing the impacts of their behavior.

As with color blindness, **political correctness** is not the goal here. This wide-ranging attempt at changing everyday communication through terminology and references (for example, "letter carrier" instead of "mailman") may have some benefit, but it often becomes the target of jokes, and it sometimes slows down deeper, more meaningful change (Morris, 2005). True, we can be aware of using language that includes others (gender-neutral language), as this creates a way of thinking that allows for more possibility. But we can also use less patronizing speech when talking to older (or younger) people, be more inclusive in our nonverbal behaviors, and so on. Becoming aware of issues in this chapter, such as subtle intolerance and invisible centers of privilege, like Whiteness, may help us be more responsible communicators. We can also create rhetoric—for example, public messages, letters to the editor, and so on—based on more egalitarian assumptions. Many of us will not create mass media, though we may make blogs or websites. Still, we can actively challenge media makers by writing letters to them or staging protests, advocating for more inclusive and positive images of different groups.

Structural and policy solutions   Social-structural solutions are more of a challenge. These typically call for some sort of social movement, such as group-based protest. As much communication research, especially intercultural research, has focused on the individual, we are not often good at visualizing this sort of change. However, sociologists have found some tools to encourage change. Solutions might range from changing the seating structure in classrooms or changing assignment structures to solutions that aim at creating jobs, reducing urban flight, equalizing opportunities, and so on. Often, such decisions, such as regional and national political decisions, are strongly influenced by lawmakers, who respond to letters. We might write letters just by ourselves, but some of us are more outgoing, have more contacts, and may successfully launch a petition campaign. In some countries, where such campaigns are not legal, citizens may need to find other solutions that work within the framework of the culture, while at the same time stretching that framework to make it more inclusive and tolerant.

Summary

We considered in this chapter the basic notion of intolerance and noted how it is central to much of our intercultural communication. We saw that intolerance has many manifestations. Some of these, such as hate crimes and genocide, are easy to notice. But in most or all societies, even if these are not present, there are more subtle forms of intolerance. We have heard some people say that these are, in some ways, worse than overt name-calling or discrimination, because people's true feelings are masked by smiles and polite behavior. We have looked at some of the mental processes that go along with intolerance, such as categorization and in-group/out-group perception, which may not be intolerant, but easily give way to stereotypes, ethnocentrism, or xenophobia. In some ways, intolerance seems to be changing, and certainly the way academic writers talk about it is changing, so that there are many debates now about where an intolerance like sexism or racism lies, whether it is explicit or hidden, whether it must be deliberate or can be determined based on the result of behavior, whether certain intolerances are strictly individual or only held in place with societal power, and so on. One thing is certain, though—all manifestations of intolerance, from social structural inequalities to psychological prejudices, are created, maintained, and resisted through symbolic activity, making the study and treatment of intolerance inherently communicative.

There are many possible factors and processes that help intolerance grow. Some of these are internal to the mind of the prejudiced person, such as thoughts and psychological needs that intolerance might fulfill. But there are also always social factors—historical relations, group-based differences, movements of groups—and with these, rhetorical and media representations of the other, which feed the stereotypes and feelings of superiority and inferiority that are internal. Laws and organizational policies can also either challenge or support inequality and intolerance. Each intolerance is different. The Protestant–Catholic division in Northern Ireland, for example, or the struggle between the *Blancos* and the *Colorados* in Colombia. Patricia Hill Collins (1990) argues that oppression of Black women in the United States, for example, is a triple oppression, based on social class, race, and sex. In the same way, any given intolerance may seem to be about religion, but is likely also about class, competition for jobs, and the personal and social insecurities of the prejudiced parties. Because of the complexity of intolerance, we have argued that in most cases, education of differences and similarities, while important, is only part of a solution. Real change will be nearer when we work together addressing individual, communicative, social, and legal sites of intolerance. Perhaps then, we will see a world that is not only more "tolerant," but also more inclusive of others and appreciative of their differences.

KEY TERMS

racism, 116

intolerance, 116

tolerance, 116

appreciation, 116

selective attention, 116

selective perception, 116

selective recall, 117

attribution, 117

fundamental attribution error, 117

self-serving (or egocentric) attribution bias, 117

ultimate attribution error, 117

stereotype, 118

categorization, 118

individuation, 118

prejudice, 119

ethnocentrism, 119

nationalism, 122

xenophobia, 122

arms-length racism, 122

redneck racism, 123

ethnophaulism, 123

hate crime, 123

ethnic cleansing, 123

redlining, 123

subtle racism, 124

symbolic racism, 124

rape myth, 125

sexism, 125

patriarchy, 125

heterosexism, 125

homophobia, 125

microaggressions, 125

contact hypothesis, 128

color blindness, 129

political correctness, 130

Discussion questions

1   The notion of **sexism** is strongly influenced by feminist authors in the West. To what degree does it extend to other cultures? If beliefs and norms in a culture support men's protection of women, and so on, is it still sexist? Why or why not?

2   Who can be racist (etc.)? As we were writing this chapter, we posted a news note on our Facebook page about a woman pilot in Brazil who ejected a male passenger who was making sexist comments about woman pilots, and one of our friends complained about the inability to discuss how women can be sexist toward men. What do you think? Can women be sexist, people of color racist, and so on? Why or why not? How do our beliefs about this inform the response we take to intolerance?

3   Read Peggy McIntosh's (1988) essay about the Invisible Knapsack. Extend her analysis to your own culture. Which of her aspects of White privilege have changed since she wrote it in 1988? What are some examples of how invisible privileges might be experienced by those with privilege?

4   Locate the Southern Poverty Law Center's website on hate groups and crimes in the United States (http://www.splcenter.org/get-informed/hate-map). What types of solution could individuals or groups enact to address hate crimes or more subtle intolerance in your country or area?

Action points

1   Conduct an analysis of media in terms of the representation of a group (such as women in sports magazines, people with disabilities in prime-time television, for example). The analysis might be quantitative (a content analysis that counts how often certain types of representation occur) or interpretive (looking at the ideas behind the images). Share your findings with the public through blogs, newspaper articles, and so on, and send your findings to the people who made the media.

2   Plan a contact event that brings together members of different groups that may not always get along. Work to include some of the factors from contact theory research that lead to successful contact, such as the possibility for dialogue and ongoing interaction after the event.

3   If your community has festivals to celebrate identity or marches that address intolerance or oppression, learn more about them and share the information with your class. If your investigation leads you to believe that this is an organization or cause you can support, join the march!

For more information

Baird, R.M., & Rosenbaum, S.E. (Eds.). (1999). *Hatred, bigotry, and prejudice: Definitions, causes, and solutions*. Amherst, NY: Prometheus Books.

Brief, A.P. (Ed.). (2008). *Diversity at work*. New York: Cambridge University Press.

González, A., Houston, M., & Chen, V. (2012). *Our voices: Essays in culture, ethnicity, and communication* (5th ed.). New York: Oxford University Press.

Ruscher, J.B. (2001). *Prejudiced communication: A social psychological perspective*. New York: Guilford.

References

Allport, G.W. (1979). *The nature of prejudice* (originally published 1954). Reading, MA: Addison-Wesley.

Ameli, S.R. (2007). Intercultural approach to Americanism and Anti-Americanism: British muslim impressions of America before and after 11 September. *Comparative American Studies*, 5(1), 37–61.

Baldwin, J.R. (1998). Tolerance/intolerance: A multidisciplinary view of prejudice. In M.L. Hecht (Ed.), *Communicating prejudice* (pp. 24–56). Thousand Oaks: Sage.

Baldwin, J.R., & Hecht, M.L. (2003). Unpacking group-based hatred: A holographic look at identity and intolerance. In L.A. Samovar & R.E. Porter (Eds.), *Intercultural communication: A reader* (10th ed., pp. 354–364.). Belmont, CA: Wadsworth.

Baldwin, J.R., & Hunt, S.K. (2002). Information seeking behavior in intercultural and intergroup communication. *Human Communication Research*, 28, 272–286.

Barker, M. (1990). Biology and the new racism. In D.T. Goldberg (Ed.), *Anatomy of racism* (pp. 18–37). Minneapolis: University of Minneapolis Press.

Barnes, J., Chesnoff, R.Z., Carter, S., Rosenberg, R., & Trimble, J. (1988). Truce in troubled waters. *U.S. News & World Report*, August 1, p. 50.

Brislin, R.W. (1991). Prejudice in intercultural communication. In L.A. Samovar & R.E. Porter (Eds.), *Intercultural communication: A reader* (6th ed., pp. 366–370). Belmont, CA: Wadsworth.

Brzuzy, S. (1998). Public policy interventions to prejudice. In M. Hecht (Ed.), *Communicating prejudice* (pp. 326–333). Thousand Oaks, CA: Sage.

Collins, P.H. (1990). *Black feminist thought*. New York: Routledge.

Collins, S. (2008) *The hunger games*. New York: Scholastic Press.

Cowell, A. (2012). In Oslo, evil demystified with civility. *The New York Times*, April 23. Accessed May 22, 2012, at http://www.nytimes.com/2012/04/24/world/europe/24iht-letter24.html?ref=andersbehringbreivik

DeAngelis, T. (2009). Unmasking 'racial micro aggressions.' *American Psychological Association*, 40 (2). Accessed March 14, 2013, at http://www.apa.org/monitor/2009/02/microaggression.aspx

Devine, P.G., & Sharp, L.B. (2009). Automaticity and control in stereotyping and prejudice. In D. Nelson (Ed.), *Handbook of prejudice, stereotyping, and discrimination* (pp. 61–87). New York: Psychology Press.

Dovidio, J.F., Ellyson, S.L., Keating, C.F., Heltman, K., & Brown, C.E. (1988). The relationship of social power to visual display of dominance between men and women. *Journal of Personality and Social Psychology*, 54, 233–242.

Dovidio, J.F., Gaertner, S.L., & Kawakami, K. (2003). Intergroup contact: The past, present, and future. *Group Processes & Intergroup Relations*, 6(1), 5–21.

Federal Bureau of Investigation (2010) *Latest hate crime statistics: Reported incidents, number of victims decrease.* Accessed April 3, 2012, at http://www.fbi.gov/news/stories/2010/november/hate_112210/hate_112210

Fowler, S.M., & Blohm, J.M. (2004). An analysis of methods for intercultural training. In D. Landis, J.M. Bennett, & M.J. Bennett (Eds.), *Handbook of intercultural training* (3rd ed., pp. 37–84). Thousand Oaks, CA: Sage.

Foxman, A.H. (2011). Norwegian attacks stem from a new ideological hate. *Anti-Defamation League*. (Originally appeared in *The Washington Post*, July 29.) Accessed May 22, 2012, at http://www.adl.org/ADL_Opinions/Terrorism/20110801-Wash+Post+Oped.htm

Gilroy, P. (2002). *There ain't no black in the Union Jack: The cultural politics of race and nation*. London: Routledge.

Glet, A. (2009). The German hate crime concept: An account of the classification and registration of bias-motivated offences and the implementation of the hate crime model into Germany's law enforcement system. *Internet Journal of Criminology*. Accessed May 22, 2012, at http://www.internetjournalofcriminology.com/Glet_German_Hate_Crime_Concept_Nov_09.pdf

Hecht, M.L., & Baldwin, J.R. (1998). Layers and holograms: A new look at prejudice. M.L. Hecht (Ed.), *Communicating prejudice* (pp. 57–84). Thousand Oaks: Sage.

Herbst, P.H. (1997). *The color of words: An encyclopædic dictionary of ethnic bias in the United States*. Yarmouth, ME: Intercultural Press.

Hewstone, M., & Ward, C. (1985). Ethnocentrism and causal attribution in Southeast Asia. *Journal of Personality and Social Psychology*, 48, 614–662.

Kelley, H. (1967). Attribution theory in social psychology. *Nebraska Symposium on Motivation*, 15, 192–238.

Kissling, E.A., & Kramarae, C. (1991). Stranger compliments: The interpretation of street remarks. *Women's Studies in Communication*, 14(1), 75–93.

Kohut, A. (2005). Arab and Muslim perceptions of the United States. *Pew Research Center Publications*.

Accessed April 12, 2012, at http://pewresearch.org/pubs/6/arab-and-muslim-perceptions-of-the-united-states

Kozol, J. (1991). *Savage inequalities: Children in America's schools*. New York: Harper Perennial.

Lau, S. (2010). Homosexuality in China. *US-China Today* (University of Southern California), March 10. Available at http://www.uschina.usc.edu/article@usct?homosexuality_in_china_14740.aspx

Mandel, R. (2008). *Cosmopolitan anxieties: Turkish challenges to citizenship and belonging in Germany.* Durham, NC: Duke University Press.

Marjoribanks, K., & Jordan, D.F. (1986). Stereotyping among Aboriginal and Anglo Australians: The uniformity, intensity, direction, and quality of auto- and heterostereotypes. *Journal of Cross-Cultural Psychology, 17*, 17–28. doi:10.1177/0022002186017001002

McConahay, J.B. (1986). Modern racism, ambivalence, and the modern racism scale. In J.S. Dovidio & S.L. Gaertner (Eds.), *Prejudice, discrimination, and racism* (pp. 99–125). Orlando, FL: Academic Press.

McIntosh, P. (1988). White privilege: Unpacking the invisible knapsack. Excerpted from P. McIntosh, *White privilege and male privilege: A personal account of coming to see correspondences through work in women's studies.* Working paper 189. Wellesley, MA: Wellesley College Center for Research on Women. Accessed August 20, 2013 at http://www.amptoons.com/blog/files/mcintosh.html

The Microaggressions Project. (2012). Accessed March 14, 2013, at http://www.microaggressions.com/

Miles, R. (1989). *Racism*. London: Routledge.

Morris, M. (2005). Political correctness. In T. Bennett, L. Grossberg, & M. Morris (Eds.), *New keywords: A revised vocabulary of culture and society* (pp. 260–262). Malden, MA: Blackwell.

Nakayama, T.K., & Halualani, R.T. (Eds.). (2010). *The handbook of critical intercultural communication.* Malden, MA: Wiley-Blackwell.

National Relief Charities Blog. (n.d.) Native American tribal names. Available at http://blog.nrcprograms.org/american-indian-tribes-names/

Neuliep, J.W., Hintz, S.M., & McCroskey, J.C. (2005). The influence of ethnocentrism in organizational contexts: Perceptions of interviewee and managerial attractiveness, credibility, and effectiveness. *Communication Quarterly, 53* (1), 41–56.

New York Times. (2012). Anders Behring Breivik (April 19). Accessed Oct 31, 2013, at http://topics.nytimes.com/top/reference/timestopics/people/b/anders_behring_breivik/index.html

Pettigrew, T. (1979). The ultimate attribution error. *Personality and Social Psychology Bulletin, 5*, 461–476.

Rattansi, A. (1992). Changing the subject? Racism, culture, and education. In J. Donald & A. Rattansi (Eds.), '*Race,' culture, and difference* (pp. 11–48). London: The Open University.

Ríos, A. (n.d.). *Mercator map of the world.* Accessed April 10, 2012, at http://www.public.asu.edu/~aarios/resourcebank/maps/page10.html

Rosenblatt, P.C. (1964). Origins and effects of group ethnocentrism and nationalism. *Journal of Conflict Resolutions, 8*, 131–146.

Ross, L.D. (1977). The intuitive psychologist and his shortcomings: Distortions in the attribution process. In L. Berkowitz, (Ed.). *Advances in experimental psychology* (Vol. 10, pp. 173–220). New York: Academic Press.

Sears, D.O., & Henry, P.J. (2003). The origins of symbolic racism. *Journal of Personality and Social Psychology, 85*, 259–275. doi:10.1037/0022-3514.85.2.259

Spagnoli, F. (2008). Hate (2): Hate crimes and xenophobia in Russia. *P.A.P. Blog*, November 14. Accessed May 22, 2012, at http://filipspagnoli.wordpress.com/2008/11/14/human-rights-facts-79-hate-crime-and-xenophobia-in-russia/

Sumner, W.G. (1940). *Folkways.* Boston: Ginn.

Tempe Daily News Tribune. (1993). FBI: Racism cause of most hate crime. 5 January, p. A3.

van Dijk, T.A. (1993). *Elite discourse and racism.* Newbury Park: Sage.

Wars in the World (2012). *List of ongoing conflicts.* March 7. Accessed March 14, 2012, at http://www.warsintheworld.com/?page=static1258254223

Where is Your Line? (2010) *The rape myth: A tool of social control* (July 11). Accessed May 22, 2012, at http://whereisyourline.org/2010/07/the-rape-myth-a-tool-of-social-control/

Zimmerman, D.H., & West, C. (1975). Sex roles, interruptions, and silences in conversation. In B. Thorne & N. Henley (Eds.), *Language and sex: Difference and dominance* (pp. 105–129). Rowley, MA: Newbury House.

Messages

With a deeper understanding of the foundations and key elements that undergird our communication, especially communication with people from different cultures or groups, we are now ready to consider the production and consumption of messages. Messages can be sent through many different channels. In this section, we consider two primary channels—verbal and nonverbal communication. But these messages are often put together in specific types of message, such as public and/or persuasive presentations (rhetoric) or mediated messages. We might think of these as "contexts" of communication, except that both rhetoric and mediated messages are, in turn, used with larger contexts, such as organizations. So we treat them here instead as secondary channels—channels that use verbal and nonverbal messages, except through public discourse or media.

Chapter 7 deals with verbal communication and language, as these relate to culture. We talk about the nature of meaning within language and some specific ideas about how language might create meaning in different cultures and how language, in turn, is impacted by social situations. We provide examples of specific ways cultural communication can differ, such as in persuasion or compliments, and discuss these in terms of some dimensions of language difference (e.g., level of formality). We close the chapter with a discussion of larger assemblage of words and meanings in the creation of cultural discourses such as myths, conversational episodes, social dramas, and cultural metaphors.

Chapter 8 introduces nonverbal communication. Since some readers may not have a background in nonverbal communication, we begin with an introduction of the basic channels of nonverbal communication, such as touch, distance, and eye contact, giving

Intercultural Communication for Everyday Life, First Edition. John R. Baldwin, Robin R. Means Coleman, Alberto González, and Suchitra Shenoy-Packer.
© 2014 John R. Baldwin, Robin R. Means Coleman, Alberto González, and Suchitra Shenoy-Packer.
Published 2014 by John Wiley & Sons Ltd.

examples of cultural difference as we go. We present the functions nonverbal communication can serve, and then turn to key issues regarding nonverbal communication that have received a lot of attention by communication scholars. One issue is whether we express or recognize emotions across cultures; another is whether there are such things as "high contact" cultures, with more eye contact and touch, and less distance. We close by covering some cultural differences in how we see time and silence.

In chapter 9, the discussion of rhetoric brings together verbal and nonverbal communication to introduce communication with a specific purpose—to persuade or influence the thoughts and behaviors of others. We relate rhetoric to culture and provide steps for understanding the rhetoric of someone of your own or a different culture. For a better understanding of rhetoric, we consider several specific traditions: African American, Chinese, Latina/o, Native U.S. American, and the Western U.S. tradition, along with the limitations of discussing such traditions. We introduce vernacular rhetoric—rhetoric used in everyday speech situations—to compare this to the public rhetoric discussed in the first part of the chapter, again with specific ethnic and regional examples.

Finally, chapter 10 presents a discussion of mediated messages. Mediated messages present language and nonverbal symbols via sound text, font, and photograph. Since media scholars sometimes use different models or approaches to communication from face-to-face researchers, we begin by discussing approaches that see media as a transmission of messages versus part of a ritual of everyday life. We discuss issues surrounding media and culture, such as how media frames our understanding of people from different groups and how cultures differ in terms of the role of media in the public sphere. Finally, we consider the Internet and new media to discuss their role in changing and preserving culture.

Chapter 7

Verbal communication: How can I reduce cultural misunderstandings in my verbal communication?

Chapter objectives

After this chapter, you should be able to:

→ Apply notions of face theory and speech acts theory to understand cultural differences in specific types of verbal communication (e.g., attempts to persuade)

→ Describe and apply various dimensions of difference in verbal communication

→ Understand and explain cultural discourses

→ Explain and give examples of cultural myths, conversational episodes, and social dramas

→ Implement general ideas of communication accommodation to understand a speech episode

Systems of language and culture: Why is talking across cultures so difficult?

Discursive elements of cultures: What happens when we join the elements of language?

Theories of conversation and culture: What happens when we actually talk to each other?

Intercultural Communication for Everyday Life, First Edition. John R. Baldwin, Robin R. Means Coleman, Alberto González, and Suchitra Shenoy-Packer.
© 2014 John R. Baldwin, Robin R. Means Coleman, Alberto González, and Suchitra Shenoy-Packer.
Published 2014 by John Wiley & Sons Ltd.

Websites from Engrish.com to *The Huffington Post* (2010) give humorous translations of signs from around the world into English, such as the notice exhorting, "Don't molest the hawks", based on the Spanish verb, *molestar* (meaning to bother); or the hotel called "The Homely Raj", probably intending homey (homelike), rather than homely (unattractive) (Murdock, 2011). Often these are funny (Figure 7.1), such as the list of mistranslated advertising slogans (of doubtful reliability) currently going around the Internet: Chevrolet trying to sell a car in Mexico called "Nova" ("no va," in Spanish, means it does not go); or "Pepsi brings you back to life", which translates into Chinese as "Pepsi brings your ancestors back from the dead" (Takingontobacco.com, n.d.).

Of course, language difficulties in intercultural communication are based on much more than translation errors. In this chapter, we discuss how different aspects of language reflect culture and can lead to cultural misunderstanding. We will touch on theories that explain how cultures differ in terms of verbal communication, as well as what happens when people of different groups and cultures talk with each other. We will end with some brief suggestions for more successful interaction.

Systems of language and culture: Why is talking across cultures so difficult?

Language refers to a system of verbal, nonverbal, and visual symbols that a group pieces together to share meaning. There are often forceful politics surrounding language, because making one language a "national language" gives those who speak that language prestige and power over others who do not speak the language well, or even who speak it with a different dialect or pronunciation than has become dominant. For example, in Québec, Canada, language politics between French and English have been longstanding. One recent

Figure 7.1 Cultural mistakes abound as people try to translate signs into other cultures. What kind of mistakes have you made while trying to speak or write in a second or third language? Source: Andrew Woodley/age fotostock/SuperStock.

policy there requires that all advertising, including in Chinese businesses and restaurants, post French as the largest language on signs and advertising (Croucher, 2006).

What do you think? In the United States, there are currently movements in some places to make English an official language—or, at least, there have been complaints about the need to "Press One for English" (http://www.youtube.com/watch?v=sEJfSIv-fU0) or for or against Ebonics (African American Vernacular English). But Tarik Rahman (2002) also talks about language politics in Pakistan, and elsewhere in this book we mention the language politics in Spain. What language politics exist in your region or culture?

In any language community, there are multiple ways of speaking (speech codes)—but people in different situations have different "communicative resources" (Philipsen *et al.*, 2005). For example, students in a classroom are guided by culture as to how (or if) to ask the teacher questions in class or challenge a teacher's mistake. Language also structures the interaction, so that certain people have the right to do some things and others to do other things. These rights are accepted and consented to by people in the situation, but sometimes challenged. In sum, language is not something we simply participate in as individuals—it is structured by history, social situations, social relations, and hierarchies.

Systems of meaning

Semantics Language researchers discuss several aspects of language that are beyond the scope of our discussion, such as writing systems, sounds that different languages make, or grammar and word order. Two main areas of language are relevant in the study of cultural communication semantics and discourse. **Semantics** is the area of language study that considers what words mean. Words have **denotation**—the relatively objective dictionary type of definition of a word, and **connotation**—the feelings (personal or social) that individuals associate with a word. Meaning comes in part from the personal experiences we have with a word. When we are little, we see a dog on the street and someone says either "puppy!" or "*viralata!*" (Brazilian Portuguese meaning "tin can-turner", or mongrel). We associate the sound or image with something we see ("reality")—either face-to-face or in a mediated text—and we get a sense of how we should feel about it. "Puppies" are cuddly and cute and want to be petted; "*viralatas*" should be avoided and left alone.

Through interaction, then, we create meanings (Berger & Luckmann, 1966), and these meanings differ from culture to culture. For example, the word "friend" translates into "amigo" in Spanish and Portuguese—but people who speak these as first languages often have different expectations and meanings for what a friend is and does than those who speak U. S. American English. In the mobile American culture, a friend may be someone one sees after a long absence and feels as if the relationship continues right where it left off. But in other cultures, friendship implies a deep sense of obligation and continued communication. At the same time, social ideologies also frame language, through the reproduction of mediated messages, politics (for example, legal definitions of what it means to be Black or White in a given country), and so on.

Some argue that meanings of words are not simply neutral, but are loaded with power implications. Groups struggle to define certain words, illustrating the notion of **discourse**. Discourse, in this sense, refers to the sets of ideas surrounding a concept. Michel Foucault (1978) talks about the history (what he calls the archeology) of words, noting how cultures and societies create notions such as mental illness, sexuality, and crime in a way that keeps certain sets of ideas in power. (For example, is same-sex sexual activity a "mental illness" or "crime" in your culture?) These meanings change over time, such as the notion of "race" in U.S. American culture (Banton, 1977), but they change through group striving, as people with different ideologies fight to make their meanings central.

What you say is what you get: the Sapir-Whorf hypothesis We have seen that cultures may differ in the way they think of language. Some writers go further to suggest that the language of a culture dictates how people within that culture can think. The **Sapir-Whorf hypothesis** posits that, in a way, language creates social reality through language structure, such as the fact that different languages make different verb tenses, word order, or words available to describe certain things (see Figure 7.2). Harry Hoijer (1991) cites examples from Navajo, Hopi, and other languages in which people from different cultures have wider or narrower sets of names for color spectrum. Thomas Steinfatt (1989) analyzes the evidence on both sides and concludes that, while language may not create a "reality" for people, it does lead people in a culture to tend to think about certain things rather than others.

Figure 7.2 The Sapir-Whorf hypothesis notes that different languages classify the world differently. This may lead people who speak these languages to think of the world in different ways or focus on different aspects of reality. Source: Whorf, 2012, Figure 15.2. © 2012 Massachusetts Institute of Technology. Reproduced by permission of The MIT Press.

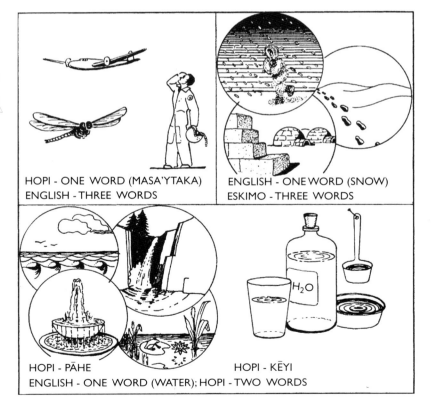

HOPI - ONE WORD (MASA'YTAKA)
ENGLISH - THREE WORDS

ENGLISH - ONE WORD (SNOW)
ESKIMO - THREE WORDS

HOPI - PĀHE
ENGLISH - ONE WORD (WATER); HOPI - TWO WORDS

HOPI - KĒYI

Speech acts and cultural communication

Another important area for intercultural communication is what we do with words—the **pragmatic** aspect of language. For example, someone tells you, "You look great". The words contain a second-person singular pronoun, "you," a linking verb suggesting how something appears, "look," and an adjective with a positive feeling behind it, "great". In one situation, this could be a compliment, but, if you have just spent all night studying and have not cleaned up before class, it could be sarcasm. It could be flattery, to your bosses' wife, or a lie, to avoid hurting someone's feelings.

This example shows us that there are many things we can do with a phrase, just as there are many ways to accomplish the same sort of act. **Speech acts theory** outlines the types of actions we perform with utterances (Austin, 1962). We follow basic rules when we communicate, as long as we are trying to cooperate with others in conversation. If we are competent, we will stay on topic, give sufficient detail but not more than is necessary, speak things we believe to be true, and speak in a way that is relatively clear (Grice, 1957; *Stanford Encyclopedia of Philosophy*, 2007). There are different types of action we can do with words—we can make statements (observations), express our feelings or opinions (compliment, curse, greet), try to influence others (hint, question, command), commit to a future act (promise, threat, vow), or change the state of things with our words (fire someone, decree something—acts that can usually only be done by people in authority). And each of these follows a set of hidden rules about what constitutes an act (an apology must be about a negative event over which a person has control and feels sincerely sorry for) or who can do it (only someone with authority can make a "pronouncement") (Nofsinger, 1991; Searle, 1969). We probably follow all of these rules without thinking about them.

Speech acts theory helps us understand cultural language difficulties. What counts as enough detail in one culture may not be the same in another culture. In one culture, someone might make a request using indirect language, which would violate unstated expectations for clarity in another culture; and the intended purpose of a message is often not what is received. We experience this in our daily lives. Deborah Tannen (1991) outlines sex-based differences in the workplace: a woman might give an order that looks and sounds like a suggestion ("you might try…"), and men might misunderstand it, with the result that women's requests are often not fulfilled by men (this explanation, neglects the possibility that men undervalue women's leadership in organizations). Shoshana Blum-Kulka (1997) illustrates such forms of indirectness in requests by analyzing a scene at an Israeli dinner table, where the father is hungry and seeks permission to make himself some food, but the mother perceives it as a complaint about what is offered, so defends her choice of rice for dinner.

In intercultural communication, people often mistake the force of a statement for what it actually looks like. Many newcomers to the United States get frustrated when people ask, "How's it going?" when they do not really want to know. While "How's it going?" can be a heartfelt request for information in the U.S., it usually serves as a greeting, and the speaker does not expect a response. In cultures that prefer indirectness, like Japan, a statement in a negotiation session like "We'll think about it" sounds like a promise for future consideration but may be a polite way to say "no".

Getting things done with language

We can see culture's impact on how we accomplish many different communication acts. These include things like making and responding to apologies, making requests, showing camaraderie, giving criticism, and gaining agreement on a project. Each area has produced rich research in cross-cultural and intercultural communication, but we will consider just four areas.

Directives   As noted earlier, **directives** (attempts to influence the behavior of or persuade another) can range from subtle hints to overt commands. Kristine Fitch (1994) found that attempts to persuade in Colombia were informed by two dimensions: *hierarchia* (hierarchy) and *confianza* (trust, relatedness), similar to power and solidarity already mentioned. People in Colombia might use a go-between or intermediary to persuade someone across status lines. People in Colorado (U.S.) tend to use politeness behaviors, giving the target of persuasion a way to avoid the imposition. Someone might say, "Hey, if you're not busy, would you be able to give me a ride?" so that the other person could reply that she or he is busy. Min-Sun Kim and Steven Wilson (1994) found that U.S. Americans and South Koreans both felt that direct requests were the clearest way to get someone to do something, but that the U.S. Americans felt such a form to be the most effective, and the South Koreans, the least effective.

Criticism   In a study of criticism, Taiwanese and U.S. American participants gave their most likely responses to situations that might yield a complaint or criticism, such as being late for an appointment, invasion of privacy by a parent, or a server's mistake at a restaurant. There were no important differences in the frequencies of options such as saying nothing or using accusing questions to criticize; but analysis of open-ended data showed that U.S. American questions about a behavior were often phrased to assume guilt on the part of the other person, where the Chinese questions were framed more to ask if the other was aware of the sender's perceptions and resulting disappointment (Chen *et al.*, 2011). Findings from conversational data suggest that some cultures prefer to soften criticism or not offer it—but for different reasons. Japanese people might avoid criticism and strong emotional displays in many cases because it shows lack of *omoiyari*—the ability to sense the pain or pleasure of another. The Japanese often do not want the other person to feel bad. Malays might engage in self-silencing to avoid having the other think badly of them. Polish speakers, however, are more likely to say things like, "Where did you get such an idea from?! You are wrong!". In fact, the ability to openly express one's perception of "disagreement, exasperation, and impatience" with the other is a sign of the feeling of openness one feels one should have in relationships (Goddard & Wierzbicka, 1997, p. 244).

Apologies   In response to an embarrassing situation, should someone make a joke, give an explanation or defense, or make an apology of some sort? Todd Imahori and William Cupach (1994) had student participants describe an embarrassing predicament of their choice. The Japanese students were more likely to describe something that had happened with someone from their in-group, and the U.S. Americans, someone from an out-group. The Japanese were more likely to feel a sense of **shame**, in the sense of negative reflection upon their group for the embarrassing situation, but the U.S. Americans, **guilt**, or a sense of personal responsibility. While people in both cultures preferred to avoid mentioning the wrong and an "apology" as the primary responses, in some situations, Americans were much more likely to use humor to lighten the situation, whereas Japanese were more likely to use **remediation**—that is, to do something concrete to make up to the injured party for the embarrassment.

Compliments Finally, Farhad Sharifian (2008) describes how Persian speakers, even when they are speaking English as a second language, give and receive compliments. The Persian notion of *adah*, a form of politeness in which one seeks to give compliments, suggests one should give many, but sincere, compliments on various aspect of the other person's life. While one may give lots of compliments, however, a contrasting notion of *shekasteh-nafsi*—modesty—leads one to downplay one's own accomplishments. In response to a prompt that one had done a great job, one participant responded with, "I owe this achievement to your efforts. If it hadn't been for your help, I would never have achieved this" (p. 62). Another study classifies the various types of compliments given in Pidgin English in Cameroon (Nkwain, 2011), such as direct appraisals ("What a beautiful blouse you have!", p. 67), or interrogative appraisals ("Where do you do your hair?", p. 68). The author suggests that the compliments, shared between people of different ethnic or tribal groups but shared in a common trade language of Pidgin, serve to build solidarity between speakers, as long as they are perceived as genuine.

Explaining the details: Seeking ways to explain differences across cultures

As we have seen, there are many different ways to make an argument, negotiate, joke, request, compliment, promise (or threat), show respect, or give instructions. Even with fluency in the logistics of a language, if we do not master the pragmatics of the culture, we will be incompetent. There are too many types of specific differences to explain here, but here we will explain several approaches researchers have used to try to explain cultural difference in language use.

Relational orientations Many scholars have defined relational orientations in two primary dimensions of interaction: power and solidarity (e.g., Brown & Levinson, 1987; Tannen, 1994). **Power** refers to the level of control over another's thoughts, feelings, or behavior. This includes communication in which one person imposes upon or yields to another. In any culture, different situations or relationships have more of a hierarchical difference, which impacts our communication. We communicate differently with our friends than with our employer, and differently with our employer than we might if we met the Queen or the Prime Minister. Another dimension of interaction is **solidarity (relational distance)**, the degree of familiarity and/or intimacy we have with another person. We tend to react differently—more formally or less rudely—to someone who is a stranger than to an acquaintance, a friend, or a close friend.

The two dimensions interact. In some cases, we might have a closer level of intimacy with a supervisor, even though she is also hierarchically above us in the organizational structure; but we might act more cordially to a stranger who is our age than one with a higher status. Deborah Tannen (1994) notes that some cultures, like the United States, associate power with asymmetry, hierarchy, and distance, and see it as the opposite of solidarity: it is difficult to be in a close relationship with a boss or status superior. Other cultures, such as one might find in Indonesia or Japan, imagine relationships that bind people together hierarchically, but also with a strong sense of solidarity. These dimensions exist in all cultures, though individual, cultural, and structural influences shape them in actual communication.

What do you think? Make a list of large or small favors or requests you could ask of someone. Now, list the ways you might ask or tell someone to do the favor. What are some ways your persuasion attempts can vary? What are some factors that influence how you shape your attempt to influence the other person? Brown and Levinson (1987) suggest hierarchy, relational closeness, and size of the imposition as three factors. How do these play out in your culture (for example, how would your request differ between a stranger and a close friend)? What other factors might influence how you shape your communication?

Face theory   As we consider these various types of action that one can accomplish with communication, we see both cultural differences and cultural similarities. Researchers have proposed several frameworks to try to make sense of a wide variety of communication behavior (verbal and nonverbal). Some seek explanations that apply across all cultures. Many authors use notions of face and politeness theory. Irving Goffman (1959) argues that we are often concerned about what he calls **face**—the image we seek to have of ourselves in interaction. We are like actors on a stage, with props, lines, and performances; but sometimes, we let others "backstage" to see more of what we are really like. Goffman (1967) argues that in interaction, we work together with others to protect and repair loss of face, because face-loss can interrupt the flow of interaction. Once face has been damaged, conversation often stops while someone makes a joke, an apology, a threat, or some other remedy, and that remedy is accepted by others—unless the most face-saving move is to say nothing, such as we do when people pass audible gas publicly in cultures where this is disapproved of (Cupach & Metts, 2006).

Penelope Brown and Stephen Levinson (1987) find evidence that in all cultures, people seek to preserve the idea that they are free and autonomous (**negative face**) as well as the idea that they are competent and qualified for some task; people also like to feel included or liked by others (the last two notions are aspects of **positive face**). (We will say more about how these relate to conflict in chapter 13.) We see an example of how cultural dimensions might be explained and predicted using notions of face in the Imahori and Cupach (1994) study noted earlier.

Cultural scripts   Other researchers, rather than try to predict behaviors, use observation and talk to people to learn the communication **scripts** used in a culture. These are cultural rules regarding expected behavior that include expectations of who does what (actors, roles), and any expected sequence of actions in a communication routine. Cliff Goddard and Anna Wierzbicka (1997), using a script approach, describe what they call a "natural semantic metalanguage" (p. 235) that uses simple words, like *people*, *something*, *say*, *think*, *know*, *good*, and *bad*, to describe a behavior in a particular culture. They use this approach to describe what they call *halus* speech—a speech form in

Malaysia in which people talk carefully with people outside of the immediate family. The cultural logic is that:

When people hear someone saying something

Sometimes they think something like this:

"This person knows how to say things well to other people; this is good."

Sometimes they think something like this:

"This person doesn't know how to say things well to other people; this is bad." (p. 242)

In a similar way, Donal Carbaugh (2005) unpacks a negative live-audience reaction to Phil Donahue, as he tries to goad Russian youth into talking about the "problem" of pre-marital sex in Russia. Carbaugh concludes that, while "public talk" and turning issues into problems is a mainstay of American talkshow television, with sex being treated very rationally, the Russians perceive sex to be a deeply emotional topic and do not perceive public television as the correct place to air public problems.

Break it down

To learn more about cultures around you, join a cultural interest group or make frequent visits to a cultural location different from your own (e.g., a different type of worshiping community, different festivals). Interact with people enough to understand how communication in that group might differ from or be similar to your own. How does your increased understanding of the communication work together to inform—and be informed by—your understanding of the background, immigration conditions, and so on, of that group? What does your experience teach you about yourself?

Dimensions of difference Instead of theories and frameworks, many authors summarize types of differences one might expect between cultures. These provide a simple way to think of how cultures can differ, as long as we realize that a) most cultures will sit between the "extremes" on any set of terms and contain elements of both aspects of a dimension; b) there will be differences within each culture based on age, social class, task at hand and so on; and c) cultures balance change and tradition in the face of globalization.

→ *Direct versus indirect*: As we have already seen, people in some cultures—depending on the relationship between individuals, the urgency of the topic, and other factors—can be very direct, even "in your face." People in some cultures can be direct and forthright in their speech. People in other cultures can be quite indirect, such as in organizational communication in Japan or Korea (though young Korean friends might make a request or joke quite directly to each other). For example, Egyptians in many cases use *musayara* speech, marked by deference, commonality, and avoidance of conflict (Zaidman *et al.*, 2008).

→ *Formal versus informal*: All cultures have situations that are more or less formal, though in some cultures, there are *more* occasions for formality than others. For example, in midwestern U.S. American classrooms, students are more informal, some even calling professors by first name (though this might differ in the southern U.S., among different ethnic cultures, or for those who have served in the armed services). In other cultures, communication in business or education situations or with status superiors demands formality.

→ **Differentiated and undifferentiated codes**: Language is differentiated when there are different **registers**, or forms and levels of formality of speech for people in different societal groups, such as based on social status. Romance languages are more differentiated than English, with both formal and informal forms for singular "you" (Spanish: tú, Usted)—though the specific rules for going from tú to Usted vary from culture to culture, even within a single Spanish-speaking country. Korean, on the other hand, has multiple levels of formality in language, and even "honorific verbs" to describe things such as eating or sleeping for those very high in status. A reporter for *Seoulbeats* demonstrates how these levels of formality apply even in K-pop, a contemporary form of popular music from South Korea (Dana, 2012).

→ **Instrumental and affective styles**: People in some cultures may be more direct and goal oriented, preferring efficient linguistic forms, while other cultures may have a preference for more emotional and expressive communication. This combines elements we discuss in chapter 4, such as being versus doing, or instrumental versus expressive. We see this in the way that offers are made in U.S. America and China. In the U.S., the correct sequence is offer → request/decline ("Would you like some iced tea?" "No, thanks." "Okay.") But in China, as in many other cultures, one should offer food or hospitality even if one is not willing or able to give it at that time, just to be polite; and the other person, even if hungry or tired, should decline the request, just to be polite. The function of such offers in these cultures, then, is to make someone feel welcome. The correct sequence becomes offer→decline→insist→[resist→double insist→]accept/decline. A larger offer may require multiple resistance and insistence turns.

→ *Exaggerated, exacting, succinct styles*: An **exaggerated style** may use language more to embellish upon reality than to describe it, as a major function of communication is to reveal the speaker's ability to use language creatively. For example, many U.S. African American males might employ boasting, rapping (romantic come-ons), and verbal games like "the dozens" (Johnson, 2000). An **exacting style** emphasizes saying what one means, giving the detail necessary—with a focus on efficiency similar to the instrumental style noted earlier. The **succinct style** reflects a cultural or personal preference for fewer words. The instrumental/exacting communication is speaker-focused, with the speaker providing the detail she or he feels the other needs, where a succinct style is listener-focused, leaving the listener to fill in the gaps (Lustig & Koester, 2010), such as in the traditional notion of British understatement or some Asian forms that include more silence and subtlety in communication.

Discursive elements of cultures: What happens when we join the elements of language?

We often interact with friends and relatives for easily identifiable reasons. We engage in conversation to exchange information and to express our feelings and judgments. However, there are times when our interactions with others have meaning beyond the immediate context and are explained by broader patterns of communication. For example, when sports fans arise for their national anthem before a game, they participate in a public ritual. The song is an expression of national pride and is a deliberate reminder of national greatness and national ideals. When fans stand, sing, remove their hats and show other signs of respect, they publicly confirm their loyalty to the state. The anthem along with other verbal (for example, a formal pledge of allegiance) and nonverbal (a flag) symbols, compose a set of meanings—or a discourse—that guides understanding and action.

These broader patterns of communication are **discursive elements of language**. Cultural myth, conversational episodes, social dramas, and metaphor are examples of discursive elements of cultures that are examined in this section. Being prepared for successful civic action requires having an understanding of the discursive elements that guide communities.

Cultural myth

Cultural myth is a narrative that is popularly told to teach preferred ways of behaving, such as a familiar story that recommends particular values and responses to situations. An example might be the U.S. American myth of the "American Dream," traditionally a view that anyone can work hard to achieve a better life (expressed in terms of monetary wealth/ security and material goods). Myths may have origins in historical events or may be anchored in values that have evolved over time. A myth is told that Buddha called all the animals to him as he ended his earthly stay. Only 12 animals answered the call, so Buddha rewarded the rat, ox, tiger, rabbit, dragon, snake, horse, sheep, monkey, rooster, dog, and bear by giving each animal its own year (Fong, 2012). People born during the year of a particular animal have the characteristics of that animal, thus giving honor to each animal. As a cultural myth, the story allows parents to recommend to their children socially valued behaviors. Though the 12 animals are assigned different traits, all have traits that point toward passion, focus, and hard work.

Myths are conveyed through a variety of methods, including popular culture. For example, the U.S. song *The Ballad of Davy Crockett*, found on a popular children's CD titled *For Our Children* (Stern & Kleiner, 1999), tells the story of Davy, who was "born on a mountaintop in Tennessee" and who was so skilled in the woods that he "kilt him a bar [killed him a bear] when he was only three." In addition to conquering the land, he fought different Native tribes and got elected to the U.S. Congress. He "saw his duty clear" and went off to fight with the Texas Revolution at the Alamo, where he met his demise in 1836. The actual Davy Crockett dropped out of school, ran away from home and angrily left Tennessee after losing an election. So why is Crockett commemorated in this song? The song emphasizes (and exaggerates) aspects of a U.S. American character that are deeply rooted in American folklore. Crockett, as the "King of the wild frontier," reinforces the goodness of turning natural resources to human use—by force if necessary. He reinforces the goodness of individualism and single-minded determination and he legitimizes the superiority of Euro-American Protestantism over other beliefs. Additional stories of characters such as Paul Bunyan and Babe the Blue Ox serve much the same purpose.

In contrast, Cherokee storyteller Gayle Ross (1986) describes how the Cherokee obtained the first sacred fire. In *The First Fire*, various animals volunteered to bring fire from a burning log that lay across the water on an island. The council first chose several birds to go to bring the fire, because they were the fastest: the raven, screech owl and the hooting owl. But the birds could not get through the thick smoke of the fire. Then the bear and the snake were chosen because they were brave and strong. But they failed as well. Finally, the tiny water spider asked to go and everyone laughed. How could the tiny spider hope to succeed when the biggest, bravest and fastest animals had failed? The water spider was allowed to try anyway. It spun a bowl in which to put a piece of coal from the fire and soon it returned to light the sacred fire of the Cherokee. The lesson is that often the "smallest and meekest" have a role in finding solutions to problems. This cultural myth emphasizes the goodness of a collectivist orientation. Action is determined through group decision-making. Instead of each animal acting individually, the council decided which animal would try to bring the fire. In the end, the least dominant animal succeeded through intelligence and patience. *The First Fire* and *The Ballad of Davy Crockett* express different cultural values and recommend different approaches for acting in the world.

Conversational episodes

A **conversational episode (CE) or communication ritual** is a routine portion of conversation that has an expected beginning and end, like ordering a meal at a restaurant, or friends exchanging details about what they did last night. Though usually brief, exchanges are important and guided by tradition. As language philosopher Judith Butler (1997) wrote, the episode "exceeds itself in past and future directions" (p. 3). In this sense, CEs are performances of cultural knowledge. When a Spanish-speaking individual is introduced to another, the common reply is "*mucho gusto*" or "nice to meet you." In Morocco, it is nearly impossible to greet someone without invoking Allah. In a CE, something specific gets accomplished: a joke is told, a bet is made, a greeting is given, much as in speech acts earlier though the CE involves more than one turn, as opposed to a hint or a threat. So, "*mucho gusto*" would be a speech act, but it would occur within an episode, typically upon first meeting someone, and would be followed with an expected follow-up, like, "*el gusto es mio*" ("the pleasure is mine"). In a different example, during the first three days of the Chinese New Year, people commonly use the expression "*gung hay fat choy*" (may you have a happy and prosperous new year) and avoid negative topics. If a speaker makes a disparaging remark and invites bad luck, the hearer replies, "*Tou heu soey dzoi geng gwa*" (spit out your saliva and speak once more) (Fong, 2012, p. 157). Some writers speak of different **discourses** as expectations and patterns of speech that occur in different situations, such as courtroom discourse, television interview discourse, or informal conversation. Who shares what in each situation is shaped by social roles, norms, and hierarchies, like other aspects of language.

POP CULTURE

In the 2009 Indian blockbuster movie, *3 Idiots*, three strangers—Farhan, Raju, and Rancho—join Delhi's Imperial College of Engineering. On the night of arrival, there is an "initiation" ceremony that involves them stripping to their underwear, singing songs, and interacting with the student leader of the initiation (Figure 7.3). In a much less formal ritual, in the 1991 U.S. movie, *White Men Can't Jump*, a group of basketball players engage in "trashtalking" (specifically, a verbal dueling game called "the Dozens," which involves "yo mama" jokes; Johnson, 2000). Initiations and trashtalking constitute communication episodes, or rituals, that serve particular functions for the communicators. What rituals do you engage in within your own culture? What functions do they serve?

Figure 7.3 Farhan, Raju, and Rancho, characters in *3 Idiots*, sing a silly song—but even silliness among friends has its hidden rules!
Source: Eros/Reliance Big Pictures/The Kobal Collection.

Social dramas

A **social drama** is a conflict that arises in a community after a social norm is violated. The violation becomes a social drama when discussion about it calls into question that social norm, and the resolution of the conflict validates, strengthens, or weakens the norm for members of the community (Turner, 1982). Social dramas can occur on an international scale, on a national scale, or at local levels. Yet even the local-level dramas can be intercultural in nature.

In 2010, the City Council in Toledo, Ohio, drafted a resolution calling for the federal government to undertake comprehensive reform of immigration policy (Messina, 2010a) as a response to controversial immigration laws passed in Arizona. The resolution was introduced by the lone Latino on the City Council. In this case, the drama centers around the response of the city leader, the mayor of the city. Through his response, we can see the four phases of a social drama:

→ Breach of the code—this is violation of an accepted rule or law.

→ Crisis—this is the talk or discussion in response to the breach.

→ Redress—this is the method for resolving the breach. Redress can be formal (a trial) or informal (public opinion). Redress can result in reintegration or dissensus.

→ Reintegration or dissensus—reintegration is forgiveness and inclusion back into the community. Dissensus means there is ongoing disagreement about the breach and its implications for the community.

In the case of the City Council resolution on immigration, the Council vote was tied, and it fell to Toledo's mayor, Mike Bell, to break the tie. He voted against the resolution (breach). The failure of the resolution created uproar in Toledo, particularly among Latina/os (crisis). Many could not understand how the mayor, who was African American, could oppose a law that was widely seen as encouraging law enforcement officers to stop using racial profiling. Many Latinas and Latinos felt that the mayor's action was a betrayal of the political alliance between African Americans and Latinas and Latinos. A columnist for *La Prensa* told the mayor "Some people have been so disappointed by your action that they have suggested simply writing you off" (Abrams, 2010, p. 7).

Ultimately, the City Council proved to have the power to redress the breach. A month later, in July 2010, the City Council passed a revised resolution. The new version directed the Ohio state legislature and the Ohio Governor not to propose or pass bills similar to the Arizona laws (Messina, 2010b). The resolution passed City Council and did not require the mayor's vote. While Mayor Bell largely has been reintegrated into the Latina/Latino political sphere, memories of this perceived betrayal linger.

Our verbal communication often is about community or national and international controversies. Our opinions become part of a larger dialogue on acceptable or reprehensible conduct. As we discuss topics with others and give our judgment on our own actions or the actions performed on our behalf (and perhaps change our judgment), we examine and prioritize our individual and cultural values. Thus, not only do social dramas shape our individual cultures, but as they arise in discussion, they become part of our intercultural dialogue.

Cultural metaphor

A **metaphor** is an association of two items. A characteristic of the more familiar item is associated with the less known item. If we talk about "saving time," we are treating time in terms of something tangible that can be saved, like money. Metaphors can have many different origins. For example "*zubda*" is an Arabic word for "the best butter or cream." *Zubda* refers to the best of what has been mixed or churned. So imagine a music CD called *The Zubda of Shakira*, which would mean "the best of Shakira" or "the essential Shakira."

Metaphors and metaphorical expressions in talk and literature have fascinated critics since Aristotle. George Lakoff and Mark Johnson (2003), a linguist and a philosopher, go so far as to say that we "live by" metaphors—they structure the very way that we think. For example, we will treat immigrants differently if we think of them as a "scaffolding for our construction economy" as opposed to a "drain on society resources." An especially helpful notion is the **metaphorical archetype**—a comparison of items that has many expressions (a "family" of metaphors, metaphorically speaking) and is deeply ingrained in a culture (Osborn, 1967). The metaphorical archetype is instantly recognized when it is used, and so assumed that it is rarely questioned. The archetypal metaphor found in President Barack Obama's 2008 campaign speeches was the metaphor of the "journey" (Darsey, 2009).

Expressions such as "the journey that led me here," "path of upward mobility," and "the road to change" allow Obama to connect to the larger narrative of America's forward motion.

Metaphors of travel and motion are not hard to come across in ordinary North American speech. Expressions such as "I see where you're going with that," and "just follow me for a second" connect motion with argument and reasoning. Other metaphors such as "being concrete," "getting to the bottom line," "getting to the point," and "the weight of evidence" all suggest a linear ("now it's time to connect the dots") orientation. The dominant U.S. culture preference for linearity (time's arrow) contrasts with Native American metaphors of circularity and *looking backward*. Another cultural difference can be seen in archetypes or metaphors for animals. All cultures use animals for different metaphoric purpose, but sometimes the meanings and feelings differ. For example, in U.S. American culture, if we call someone a "rat," that person is "contemptible...sneaky, disloyal, and hated" (Smith-Marder, 2002, p. 55). But in many cultures, such as India, China, and ancient Egypt and Rome, the rat is revered (though in Rome, it depended on the color of the rat).

What do you think? Imagine an orientation that was grounded in recurring growth (birth-to-death-to-birth) rather than travel. The struggle to adopt policies that ensure a sustainable use of natural resources can be seen as a struggle over metaphors. Which metaphor families will prevail: metaphors of linear development or metaphors of growth?

As critical observers and participants in cultures, we are reminded that discursive elements of cultures serve a variety of purposes. The words and expressions that existed before us may have become popular to further marginalize a specific population or region or to privilege a particular cultural value or view of something, like success, beauty, or human nature. We should not automatically accept the verbal options given to us. We should always reflect upon who is served or under-served by a particular narrative, metaphor, or conversational episode. Typically, we view the breach of a code as negative. But we should ask: did that code need to be violated to advance social justice? Is dissensus *the* right outcome to achieve social justice?

Theories of conversation and culture: What happens when we actually talk to each other?

We have looked at what happens within each culture, either in terms of forms of languages (apologies, compliments) or in terms of larger levels of discourse and meaning (metaphors, rituals). But what happens when people from different cultures communicate? To the extent that differences in expectations for different behaviors are beyond our awareness, when someone else requests, criticizes, compliments, or greets in a way we do not expect, we will give meaning to their behavior based on our own cultural norms (**attribution**, see chapter 6). In many cases, this can lead to a negative evaluation or simply to misunderstanding. Here we introduce one theory that has gained much attention, and then address issues of dominance and power in intergroup communication.

Communication accommodation theory

Often people with different speaking styles communicate with each other, even from within the same nation. Basil Bernstein (1966) stated that the social situation, including communicative context (for example, a job interview versus a party) and social relationships (for example, peers versus status unequals), dictates the forms of speaking used in a particular situation. Bernstein suggested that in all cultures, there are different types of codes. A **restricted code** is a code used by people who know each other well, such as jargon or argot. **Jargon** refers to a vocabulary used by people within a specific profession or area (such as rugby players or mine workers), while **argot** refers to language used by those in a particular underclass, often to differentiate themselves from a dominant culture (e.g., prostitutes, prisoners). However, as people get to know each other better, even good friends can develop this sort of linguistic shorthand, speaking in terms or references that others do not understand. In an **elaborated code**, people spell out the details of meaning in the words in a way that those outside of the group can understand them. This switching back and forth between codes is called **code-switching**. Effective communicators should be able to speak in restricted codes appropriate to their context, but also know how to switch to elaborated code (for example, to include outsiders)—to change their vocabulary, level of formality, and so on, to match the audience and social occasion.

Break it down

Tell about a time that you moved back and forth between an elaborated and a restricted code. This might have happened at a workplace, if your work has a specific jargon, or even as you move between slang your friends use and the talk you use with parents or teachers. What are some ways that "code-switching" can be effective or ineffective in communication? How can we use an awareness of others around us (such as international students) to use code-switching appropriately to make their communication adjustment easier and to make them feel more accepted?

Based on the notions of different codes within a community, as well as code-switching and other theoretical ideas, Howard Giles and his colleagues introduced **communication accommodation theory** (Giles & Noels, 2002; Gallois *et al.*, 2005). This theory predicts how people adjust their communication in certain situations, the factors that lead to such changes, and the outcomes of different types of changes.

In the U.S. television series, *Lost*, through a series of flashbacks and present communication, we observe the speech of Jin Kwon (Daniel Dae Kim), a Korean man, the son of a fisherman, but hired by a wealthy restaurant owner. In some cases, his communication is respectful, indirect, deferential; in others, it is direct, friendly or aggressive, and nonverbally more expressive. In some cases, he might change his behavior to be more like that of the person with whom he is speaking (**convergence**), and in others, he might make no changes in his behavior (**maintenance**) or even highlight his own style to mark it as different from that of the other group (**divergence**). Jin can change his behavior in terms of nonverbal behavior (distance, posture, touch, etc.), paralinguistic behavior (tone of voice, rate of speech, volume, etc.), and verbal behavior (word choice, complexity of grammar, topic of conversation, turn-taking, etc.). Many things influence shifts in his speech, such as the status and power of the other communicator, the situation, who is present, communication goals (for example, to seem friendly, or to show status or threat), the strength of his own language in the community, and his communication abilities.

Communication and sites of dominance

Convergence can often go wrong. Giles and Noels (2002) explain that, although converging is usually well received, we can **overaccommodate**, or converge too much or in ineffective ways, by adjusting in ways we might think are appropriate, but are based on stereotypes of the other. People often speak louder and more slowly to a foreigner, thinking that they will thus be more understandable. Overaccommodation also works in situations of dominance. For example, younger people often inappropriately adjust their communication when talking with elderly people. Often called **secondary baby talk**, this includes a higher pitch in voice, simpler vocabulary, and use of plural first-person ("we"—"Would we like to put our coat on? It's very cold outside"). While some older people find this type of communication comforting, especially from health workers, some feel it speaks down to them and treats them as no longer competent. A similar feeling might be experienced by Blacks in the United States when Whites use **hyperexplanation**. This inappropriate form of adjustment also includes use of simpler grammar, repetition, and clearer enunciation. But Harry Waters (1992) suggests that it is a behavior some Whites engage in while talking with Blacks (or other minority members)—perhaps based on real communication differences or perhaps based on stereotypes, but certainly leaving hurt feelings or resentment on the part of the Black listeners.

Writers have outlined the ways in which word choice, turn-taking and length, or topic selection may also serve to exclude others, often without us even being aware of it (Fairclough, 2001; Tannen, 1994). Don Zimmerman and Candace West (1975) found that while women "overlapped" speech turns in talking to men, often with "continuers" ("mm hmm," "yes") that continued the turn of the male, men were more often likely to interrupt women, often taking the turn away from them. And when women did interrupt men, the men did not yield the turn to women, while women did yield the turn to men. Jennifer Coates (2003), observing storytelling, found that men and boys often framed themselves as heroes, as being rebels or rule-breakers. In analysis of family communication, she found that there is "systematic" work done by all family members in many families to frame the father as either the primary story teller or the one to whom children tell their stories. Coates concludes, "Family talk can be seen to construct and maintain political order within families. . . . to conform roles and power structures within families" (p. 158), giving men more power in most mixed-gender storytelling over women. We can see that each aspect of verbal communication could be used in ways to impose power over others, often based on group identity, cultural difference, maintenance of group power, or, simply put, prejudice.

Summary

Our focus in this chapter has been on various aspects of verbal communication as these relate to culture and intercultural communication. We considered elements that make up the language system—from the smallest parts of sound (phonemes) to language woven into myth, ritual, and practice. We considered perspectives of language and culture, such as whether linguistic relativity is a valid concept, that is, whether the language that a culture speaks creates the reality that the speakers of that language inhabit. We gave special attention to the use of language in building myth, communication episodes, and social dramas.

Beyond lists of dimensions of language variation (e.g., formal to informal), we provided some overarching ideas to explain how these might vary across cultures, such as speech acts and face theory. We considered explanations of what happens when people of different groups or cultures speak to each other, through the notion of communication accommodation. Finally, we suggested ways that people use verbal language, perhaps without intention, to reinforce power structures and social discourses, such as discourses of traditional gender roles or ideas of group stereotypes.

An understanding of the elements of language and how they can differ among cultures is useful as we engage ourselves with a multicultural world. Realizing how adjusting our language to others can often be helpful may help us to be aware of our own communication behavior when interacting with others. And, while our focus has been on how language might oppress others with or without intention, we can use this knowledge to speak more respectfully with others. Indeed, many scholars today are using this knowledge to give those who are in groups that dominant culture subordinates new ways of speaking that provide more equality of power among communicators.

KEY TERMS

language, 138
semantics, 139
denotation, 139
connotation, 139
discourse, 140
Sapir-Whorf hypothesis, 140
pragmatics, 141
speech acts theory, 141
directive, 142
shame, 142
guilt, 142
remediation, 143
power, 143
solidarity (relational distance), 143
face, 144
negative face, 144
positive face, 144

scripts, 144
differentiated and undifferentiated
    codes, 146
register, 146
instrumental and affective styles, 146
exaggerated style, 146
exacting style, 146
succinct style, 146
discursive elements of language, 147
cultural myth, 147
conversational episode (CE) or
    communication ritual, 148
discourse, 148
social drama, 149
metaphor, 150
metaphorical archetype, 150
attribution, 151

restricted code, 152
jargon, 152
argot, 152
elaborated code, 152
code-switching, 152
communication accommodation theory, 152
convergence, 152

maintenance, 153
divergence, 153
overaccommodate, 153
secondary baby talk, 153
hyperexplanation, 153

Discussion questions

1 What mythic stories were you told as a child that influenced your values and decisions?

2 What metaphors do you commonly use in your talk? How do these work to create shared meaning with the people you are speaking with? What cultural assumptions and values do these reflect?

3 Visit a website that includes different mistranslations, such as in signs (e.g., http://www.engrish.com; http://www.lonelyplanet.com/blog/2011/10/20/12-funny-lost-in-translation-photos/) for mistranslations into English. If English is not your first language, find examples in your language of English-speakers' efforts to speak your language). See if you can describe how meaning is violated in the mistranslation (sounds, grammar, word meanings, pragmatic level).

4 Give an example of a time when you adjusted your behavior toward another person (especially of another age, ethnic, class or other group). Include how you adjusted, various factors that may have influenced your adjustment, and outcomes—your feelings/perceptions or relational outcomes. What are some advantages or disadvantages of adjusting your behavior toward someone? Are there times not to do so, or to adjust your communication away from someone?

5 What are the advantages and disadvantages to a country having a single national language? Think broadly both about economic advantages and about aspects of prestige for various groups. Do some investigation: does your country or state have an official language?

Action points

1 See what opportunities there are in your area to serve as a language instructor or tutor. Often there are volunteer agencies to teach people the local language (e.g., in the U.S.), or to teach visitors the local customs, immigration information, and so on.

2 Review recent events at your school or within your city. What social dramas can you identify? Were existing values reaffirmed or weakened?

3 Identify metaphorical expressions from five different cultures. How do these metaphors reflect distinctive ways of understanding the world?

4   Analyze jokes that are popular in your culture (either among comedians or among you and your friends). What are some ways the jokes build or support lines of power (e.g., putting some groups over others)? Discuss in class or with friends appropriate ways to address jokes that cast people as "Other," when you hear them.

For more information

Fairclough, N. (2001). *Language and power* (2nd ed.). Harlow, England: Pearson.

Jackson, J. (Ed.). (2012). *The Routledge handbook of language and intercultural communication.* London: Routledge.

Johnson, F. (2000). *Speaking culturally: Language diversity in the United States.* Thousand Oaks, CA: Sage.

Ng, S.H., Candlin, C.N., & Chiu, C.Y. (Eds.). *Language matters: Communication, culture, and identity.* Hong Kong: City University of Hong Kong.

Spencer-Oatey, H. (Ed.). (2008). *Culturally speaking: Culture, communication, and politeness theory.* London: Continuum.

References

Abrams, A. (2010). An open letter to Toledo's Mayor Mike Bell. *La Prensa*, August 13.

Austin, J.L. (1962). *How to do things with words.* Cambridge MA: Harvard University Press.

Banton, M. (1977). *The idea of race.* London: Tavistock.

Berger, P., & Luckmann, T. (1966). *The Social construction of reality: A treatise in the sociology of knowledge.* Garden City, NY: Doubleday.

Bernstein, B. (1966). Elaborated and restricted codes. In A. Smith (Ed.), *Culture and communication* (pp. 427–441) New York: Holt, Rineholt, & Winston.

Blum-Kulka, S. (1997). Discourse pragmatics. In T.A. van Dijk (Ed.), *Discourse as social interaction* (pp. 38–63). London: Sage.

Brown, P., & Levinson, S. (1987). *Politeness: Some universals in language use.* Cambridge: Cambridge University Press.

Butler, J. (1997). *Excitable Speech: A politics of the performative.* New York, NY: Routledge.

Carbaugh, D. (2005). *Cultures in conversation.* Mahwah, NJ: Lawrence Erlbaum Associates.

Chen, Y.-S., Chen, C.-Y. D., & Chang, M.-H. (2011). American and Chinese complaints: Strategy use from a cross-cultural perspective. *Intercultural Pragmatics, 8*(2), 253–275. doi:10.1515/IPRG.2011.012

Coates, J. (2003). *Men talk.* Malden, MA: Oxford.

Croucher, S.M. (2006). The impact of external pressures on an ethnic community: The case of Montreal's *Quartier Chinois* and Muslim-French immigrants. *Journal of Intercultural Communication Research, 35,* 235–252.

Cupach, W.R., & Metts, S. (2006). Face management in interpersonal communication. In K.M. Galvin & P.J. Cooper (Eds.), *Making connections: Readings in relational communication* (2nd ed.) (pp. 164–171). Los Angeles, CA: Roxbury.

Dana. (2012). Korean through K-Pop 101: Navigating speech formality. *Seoulbeats*, August 9. Accessed March 15, 2013 at http://seoulbeats.com/2012/08/korean-through-k-pop-101-navigating-speech-formality

Darsey, J. (2009). Barack Obama and America's journey. *Southern Communication Journal, 74,* 88–103.

Fairclough, N. (2001). *Language and power* (2nd ed.). Harlow, England: Longman.

Fitch, K.L. (1994). A cross-cultural study of directive sequences and some implications for compliance-gaining research. *Communication Monographs, 61,* 185–209.

Fong, M. (2012). Communicating good luck during the Chinese New Year. In A. González, M. Houston & V. Chen, (Eds.). *Our voices: Essays in culture, ethnicity, and communication* (5th ed., pp. 154–157). New York, NY: Oxford University Press.

Foucault, M. (1978). *The History of sexuality: An introduction* (Vol. 1, Trans. R. Hurley). New York: Vintage.

Gallois, C., Ogay, T., & Giles, H. (2005). Communication accommodation theory. In W.B. Gudykunst (Ed.),

Theorizing about intercultural communication (pp. 121–148). Thousand Oaks, CA: Sage.

Giles, H., & Noels, K. (2002). Communication accommodation in intercultural encounters. In J.N. Martin, T.K. Nakayama, & L.A. Flores (Eds.), *Readings in cultural contexts* (2nd ed., pp. 117–126). Mountain View, CA: Mayfield.

Goddard, C., & Wierzbicka, A. (1997). Discourse and culture. In T.A. van Dijk (Ed.). *Discourse as social interaction* (pp. 231–257). London: Sage.

Goffman, E. (1959). *The Presentation of self in everyday life*. New York: Doubleday.

Goffman, E. (1967). *Interaction ritual: Essays on face-to-face behavior*. New York: Pantheon.

Grice, H.P. (1957) Meaning. *The Philosophical Review*, 66, 377–388.

Hoijer, H. (1991). The Sapir-Whorf hypothesis. In L.A. Samovar & R.E. Porter (Eds.), *Intercultural communication: A reader* (6th ed., pp. 244–251). Belmont, CA: Wadsworth.

Huffington Post (2010) Lost in translation: Funny signs & text from around the world, October 15. Accessed July 12, 2012, at http://www.huffingtonpost.com/2010/10/15/funny-signs-from-around-the-world_n_763727.html#s156821

Imahori, T.T., & Cupach, W.R. (1994). A cross-cultural comparison of the interpretation and management of face: U.S. American and Japanese responses to embarrassing predicaments. *International Journal of Intercultural Relations*, 18, 193–219.

Johnson, F. (2000). *Speaking culturally: Language diversity in the United States*. Thousand Oaks, CA: Sage.

Kim, M.-S., & Wilson, S. (1994). A cross-cultural comparison of implicit theories of requesting. *Communication Monographs*, 61, 210–235.

Lakoff, G., & Johnson, M. (2003). *Metaphors we live by*. Chicago: University of Chicago Press.

Lustig, M.W., and Koester, J. (2010). *Intercultural competence: Interpersonal communication across cultures* (6th ed.). Boston: Allyn and Bacon.

Messina, I. (2010a). Bell tiebreaker over Ariz. Immigration law rankles some on City Council. *Toledo Blade*. Accessed March 26, 2012, at http://www.toledoblade.com/local/2010/07/22/Bell-tiebreaker-over-Ariz-immigration-law-rankles-some-on-City-Council.html

Messina, I. (2010b). Immigration measure revived City Council condemns Arizona law. *Toledo Blade*. Accessed March 26, 2012, at http://www.toledoblade.com/local/2010/08/04/Immigration-measure-revived-City-Council-condemns-Arizona-law.html

Murdock, A. (2011). Lost in translation: Our top 20 picks. *The lonely planet*. Accessed March 26, 2012, at http://www.lonelyplanet.com/blog/2011/11/24/lost-in-translation-our-top-20-photos/

Nkwain, J. (2011). Complimenting and face: A pragma-stylistic analysis of appraisal speech acts in Cameroon Pidgin English. *Acta Linguistica Hafniensia: International Journal of Linguistics*, 43, 60–79. doi:10.1080/03740463.2011.589992

Nofsinger, R.E. (1991). *Everyday conversation*. Prospect Heights, IL: Waveland.

Osborn, M. (1967). Archetypal metaphor: The light-dark family. *The Quarterly Journal of Speech*, 53, 115–126.

Philipsen, G., Couto, L.M., & Covarrubias, P. (2005). Speech codes theory: Restatement, revisions, and response to criticisms. In W.B. Gudykunst (Ed.), *Theorizing about intercultural communication* (pp. 55–68). Thousand Oaks: Sage.

Rahman, T. (2002). *Language, ideology, and power: Language learning among the Muslims of Pakistan and North India*. Karachi, Pakistan: Oxford University Press.

Ross, G. (1986). *To this day: Native American stories*. Audiocassette. Fredericksburg, TX: Gayle Ross.

Searle, J.R. (1969). *Speech acts: An essay in the philosophy of language*. Cambridge: Cambridge University Press.

Sharifian, F. (2008). Complimenting and face: A pragma-stylistic analysis of appraisal speech acts in Cameroon Pidgin English. *International Journal of Linguistics*, 43, 60–79. doi:10.1080/03740463.2011.589992

Smith-Marder, P. (2002). The rat as archetype. *UPYP*, 43, 50–64.

Stanford encyclopedia of philosophy. (2007). Speech acts. Accessed July 14, 2012, at http://plato.stanford.edu/entries/speech-acts/

Steinfatt, T. (1989). Linguistic relativity: Toward a broader view. In S. Ting-Toomey & F. Korzenny (Eds.), *Language, communication, and culture* (pp. 35–75). Newbury Park: Sage.

Stern, S., & Kleiner, H.J. (1999). *For our children*. Santa Monica, CA: Elizabeth Glaser Pediatric AIDS Foundation.

Takingontobacco.com (n.d.) *Some humorous cross-cultural advertising gaffes*. Accessed July 12, 2012, at http://www.takingontobacco.org/intro/funny.html

Tannen, D. (1991). How to close the communication gap between men and women. *McCall's*, May, 118(8), 99–102, 140.

Tannen, D. (1994). *Gender and discourse.* Oxford: Oxford University Press.

Turner, V. (1982). *From ritual to theatre: The human seriousness of play.* New York, NY: PAJ Publications.

Waters, H. Jr. (1992). Race, culture, and interpersonal conflict. *International Journal of Intercultural Relations, 16,* 437–454.

Whorf, B.L. (2012). *Language, thought, and reality,: Selected writings of Benjamin Lee Whorf* (2nd ed.), Eds. J.B. Carroll, S.C. Levinson, & Penny Lee. MIT Press.

Zaidman, N., Te'eni, D., & Schwartz, D.G. (2008). Discourse-based technology support for intercultural communication in multinationals. *Journal of Communication Management, 12,* 263–272.

Zimmerman, D.H., & West, C. (1975). Sex roles, interruptions, and silences in conversation. In B. Thorne & N. Henley (Eds.), *Language and sex: Difference and dominance* (pp. 105–129). Rowley, MA: Newbury House.

Chapter 8

Nonverbal communication: Can I make nonverbal blunders and not even know It?

Chapter objectives

After this chapter, you should be able to:

→ **Differentiate functions of nonverbal communication as it relates to verbal communication**

→ **Describe different cultural views of silence**

→ **Summarize perspectives on the universal expression of emotion**

→ **Explain and evaluate the notion of the contact cultures as an explanation of cross-cultural differences in nonverbal communication**

→ **List and define three different ways of thinking about cultural differences in time orientation**

Forms and functions: How should we act nonverbally when in another culture?

Issues in nonverbal communication: How can I compare several cultures at the same time?

Nonverbal expectancy violations: What does your nonverbal behavior mean?

Intercultural Communication for Everyday Life, First Edition. John R. Baldwin, Robin R. Means Coleman, Alberto González, and Suchitra Shenoy-Packer.
© 2014 John R. Baldwin, Robin R. Means Coleman, Alberto González, and Suchitra Shenoy-Packer.
Published 2014 by John Wiley & Sons Ltd.

n March of 2010, former U.S. Presidents George W. Bush and Bill Clinton traveled to earthquake-devastated Haiti in support of the Clinton-Bush Haiti fund. In a now-famous gesture, after shaking hands with Haitians, Bush appeared to discretely wipe his hand on Clinton's shirt (Muskus, 2010; Figure 8.1). A video of the gaffe has gone viral. Some Internet bloggers and commentators (e.g., Richard Adams, 2010) attribute the gesture to Bush's timeliness as opposed to Clinton's desire to have contact with people: Bush may simply have been touching Clinton's shoulder to hurry him on. Others complain about the rudeness of the gesture of using a former President as a personal handkerchief. Still others cite the gesture as ongoing evidence of Bush's over-zealous desire for personal cleanness. Finally, some use the gesture to support claims that Bush is racist, comparing it to a similar event when he shook hands with Barack Obama and then immediately turned to an aide for a glob of hand sanitizer.

The gesture and the following storm of opposing interpretations illustrate several points about nonverbal communication. First, nonverbal behavior can sometimes have clear meaning; but it is frequently ambiguous. If someone looks too long at you, it might be a gesture of personal or sexual interest or a hint that you have something hanging out of your nose. A pat on the shoulder can show affection or it can indicate that the other person sees you with pity and as someone of lower social status. If someone stands closer than you expect, it might mean he cannot hear you very well or that he likes your cologne.

Another lesson we can draw from this event is that the meaning of nonverbal behaviors (like verbal and mediated behavior) is negotiated. The meaning that someone intends with a behavior—if in fact the person has any meaning in mind—is often not the meaning others take from the behavior. People make decisions about us—to continue a relationship, to avoid future contact, to give us a job, and so on—not based on what *we* mean by a behavior, but by the meanings *they* give to it.

This leads to our third point: people give meaning to nonverbal behavior within a variety of contexts. If we interpret Bush's behavior as a hand wipe, we would understand it in terms of the individuals' relationship. The relational context might reflect interpersonal distance or status difference: a pat (or wipe) on the shoulder from a stranger, a subordinate

Figure 8.1 President George Bush's "hand wipe" on the shoulder of former President Bill Clinton in Haiti must be understood in terms of other contexts, such as how he interacts with Haitians in other situations.
Source: Brooks Kraft/Corbis.

....

ON THE NET

The notion of a *faux pas* (literally, "false step") applies to any sort of breaking of etiquette or cultural norm, within a culture or between cultures—so when American actor Richard Gere publicly kissed Indian star Shilpa Shetty in 2007, even though their motives were to raise funds for HIV-AIDS, it was a major (nonverbal) *faux pas*. Writers summarize the types of *faux pas* that one might commit in other cultures. Do an Internet search of "cultural *faux pas*—list" and bring a list of faux pas, about travel in general, or about a specific culture, to class. How many of the *faux pas* deal with nonverbal behaviors? What attributions might someone in the culture in question make about you if you commit this *faux pas*?

....

or a superior, might mean something different from a pat from a friend or someone of our own status. Was it rude? We would want to know if Bush uses a similar gesture with his wife or children. A second context is previous behavior and experiences of the individuals. Does Bush have a history of avoiding germs? If so, it may simply be a cleanliness behavior. We might interpret it as racist, but only if Bush does not engage in similar behaviors with people of his own race or if there is other evidence to support such a claim. A third context would be situation. Bush has just been in a crowd of people, and he might be in a hurry. We can see how commentators have used the situation to draw their conclusions of the behavior. In the same way, if someone stands too close to us, we interpret it based on our relationship, on the situation (are we in a crowded party?), and on the location (is it an otherwise empty public restroom?). Each of these contexts sheds light on how we interpret nonverbal behavior.

An important context of nonverbal communication is the "speech episode"—what is going on in the situation: a touch on the shoulder may mean one thing in a moment of tenderness or comforting, but in an "argument" episode, the same sort of touch may not be welcome (Cronen *et al.*, 1988). This relates to one of the most important contexts of nonverbal communication, and that is the context of verbal communication. Finally, nonverbal behaviors are understood in the context of culture. Often people in one culture use nonverbal behaviors—distance, eye contact, gestures, and so on—that are misunderstood by people in other cultures. Thus, our cultures form a large part of how we negotiate and understand nonverbal behaviors. These last two contexts are central to this chapter. We will introduce these together, covering basic forms and functions of nonverbal communication, and then turn to four main questions that culture raises for understanding specific types of nonverbal behavior.

Forms and functions: How should we act nonverbally when in another culture?

The beginnings of intercultural communication as a discipline are tied to the study of nonverbal communication. The U.S. government brought together a group of scholars in the Foreign Service Institute in the 1940s to 1950s to better understand cultures around the world (Leeds-Hurwitz, 1990). Using language as a framework, these scholars saw nonverbal communication and culture as patterned, regular, and predictable. Researchers from linguistics, anthropology, and other disciplines, like E.T. Hall, George Trager, and Ray Birdwhistell, began a systematic study of various aspects of nonverbal communication, seeing it as central to the "silent language" or "hidden dimension" of culture (Hall, 1966; 1973). We will consider these briefly, turning to deeper issues later.

Channels (forms) of nonverbal communication

Nonverbal communication has been classified into a variety of channels. **Kinesics** deals with body movement, including gestures, stance, gait (how one walks), posture, and facial expressions of emotion. We have heard the stereotype that people from some cultures are more likely to "talk with their hands." David Matsumoto and Hyi-Sung Hwang (2013) arranged for coders from six world regions to code recognizable gestures in their cultures, and in different cultures found gestures with exact verbal meanings from "goodbye," to "Namaste," and from "ward off bad luck" to "I have to pee" (p. 5).

Haptics refers to the study of touch. Edwin McDaniel and Peter Andersen (1998), observing touching behavior at an international airport with follow-up questions to passengers, found that people from northern Asian cultures were less likely to touch than those of southern Asian, Caribbean, Latin American, U.S., or northern European cultures (with no differences in the last five groups). Closeness of relationship (e.g., lovers versus friends) may determine touch behavior (e.g., Williams & Hughes' 2005 naturalistic study of touch in Italy), and nonverbal researchers note that touch relates also to topic of conversation, furnishings/physical environment, and other factors. Researchers have found differences within nations; for example, Asian Americans tend to avoid touch from brothers and sisters more than European Americans, though the difference is small (Avtgis & Rancer, 2003).

Proxemics pertains to a culture's use of space. Hall (1966) wrote a book describing space as a "hidden dimension" of culture. Hall suggests that there are different dimensions for communication that is intimate (between lovers or spouses), personal (between friends), social (between acquaintances, say, in public settings, restaurants, and so on), and public (between people talking across a distance). These, along with topic, posture (sitting/standing), and relationship may influence how close people choose to be. Different cultures prefer different amounts of distance at each level, a point we will return to below. Thus, a person from a culture who likes less space may try to reduce distance between speakers, while someone from a culture where people tend to prefer more space may instinctively move away, with the result that the one subtly begins to "chase" the other around the room.

Another aspect of distance is **territoriality**, how a person or group perceives of and marks territory. For example, where the U.S. American might give a guest a "tour of the house" (perhaps to show off the "goods" he has obtained), in another country, you might be friends with someone for years but never get beyond the front room of the house. In terms of public place, in some national cultures, it is common, if someone is sitting alone at a café table, for someone else to join her, seeing only that person's side of the table as her territory. In another country, people consider the whole table to be that person's temporary territory.

Oculesics pertains to a culture's use of eye behavior, particularly gaze. For example, cultures (as well as people of different sexes) differ in how much they maintain eye contact while speaking versus listening. Differences in this behavior are very subtle and may not be noticed, but might still impact whether one sees the other person as distant, invasive, threatening, and so on (probably interacting with stereotypes one already has of the other group; see chapter 6).

Paralinguistics is a term that some use to describe voice patterns—the characteristics of voice and vocalization that are not verbal, but not strictly nonverbal either. This can include things such as rate of speech, volume, intonation, pronunciation, tone of voice, and other vocalizations such as sighs, laughter, grunts, and so on. People in some cultures may speak in regular conversation more loudly than those in other cultures. Indeed, loudness is a stereotype that those in many national cultures have of Americans, but also a stereotype White and Black Americans have of each other (Leonard & Locke, 1993). Paralinguistics include the notion of verbal pauses or backchanneling. There is a variety of types of pause in conversation (Clark & Clark, 1977), such as vocalized pauses when someone is thinking of something. In the United States, one might say "um," "er," or the growingly prevalent and annoying "like;" but in Spanish-speaking cultures one would say "Este…". **Backchanneling**, the subtle verbal, nonverbal, and paralanguage cues we use to indicate we're listening may also be cultural, both as to when we give them and as to the content of the channeling. Harry Waters (1992) suggests that Black and White Americans give backchannel cues at different times and for different reasons, and Laura Sicola (2005) relates her own experience of returning from Japan, using only "*mm mm*" as a backchannel devise, rather than the socially accepted variety of "yeah", "okay", and "right."

What do you think? Cultural training books such as *CultureGrams* (Proquest, 2009) and *Kiss, Bow, or Shake Hands* (Morrison *et al.*, 1994) list etiquette tips for visiting countries around the world. Note the observations about the following cultures from *Kiss, Bow, or Shake Hands*. Which of the channels mentioned in this section do they exemplify?

→ Bolivia: Keep your hands on the table, not in your lap, while dining.

→ Egypt: Speakers stand much closer than in some countries, such as America. Don't back away if the other speaker stands closer than you expect.

→ Hungary: Use a handshake both when greeting and saying goodbye. Men follow a sequence: handshake, embrace, cheek-to-cheek contact (similar to fake "kiss")—left cheek then right.

→ Malaysia: Don't express anger in public, or you will be seen as someone who lacks self-control, and you will lose face.

→ Philippines: Speak in "quiet, gentle tones" to show respect and discretion and promote harmony. Loud talk is only for when you are "boisterously happy" (p. 292).

→ Romania: Bring your shorts! But only expect to wear them to the beach or in the country, not in the city.

→ Russia: As a business visitor, be punctual; but for Russians, "patience, not punctuality, is considered a virtue" (p. 317). Russians may be one to two hours late for an appointment.

→ Sweden: Toasts are formal—and allow people older than you to toast first. If your host seats you next to the hostess, you might be expected to make a speech.

If you know someone from these cultures, ask if these generalizations are true for their countries. Are there exceptions or conditions to these rules? How do rules from these countries compare to rules in your own culture? What might be some historical, social, or cultural reasons the rules are in place?

Functions of nonverbal communication and relations to verbal communication

As the above forms of nonverbal communication illustrate, different behaviors serve different functions and exist in different relationships to verbal communication. Nonverbal behavior, together with verbal, can accomplish several tasks (Burgoon *et al.*, 1996; Knapp & Hall, 2006). These include showing emotion (affect display), showing attitudes and our relationship to others, revealing our moods and personality, marking our identities, managing turn-taking, and releasing emotional or nervous tension. Culture can differ on several of these dimensions. For example, John Gumperz (1982), through discourse analysis, describes an ineffective interaction between an Indian studying in Britain and a British financial aid agent. Many of the difficulties were due to **prosody**, or the vocalic shaping of utterances, including pitch, volume, tempo, and rhythm. Due to different intonation patterns between Subcontinental Asian and British English, the British university employee thought the student was continuing to ask for confirmation.

Nonverbal behaviors also work together with verbal communication. Nonverbal behaviors can clarify or accent what the verbal behaviors say, or they can contradict each other—as happens in sarcasm. They work together in turn-taking. Head nods, eye contact, intonation, and body posture shifts all work in very subtle ways for us to hand the turn to each other. And these can differ from culture to culture. For example, Han Li (2006) had Canadian and Chinese participants pretend to be patients and doctors, and interact with each other. The groups used different verbal and nonverbal turn-taking signals ("backchannels") in interaction. For example, a head nod or "mm hmm" in one culture might mean "I am paying attention," but in the other culture it might mean, "I understand what you are saying" (p. 111). The researchers linked these differences to the fact that the groups had less ability to recall what had happened in intercultural as opposed to same-culture interactions.

Finally, some gestures have an explicit verbal translation that is known among most members of a group (that is, it is an **emblem**; Richmond *et al.*, 2008). These are used intentionally to convey verbal meanings, such as "okay," "he's cheap," "go away," "check please," "money," or "she's crazy" (see, for example, the study by Matsumoto & Hwang, 2006, mentioned above). With emblems, a nonverbal behavior can substitute a verbal behavior or repeat the same message as the verbal behavior.

The distinct verbal meanings of emblems often lead to trouble in intercultural communication. We can make mistakes in many of the areas (speaking louder or quieter than cultural norms, gesturing when we shouldn't, and so on), but emblems often create trouble as they

ON THE NET

The subject of gestures around the world is a popular topic for bloggers, journalists, and business and academic writers. Look on the Internet for "gestures around the world" or similar search words (e.g., http://www.youtube.com/watch?v=BM9Iu4OQXAw). Locate a list of gestures and what they mean in different cultures. Much of the sites are "popular"—that is, not supported by systematic evidence. Now do a search including "gestures" and "culture" on a site like Google Scholar (http://scholar.google.com/). What research on gestures and culture have researchers done? How might this research be useful?

are linked to specific verbal meanings in the culture. Holding out your hand to say "enough" is an illustrative behavior in the U.S., meaningless by itself. But in Greece, it means, "Eat feces"—or something similar (Cameron, 2008). Sometimes an emblem in one culture is also one in another, but with an entirely different meaning. The circled thumb and finger with fingers outspread means "okay" in the U.S.A., "money" in Japan, "homosexual" in Turkey, and "screw you" in several Latin American cultures (Siljerud, 2008). The V-sign (index and middle finger extended) has many meanings, some offensive, and can vary depending on whether the hand faces the sender or receiver. And holding the middle fingers of with one's thumb, palm facing another person, with pinky and forefinger extended (Figure 8.2) can mean—depending on how it is used—a symbol of the occult (the Devil's horns); rock n' roll; to ward off bad luck; or a sign of solidarity with a Texas college football team (Hook 'em Horns!). And two fingers behind someone's head can be cute "bunny ears" to harmlessly mess up a photo, or an indication that a man's girlfriend or wife is cheating on him.

Figure 8.2 Gestures in different cultures often have different meanings—and some of these might be quite offensive. Source: Clandestini/Westend 61/Corbis.

Issues in nonverbal communication: How can I compare several cultures at the same time?

As we have noted above, many writers have provided lists of behaviors, and it is easy to find "how-to" lists about what (not) to do in this culture or that. Some researchers have looked beyond individual cultures to provide frameworks or discuss issues that cut across cultures. In this section, we will summarize four specific issues that have received attention in intercultural literature.

Issue number 1: I can understand your facial expression—but does it mean what I think it means?

Many researchers suggest that emotional expression is culturally learned (Matsumoto, 1991). This is something that ethnographers of communication have supported. At the same time, others argue that expression of emotion is universal. Countless studies over the years by many authors have looked at the ability of people in different cultures to recognize the same emotions. Researchers have established firmly that six emotions are recognized around the world: sadness, happiness, anger, disgust, surprise, and fear. Using a carefully developed measure known as the Facial Action Coding Scheme, Paul Ekman, Walt Friesen, and other researchers (1987) found that participants in 10 different countries around the world recognized these emotions with a high degree of accuracy—over 90% in most cases. Agreement was lower for countries with less exposure to White or Western cultures (e.g., Sumatra). A study in Ethiopia (Ducci *et al.*, 1982) found that people in rural areas agreed less on the meanings of the emotions than those in the city, perhaps due to the higher television exposure of those in the city. Supporting this, Ekman *et al.*'s (1987) study above did find that people from Western cultures rated the emotions (in the photos of Whites) more intensely than did those from Asian cultures.

So, is emotional expression universal? Ekman and Friesen (1969), the same scholars who established the universal recognition of emotion, above, had Japanese and American participants watch films, some mild and some containing graphic violence. The researchers found that when participants were alone in the viewing room, those from both cultures showed the same emotion, but when they were aware of a researcher sitting in the room observing, the Japanese tended to shield or mute their emotional displays. This study demonstrates that people in all cultures may also *show* emotions the same way, but that there are cultural expectations about when, how much, and with whom to show emotions—what the authors call **display rules**. A comparison of advertisements in South Korea and the United States found display rules to be at work in media as well as face-to-face communication. South Korean models used fewer hand gestures, showed less skin, and touched less than American models. Regarding facial expression specifically, they smiled less and were overall less expressive (Kim, 1992).

As noted in chapter 2, intercultural researchers have taken different approaches to understanding this tension. From a critical perspective, for example, researchers have noted that expressions of emotion may actually reinforce traditional social structures. We saw in chapter 7 how power could come to play in verbal communication. Although some research shows minimal difference in U.S. American men and women's nonverbal behavior, other research suggests that both women and men might, even without knowing it, reinforce and consent to male power in group or organizational settings and in other face-to-face or mediated communication, such as through silence, tone of voice, volume, touch, eye contact, facial display, and use of distance. From a humanistic perspective, Donal Carbaugh (1994), a scholar who does primarily observational research (ethnography of communication), suggests that facial expression is specific to cultures and can best be understood by an approach that looks at the rules of each culture in its own context.

Break it down

This week, think carefully about your own nonverbal display toward people of different groups. Do you treat them equally? Do you show tolerance or acceptance in your nonverbal behavior, or arrogance, offishness, or disrespect? How could you use nonverbal gestures, from facial display to posture to "paralinguistics" to include others?

Issue number 2: Why are you standing so close to me? Space and other aspects of contact

A second issue in intercultural research surrounds Hall's (1966) notion of **contact cultures**. In high-contact cultures, people tend to seek more sensory input during face-to-face interaction. This involves several channels of nonverbal communication—increased eye contact and touch between communicators and decreased distance and body angle. People talking who are members of a high-contact culture are more likely to look at each other more, touch more, stand closer together, and stand more face-to-face, rather than at a wider angle. As with most cultural dimensions and frameworks (e.g., individualism-collectivism, chapter 4), it might be better for us not to think of cultures in terms of a dichotomy of "high-" and "low-contact," though this is the way that many writers and organizational trainers frame them. Rather, we might think of cultures as *higher* or *lower* in contact behaviors than other cultures.

Today, many researchers consider Hall's research, on which understandings of contact are based, to be based on personal stories, but without systematic research behind it. Still, many studies support the idea of contact cultures. Researchers had students from Japan, the United States, and Venezuela talk with people from their own country (Sussman & Rosenfeld, 1982). When speaking their own language, Venezuelans sat closer than U.S. Americans, who sat closer than Japanese, though among participants from all three nations, women sat closer together than did men. A more recent study on mediated communication finds that Asian partners use more distance between their avatars when communicating than Europeans—but they adjust to closer distances when interacting with Europeans (Hasler & Friedman, 2012).

At the same time, some research raises questions about a blanket application of the idea of contact cultures. Robert Shuter did two studies using photographs of people in public places. First (1976), he found differences in contact, eye contact, and distance between Costa Rica, Panama, and Colombia—three nations, side by side, all in Latin America. This challenges the idea of clustering all Latin Americans as high-contact in all aspects of the construct. Then (1977), he studied different people communicating in Italy, Germany, and the United States. He found culturally specific expectations for touching, whether one is in a same-sex dyad or a cross-sex dyad. A similar study of naturally occurring behavior in several major European cities both supported and contradicted Hall's notion of contact cultures. Sometimes people from neighboring nations used contact differently: Irish and Scottish participants used more touch with each other than the English (Remland *et al.*, 1995). Likely, especially if they assume each other to be culturally similar, people from different nations or even within a nation might draw mistaken conclusions about the other person's intentions, feelings, or character, because the other touches, looks, or uses distance differently. Even in so-called low-contact cultures, young people might hug and touch their friends, laugh, and use louder volume in some contexts. Contact might relate to the fact that the people involved are close friends and are younger.

In sum, the idea of contact cultures may be useful in some ways as a general framework. If we go to Mexico, people may, indeed, stand closer. If we go to India, Pakistan, or China ("low-contact" cultures), people *may* stand further away or use less eye contact. We must keep in mind that even if people stand closer, this does not mean that all contact behaviors will coincide with distance—especially in terms of male-female behavior. In addition, how close people stand—as well as how much they touch, how much they look at each other, and so on may be dictated by cultural rules that are best learned in the culture itself and that will be impacted by things such as the topic of the conversation, the environment, and aspects of the communicators such as age, status, co-cultural group, personal disposition toward contact, and relationship (Figure 8.3).

Figure 8.3 People in different cultures have different expectations for use of interpersonal space, eye contact, and touch, though these are always influenced by situation, relationship, and other factors. Here, people in Udaipur, India share a bus ride. Source: Imagebroker.net/ SuperStock.

Chapter 8   Nonverbal communication: Can I make nonverbal blunders and not even know It?

169

What do you think? Some people argue that there are nonverbal differences between racial groups in the United States (for example, Blacks and Whites, Booth-Butterfield & Jordan, 1989). Others (e.g., Halberstadt, 1985) find that other factors, such as socio-economic status and level of education, may explain much of such differences and that, within a social class grouping, such differences may not exist. Think about social, class, sex, age, or ethnic cultures where you live. What are some differences and similarities in different channels of nonverbal behavior, such as use of space, expression of emotion (including to in-groups versus out-groups), and so on? Where there are differences, what underlying values or social and historical influences might explain those differences? For example, are there power structures that limit who can behave nonverbally in different ways? What is a possible danger of focusing on such differences?

Issue number 3: Does anybody really know what time it is?

The concept of time presents less of an issue in the study of intercultural communication than it is an area with different categorization systems and ways to think—and great implications for our social behavior. Specifically, researchers have proposed three different frameworks that we can consider: past/present/future time; monochronic versus polychronic time; and formal versus informal time.

First, as we saw in chapter 4, Kluckhohn and Strodtbeck (1973) discuss among their value orientations the notion of past, present, or future time orientations. People in cultures that orient toward the past are likely to resist change and will value tradition. Those in cultures that are future-oriented are more likely to value change, including valuing progress, probably by some measurable or visible definition. And people who live in cultures that focus on the present may focus on the present enjoyment of life. It is possible that people in any national culture who live in poverty are more present-focused, as they may be concerned more about where the next meal comes from than "saving for a rainy day." At the same time, whole cultures may value one orientation over the other. The United States has traditionally been a future-oriented culture, where (middle- and upper-class people) save and look to the future—and also buy all kinds of insurance for protection from future disasters (health, life, disability, flood, pets). Latin American cultures have tended to include norms that suggest a present focus. The somewhat stereotypical notion of a *mañana* culture, where one shows up late for many appointments, may actually reflect a focus on present relationships. Others have argued that, within the United States, White American culture values being "on time," while African American culture more takes a view of being "in time" (Johnson, 2000)—that is, the present task, discussion, or relationship may be more important than being in a certain location at a particular time on the clock.

A time dimension well-known among interculturalists is Hall's (1983) notion of polychronic and monochronic time. People in **monochronic cultures** (or M-time cultures) tend to do tasks one at a time (e.g., the North European system), and those in **polychronic cultures** are able or prefer to do several things at once (what Hall calls the "Mediterranean model"). In monochronic cultures, people speak of saving, spending, and wasting time, and time is seen more linearly. The focus is often more on task accomplishment. In polychronic cultures, on the other hand, people treat time more flexibly. We might see this in how one treats time for appointments (focusing on the present relationship or activity rather than the time on a clock), or even on meeting with different people at the same time. Hall notes that we might see this orientation even in professions, such as in academia. In M-time cultures, a student might prefer to work on one project at a time, bringing it to completion before beginning another; the P-time student might jump back and forth between projects at the same time.

Hall contends that "P-time stresses involvement of people and completion of current transactions" (1983, p. 46), such that the conversation one is currently in often has precedence over a marked schedule. M-time people often compartmentalize appointments and engagements and might even stop a conversation in order to arrive at some location at a designated time on the clock. As with other dimensions, people who prefer one or other of the types of time exist in all cultures—and they often frustrate each other. If you are a P-time person on a group project with an M-time person, you might feel the M-time person is inflexible and too task-focused. You might prefer working on different parts of the project at one time or prefer "multi-tasking." But if you are an M-time person working with a P-time partner, you may feel your partner is not task-focused and may find she or he has difficulty with task completion.

Finally, some have discussed the distinction between formal and informal time. **Formal time** pertains to a specific time on the clock. This holds true especially in the digital age. Now, when we ask our friend what time she woke up, she might say, "10:13." **Informal time** includes the host of expressions that we use in our cultures to refer to more vague expressions of time, such as "after a while," "later," and so on. Informal time expressions are more likely to create cultural dilemmas than formal ones. On one hand, someone from one culture might use an expression like, "See ya later," meaning another day, while the other communicator may think "later" implies sometime during the same day. "Don't take too long…"—but how long is too long? Beyond the verbal expressions, we see that each culture has different temporal orientations for all activities, including the pace of work, the expected length of courtship, or how long the spaces between speech turns should be.

Issue number 4: Why are you being so quiet? Cultural understandings of silence

Writers have tried to understand silence from the point of view of specific cultures. For example Satoshi Ishii and Tom Bruneau (1994) suggest that there are different "silences." People from Japan and other cultures might use silence for any number of reasons. It might be to show disagreement, as a response to something someone else has done that might be embarrassing, or simply to show respect, and that one is thinking about an idea the other has proposed. Indeed, often, the best response to a beautiful sunset or one's deepest sentiment of love for another is silence, and not the words that so permeate United States and other Western cultures.

Using ethnography, Keith Basso (1970) investigated uses of silence by people in the Apache nation in North America. After much observation, he noted that people used silence in particular situations, such as when placed with a new worker on a job, when one was first married, or when someone raised her or his voice in a public setting, like a bar. Looking for what held these instances together, Basso concluded that people may use silence in situations of uncertainty, a proposition later called **Basso's hypothesis**. He illustrated how each of these situations, culturally, was a situation of uncertainty. You wouldn't know the new worker for a few days; husbands and wives had no contact prior to their wedding and had not been raised around people of the opposite sex; and the person who yells must be crazy, so one is safest to respond in silence. Charles Braithwaite (1990) extended Basso's hypothesis by looking at research accounts of the use of silence in many different cultures. He added the notion that people in all cultures may use silence as a marker of status, either to respect someone of higher status or disdain someone of lower status, if they are aware of status differences.

Nonverbal expectancy violations: What does your nonverbal behavior mean?

One of the benefits of the drive by Hall and his colleagues to gain a new understanding of intercultural communication (chapter 1; Leeds-Hurwitz, 1990) is that they directed the focus of those wanting to learn about other cultures away from culture as a broad, complex phenomenon. Instead, they focused on cultural specifics, dimensions that we have seen in several chapters, but especially in regard to nonverbal communication (monochronic/polychronic, high/low contact). One of the disadvantages of such frameworks is that they often oversimplify cultures. In fact, people holding all orientations exist in all cultures (though there may be ends of a continuum that a culture prefers); there might be differences between how people use time, space, or facial display of emotions, according to their occupations, the region of the country in which they live (e.g., rural versus urban), or their age and sex. The alternative to simplistic frameworks is to learn the specifics of each culture from the sorts of guides we introduced in the "What do you think?" textbox on cultural training books earlier in this chapter. These can be very useful in that one can learn the specific verbal and nonverbal behaviors that will be more or less effective, generally speaking, in a given culture. But the result of this sort of learning is that one must learn long lists of behaviors. We are left wondering if there are not ways of simplifying the long lists of behavioral preferences with some sort of theory, as theories can provide us with a nice shorthand of understanding.

As interesting as nonverbal behavior is, it has less theory than many areas of intercultural communication. One area of theorization, though it may not rise to the level of a theory, is Hall's notion of high- and low-contact cultures, mentioned above. Others have used Hofstede's dimensions (chapter 4) to understand nonverbal behaviors in general (Hecht *et al.*, 1989) or specific aspects of behavior. For example, Matsumoto (1991) predicts that high power-distance cultures will have a greater difference in display rules between those with status difference than low power-distance cultures. So, in Malaysia, one would be much less likely to show anger or extreme happiness to a boss, but would use more discretion in showing emotion, than in Australia.

Other researchers are investigating the idea of communicative immediacy across cultures. **Immediacy** refers to verbal and nonverbal behaviors that show warmth, liking, and affiliation. These include things such as forward body lean, smiling, tone of voice, use of other's name, and so on. On the surface, for example, we might think that students in high power-distance cultures would prefer less immediate instructors. Instructors might use fewer smiles, not use students' names, and stand behind the podium to deliver a lecture, instead of using an interactive (more immediate) style. However, different studies show that in several cultures studied, including Australia, Finland, Puerto Rico, France, South Korea, and the U.S.A., immediacy—especially nonverbal immediacy—is linked to better learning outcomes (McCroskey *et al.*, 1996; Roach *et al.*, 2005).

Culture and the expectancy violations model

Judee Burgoon proposed one of the more commonly mentioned theories relating to nonverbal communication. In 1978, she (with Hale, 1988) proposed her expectancy violations model, primarily in response to other theories that tried to explain what happens when someone stands too close. Previous theories suggested that, for different reasons, someone violating our special expectations would lead to negative responses and, if they had moved too close, we would move away. Burgoon noted that this is often not the case, such as when we perceive the other communicator as rewarding or attractive in some way. Her expectancy violations model suggests that we have **expectancies**—expectations for communication behavior based on our culture, our personal preferences, and our knowledge of the other communicator. When someone violates these behaviors, it draws our attention and we (almost instantly) evaluate the behavior (**behavior valence)** and the communicator (**communicator reward valence**). If both are positive, we may respond positively to the violation. In fact, a violation of expectations may be more helpful than going along with behavioral norms, because it might remind the other communicator that they like us as communicator, so their liking, as well as our message, may work to persuade them of our communication goals. If both are negative, then the response to the violation will be negative. But if the behavior is ambiguous, such as a glance longer than one would expect or a pat on the shoulder, we will interpret it based on whether we see the communicator as rewarding.

Burgoon (Burgoon & Hubbard, 2005) has outlined the usefulness of the approach in areas of intercultural communication. She has noted, for example, that often whether someone violating expectations in a new culture is perceived as "cute" and endearing, or as "weird" and unacceptable will depend on whether the people in the culture see the communicator as possibly rewarding. Burgoon also uses Hofstede's dimensions, noting, for example, that in a high uncertainty avoidance culture, people will likely be less accepting of violations to communication expectations and may define these expectations more narrowly. Countries with lower power distance (her example is the United States, though it is actually toward the middle of power-distance cultures) may have fewer rules about certain verbal and nonverbal behaviors. Burgoon suggests that we must think about aspects of the communicator (for example, status, sex, age), the relationship between communicators, and the context to understand what violations are important, how they are perceived, and how people respond to them.

Burgoon's theory has much potential for intercultural communication researchers and those who travel to other cultures. It lets us know that we must be aware of cultural specifics, influenced by cultural values, in terms of nonverbal expectations. Knowing the underlying values may help us anticipate nonverbal expectations, even if we don't know the specifics. But, importantly, her theory suggests that if we are positive, well-intentioned communicators, those in other cultures may be more lenient in overlooking our more subtle cultural mistakes. What we do not yet know is if people in other cultures expect us to act like people in their culture or people from our own culture. Future research still needs to investigate the degree to which violating others' *stereotypes* of behavior of people from our own nation will work for or against us in intercultural communication.

What do you think? Think about a time that someone violated what you expected, especially in terms of nonverbal communication. Did they violate your cultural expectations, your expectations of the individual, or what you would have wanted to happen personally? Did the violation have a pretty clear meaning, or was it open for interpretation? What did you think about the person who violated your expectation (pretty? rude? smelly?)? Finally, how did you respond? In what way does your experience support or contradict the expectancy violation theory?

Culture and meaning: Semiotics

The main approaches we have introduced above are all "social scientific" in focus (see chapter 2), seeking to make predictions about outcomes with variables. Not all nonverbal intercultural research follows this model. As noted above, some in ethnography of communication have sought culturally unique patterns of behavior, such as how a group uses silence or expression of emotion. Another humanistic approach that often has a critical edge is semiotics. **Semiotics**, a cross-disciplinary approach that looks at how meaning is conveyed through "signs," is a very large field, with some of its own journals (e.g., *Semiotica*), and a full explanation of it would take more than this chapter—or book. Just a few concepts can help us see its usefulness in understanding nonverbal communication.

Semiotics focuses on the symbolic nature of communication, noting that when we communicate, we assemble sounds or images to represent ideas. Several writers began looking at semiotics (e.g., Peirce, 1991). One of the key writers, French linguist, Ferdinand de Saussure (1983) describes the nature of signs and language, noting the nature of linguistic signs. Specifically, he noted how we use a word, like "arbor"—either visually or orally (a "sound pattern")—to represent a reality, like a real tree ("concept," p. 67). Over time, meaning might shift, so that the same sound pattern might now refer to something different (e.g., a "family tree"). The Italian author, Umberto Eco (1976), in addition to writing famous books-turned-into-movies, also philosophized on semiotics, noting that semiotics is "the discipline studying everything that can be used in order to lie" (p. 7). Already, we see the nonverbal aspect of signs: someone can use make-up, a wig, false eyelashes, platform shoes, and so on to "represent" some image or identity that may or may not be the truth (Berger, 2005)! Since words and nonverbal signals can also be used to lie, they can also have "sign" value.

A good nonverbal example of a sign is a wink. The wink "represents," or, in semiotic language, "signifies" something. It might mean that you like someone, or it might suggest that you and the other person have a hidden meaning, like an inside joke or arrangement. The object or idea it represents is the **signified**, and the sound or image that represents it is the **signifier** (Fiske, 1990). The **sign** is the combination of the signified and the signifier and the relationship between them (Barthes, 1968).

We often represent ideas with several images, gestures, and sounds, and these are borrowed from our culture from a set of related sounds/images that represent the idea (a **code**). Whether we are making a magazine advertisement or getting dressed in the morning, and we want to put together an image of "cool," or "sexy," or "professional," we put together a set of signifiers. "Cool" (an ever changing code!) might be represented—at a particular time and among a particular age group in U.S. American culture—by making sure one's tattoo or body piercing is seen, wearing certain clothes, and even walking or holding oneself a certain way (not to mention "coolly" appropriate verbal behaviors). The code can be the set of various symbols we use to illustrate "cool," but it is also the culturally agreed-upon ideas linked to "cool" in society at the time. When we put signs from the "cool" code together (nonverbally, or in media, or in a spoken message) with signs from other codes, we now have **sign systems**. For example, someone applying for a job might blend signs (scents, behaviors, words) of professionalism, but also of physical beauty, and, depending on the job, either conformity or forward-thinking.

The assembling of signs to create ideas—through our dress, gait, scent, posture, gesture, and so on, is a rich field of semiotic meaning. In fact, though communication nonverbal scholars often do not say much about semiotics, semioticians outside of communication say a lot about nonverbal behavior. Even if different cultures have similar values (e.g., respect for the status of the other communicator), they might have a different relationship between signifier and signified. In one culture, one might show respect by looking down, but in the other, by looking the other communicator in the eye. Some researchers (e.g., Leeds-Hurwitz, 1993) suggest semiotics as a tool not only for understanding nonverbal behavior, but also all aspects of culture myth, artifact, and behavior.

Finally, semiotics can have implications for power in communication. Not only do we always encode personal power differences in verbal and nonverbal communication, such as by using posture, tone of voice, volume, and so on to establish power over another or consent to that person's power over us—some researchers in this area consider how in media imagery, we use sign systems to battle over correct ideas (or better said, **ideologies**, see chapter 5). We frame a certain idea as democratic—or beautiful or successful or respectful—by placing it with other ideas, and no set of ideas is politically neutral. In the same way, one could argue that if we buy into a culture's notion of how to act and dress in a particular code of "beauty"—one that is probably crafted and promoted by advertisers and product-makers who benefit by us having that particular view of beauty—we are buying into a set of ideas that (1) excludes the appearance of some by promoting a narrow set of standards, and (2) gains control over our own expression, as we buy into it often without thinking. People often battle over beauty standards, either within themselves or against a dominant culture.

· ·

ON THE NET

Read or watch the story of Bryon Widner and how he changed his appearance to reflect a new identity (e.g., http://www.youtube.com/watch?v=4bkTTEGfjgI). What ideas might his original tattoos refer to as "signifiers," using the notion of semiotics (Figure 8.4)? How about the "collage" of tattoos as a whole? Think of another group (sports fans, "punk rockers," etc.). What aspects of appearance can you identify that they use? How might aspects of physical appearance work together with other aspects (way of walking, bodybuilding to change physical appearance, posture, use of gesture) to serve as a "code" for a particular identity? How do you represent *your* identities through nonverbal communication?

· ·

Figure 8.4 How do the various aspects of body ornamentation (hair style, tattoos) of this member of the group Blood and Honour USA reproduce and borrow from a semiotic "code" of meanings?. Source: Jean-Patrick di Silvestro/Corbis.

Summary

In this chapter, we considered issues related to nonverbal communication and culture. We first described basic aspects of nonverbal communication—the functions it serves, various channels of nonverbal and paralinguistic behavior, and its possible relations to verbal communication. We then investigated four specific areas of nonverbal communication research and practice as these related to culture—issues of "contact cultures," universally recognized facial expression of emotion, use of time, and use of silence. Finally, we explored some theories that seek to understand why or how people use nonverbal and verbal communication (we really cannot separate these). Some seek to predict how people might respond to violations of our nonverbal expectations or how someone might use nonverbal behaviors based on cultural values.

Other researchers explore nonverbal communication in ways that show culturally specific rules for behavior, or even how we might use nonverbal communication in ways that support or challenge power structures. It is here, perhaps, that nonverbal behavior meets civic engagement. We can use appropriate nonverbal behavior—dressing and acting for the part—as part of our own engagement efforts—showing respect and interest nonverbally when we are working in part of a civic project or taking part in community action to promote change. We can also be aware in our daily interactions how we often draw conclusions and might even have our prejudices triggered by the nonverbal behavior of others, especially from other cultures, as in the reference to "smell culture" in chapter 5, or how they subtly exclude others, maybe even without our awareness.

Regardless of how we think about culture and cultural difference (as prediction, as in-depth explanation, or as passing on and resisting power), a clearer understanding both of nonverbal differences and the subtle—and not-so-subtle—meanings of nonverbal behaviors can both make us better intercultural communicators and help us to recognize ways in which our own nonverbal behaviors may hurt or help the dignity of others.

KEY TERMS

faux pas, 161	formal time, 170
kinesics, 162	informal time, 170
haptics, 162	Basso's hypothesis, 170
proxemics, 162	immediacy, 171
territoriality, 162	expectancies, 172
oculesics, 162	behavior valence, 172
paralinguistics, 163	communicator reward valence, 172
backchanneling, 163	semiotics, 173
prosody, 164	signified, 173
emblem, 164	signifier, 173
display rules, 166	sign, 173
contact cultures, 167	code, 173
monochronic cultures, 169	sign systems, 174
polychronic cultures, 169	ideologies, 174

Discussion questions

1 Think about different co-cultural groups in your own culture. Do you think that there are nonverbal differences between the groups (for example, between men and women; older or younger; if you are in the United States, Blacks, Whites, Latinos, or other groups)? Explain possible differences in terms of the specific channels that we mention in this chapter. If possible, ask a member of the groups in question to verify if your understandings are correct.

2 What are some specific display rules for your own cultural group? For example, when might you exaggerate or mute an emotional expression? Or, to think of it differently, how might you show great joy or displeasure to a boss? How should you respond when you receive a gift you do not like? Are there different display rules for men and women?

3 Many intercultural authors focus on how cultures might represent a fairly *consistent* set of behaviors (e.g., how they use touch, contact, facial expressions the same way). But very often, groups surprise us! We think that Koreans will show subdued emotions, then we see young friends showing great happiness and laughing loudly. Choose a specific channel of behavior (e.g., touch). Instead of focusing on similarities, describe the *differences* among people of your cultural group. What are some things that might influence how the channel is used?

4 In this chapter, we do not talk about interpersonal power—that is, who might have more power in a situation (this may not be *formal* power!). What are some nonverbal and paralinguistic ways one communicator might show—or try to establish—power over another communicator?

5 Do you think that more meaning lies in nonverbal or verbal communication? Justify your answer.

Action points

1   Talk to someone who belongs to a group different from you, such as an immigrant or international traveler to your culture, a person in a wheelchair (if you are not), someone with a different sexual orientation, or of a different racial group. Ask about how people might use nonverbal and paralinguistic communication in a way that shows disrespect. Share the ideas with your class. What are some behaviors *you* might need to change, if any?

2   Many people use nonverbal markers (tattoos, clothing, jewelry, etc.) to mark identities. But we can also use these to support important causes or raise awareness for issues. Think about an issue or cause or belief that is important to you. Find a nonverbal marker that represents this identity and wear it to class and talk about it.

3   While it is not good to be overly self-analytical, take a self-inventory of ways you might act around people of different groups. If you know someone who will be honest, and you are ready for an open discussion of your behavior, ask a friend in another group to give you feedback on behaviors of people from your own group, and of your own nonverbal behavior.

For more information

DeVito, J.A., & Hecht, M. (Eds.). (1990). *The nonverbal communication reader*. Prospect Heights, IL: Waveland.

Hall, E.T. (1973). *The silent language*. New York: Anchor.

Leeds-Hurwitz, W. (1993). *Semiotics and communication: Signs, codes, cultures*. Hillsdale, NJ: Lawrence Erlbaum Associates.

Manusov, V., & Patterson, M.L. (Eds.). (2006). *The SAGE handbook of nonverbal behavior*. Thousand Oaks, CA: Sage.

Molinár, P., & Segerstråle, U.C.O. (1997). *Nonverbal communication: Where nature meets culture*. Mahwah, NJ: Lawrence Erlbaum Associates.

References

Adams, R. (2010). George Bush's clean hands in Haiti. Richard Adams' Blog, *Guardian*, March 24. Accessed July 28, 2012, at http://www.guardian.co.uk/world/richard-adams-blog/2010/mar/24/george-bush-handshake-haiti-clinton

Avtgis, T.A., & Rancer, A.S. (2003). Comparing touch apprehension and affective orientation between Asian American and European American siblings. *Journal of Intercultural Communication Research, 32*(2), 67–74.

Barthes, R. (1968). *Elements of semiology* (Trans. A. Lavers & C. Smith). New York: Hill & Wang.

Basso, K. (1970). To give up on words: Silence in the Western Apache culture. *Southwestern Journal of Anthropology, 26*, 213–230.

Berger, A.A. (2005). *Media analysis techniques* (3rd ed.). Thousand Oaks: Sage.

Booth-Butterfield, M., & Jordan, F. (1989). Communication adaptation among racially homogeneous and heterogeneous groups. *Southern Communication Journal, 54*, 253–272.

Braithwaite, C.A. (1990). Communicative silence: A cross-cultural study of Basso's hypothesis. In D. Carbaugh (Ed.) *Cultural communication and intercultural contact* (pp. 321–327). Hillsdale, NJ: Lawrence Erlbaum.

Burgoon, J.K., Buller, D.B., & Woodall, W.G. (1996). *Nonverbal communication: The unspoken dialogue* (2nd ed.). New York: McGraw-Hill.

Burgoon, J.K., & Hale, J.L. (1988). Nonverbal expectancy violations: Model elaboration and application to immediacy behaviors. *Communication Monographs, 55*, 58–79.

Burgoon, J.K., & Hubbard, A.S.E. (2005). Cross-cultural and intercultural applications of expectancy violations theory and interaction adaptation theory. In W.B. Gudykunst (Ed.), *Theorizing about intercultural communication* (pp. 149–171). Thousand Oaks, CA: Sage.

Cameron, T. (2008). 7 innocent gestures that can get you killed overseas. *Cracked.com*. Accessed September 9 2011, at http://www.cracked.com/article_16335_7-innocent-gestures-that-can-get-you-killed-overseas.html

Carbaugh, D. (1994). Toward a perspective on cultural communication and intercultural contact. In L.A. Samovar & R.E. Porter (Eds.), *Intercultural communication: A reader* (pp. 45–59). Belmont: Wadsworth.

Clark, H.H., & Clark, E.V. (1977). *Psychology and language: An introduction to psycholinguistics.* New York: Harcourt Brace Jovanavich.

Cronen, V.E., Chen, V., & Pearce, W.B. (1988). Coordinated management of meaning: A critical theory. In Y.Y. Kim & W.B. Gudykunst (Eds.), *Theories in intercultural communication* (pp. 66–98). Newbury Park, CA: Sage.

Ducci, L., Arcuri, L., Georgis, T., & Sineshaw, D. (1982). Emotion recognition in Ethiopia: The effect of familiarity with Western culture on accuracy of recognition. *Journal of Cross-Cultural Psychology*, *13*, 340–351.

Eco, H. (1976). *A Theory of semiotics.* Bloomington: Indiana University Press.

Ekman, P., & Friesen, W.V. (1969). The repertoire of nonverbal behavior: Categories, origins, usage, and coding. *Semiotica*, *1*, 49–98.

Ekman, P., Friesen, W.V., O'Sullivan, M., Chan, A., Diacoyanni-Tarlatzis, I., *et al.* (1987). Universals and cultural differences in the judgments of facial expressions of emotion. *Journal of Personality and Social Psychology*, *53*, 712–717.

Fiske, J. (1990). *Introduction to communication studies* (2nd ed.). London: Routledge.

Gumperz, 1982. *Discourse strategies.* Cambridge: Cambridge University Press.

Halberstadt, A. (1985). Race, socioeconomic status, and nonverbal behavior. In A.W. Siegman & S. Feldstein (Eds.), *Multichannel integrations of nonverbal behavior* (pp. 227–266). Hillsdale, NJ: Lawrence Erlbaum Associates.

Hall, E.T. (1966). *The hidden dimension.* New York: Doubleday.

Hall, E.T. (1973). *The Silent language.* New York: Anchor.

Hall, E.T. (1983). *The dance of life: The other dimension of time.* New York: Anchor.

Hasler, B.S., & Friedman, D.A. (2012). Sociocultural conventions in avatar-mediated nonverbal communication: A cross-cultural analysis of virtual proxemics. *Journal of Intercultural Communication Research*, *41*, 238–259.

Hecht, M.L., Andersen, P.A., & Ribeau, S.A. (1989). The cultural dimensions of nonverbal communication. In M.K. Asante & W.B. Gudykunst (Eds.), *Handbook of intercultural communication* (pp. 163–185). Beverly Hills, CA: Sage.

Ishii, S., & Bruneau, T. (1994). Silence and silences in cross-cultural perspective: Japan and the United States. In L.A. Samovar & R.E. Porter (Eds.), *Intercultural communication: A reader* (7th ed.). Belmont, CA: Wadsworth Publishing.

Johnson, F. (2000). *Speaking culturally: Language diversity in the United States.* Thousand Oaks, CA: Sage.

Kim, M.-S. (1992). A comparative analysis of nonverbal expressions as portrayed by Korean and American print-media advertising. *Howard Journal of Communications*, *3*, 317–339.

Kluckhohn, F.R., & Strodtbeck, F.L. (1973). *Variations in value orientations* (2nd ed). Westport, CT: Greenwood.

Knapp, M.L., & Hall, J.A. (2006). *Nonverbal communication in human interaction* (6th ed.). Belmont, CA: Wadsworth.

Leeds-Hurwitz, W. (1990). Notes in the history of intercultural communication: The Foreign Service Institute and the mandate for intercultural training. *Quarterly Journal of Speech*, *76*, 262–281.

Leeds-Hurwitz, W. (1993). *Semiotics and communication: signs, codes, cultures.* Hillsdale, NJ: Lawrence Erlbaum Associates.

Leonard, R., & Locke, D.C. (1993). Communication stereotypes: Is interracial communication possible? *Journal of Black Studies*, *23*, 332–343.

Li, H. (2006). Backchannel responses as misleading feedback in intercultural discourse. *Journal of Intercultural Communication Research*, *35*, 99–116.

Matsumoto, D. (1991). Cultural influences on facial expressions of emotion. *Southern Communication Journal*, *56*, 128–137.

Matsumoto, D., & Hwang, H. (2013). Cultural similarities and differences in emblematic behaviors. *Journal of Nonverbal Behavior*, *37*, 1–27.

McCroskey, J.C., Fayer, J.M. Richmond, V.P., Sallinen, A., & Barraclough, R.A. (1996). A multi-cultural examination of the relationship between nonverbal immediacy and affective learning. *Communication Quarterly*, *44*, 297–307.

McDaniel, E., & Andersen, P.A. (1998). International patterns of interpersonal tactile communication: A field study. *Journal of Nonverbal Behavior, 22*(1), 59–75.

Morrison, T., Conaway, W.A., & Borden, G.A. (1994). *Kiss, bow, or shake hands: How to do business in sixty countries.* Holbrook MA: Adams Media Corporation.

Muskus, J. (2010). George Bush wipes hand on Bill Clinton's shirt after shaking hands with Haitians. *Huffington Post*, May 24. Accessed July 28, 2012, at http://www.huffingtonpost.com/2010/03/24/george-w-bush-wipes-hand_n_511188.html#s76480

Peirce, C.S. (1991). *Peirce on signs* (Ed. J. Hoopes). Chapel Hill: University of North Carolina Press.

Proquest. (2009). *CultureGrams* Provo, Utah: Proquest.

Remland, M.S., Jones, T.S., & Brinkman, H. (1995). Interpersonal distance, body orientation, and touch: effects of culture, gender, and age. *The Journal of Social Psychology, 135*, 281–297.

Richmond, V.P., McCroskey, J.C., & Hickson, M.L., III. (2008). *Nonverbal communication in interpersonal relations* (6th ed.). Boston: Pearson.

Roach, K.D., Cornett-DeVito, M., & DeVito, R. (2005). A cross-cultural examination of instructor communication in American and French classrooms. *Communication Quarterly, 53*, 87–107.

Saussure, F. de. (1983). *Course in general linguistics* (Ed. C. Bally & A. Sechehaye, Trans. R. Harris). La Salle, IL: Open Court.

Shuter, R. (1976). Proxemics and tactility in Latin America. *Journal of Communication, 26*, 46–52.

Shuter, R. (1977). A field study of nonverbal communication in Germany, Italy, and the United States. *Communication Monographs, 44*, 298–305.

Sicola, L. (2005). "Communicative lingerings": Exploring awareness of L2 influence on L1 in American expatriates after re-entry. *Language Awareness, 14*, 153–169.

Siljerud, P. (2008). The meaning of the OK hand gesture around the world—Learn the meaning of hand gestures. *Ezine@rticles*. Accessed September 9, 2011, at http://ezinearticles.com/?The-Meaning-of-the-OK-Hand-Gesture-Around-the-World---Learn-the-Meaning-of-Hand-Gestures&id=1640238

Sussman, N.M., & Rosenfeld, H.M. (1982). Influence of culture, language and sex on conversational distance. *Journal of Personality and Social Psychology, 42*, 66–74.

Waters, H. Jr. (1992). Race, culture, and interpersonal conflict. *International Journal of Intercultural Relations, 16*, 437–454.

Williams, D.E., & Hughes, P.C. (2005). Nonverbal communication in Italy: An analysis of interpersonal touch, body position, eye contact, and seating behaviors. *North Dakota Journal of Speech & Theatre, 18*, 17–24.

Chapter 9

Rhetoric and culture: How does my culture relate to persuasive writing and speaking?

Chapter objectives

After this chapter, you should be able to:

→ Understand rhetoric as a unique aspect of communication

→ Explain how rhetoric and culture are interrelated

→ Identify examples of rhetorical traditions

→ Understand and explain vernacular rhetoric

→ Reflect a greater understanding and appreciation for the complexities of trying to persuade multicultural audiences

Rhetorical communication: How does culture inform persuasion?

Vernacular rhetoric: How does everyday communication seek to persuade?

Intercultural rhetoric: What are the implications for civic engagement?

Intercultural Communication for Everyday Life, First Edition. John R. Baldwin, Robin R. Means Coleman, Alberto González, and Suchitra Shenoy-Packer.
© 2014 John R. Baldwin, Robin R. Means Coleman, Alberto González, and Suchitra Shenoy-Packer.
Published 2014 by John Wiley & Sons Ltd.

The process of learning about cultures is important and complex. Sometimes this process is comically shown in popular entertainment. The 2008 U.S. film, *The Other End of the Line* (produced by Ashok Amritraj and directed by James Dodson), depicts a very fundamental rhetorical strategy: building commonality between speaker and audience. *The Other End of the Line* is about a young man, Granger Woodruff, who needs to resolve problems with his credit card over the telephone. He thinks that the credit card agent is Jennifer David, in San Francisco; in fact, she is actually a woman called Pryia who works in a call center in Mumbai, India. Before the Indian operators are allowed to answer calls from U.S. customers, they have to take classes in U.S. popular culture. They are taught to distinguish Sarah Michelle Gellar from Sarah Jessica Parker. They are taught the difference between a burger from Wendy's and a burger from Burger King and McDonald's.

Why? Literary critic Kenneth Burke famously wrote that we persuade others by speaking their language and knowing their ways. For Burke, persuasion hinges on our ability to create commonality or **identification** with others because "identification is compensatory to division" (Burke, 1969, p. 22). **Division** consists of the differences in beliefs and ways of interacting that might create conflict. Not only do people live differently, they express themselves differently. In this case, the Indian agents are taught how to close the cultural divide and establish a common ground with U.S. callers in order to gain their trust, answer their questions and keep them as customers.

The Other End of the Line helps us to understand the relationship between rhetoric and culture. In order for Pryia to identify with Granger, she must learn his cultural references and apply them in conversation. This chapter explains rhetorical communication as a cultural activity and describes implications for rhetorical action and civic engagement in a multicultural world.

Rhetorical communication: How does culture inform persuasion?

Following Burke, we define **rhetoric** and **rhetorical action** as the use of symbols to "induce cooperation" (Burke, 1969, p. 43). Within and across communities, there is an ongoing tension between identification and division, and rhetoric mediates this tension. In the U.S. Cold War with the former Soviet Union, political and cultural differences were emphasized in order to establish one side as superior to the other. In the 1970s, both engaged in a rhetoric of détente that instead emphasized mutual interests. **Rhetorical communication** is a message that is planned and adapted to an audience (or audiences) (Herrick, 2009, pp. 8–9). When President Obama spoke to the U.S. and the international community on June 15, 2010, about the oil spill in the Gulf of Mexico, he wanted to reassure the nation that adequate steps were being taken to protect the environment and the economy of the Gulf region. Verbally, the president described the government's efforts to assemble scientific expertise and explained how BP was being directed to cap the out-of-control well. There was a visual strategy also: President Obama delivered the speech from the White House, and the fact that he was speaking from the Oval Office—the president's primary office—conveyed to domestic and international audiences that the severity of this disaster was understood at the highest level of government.

Rhetorical communication occurs not only publicly but also in interpersonal situations. With observation, we can discover that seemingly small pieces of talk can display the planned and identification-seeking quality of rhetorical interactions. At a U.S. university, a graduate student from X'ian, China, records her voicemail message to end with "See 'ya." A bank teller from the Catalan region of Spain, who is working in a town in the midwestern United States, closes each conversation with the expression, "Have a good one!" In each instance, the goal is to create a sense of shared identity by incorporating local expressions. While the Spanish bank teller might occasionally end a conversation by saying "*Ciao,*" her hope is that she has still adapted her way of talking to the U.S. listener.

So how do we know what persuades people? How do we know what kinds of arguments and information will lead people into positive relationships and mutual action? In order to be persuasive, speakers need to employ more than knowledge of a particular topic; they must also draw upon cultural knowledge. Rhetorical action does not take place in a vacuum. It is created within, and reflects, a cultural context. As language scholar Fern Johnson observes, "Rhetoric arises from cultural contexts rather than being universal, and rhetorical communication is perceived and evaluated through cultural frames" (2000, p. 37). In the next section, we explore the concepts that critics of rhetorical communication have developed for understanding the connections between rhetoric and culture.

What do you think? Think of a recent persuasive campaign. The campaign might have been to pass a local ordinance, student government elections, or state or national elections; or it might have been a public announcement about a social problem or policy. Whatever the case, the speaker (advocate) will be urging a particular view of the world or a particular action. How did the advocate(s) seek to create identification with the audience? What shared values did they associate with their cause? What common images did they associate with their cause? How do you decide whether an advocate shares your views?

Rhetorical traditions: How do people in different cultures try to persuade?

The concept of the **rhetorical tradition** has greatly added to analysis of rhetoric and cultures. The notion is simple and intuitive: we should try to understand rhetorical communication in terms of the historical and social influences and ethnic practices of the speakers (Garrett, 2000; Garrett & Xiao, 1994).

The work of interpretive scholar Gerry Philipsen provides a clear example of analysis that places a speech within a rhetorical tradition. Philipsen (1992) examined a speech given by Richard J. Daley, the long-term mayor of Chicago. Mayor Daley had been criticized by a member of city council for making appointments to city jobs on the basis of family connections and favoritism rather than expertise and qualifications. Daley lashed out at his accuser by associating him with "hypocrites and fakers" (p. 46) who only wanted to criticize the city. Daley's speech praised one appointee's mother for having raised such a fine son—a son worthy of working for the City of Chicago. Philipsen placed Daley's speech and style of governing within the expectations of the working class neighborhoods of South Chicago. There, people watched out for one another, defended their families and rewarded loyalty according to a hierarchy that was commonly understood. Philipsen traced the neighbor-hood norms and Daley's response to criticism to a centuries-old Irish "code of honor" that requires immediate and harsh defense in the face of disrespect. Outside of this tradition, Daley's speech was described as incoherent and egotistical, but within that tradition he was seen as being true to the code of honor.

When two differing cultural perspectives come together in public or interpersonal persuasion, we have an instance of **intercultural rhetoric.** Mayor Daley was speaking from one cultural perspective (working-class Irish American) and the mainstream media were assessing the speech from their cultural perspective (conventional Western journalism and Western deliberative politics). Making sense of intercultural rhetoric requires that we adopt a provisional attitude, "check the impulse to condemn," and work to understand a speech "on its own terms" (Philipsen, p. 48).

Rhetoric scholars have identified steps for the analysis and assessment of intercultural rhetoric. These steps are useful guides for gaining a cultural understanding of public discourse and persuasion. As listeners and observers, we should:

1 Delineate historical relations between the speaker's culture and that of the audience.

2 Identify those elements of a speaker's culture that normally determine the speaker's style of presentation.

3 Specify any preconceptions the audience may have of the speaker.

4 Identify public expectations regarding the address.

5 Describe expectations from an understanding of cultural presuppositions as well as the rhetorical legacy of the form of communication.

6 Examine the significance of the specific rhetorical medium (speech, poem, proclama-tion, etc.) in the speaker's culture.

7 Examine the speaker's style of discourse broadly to include the various structures, images, content, strategies, and appeals of a rhetorical piece.
(Adapted from Hammerback & Jensen, 1994; Starosta & Coleman, 1986)

With these guides in mind, we can turn to examples of political activism and delibe-ration and their rhetorical traditions. These public discourses are selected because they co-exist with the dominant Euro-American tradition that emphasizes objectivity and individuality.

What do you think? How would you describe the typical methods of persuasion in your country or culture? Why are these methods effective? On the Internet, search to find the roots or traditions that guide the rhetoric in your culture (e.g., Arabic rhetoric, Western rhetoric, Chinese rhetoric, Indian rhetoric). How much are we taught about approaches to persuasion that come from different roots or traditions?

African American tradition: Rooted in resistance

African American voices have delivered powerful critiques and affirmations of U.S. social and cultural structures. In the 20th century, Angela Davis and Malcolm X provided alternative histories and social theories to counter the prevailing Puritan myth. In literature, James Baldwin, Maya Angelou, and August Wilson dramatized the lasting effects of marginalization as well as irrepressible hope in the lives of their characters. From the pulpit, the Reverends Dr. Martin Luther King, Jr., Jesse Jackson, and Al Sharpton mobilized audiences to advance civil rights. In each case, they reminded the United States that its collective memory included the creation of a labor pool obtained by force and currency. The African American rhetorical tradition begins with Africa, but it is a unique blend of African and Western cultural influences.

African American rhetoric locates an origin—Africa—that taps "a core African value system" that creates similarities in the social lives of Blacks of African descent wherever they are found (Collins, 1989, p. 755). The rhetorical qualities of the African tradition focus on the "almost universal African regard for the power of the spoken word" (Smith, 1970, p. 265). The primary African legacy was a belief in "the transforming power of vocal expression" (Smith, 1970, p. 265). Through words, slaves of various ethnicities from different regions of West and Central Africa could create a common identity as well as transcend (if only temporarily) the horrors of their captivity and servitude through song and lamentation. In this tradition, language and **paralanguage** (tone, volume, speech rate, etc.) are creative tools for expressing the whole range of human emotion and feeling. Language use is characterized by improvisation and inventiveness, as seen in original rap music or verbal dueling games like "the dozens" (Johnson, 2000).

This core belief in the power of language together with remnants of African religious traditions combined with Western denominations of Christianity to produce in post-slavery a form of worship and expression that centered on freedom. The formation of the African Methodist Episcopal (A.M.E.) church in 1816 created a space for Christian worship free from the judgments and constraints of mainstream Christianity (Weaver, 1991). The church service became a counterpoint to mainstream exclusion and invisibility. The free involvement of the worshippers was a metaphor for the inclusion that mainstream society often denied African Americans. In the Black Church, "worshippers experience a catharsis through the freedom in which they are allowed to express themselves" (Hamlet, 2011, p. 113). Freedom in the church service is expressed by singing, calling out to the preacher during the sermon, standing, and moving and clapping with the music.

The preacher is the focal point of the church service. The preacher "has an individualized style which is drawn from the larger paradigm of performance" that displays improvisation and inventiveness (Weaver, 1991, p. 59). The successful preacher performs the Biblical text dynamically, using repetition, analogy, and rhyme, and sometimes singing the sermon with stomping, hollering, and dramatic pause. The spirituals, as well as other musical forms such as jazz and blues, "represent a continuous linkage with the rituals and arrangements of West Africa" (Asante, 1980, p. 75). It is out of this tradition that the most influential African American speakers emerged.

When most people think of an African American presidential candidate, they often think of Barack Obama, the Senator from Illinois. It is natural to reference Senator Obama because he was elected U.S. President in 2008. Fewer will remember that 20 years earlier, another African American, Jesse Jackson, ran for U.S. President (and that, in 1972, an

African American female, Shirley Chisholm, sought the Democratic nomination—and faced three assassination attempts). The Reverend Jesse Jackson, also from Illinois, inherited the mantle of social justice spokesperson after the Civil Rights Movement. Jackson headed the Chicago-based Operation PUSH that championed policies that empowered the working class and those in poverty.

On July 20, 1988, the Reverend Jackson addressed the Democratic National Convention, in Atlanta Georgia, as a presidential candidate. Jackson delivered the speech, "Common Ground and Common Sense" (Sullivan, 1993) amid speculation over whether he would be named to the Democratic ticket as vice-presidential candidate or throw his support behind another candidate. Rosa Parks and Aaron Henry were in attendance. Jackson recognized these icons of activism and also noted that the tomb of Martin Luther King, Jr. lay only a few miles from the convention site. Jackson began his speech by noting that the country was at a crossroads: "Shall we expand, be inclusive, find unity and power? Or suffer division and impotence?" Jackson used Biblical references and imagery, naming Jerusalem as the intersection where different people, different cultures, and different civilizations "could meet and find common ground" (Sullivan, 1993, p.8).

He urged "common sense" that would inform U.S. domestic and foreign policy. "I just want to take common sense to high places," he declared, by saving family farms, reducing tax loopholes for the wealthy, increasing health care and education, and supporting human rights internationally. The rhythmic quality of the speech, together with its religious imagery and personal stories "are vital for the Black speaker who represents an oral tradition" (Sullivan, 1993, p. 5). Jackson attempts to reframe or transform the aims of political action. The "real world" requires the support of various "basic principles" that will compose a new moral authority. Parts of Jackson's speech illustrate the transformative potential of words:

> This generation must offer leadership to the real world. We're losing ground in Latin America, the Middle East, South Africa, because we're not focusing on the real world.
> That real world.
> We must use basic principles, support international law. We stand to gain the most from it.
> Support human rights; we believe in that.
> Support self-determination; we'll build on that.
> Support economic development; you know it's right.
> Be consistent and gain our moral authority in the world!
>
> (Jackson, 1988, p. 652)

Like Mayor Daley, who spoke guided by his Irish American rhetorical tradition, Jesse Jackson spoke from within an African American rhetorical tradition. Sensing the cultural difference, some did not believe that "Common Ground and Common Sense" met the expectations of mainstream political discourse. However, the vast majority concluded that Jackson reached across cultural communities to create an inspiring national vision (Sullivan, 1993).

Chinese tradition: Rooted in social reflection

The Chinese rhetorical tradition draws from spirituality and philosophy, folklore and the arts, and contains the culturally distinctive values of "*tao* (Way), *sheng* (life-giving, production), *ren* (love) and *tian* (Heaven)" (Xiao, 1995, p. 87). The Chinese speaker can "anchor" arguments to these values and create identification with an audience (Garret & Xiao, 1994).

Figure 9.1 In order to gain the people's support, Mao Zedong blended his Communist ideology with traditional Chinese rituals. Source: David Pollack/Corbis.

紧跟伟大领袖毛主席奋勇前进！

Perhaps the best known example of the merging of rhetoric and Chinese tradition is found in the rule of Mao Zedong, one of China's most famous leaders.

Mao Zedong (Figure 9.1) ruled China for over 33 years until his death in 1976. As Chairman of the Communist Party of China, he devised a socialist "Cultural Revolution." Mao sought to eliminate private wealth and the affluent class was persecuted and largely eliminated. Millions died, either executed for harboring Western sentiments or due to starvation as the country's infrastructure declined. Still, Mao was worshipped as a god (Huang, 1997). Masses of young people joined the Red Guards and they passionately enforced Mao's socialist dictates. How was he able to create such devotion and loyalty? One part of the answer involves Chinese ancient traditions and their modern rhetorical application. Sharong Huang (1997) studied the cultural elements in Cultural Revolution rhetoric. He found that:

> Traditionally, the Chinese are religious people. Some believe in Buddhism, some in Taoism, and some in other religions such as Islam and Christianity. During the [Cultural Revolution Movement], all kinds of religions were abolished. Many Buddhist and Taoist temples were burned down by the Red Guards. However, the Chinese people were used to worshipping. If they were not allowed to worship the old gods, they looked for a new one to worship. Naturally, Mao became the only god for them. (p. 130)

Mao understood the persuasive power of tradition as he crafted his strategies to closely match existing social understandings (Cai & González, 1997). Mao's strategy was to adapt centuries-old customs and beliefs to his Cultural Revolution ideology. For example, the people had followed the teachings of Confucius for over 2000 years. Mao adapted the Confucian model of family authority and hierarchy to his leadership. As "father" of the Chinese people, Mao's moral authority was absolute (Teiwes, 2010). This was an assertion people could accept. Additionally, the ritual study and repetition of Mao's sayings mirrored the learning of Confucian thought. The hyperbole used to describe Mao and his actions borrowed from classical Chinese poetry and forms of address in the Chinese dynasties. Finally, the daily political gatherings where people shouted slogans and moved together in a "loyalty dance" mirrored the collectivism of Chinese society (Huang, 1997, p. 134).

From the standpoint of rhetoric and culture, it is important to observe that Mao did not create a new rhetorical strategy to gain and maintain power. He did not borrow from the outside—the West—to legitimize his rule. He utilized the values and rituals of the people he sought to dominate. At the same time, China serves as an excellent case study in the way that rhetoric changes. Mei Zhong's (2003) outline of major historical points that impacted Chinese language may also have relevance to the study of rhetoric. She notes five distinct eras of Chinese language, starting from the New Culture era, in which writing moved from an "ancient literature" style to a "new and fresh style that is coherent with spoken language" (p. 207), making writing more accessible for the average person. She discusses the impact of Mao Zedong, as we have noted earlier, but then highlights the anti-intellectualism of the Cultural Revolution era. She notes that modern rhetoric is being influenced by an "All Around Open and Western Influence Era" (p. 213). Her observations are specifically about language, such as the turn in the 1990s from addressing people as "Comrade" to "Mr." and "Ms.". But they have implications for rhetoric in showing us that, while strongly influenced by its Communist past, Chinese rhetoric continues to evolve with new historical and philosophical influences.

Latino/a tradition: Rooted in revolution

Mexican social essayist and critic, Octavio Paz, attempted in his writings to capture the essences of Mexican culture. Recipient of the 1990 Nobel Prize in Literature, he described a national character that largely avoids public discourse except in the cause of revolution (Paz, 1961; 1972). For Paz, the Mexican—who has withstood the traumas of multiple invasions, natural disasters, and political instability—finds safety in ambiguity and withdrawal from public expression. This tendency to withdraw is shattered in the case of fiesta and revolution. The rhetorical challenge faced by Mexican Americans (U.S. citizens of Mexican descent) was to balance the tension between silence and advocacy. This challenge was successfully met by activist Cesar Chavez (Figure 9.2).

Born in Arizona in 1927, Chavez experienced first hand the poor treatment given to migrant farmworkers by growers, the state and federal government, and by those who would exploit the low status of the workers. With Dolores Huerta—who in 2012 received the Presidential Medal of Freedom—Chavez co-founded the United Farm Workers. Their goal was to unionize the California farmworkers so that they could for the first time enter into legally binding agreements with the growers. This would assure humane treatment and better wages. Perhaps Chavez is best known for leading a national boycott of California grapes and their products. Any aficionado of merlot or pinot noir wine will understand the significance of the California grape crop. But to be successful, Chavez first had to gain credibility as a public advocate among a people who tended to reject public advocacy.

A recent biography of the life and activism of Cesar Chavez, *The Fight in the Fields: Cesar Chavez and the Farmworkers Movement*, lists major influences upon Chavez as Saint Francis of Assisi, the writings of Saint Paul, and biographies of U.S. labor leaders John L. Lewis and Eugene Debs, Machiavelli, Alexis de Tocqueville, and Mahatma Gandhi (Ferriss & Sandoval, 1997, p. 47). While these were no doubt important influences, this list must be considered

Figure 9.2 Farm labor
activist Cesar Chavez drew
upon traditional Mexican
oratory.
Source: Bettmann/Corbis.

partial for a man who coined the slogan, "*sí se puede*" [yes, it can be done] and who called his activism "*el movimiento*" [the movement]. To gain recognition and establish identification, Chavez countered the "ideology of silence" (González, 1989) and drew upon the revolutionary rhetoric of Mexican leaders who fought to maintain a close connection between the people and the land that they toiled.

To best understand Chavez and his tactics, we need to place them "within the context of their own rhetorical tradition, a tradition anchored in Mexican history and developed from the Mexican American's culture and experiences" (Hammerback & Jensen, 1994, p. 54). The issuance of guiding principles and proclamations for persuasive movements—called "plans"—is patterned after the political plans issued during Mexico's revolutionary era in the 1800s. A plan was typically named for the city in which it was written and it could list grievances, provide a rationale for action, and announce proposed actions to redress injustice or specific problems. The Plan of Tomé and the Plan of Ayala (which dealt with agriculture and land rights) are among Mexico's most famous plans (Hammerback & Jensen, 1994).

Additionally, Chavez and his associates were influenced by Emiliano Zapata, a military leader of the Mexican Revolution of 1910, who championed land reform. They were also fond of quoting much-celebrated Mexican President Benito Juarez's most famous saying: "*el respeto al derecho ajeno es la paz*" (to respect the rights of others is peace). Chavez named his movement newsletter *El Malcriado*, after a Revolutionary-era newspaper. Cartoons satirized California landowners and politicians in *El Malcriado* in much the same way as the Mexican ruling elite was satirized in Mexican newspapers.

The Plan of Delano, written in 1966, was intended to generate public support for farmworkers who were striking in nearby vineyards and to reinforce the resolve of farmworkers who were paid low wages and forced to live in shacks by the fields. Though written in the 1960s, the Plan of Delano was modeled after Zapata's Plan of Ayala of

1911. The early inspiration for the movement came from the Mexican Revolution. The plan was an important persuasive tool since it could be read in both Spanish and English and could be copied and delivered to many workers and politicians. The plan stated that the workers were entitled to fundamental human rights, that the workers' belief in God would ensure their endurance, and that they were united in their cause (Hammerback & Jensen, 1994).

Without doubt, Cesar Chavez was influenced by the early labor leaders, and peace activists such as Gandhi and Martin Luther King, Jr. However, including the rhetorical tradition of Mexico lends a fuller explanation of how Chavez achieved identification with the farmworkers whose trust he needed.

Break it down

Many college campuses have student organizations that are involved in political activism or focused on promoting the interests of a particular ethnic or identity group. For example, at a U.S. university, you might find organizations aimed at fighting global warming, advocating human rights around the world (Amnesty International), or encouraging vegetarianism. Or you might find student groups focused on African American, Latina/Latino, Deaf, GBLT, or other identity groups.

Locate a particular group and get permission to analyze its messages (for example, its recruiting messages, motivational speeches at activities). Do the style, form, and content of the message (that is, the rhetorical strategies) seem appropriate and effective for their audience? If such a group wanted recommendations, what recommendations would you make for more effective messages?

Native American tradition: Rooted in nature

An important cultural value among many Native American communities is a "circular and flexible" notion of time (Shutiva, 2012, p. 134). When enacted, this approach to time would observe the connectedness of the present to the past. This approach also would observe approximate times for the beginning and ending of events. The people and the event itself—rather than time—are the controlling factors. This approach is in contrast to the dominant Western notion of linear and exact time. Whenever we expect punctuality or when we say that we've "moved beyond" or "gotten over" something, we are enacting the linear notion of time (see chapter 9).

In public advocacy, these differing values are apparent. In Arizona, a dispute arose over a proposed astronomical observatory on Mount Graham (Carbaugh & Wolf, 2000). The four tribes of the Western Apache Nation regarded the mountain as a sacred space, a place of worship for generations that connected modern Apaches to their past. The tribes argued that it must be protected; and one way to protect the space against outside interference and show reverence was not to speak about it. The belief was that the time-tested sacredness of the space was self-evident and beyond argument.

The astronomers and the scientific community, on the other hand, regarded the site as ideal for astronomical research: the sky was clear most of the time, it was elevated, it was away from light pollution, and it was near to a major university. Yet, when the scientific community tried to engage the Apache leaders, they were met with silence. While the Apache leaders enacted silence to revere and protect, the scientists interpreted their behavior as indicating a lack of knowledge and a disregard for progress. This is an example of a problem of **mutual intelligibility** (Carbaugh & Wolf, 2000, p. 21). Mutual intelligibility refers to the common meanings and interests people share in order to understand each other. Mutual intelligibility is necessary for identification. This case illustrates the importance of notions of time in framing the significance of places and determining uses for places. When rhetoric is practiced from traditions that are very different from one another, mediating disputes is difficult.

While several telescopes have been operating on Mount Graham (*Dzil Nchaa Si An*, in Apache) since the 1990s and a new Large Binocular Telescope (LBT) was dedicated in 2004, Native American and environmental groups continue to seek limitations on the use of the site (Saunders, 2010).

A second example reveals how rhetorical traditions influence advocacy. Competing notions of time are captured by the metaphors "time's arrow" and "time's cycle" (Lake, 1991). The arrow represents linear time and the mainstream Euro-American values that are associated with it: social progress, improvement, development, and innovation. The cycle represents circular time and several prevalent Native American values: the natural world and its rhythms, the knowledge of myths and rituals handed down from the past, and the interdependence of all things (often symbolized by the hoop). Notably, this circular view of time of Native Americans in the United States is very similar to a cyclical and natural view of time held by Aboriginals in Australia (Silverman, 1997).

These distinct metaphors converged as the U.S. government and Native American protesters clashed in 1973 at Wounded Knee, South Dakota. Members of the American Indian Movement (AIM) occupied Wounded Knee for 71 days to protest the terrible living condition on the Pine Ridge Reservation. AIM members protested the leadership of Richard A. Wilson, tribal chair of the reservation, whom they accused of nepotism in steering the few jobs available on the reservation to family and friends. The U.S. government deployed troops, weapons, and vehicles to Wounded Knee to force out the protesters. The troops killed two protesters, and one U.S. Marshall was wounded by a gunshot.

Our interest in rhetorical communication focuses our attention to the ways in which participants frame their purposes and actions. The mainstream Euro-American perspective portrays Native American activism as "hopelessly out-of-date," since society has moved on (Lake, 1991, p. 129). From the perspective of time's arrow, history cannot be changed and what matters is what is done today, rather than dwelling on the past. Rhetorically, this allowed the government to dismiss the grievances of the protestors and make their unlawfulness the main factor for consideration and response.

From the perspective of time's cycle, the material conditions at Pine Ridge warranted action, but equally important was the need to restore tribal identity; that is, to reconnect tribal ways to the past. As imposed from the larger society, the poverty on the reservation interrupted the observance of ritual, breaking the circle of tradition. Protest rhetoric was concerned with transcendent meanings—meanings that encompassed past, present, and future—in ways the government and the general public could not understand. In seeking to restore time's endless cycle, the protesters at Wounded Knee enacted "a group-tribalistic approach to life, [where] time is meaningless" (Lake, 1991, p. 135).

Western tradition: Rooted in argument

The Greek philosopher Aristotle has had an enduring and immense influence on Western politics, ethics and communication. In *The Rhetoric* (Cooper, 1960), he made a distinction that would be reflected in public speaking for more than two millennia. For Aristotle, **dialectic** was the formal objective method of reasoning and arriving at truthful claims, and "rhetoric" was the "counterpart of dialectic," that is, **rhetoric** was the discovery of the means for persuading an audience that would include "common knowledge and accepted opinions" (Cooper, 1960, p. 6). This distinction between dialectic and rhetoric made the latter a practical art. The skilled persuader was a person who understood audience values and preferences and who could establish credibility and goodwill with an audience. In seeking agreement with one's position, the speaker implicitly attacked all other positions. The adversarial model for public deliberation was launched as Aristotle advised: "You have to upset the opposite hypothesis, and frame your discourse against that as if it were your opponent" (p. 141).

Today, this practical, competitive, and objective approach to public speaking remains. This Western speech tradition is sometimes referred to as the Euro-American or dominant-culture speech tradition. Several contemporary qualities of speech consistent with this tradition are: self-assertive and goal-oriented statements; the desire to be right; a preference for objective information; and a future-oriented perspective. Public speaking classes today cover audience analysis, building credibility, anticipating and addressing counter arguments, use of evidence, and other topics that originate with the Greek formulations of effective persuasion.

So foundational is the analytical nature of the Western rhetoric that intercultural scholars occasionally warn of its limitations. For example, Hall (1976/1989) remarked that "we Westerners . . . find ourselves deeply preoccupied with specifics . . . to the exclusion of everything else" (p. 123). Hall's point is that because scientific or logical demonstration involves precise and controlled conditions, it is almost impossible to think and argue in a way that integrates conclusions from various ways of knowing. *An Inconvenient Truth*, the 2006 Academy Award-winning documentary film with former U.S. Vice President Al Gore, was impressive not because it presented different bodies of knowledge that holistically converged on a conclusion of global warming, but for the overwhelming amount of scientific data on global changes. The documentary also was impressive in the way it presented a seemingly inescapable future vision of a depleted planet. The persuasiveness of the argument was anchored in three very powerful Western cultural values: science, the future, and casual delivery.

If we return to the contrast between time's arrow and time's cycle, we see that the Western tradition of linear time privileges the future and treats the Native American past as savage and outdated (Lake, 1991). The competitive model of argument does not seek accommodation. It seeks a winner, locking the U.S. government and indigenous concerns in an either/or conflict: each side is either right or wrong. Similarly, the conflict at Mount Graham reveals that the scientists and the broader community in Tucson required a "precise explanation" from the Apaches of the mountain's significance (Carbaugh & Wolf, 2000, p. 22) making a historical or spiritual account unacceptable. In other words, the community in power sought an argument it could recognize rather than an argument the Apaches could deliver.

In the U.S., the examination of the invisible and assumed centrality of Western power is known as Whiteness Studies. This work attempts to reveal the ways in which Whiteness—as a social position—exerts privilege (Nakayama & Krizek, 1995). For example, when NBA Commissioner David Stern imposed a dress code in 2005 that mandated suits and ties and prohibited hip-hop style clothing, he claimed race had nothing to do with his decision. In the face of opposition from African American players, Stern was able to mask any accusation of racism by claiming that it was appropriate for management to expect that players have a "traditional" business appearance. Yet he reinforced racist stereotypes about African Americans when he claimed that the European American (White) business look would improve the NBA's reputation and the urban look would hurt the NBA's reputation (Griffin & Calafell, 2011, p. 127). Similarly, the television sitcom *Friends* has been interpreted to represent the inherent goodness of Whiteness, as the characters lead largely superficial and privileged lives while maintaining a non-diverse circle of friends (Chidester, 2008). This criticism can also be directed toward a more recent television show, *Girls*.

The Western speech tradition and performances of Whiteness are powerful in their prescriptive force and in their ubiquitous quality. When high school officials in suburban Washington, D.C. refused to award Thomas Benya his diploma because the bolo tie he wore to commencement was not considered a "traditional" tie (Manning, 2005), the officials uncritically reinforced the management/worker divide created during the Industrial Revolution, which made the knotted tie the sign of authority and success. The competitive speech model, the preference for objective data as evidence, and the future orientation of speeches emerge from particular cultural values that have been made universal. As practitioners of intercultural communication, we always must be aware of the dominant culture practices and what these practices imply for our interactions with those who speak from speech traditions of their own.

Limitations when considering rhetorical traditions

The concept of the rhetorical tradition is very useful when considering the relationships among rhetoric, culture, and intercultural communication. As with all explanatory tools, there are some precautions. Rhetorical traditions, especially those that span centuries (like Chinese, Arabic, and European traditions) change over time. Traditions—their meaning and significance—are themselves subject to perspective and interpretation. For example, Garrett reminds us that "the Chinese tradition" had different emphases in different dynasties; sometimes Confucianism guided discourse and at other times Buddhism guided discourse (Garrett, 2000, p. 60). Contemporary Chinese discourse is guided by a blend of previous emphases.

Further, Garrett observes that the discourse we would consult to construct the Chinese rhetorical tradition was written by the elite for the elite. The historical record emerges from the concerns and interests of the "well-off, educated, male elite" (p. 60). In other words, it only partially reflects Chinese thought and practice.

Finally, in approaching contemporary Chinese rhetoric, how do we distinguish what is genuinely Chinese from Western influence? This question applies to African rhetoric as well. The "I am African" speech delivered by Thabo Mbeki in 1996 was inspired as much by the "Camelot vision" of the Kennedy presidency as by traditional South African influences (Sheckels, 2010). The lesson here is that any "tradition" is never as straightforward as we might suspect. As students of culture and inclusion, we are obligated to interrogate and acknowledge the selective quality of traditions.

ON THE NET

Search an online speech bank for a speech from someone in a country or co-culture besides your own. Think about the content of the speech and how the speaker tries to persuade the audience. Do you see evidence of the types of rhetorical traditions represented here? How is the speech different in style, structure, and type of argument than the rhetorical tradition in your own country?

There are different speech databases to choose from. For example, http.thespeechsite.com contains transcripts of speeches from Malcolm X, Aung San Suu Kyi, and Sadako Ogata, as well as student speeches from several countries. http://americanrhetoric.com has text, audio, or visual reproduction of more than 5000 speeches; its databank, which lists speakers alphabetically, provides links to speeches by Elie Wiesel, Dmitry Medvevev, Rev. Al Sharpton, Coretta Scott King, Mother Theresa, Swami Vivekananda, Zainab Al-Suwaij, and many others. BlatantWorld.com specifically focuses on world social issues; its "speeches" link (http://www.blatantworld.com/speeches.html) gives access to speeches from different parts of the world. Or you might find other databases that give speeches of a particular speaker, such as Martin Luther King, Jr. (http://www.mlkonline.net/speeches.html).

Vernacular rhetoric: How does everyday communication seek to persuade?

While an understanding of rhetorical traditions is important in placing a speech or text in a cultural context, another exciting concept is also available. **Vernacular discourse** refers to locally produced meanings; that is, speech that has been adapted to audiences to elicit persuasion or cooperation by taking the form of the everyday communication of the community in which the speech occurs. Critical focus is upon marginalized communities because vernacular discourse "makes visible power relations among subjects" (Calafell & Delgado, 2004, p. 6). Since local meanings often function persuasively to mediate relationships between marginalized and dominant communities, we also use the term **vernacular rhetoric**.

Vernacular rhetoric in Africa

In the early 2000s, the Feminist International Radio Endeavor (FIRE) expanded its South American operations to Sub-Saharan Africa. The goal of FIRE was to facilitate community radio broadcasting that centered on women's voices and women's issues (Gatua *et al.*, 2010). Through a variety of means, including audiotapes, or recorded content, and the Internet, FIRE created programming for tens of thousands of women and their families.

The programs created by FIRE contained many vernacular elements. In countries such as Kenya, Nigeria, Uganda, Burundi, and Congo, FIRE used community radio to promote local issues in locally understood ways. Radio in Africa remains an affordable, accessible, and versatile communication medium. First, FIRE sponsored workshops to train women journalists. Many African countries have no independent media, only state-owned media.

The FIRE-trained journalists are aware of community issues, and know how to create independent content for local media. Second, the program content reflects community issues. Circumstances vary across the continent. At times, information about food, employment, and health may be most important. At other times, illiteracy and general education may be most important. Community radio can quickly address topics that are immediately relevant to the community. Third, programs were recorded and broadcast in local dialects. UNESCO estimates that there are more than 2000 languages and 4000 dialects spoken on the continent. FIRE recorded programs in the dialect of the community as opposed to a "standard" dialect. This ensured that a maximum number of listeners would be able to understand the information delivered (Gatua *et al.* 2010).

A second example of vernacular rhetoric in Africa is the Knowledge Center project in Ihiala, Nigeria (Ha *et al.*, 2008). This project provided free Internet service to the people of Ihiala. A special website was established that allowed farmers to share information with each other. The farmers found the website to be informative and enjoyable since the local knowledge of the community was the basis of its content. The farmers were able to socialize via the website using references to places, people and events that were well understood.

FIRE and the Knowledge Center engaged in vernacular rhetoric as they empowered communities to respond to self-identified priorities. Further, the community members engaged radio and the website to persuade the community to avoid infection, read more, or grow better crops, in their own dialect and with well-understood community meanings. These practices often resist larger government structures that centralize the needs of capital cities and urban areas to the neglect of smaller and remote villages.

POP CULTURE

With its Creole imagery, King Cakes and Krewes, Mardi Gras is a ritual that is truly identified with New Orleans (Figure 9.3). Mardi Gras is an example of a vernacular celebration. What vernacular celebrations surround you?

Figure 9.3 Mardi Gras is a local celebration on the eve of the Christian Lenten period. Source: Atlantide Phototravel/Corbis.

Figure 9.4 Pagne. The pagne worn by African women reflect positions on local and national politics.
Source: Antoine Gyori/Sygma/ Corbis.

A third example of vernacular rhetoric also comes from the Sub-Saharan region of Africa. In this example, the main rhetorical medium is clothing. *Pagne* refers to the cloth worn by women in Western Africa (Figure 9.4). Women in the African nation of Côte d'Ivoire communicate their perspectives on a variety of local issues through pagne designs (Hagan, 2010).

Each pagne is given a name in the local marketplace. The women who sell them suggest names for each pagne to the customers. After several tries, a name is agreed upon by the woman buying the pagne and the purchase is completed. Pagne names can be associated with well-known proverbs, political positions and even specific political personalities. By wearing a pagne, the woman may visually express her support for equity and fairness when her verbal support may be prohibited. Pagne can indicate the status of the wearer, since pagne elements (imported or local, fancy or plain, etc.) convey information about the social class of the wearer (Hagan, 2010, p. 150).

The pagne works rhetorically to mediate relations between men and women. In many postcolonial nations, traditional African kinship structures in which women's roles were valued were replaced by European structures that privileged male participation. The woman signifies her support for traditional communal structures through the pagne she wears. As vernacular rhetoric, pagne is a way for women in a community to critique and resist patriarchy and the slowness of government reform.

Vernacular rhetoric in South Toledo, Ohio

The Old South End of Toledo, Ohio, is generally known as a lower working-class neighborhood. Its residents are mostly Latino and African American. The neighborhood sits south of the downtown area and it is bordered on the south by the Maumee River. A traveler driving south on Broadway enters the South End by passing through the I-75 freeway underpass. The underpass serves as an informal gateway into the neighborhood and it serves for most Toledoans as a symbolic reminder of the marginalized status of the community.

Figure 9.5 This mural in the Old South End of Toledo, Ohio, provides an interpretation of the local Latina/o experience.
Source: Reproduced courtesy of Bowling Green State University.

In 2010, local artists and art students from a nearby university painted a mural on one of the pylons underneath I-75 along Broadway Avenue. A casual glance at the mural reveals images that are instantly recognizable: Frida Kahlo, Cesar Chavez, Emiliano Zapata (Figure 9.5). But a closer look reveals local references: a cardinal (the state bird of Ohio), a nearby suspension bridge, a barge hauling grain up the nearby Maumee River, and a nearby church. The significance of these references might not be understood to an out-of-town visitor, but they would be known to a Toledo resident.

Further, the mural displays the faces of two prominent Latina activists: Aurora González and Sofia Quintero. Both women worked to improve the living conditions of residents of South Toledo and were very influential in local government. Also, the mural displays— front and center—the *calavera* (skull) character that many observers associate with the religious observance of *Dia de los Muertos* (Day of the Dead). The *calavera* character originated in early 20th century Mexico to critique the excesses of the European-influenced Mexican bourgeoisie. Together with the faces of González and Quintero, the *calavera* delivers a local commentary on the social and economic marginalization of South Toledo.

Obviously, we are receptive to persuasive communication that does not have us specifically in mind. Many political messages and advertisements are created far away from us and are directed to general publics. Still, in response to these messages, we might make a campaign contribution, volunteer for a charitable cause, or buy a product. Television or web messages can be so common that we might not notice persuasion that has nearby origins. Further, we might not notice the special power of vernacular discourse. A recent study of the community impact of murals in Philadelphia, Pennsylvania, identified the special influence of locally created art:

1   Murals that closely matched the input of the nearby residents were most favorably received.

2   Affirming or positive images in the murals tended to smooth over conflicts among diverse identities.

3 Murals encouraged a sense of neighborhood pride and delight.

4 Murals encouraged a sense of empowerment and resistance to negative forces outside the neighborhood.
(Adapted from Moss, 2010)

Vernacular rhetorics are important in the study of intercultural communication, because they lead us to the distinctive and highly detailed meanings of cultures. Those images, slogans, or other appeals that are invented locally have much to offer the outsider. Recognizing those appeals and asking residents about their significance will allow us to better understand communities that are new to us.

Intercultural rhetoric: What are the implications for civic engagement?

In the spring of 2011, a wave of revolt broke over the Middle East. In Tunisia, Egypt, Syria, and Yemen, governments were pressured to reform. In Bahrain, Morocco, and Mauritania, protests surprised leaders and the international community. The revolt in Libya against the 30-year rule of Colonel Moammar Gadhafi was the most violent. As Gadhafi refused to concede, protests turned into armed conflict. From all of these protests, a single face emerged whose story seemed to summarize the repression many in Libya experienced. Eman al-Obeidy claimed that, in the early days of the revolt, she had been assaulted and raped by Gadhafi's soldiers. She was arrested after making her accusations and later released (Figure 9.6). Gadhafi's representatives countered by labeling al-Obeidy a drug user and prostitute. News video showed al-Obeidy being slapped and pushed by government repre-

Figure 9.6 Protesters in the Middle East reach across cultures to gain support for the freedom of Iman al-Obeidy. Source: Chip Somodevilla/Getty Images.

sentatives at a news conference. In an interview with Anderson Cooper on CNN in early April 2011, al-Obeidy described her brutal treatment and her fear. Then she asked to speak directly to the U.S. viewers. "We are a peaceful people," she began, "and we are not members of al-Qaeda. We are a peaceful people and we are moderate Muslims, not extremists, and we are not asking for anything except for our freedom" (CNN, 2011.)

If we scan our environment, we will observe that people from cultures and nations other than our own are attempting to persuade us. People are attempting to build relationships with us and they invite us to consider new ways to understand the world through arguments, testimonies, and powerful images. These communicative actions are intercultural rhetoric. In the case of Iman al-Obeidy (also spelled Eman al-Obeidi), we see that she was attempting to build identification with U.S. viewers through a familiar and admirable narrative: standing up to tyranny for the cause of freedom. In effectively reaching across significant cultural differences, she was able to build support for U.S. and NATO military actions in Libya.

Communication scholars have reflected upon the possibilities for civic engagement in the communities where they conduct their research. While typically working in situations less severe than that faced by al-Obeidy, activist-scholars have an opportunity to take "action that attempts to make a positive difference in situations where people's lives are affected by oppression . . . conflict, and other forms of cultural struggle" (Broome *et al.*, 2005, p. 146). Many of us who have studied rhetorical communication (perhaps as undergraduate or graduate students) are in a position to assist local nonprofit organizations or neighborhood community centers. As volunteers, we might assist residents by holding public speaking workshops, evaluating arguments in petitions or other documents, writing announcements for the local media, teaching interviewing techniques, or conducting an audience analysis in advance of a public forum. As with al-Obeidy, these activities often require us to reach effectively across cultural divides.

To work productively as an intercultural advocate involves several key considerations. The primary orientation is an ethic of **speaking with** members of a community in one's efforts to advance issues important to them (Alcoff, 1991), rather than speaking to them.

"Speaking with" means that the advocate understands and accepts the common knowledge of a community through extensive contact with its members. The advocate is allied with the interests—the "real issues"—of the community, and works with its members on issues the members have identified as important (Broome *et al.*, 2005, p. 169). The ethic of speaking with includes the following guides:

1   Begin, proceed, and end honestly and respectfully.

2   Enter into active dialogue and participation with community residents.

3   Seek to understand the broader social structures that silence the community or suppress its interests.

4   Be prepared to challenge those structures at public meetings or in public forums.

5   Assist and facilitate the expression of those who do not have access to communication media.

6   Be willing to reciprocate; that is, share your academic knowledge when appropriate, but never consider it "better than" local knowledge.
    (Adapted from Broome *et al.*, 2005)

Maybe some day we will have the chance to reach across cultural lines as global citizens. We may be faced with empowering Latin American and African women to use radio programming to help their communities or maybe we will be faced with asking residents in an urban neighborhood about the kinds of images they would like to see painted on the sides of buildings and homes. In the same vein, maybe someone in another culture will need to reach across lines to help us in some way, either in terms of material goods or to understanding things about our own culture that we cannot see from our perspective. Successfully meeting these goals interculturally—learning to speak with— requires us to learn about new sources of influence and new ways to create identification.

Summary

In this chapter, we have learned that rhetoric and culture are closely bound concepts. Rhetorical communication is designed to persuade people to accept an action or belief. Rhetorical communication can also be designed to mediate relationships and contrasting beliefs. Identification is a key rhetorical strategy. Identification means promoting a common identity that then allows cooperation and harmony. Identification is the remedy to division.

There is no single standard for persuasion and mediation. Cultures produce distinctive rhetorical traditions. What counts as believable and influential varies from culture to culture. Intercultural rhetoric refers to situations where at least two rhetorical traditions meet. When Dr. Martin Luther King, Jr. gave the "I Have A Dream" speech in Washington, D.C. in 1964, the vernacular rhetoric of southern African American preachers met Euro-American expectations. This speech continues to be an example of successful intercultural rhetoric because listeners from various cultural backgrounds understand, accept, and are inspired by King's imagery and delivery.

For successful civic engagement, we should have an awareness of the rhetorical traditions that influence how community members seek to persuade others. Practicing an ethic of speaking with community members means that our interests are aligned with those of community members. Speaking with also obligations us to understand and challenge inequities that disadvantage the community.

KEY TERMS

identification, 181

division, 181

rhetoric, 181

rhetorical action, 181

rhetorical communication, 181

rhetorical tradition, 182

intercultural rhetoric, 183

paralanguage, 184

mutual intelligibility, 190

dialectic, 191

vernacular discourse, 193

vernacular rhetoric, 193

speaking with, 198

Discussion questions

1   How do you attempt to create identification with others? In social settings? At work? At school? Do you think about how others are attempting to create identification with you?

2   Make a list of three public figures you admire. What rhetorical tradition (or traditions) helps to explain how these individuals relate to audiences? What rhetorical tradition guides what these individuals say and do?

3   What is the presence of vernacular terms and meanings on Facebook? On YouTube?

4   Have you ever *spoken with* members of a community on a particular issue? How did you build the relationship? What was the outcome?

Action points

1   In 2010, members of the Iroquois lacrosse team were denied travel to England to compete in the lacrosse world championships. To respect the sovereignty of their native nation—the Iroquois Confederacy—team members would not obtain U.S. passports. Yet due to new rules by Homeland Security, the U.S. and England required that team members have U.S.-issued identification. Research this case. How did this situation end?

2   Conduct a Google search for Mount Graham. Why is this a unique location for Native Americans, scientists, and environmentalists? What current actions are underway to resist development of this area?

3   Pick a local magazine or newspaper and look through its advertisements. How can you tell the local advertisements from the chain or national advertisements? Do the local advertisements reflect "what everybody knows" about your area?

For more information

Hagan, M.A. (2006). Culture, communication, and identity in the Cote d'Ivoire: *Le pagne parle*. In M.P. Orbe, B.J. Allen, & L.A. Flores (Eds.), *The same and different: Acknowledging the diversity between and within cultural groups* (pp. 193–125). Washington, D.C.: National Communication Association.

Joseph, W.A., Wong, C., & Zweig, D. (Eds.). (1991). *New perspectives on the cultural revolution.* Cambridge: Harvard University Press.

Meisner, M. (2007). *Mao Zedong: A political and intellectual portrait.* Cambridge: Polity.

Rogers, R.A. (2009). "Your guess is as good as any": Indeterminacy, dialogue, and dissemination in interpretations of Native American rock art. *Journal of International and Intercultural Communication, 2,* 44–65.

Shi, Y. (2008). Chinese immigrant women workers: Everyday forms of resistance and "coagulate politics". *Communication and Critical/Cultural Studies, 5,* 363–382.

Sorrells, K., & Nakagawa, G. (2008). Intercultural communication *praxis* and the struggle for social responsibility and social justice. In O. Swartz, (Ed.), *Transformative Communication studies: Culture, hierarchy and the human condition* (pp. 17–43). Leicester, UK: Troubador Press.

References

Alcoff, L. (1991). The problem of speaking for others. *Cultural Critique, 20,* 5–33.

Asante, M.K. (1980). *Afrocentricity: The theory of social change.* Buffalo, NY: Amulefi Publishing.

Burke, K. (1969). *A rhetoric of motives*. Berkeley, CA: University of California Press.

Broome, B., Carey, C., De la Garza, S. A., Martin, J.M., and Morris, R. (2005). "In the thick of things": A dialogue about the activist turn in intercultural communication. In W.J. Starosta & G. Chen (Eds.), *Taking stock in intercultural communication: Where to now?* (pp. 145–175). Washington, DC: National Communication Association.

Cai, B., & González, A. (1997). The Three Gorges Project: Technological discourse and the resolution of competing interests, *Journal of Intercultural Communication, 7*, 101–111.

Calafell, B.M., & Delgado, F.P. (2004). Reading Latina/o images: Interrogating *Americanos. Critical Studies in Media Communication, 21*, 1–21.

Carbaugh, D., & Wolf, K. (2000). Situating rhetoric in cultural discourses. In A. González & D.V. Tanno (Eds.). *Rhetoric in intercultural contexts* (pp. 19–30). Thousand Oaks, CA: Sage.

Chidester, P. (2008). May the circle stay unbroken: *Friends*, the presence of absence, and the rhetorical reinforcement of whiteness. *Critical Studies in Media Communication, 25*, 157–174.

CNN (2011). Alleged Libyan rape victim speaks out. *Anderson Cooper 360*. Accessed April 23, 2011, at http://www.cnn.com/video/data/2.0/video/world/2011/04/05/ac.woman.talks.pt2.cnn.html

Collins, P.H. (1989). The social construction of Black feminist thought. *Signs: Journal of Women in Culture and Society, 14*, 745–773.

Cooper, L. (Tr.) (1960). *The rhetoric of Aristotle*. Englewood Cliffs, NJ: Prentice-Hall.

Ferriss, S., & Sandoval, R. (1997). *The fight in the fields: Cesar Chavez and the farmworkers movement*. New York, NY: Harcourt Brace.

Garrett, M.M. (2000). Some elementary methodological reflections on the study of the Chinese rhetorical tradition. In A. González & D. V. Tanno (Eds.). *Rhetoric in intercultural contexts* (pp. 53–63). Thousand Oaks, CA: Sage.

Garrett, M.M., & Xiao, X. (1994). The rhetorical situation revisited. *Rhetoric and Society Quarterly, 23*, 30–40.

Gatua, M.W., Patton, T.O., & Brown, M.R. (2010). Giving voice to invisible women: "FIRE" as model of a successful women's community radio in Africa. *The Howard Journal of Communications, 21*(2), 164–181.

González, A. (1989) "Participation" at WMEX-FM: Interventional rhetoric of Ohio Mexican Americans. *Western Journal of Communication, 53*, 398–410.

Griffin, R.A., & Calafell, B.M. (2011). Control, disipline, and punish: Black masculinity and (in)visible whiteness in the NBA. In M.G. Lacy & K.A. Ono (Eds.). *Critical rhetorics of race* (pp. 117–136). New York, NY: NYU Press.

Ha, L., Okigbo, R.N., & Igboaka, P. (2008). Knowledge creation and dissemination in sub-Saharan Africa. *Management Decision, 46*, 392–405.

Hagan, M.A. (2010). Speaking out: Women, *pagne*, and politics in the Cote d'Ivoire. *The Howard Journal of Communication, 21*, 141–163.

Hall, E.T. (1976/1989). *Beyond culture*. New York, NY: Anchor Books.

Hamlet, J. (2011). The reason why we sing: Understanding traditional African American worship. In A. González, M. Houston, & V. Chen (Eds.). *Our voices: Essays in culture, ethnicity, and communication*, (5th ed., pp. 112–117). New York, NY: Oxford University Press.

Hammerback, J.C., & Jensen, R.J. (1994). Ethnic heritage as rhetorical legacy: The Plan of Delano. *Quarterly Journal of Speech, 80*, 53–70.

Herrick, J.A. (2009). *The history and theory of rhetoric: An introduction*. (4th ed.) Boston: MA: Allyn & Bacon.

Huang, S., (1997). Ritual, culture, and communication: Deification of Mao Zedong in China's cultural revolution movement. In A. González & D.V. Tanno (Eds.), *Politics, communication, and culture* (pp. 122–140). Thousand Oaks, CA: Sage.

Jackson, J. (1988). Common ground and common sense. *Vital Speeches of the Day, 54*, 649–653.

Johnson, F.L. (2000). *Speaking culturally: Language diversity in the United States*. Thousand Oaks, CA: Sage.

Lake, R.A. (1991). Between myth and history: Enacting time in Native American protest rhetoric. *Quarterly Journal of Speech, 77*, 123–151.

Manning, S. (2005). Bolo tie creates bind for graduating senior. *The Seattle Times*, June 11. Accessed March 25, 2013, at http://seattletimes.com/html/education/2002329323_tie11.html

Moss, K.L. (2010). Cultural representation in Philadelphia murals: Images of resistance and sites of identity negotiation. *Western Journal of Communication, 74*, 372–395.

Nakayama, T.K., & Krizek, R. (1995). Whiteness: A strategic rhetoric. *Quarterly Journal of Speech, 81*, 291–309.

Paz, O. (1961). *The Labyrinth of Solitude: Life and thought in Mexico*. (Trans. L. Kemp.) New York: Grove Press.

Paz, O. (1972). *The other Mexico: Critique of the pyramid*. (Trans. L. Kemp.) New York: Grove Press.

Philipsen, G. (1992). *Speaking culturally: Explorations in social communication*. Albany: SUNY Press.

Saunders, D. (Sept. 29, 2010). Apache opposes telescope permit renewal. *Mount Graham Coalition*, September 29. Accessed on March 27, 2011, at http://www.mountgraham.org/

Sheckels, T.F. (2010). The rhetorical success of Thabo Mbeki's 1996 "I Am an African" address. *Communication Quarterly, 57,* 319–333.

Shutiva, C. (2012). Native American culture and communication through humor. In A. González, M. Houston, & V. Chen (Eds.), *Our voices: Essays in culture, ethnicity and communication* (5th ed., pp. 134–138). New York: Oxford University Press.

Silverman, E.K. (1997). Politics, gender, and time in Melanesia and Aboriginal Australia. *Ethnology, 36*(2), 101–122.

Smith, A. (1970). Socio-historical perspectives of Black oratory. *Quarterly Journal of Speech, 56,* 264–269.

Starosta, W.J., & Coleman, L. (1986). Jesse Jackson's "Hymietown" apology: A case study of interethnic rhetorical analysis. In Y.Y. Kim (Ed.), *Interethnic communication* (pp. 117–135). Beverly Hills: Sage.

Sullivan, P.A. (1993). Signification and African-American rhetoric: A case study of Jesse Jackson's "Common Ground and Common Sense" speech. *Communication Quarterly, 41,* 1–15.

Teiwes, F.C. (2010). Mao and his followers. In T. Cheek (Ed.), *A critical introduction to Mao* (pp. 129–157). New York: Cambridge University Press.

Weaver, M.S. (1991). Makers and redeemers: The theatricality of the Black Church. *Black American Literature Forum, 25,* 53–62.

Xiao, X. (1995). China encounters Darwinism: A case of intercultural rhetoric. *Quarterly Journal of Speech, 81,* 83–99.

Zhong, M. (2003). Contemporary social and political movements and their imprints on the Chinese language. In L.A. Samovar & R.E. Porter (Eds.), *Intercultural communication: A reader* (10th ed., pp. 206–223). Belmont, CA: Wadsworth.

Chapter 10

Culture, communication, and media:
How do media shape our views of others?

Chapter objectives

After this chapter, you should be able to:

→ Compare mediated communication to face-to-face communication

→ Outline Lasswell's model of mediated communication

→ Contrast the transmission and the ritual views of media communication

→ Evaluate the role media communication plays in terms of intercultural communication

→ Define the notion of the public sphere and understand its implications for us as citizens

→ Apply media framing to the representation of a particular identity, such as gender

→ Discuss ways in which media can distort our image of people of different cultures or groups, but can also be used in social and political action

Effects and rituals: What role do media play in our lives?

Democratic discourse and diversity: What issues do media present to me as a citizen?

Media and cultural identities: Who are "we" now?

Beyond traditional media: How do new media and culture shape each other?

Intercultural Communication for Everyday Life, First Edition. John R. Baldwin, Robin R. Means Coleman, Alberto González, and Suchitra Shenoy-Packer.
© 2014 John R. Baldwin, Robin R. Means Coleman, Alberto González, and Suchitra Shenoy-Packer.
Published 2014 by John Wiley & Sons Ltd.

edia complicate our fundamental understandings of communication as a message sent from a sender to a receiver. We can explore the nature of mediated communication more fully with a provocative communication example from a 2009 headline appearing in Cambodia's *Phnom Penh Post* (Rith, 2009):

Hun Sen Decries Reliance on Foreign Styles in the Arts: Premier Says Cambodian Artists should Reflect Khmer Tradition rather than Incorporating "Other Countries' Styles" in their Work.

This newspaper headline evidences just how quickly mapping the communication process can turn complicated. For example, we can ask, "Who is the sender of the message?" and in doing so come up with several answers—the Premier Hun Sen, or the author of the article or, perhaps, the newspaper editor, or even the newspaper itself!

Effects and rituals: What role do media play in our lives?

Lasswell's model of (mediated) communication

Harold Lasswell (1948/1967) suggests that sorting out communication patterns requires an understanding that they occur on multiple, often circuitous levels, rather than a single, linear one. Lasswell asks—and poses as a model (sometimes called **Lasswell's model of communication**) to media researchers—this multi-part question: "Who, says what, in which channel, to whom, with what effect?"

In the earlier headline from the *Phnom Penh Post*, unlike face-to-face models (chapter 2) that would focus on the premier as the sender and the reporter as the receiver, Lasswell's model is concerned with effects of mediated messages. The reporter becomes the "who," though there may be other "who's," such as the newspaper editor who is also filtering the message. The reporter covers "what" the premier has told the reporter. The reporter delivers this message to the reading audience ("whom") through coverage of the premier's remarks in the "channel" of the *Post*. The *Post* can also be understood using the language of a "medium"—a technological agent that facilitates the dissemination of a message. Again, the overall "effect" is unknown, but we do know of one desired effect, which is to *inform* readers of the premier's sentiments. The point of the model is that, if we change the who (e.g., the UK's BBC or Qatar's Al Jazeera as opposed to *The Phnom Penh Post*), the channel (e.g., print versus online versions of the paper), the what (the content of the report, presence of images, and so on), or other elements, the message might have different effects. Some add that we must also consider the context of the message to understand effects. For our purposes, the context could be the culture of the sending and receipt of a given message, but as we consider sex, ethnicity, and other within-cultural divisions as relevant cultural contexts, it must also consider the political, social, and cultural power contexts within the boundaries of a nation (Lee & Baldwin, 2004).

Today's media climate makes Lasswell's approach, just like the information-sending model it parallels (chapter 3), too simple. About a century ago, media researchers theorized about the notion of direct effects—how media have a strong and direct influence on an audience that is perceived to be pretty passive and homogenous. Now they take a more complex view. One modification is a two-step flow of media, where media influence our opinion leaders, like doctors, teachers, and politicians. But most recent views see the effects of media flowing both from media to opinion leaders to individuals, and back the other way, with media impacting governments and cultures, cultures impacting media, individuals influencing and being influenced by their social networks, and, with increasing participation and new media, having effects directly on media outlets. On many online news sources, for example, countless posts from readers follow the story, framing and modifying our understanding of it. This is relevant for culture; as **media dependency theory** suggests, people's reliance on the media is influenced by—but also influences—their social networks, which are, in turn, influenced by (and influence) the complexity of society and the role of media in society in general (deFleur & Ball-Rokeach, 1982).

The transmission view versus the ritual view

Communication theorist James Carey (1989) describes Lasswell's model of the process of communication as the "transmission view" of communication. The **transmission view of media communication** is defined by terms such as imparting, sending, giving, or *transmitting* information from sender(s) to receiver(s). Carey's transmission view, like Lasswell's model, accounts for the presence of mass media. However, Carey adds that, frequently, beyond the transmission of messages, or even broadcast or digital signals, communication has a vital ability to *control*. When Carey talks of *control*, he is referring to communication's ability to manage and manipulate barriers such as distance or time. The impacts of mass communication can be far-reaching and not limited by space or geography. This also means that communication can take control of time. That is, communication need not be limited by time of day or time zones. Writers in different areas of theory talk about how media might be related to overt control and power plays, such as in the radio airing of Stalinist Communist messages, and then democratic ideological messages in the 1956 uprising in Hungary (Szemere, 1992). The control can also be through shaping ideology. Even media coverage differs, such as in the way American and Japanese media framed "3/11," the 2012 earthquake and tsunami that hit Japan (Chattopadhyay, 2012).

Importantly, Carey argues that there is an even more complex way to think about communication—the **ritual view of media communication**. The ritual view of communication includes the transmission view but adds a definition of communication as a sense of interactivity. Communication is not one-way. It is embedded in culture and is marked by cultural dynamics such as participation, fellowship, association, and commonness. In this innovative, extended version, Carey maintains that communication relies upon and circulates shared constructions of social meaning and representations of shared beliefs. Communication necessarily involves and influences common patterns of behavior, interactions, and that which is deemed socially and culturally significant, rather than merely passing on information. This means that communication projects a society's ideals and is part of how people live as social beings. Mass media embody the material form of these ideals by putting them into news stories, music recordings, situation comedies, and the like. As such, media not only describe, but also shape our evolving social world and our practices as people. At the same time, because the ritual view sees media reality as social and participative, it also allows room for social action and change, as people influence that view.

The ritual view allows us to consider the role and function of media in intercultural communication in more depth. It helps us to understand how media facilitate the production of our cultural realities and, consequently, how we live within and under those realities. The ritual view challenges us to bear in mind not only the transmission of information, but also the deeper meanings behind that information, why it's being elaborated and shared, and what it suggests about the source of that information's view of the world. Specifically, the ritual view, when applied to questions around the presentation of cultures, asks: How are our cultural understandings created or mediated? How do media construct cultural messages? That is, how do they select foci, assemble the message, and present it?

The role of media in intercultural communication

When media decide how to tell stories about the world, from particular perspectives and with particular facts highlighted as key, they impact culture and communication in at least three ways. First, one culture's frames—or interpretive terms of reference that shape how one understands a story—may impact the understandings of other cultures or nations, for good or harm. For example, foreign visitors to the United States may expect the country to look like the places in Hollywood movies. If the settings of popular films tend to show upper-class neighborhoods in New York or California, visitors may expect all of the country to fit this frame of America as affluent and opulent. Second, media create *frames that we use to understand cultural difference* within our own society. For example, mediated representations of Latinos within the United States tend to focus on several levels of difference, some of which can affect policies. Some stories about Latinos focus on the story of immigration to the United States and working hard to advance to a better livelihood. Other stories depict Latino immigration as primarily illegal and the source of social ills. Yet another frame shows Latino labor as vital to the economy. These frames are important because they imply different types of immigration policies as being appropriate. Finally, media *produce and reproduce the meanings of our own culture*, serving as a primary means of cultural transmission within a single culture. We are often not even aware of how media construct, alter, or transmit notions of success, beauty, nationalism, true love, or other cultural norms, and recognizing the media's role can give us more power to understand them.

These messages are not created in a power vacuum. In each society, groups have unequal access to the production of images. Thus, as we will see below, in U.S. American culture, much media content supports the interests and privilege of (White, heterosexual, middle-class) men. Countless studies talk about how media represent women frequently as objects for male desire, with restrictive notions of beauty (e.g., Jean Kilbourne's *Killing Us Softly* video series), or how the media construct the identities of all groups—both majority and minority—within a culture. For example, Anastacia Kurylo (2012) outlines how U.S. American media socially construct what it means to be "Asian," ending with an analysis of how people on an online discussion board exemplify "Linsanity," a short-lived obsession with Chinese American New York Knicks player Jeremy Lin. Authors across the world are beginning to consider power and social constructions within their own nations.

Furthermore, the messages are not merely received by passive audiences. Individuals often create new messages, face-to-face and mediated, that they use to interpret media images or resist their meanings. This leads us to new culturally related questions about media: How are cultural messages used, maintained, or transformed? How do we negotiate the representations of culture—which do we believe and trust, and what do they mean to and for us?

Democratic discourse and diversity: What issues do media present to me as a citizen?

Given media's ability to circulate information and to include messages that may be negative or inaccurate, some of us might be tempted to call for censorship of troublesome messages, removing them from our media. Indeed, it is not hard to imagine how our world might be a better place without persistent stereotypes and other disruptive frames that work to derail egalitarian intercultural communication. Most countries place some degree of restriction on the types of messages that media can include, from what journalists can report about to the level of nudity or sex available on public broadcasting. Some of these restrictions might cover what one can or cannot say about other cultures, such as whether someone can print denials of the Holocaust or reproduce anti-Islamic comic strips.

Some nations, on the other hand, promote freedom of expression, an ideal that tolerates the existence of stereotypical, racist, sexist, or other derogatory images of different groups. United States culture provides an excellent example of this dilemma: what we must come to terms with is that the freedom of expression sometimes means tolerating the most intolerant voices out there, such as hate groups. Freedom of expression is guaranteed by the U.S. Constitution, as well as guiding documents of other countries. While not all democratic countries protect this freedom as vigorously, the balance between freedom and sensible limits on expression is a difficult one for all of them. The First Amendment of the United States Constitution states:

> Congress shall make no law respecting an establishment of religion, or prohibiting the free exercise thereof; or abridging the freedom of speech, or of the press, or the right of the people peaceably to assemble, and to petition the government for a redress of grievances.
> (The First Amendment to the Constitution, ratified December 15, 1791)

With these powerfully penned words, speech, the press and the right of people to gather—modes of communication—were recognized in the United States' most important legal document. The First Amendment functions to ensure that the citizenry is afforded the right to communicate. The right to free speech enshrined in a written constitution is a privileged position not held by the communications media in any other country (Tebbel, 1976). The fundamental promise of the First Amendment is not simply that we have a right to speak; rather, it also formalizes that we have a right to speak and hear others on all sorts of matters, whether they relate to the government or not. The First Amendment permits Americans to contribute to the **public sphere**—amorphous communities where discourse is exchanged, to advance democratic, public participation in the contribution and circulation of ideas (Calhoun, 1992; Habermas, 1989). In extending this right of speech to the press and to the people, no distinction is made between the speech of individuals like you and me, or modern media organizations such as *The Los Angeles Times* newspaper, the Comedy Central television network, radio talkshow host Sean Hannity, or the website blackamericaweb.com. Under the First Amendment, all are afforded the right to have their say—to contribute to the public sphere—and to be heard (if we want to listen).

Gonen Dori-Harcohen (2012) argues that the media help to create the public sphere, especially when they give people a way to air their voice, something central to civic and political engagement. Using the *speaking* framework (see chapter 4), Dori-Harcohen compares U.S. American and Israeli radio talkshows. U.S. talk radio programs tend to be "talk back" shows, where callers call in, but the focus of the show is on the host like Rush Limbaugh, conservative political commentator whose syndicated radio programs reach approximately 600 markets. What is notable about U.S. talk radio is how personalities such as Limbaugh manage callers, usually with a focus of persuading them that "Rush is right!" (p. 157). By contrast, the Israeli shows, while having hosts and callers (participants), have a different "act sequence" and "end" (purpose). The callers get most of the time, and, since the shows are on public stations—not commercial as in the U.S.—the host seeks to remain neutral, merely managing conversation.

Freedom of speech ensures that any one of us, as individuals or even as media corporations, is permitted to express ourselves. The freedom of expression is what allows us to be who we are in public, as well as to display our beliefs and cultural practices in our communities. U.S. Supreme Court Justice Thurgood Marshall once explained the importance of the First Amendment in this way: "The First Amendment serves not only the needs of the polity, but also those of the human spirit; a spirit that demands self-expression" (*Procunier v. Martinez*, 1974). However, the First Amendment does more than provide space for self-expression, it also encourages public debate. Without public debate over issues, democracy and self-governance are simply impossible. There can be elections, but there would be no way for people to discuss the issues that make elections meaningful.

There are, however, some limits to the freedom of speech. For example, neither libelous (written) nor slanderous (oral) speech is protected. Likewise, there is no protection for speech that might incite what some people call imminent lawless action, such as a riot, or that could prompt immediate danger—for example, falsely yelling "fire!" in a crowded theater. Child pornography, which has been deemed indecent and obscene, is not protected speech in the U.S. either. Still, in U.S. media, all sorts of provocative speech are protected, even while many have tried to limit this protection in certain instances. Some of the most important legal cases have centered on the rap album, *As Nasty as They Wanna Be*, by the rap group 2 Live Crew, and on the adult pornography magazine, *Hustler*. Both had been cited for being obscene, although ultimately neither had their message or expression suppressed.

What do you think? What might these U.S.-produced "expressions" communicate to other cultures about, for example, the prevalence of guns, youth culture, socio-economic class, or our education-sports systems? Does the notion of freedom of expression hold up in the modern world of global media? What might be lost, or gained, if we begin to put limits on speech, with the implications of intercultural understanding kept in mind?

The question for us becomes whether we are absolute in our commitment to these freedoms under any circumstances. Supreme Court Justice Hugo Black said in 1960 that there are absolutes in the Constitution. For him, the wording in the country's main legal document that says Congress *shall* make no law means just that. In other words, freedom of expression is to be protected at all costs. However, did Black consider that some free expression can have horrific effects? For example, several media presentations have been linked to tragic acts of violence. Ozzy Osbourne's song, *Suicide Solution*, was said to have prompted an Osbourne fan's suicide. The Hughes Brothers' film, *Menace II Society*, has been cited as playing a contributory role in a copy-cat murder. The five-time Academy Award-winning film *The Deer Hunter*, with its Russian Roulette sequences, and the film, *The Program*, which depicts college football players playing chicken—a dangerous game with oncoming cars on a freeway to see who is the bravest—continue to be linked to copy-cat deaths. While these events seem not to be related to culture, as we consider the cultural transmission and creation of values noted earlier, we see that media can contribute to what some have called a culture of violence in America (Leonard, 1997). (See also Figure 10.1.)

Similarly, free expression in one part of the world can now be received in other parts of the world; this means that what one public figure says can cause crises in international relations, or even street protests. When, in 2005, the Danish newspaper *Jyllands-Posten* published 12 editorial cartoons depicting Mohammad, the prophet of Islam, some Muslims from around the world called the images blasphemous, and some responded with protest. Since then, dozens of (mostly Western) newspapers have reprinted the cartoons, prompting additional concerns about ignorance, insensitivity, and even arrogance. These events can result in serious international problems. People debate whether in this media age, freedoms of expression that lead to actual harms must be protected.

Figure 10.1 Poster of Hit-Girl from the film *Kick Ass* (2010). How does this image (or, if you have seen it, the movie) represent teen culture, gender identities, and violence in America? Source: Marv Films/The Kobal Collection.

What do you think? Many in the United States argue that freedom of speech is a bedrock principle that should not be modified. Do you think freedom of speech in cases of hate speech (on campus, in journalism, on the Internet) should be allowed? Why or why not?

How about in times of international crisis? For example, China has a policy of freedom of the press (complicated by differing government, journalistic, and public views) that focuses on the social responsibility and self-discipline of the press (for example, not to create unrest in a country of enormous size). The government perceives problems with unlimited freedom of expression and might even see Western freedom not as freedom of the press but as freedom of "media tycoons," politicians, and lobbyists (Zhong Xin and Chen Xuan, personal communication, April 15, 2013).

How do you feel about a country's freedom to dictate what forms of communication enter and leave the country? Should countries have "media autonomy," or should a free press reign? Interestingly, according to Thomas McPhail (2006), the U.S. left UNESCO for several years in 1983, in part over this issue.

Media and cultural identities: Who are "we" now?

Digital media and social movements

We Shall Overcome (1947), written by Charles Tindley. *Say it Loud, I'm Black and I'm Proud* (1968), written and sung by James Brown. *Born in the U.S.A.* (1984), written and sung by Bruce Springsteen. *Self Destruction* (1989), performed by rap artists participating in the Stop the Violence movement. Social change and political movements often come with a soundtrack, and these are just a very few of the song titles over the course of U.S. history that have provided the unifying beat. In the U.S., the labor movement, the civil rights movement, the feminist movement, the Viet Nam war protest movement, the Black power movement, lesbian, gay, bisexual & transgender (LGBT) social movements, environmental movements, and anti-violence movements, to name a very, very few, made music instrumental to advancing collective action. In countries around the world, musicians and artists have used their craft to call for social justice and reform.

Music often functions as a rallying cry, transmitting to the masses issues that require attention, if not change. For example, the rap group Public Enemy spoke out against poor public services in underclass communities in their song *9-1-1 is a Joke*. The hymn *We Shall Overcome* was first associated with the U.S. labor movement of the 1940s, then with the U.S. civil rights movement of the 1960s, and most recently with China's Tiananmen Square protest for democratic reform in the 1980s. The popularity of its message and the reach of *We Shall Overcome* evidences that music, when disseminated through mass media, can transcend time, cultures, and place, as well as circumstance. While these art forms and acts do transmit messages, they also inspire and mobilize people, showing the power of communication in social movements. Recent groups like Green Day (*Welcome to Paradise*, 1994), Twenty-One Pilots (*Guns for Hands*, 2013), and the Manhattan Gypsy band, Gogol Bordello (*Immigraniada*, 2010) continue to weave social issues and the desire for culture change into their music.

Media can also be used to propel social action in specific instances. In 2007, thousands of protesters, most of them college students from across the U.S., descended on the small town of Jena, Louisiana. They gathered there to speak out against what they believed was the inequitable legal treatment of six Black, male, high school students. The six youths had become involved in a physical altercation with some of their White, male classmates after discovering a noose—used in this context to symbolize racial hatred—hanging from a tree on school grounds. The White students were suspended from school for hanging the noose. But, for their participation in the schoolyard fight, only the six Black youth (the "Jena Six") were charged with attempted murder. As news broke of the charges, several activist initiatives in support of the Jena Six emerged. Almost immediately, college students at historically Black colleges and universities such as Howard University, Spelman College, and North Carolina A&T turned to listserves, social networking sites, and blogs, not only to inform those in their communities about the plight of the Jena Six, but also to organize a protest march in the town of Jena. Their goal was both to inform the public, and to effect change.

Information spread quickly and ended up in the digital inboxes of important leaders such as Martin Luther King III, Rev. Jesse Jackson, Rev. Al Sharpton, Dennis Coutland Hayes (interim president of the National Association for the Advancement of Colored People, or NAACP), and Representatives Maxine Waters, D-CA, and Sheila Jackson Lee, D-Texas. Many of these leaders joined the students in Jena, while also lobbying the House Judiciary Committee to look into the actions of Jena's prosecutor. Over a few days, across the country, communities were mobilized. The result was approximately 20,000 college students, adults, and civic leaders descending on Jena calling for justice and change. Five of the six students eventually pleaded no contest to lower crimes and were fined $500 and sentenced to seven days of unsupervised probation. One, Mychal Bell (Figure 10.2), was charged with second-degree battery and was sentenced to 18 months in prison. He went to prison as a 16 year-old and served more than a year. We see that media—here, digital media—serve not only as a tool for passing on prevailing views of reality, but for mobilizing social change and possibly changing social structure.

Figure 10.2 Mychal Bell, from Jena, Louisiana, became the center of a debate over racial equality and the fulcrum for a massive computer-mediated information campaign.
Source: Alex Brandon/AP/Press Association Images.

Break it down

Technologies researchers Hargittai, Gallo, and Kane (2008) argue that it is common to find web-links that direct us to the writings of conservative and/or liberal bloggers. But other writers say we avoid "cognitive dissonance" by not exposing ourselves to new opinions. Consider whether your use of the web exposes you to dissenting political positions, or do you favor websites that only offer information that is in line with your ideological position? How can exposure to dissenting opinions help you to make better contributions to the public sphere? How might addressing dissent work to facilitate cross-cultural understanding? How might digitally organized social movements effectively incorporate dissent into the rallying cry?

Choose a political or social issue that is important to you. Find one site that advocates or seeks change on behalf of your issue. Now find one that opposes it and read it carefully. How does this site help you to see your issue differently?

Gender media frames: The social acceptability of showing breasts

So far, we have learned much about media's great potential to impact or facilitate intercultural communication and to mobilize people. Media are useful in the transmission of information, they reveal and reflect our cultural customs, they assist us in having our say and being heard, and they even help us have an effective rallying cry for collective action.

However, as we noted before, mediated communication does not always take place objectively and without bias. Rather, media can, as Tuchman (1978, p. ix) explains, "actively set the frames of reference that readers or viewers [or receivers] use to interpret and discuss public events." Frames lead readers to understand a given event, tale, or theme in a certain way. **Media frames** function as much more than presenters of a story. Rather, they also suggest the issues and controversies surrounding the story. Frames organize the communication or, as Gamson and Modigliani (1989) call it, the "story line," while providing meaning about events associated with the communication. It is important to note that each story can have more than one frame, though media may focus on certain frames over others.

One provocative example of biased framing is the coverage of survivors' actions during the aftermath of 2005's devastating hurricane Katrina in New Orleans, Louisiana. As news agencies' photographs reveal, some survivors who entered storm-hit stores to take goods to eat were described as "looting" food, while others were classified as "finding" food (Figure 10.3). In both cases, taking food without paying is stealing, but "looting" is condemning language while "finding" is neutral. In some media reports, Blacks who took food from stores were labeled looters, while non-Blacks were framed as finders.

(a)

Figure 10.3 a) "A young man walks chest deep in flood waters after **looting** a grocery store," August 30, 2005. b) "Two residents wade chest deep after **finding** bread and soda in a grocery store," August 29, 2005. Note the highlighted words in these two news stories. How do the stories frame the taking of food differently? What might account for this difference in framing?
Source: a) Dave Martin/Press Association Images; b) Chris Graythen/Getty Images.

(b)

Consider the case of Janet Jackson's "wardrobe malfunction," in which part of her breast was uncovered during the 2004 Superbowl (U.S.A.) (Figure 10.4). How might the media be (uncritically) favoring an understanding of gender roles? How is the media defining and/or restricting the debates surrounding the sexualization of bodies? What assumptions does the news media advance about femininity and masculinity (the performance of gender roles)?

(a)   (b)

Figure 10.4 Justin Timberlake assists Janet Jackson in a "wardrobe malfunction," causing a scandal in the 2004 Superbowl, but frequently bares his own breasts with no consequence.
Source: a) John Zich/Corbis; b) AF archive/Alamy.

Rarely, however, are media frames so easily identified. For example, the presentation of **gender**—the cultural and social expectations of one's sex—tends to include frames that reproduce dominant notions of femininity and masculinity. Before you read on, consider Textbox 10.6 about two different images of partial nudity.   *For example, in an image*

In the first illustration in the Pop Culture textbox earlier, Janet Jackson is seen with Justin Timberlake during the 2004 Superbowl halftime show. She is shown quickly covering her breast. On many occasions, Justin Timberlake performs shirtless or tears off his shirt and throws it to the audience, therefore with both his breasts, supported by well-developed pectoral muscles, proudly on display. Unlike the "looting" versus "finding" images from hurricane Katrina, the images of Jackson versus Timberlake do not so starkly reveal a potential bias. Still, they have implications for how we produce and reproduce meanings of gender.

The Jackson image relates to what has been called "nipplegate," a controversy surrounding the live broadcast of the Superbowl halftime show. The controversy centers on how Janet Jackson and Justin Timberlake, two of pop music's biggest stars, took the stage for a rare, sexy duet. Singing his own song *Rock Your Body*, Timberlake adopted a performance of a pursing male suitor, while Jackson took on the role of the coquettish female. At the end of the song, in a pre-planned bit of choreography that coincided with the lyrics, "You'll be naked before this song is done," Timberlake ripped off part of Jackson's outfit. Though the broadcast image in question lasted only 9/16th of a second, viewers got a glimpse of a woman's breast on live television. The public uproar and legal repercussions over American broadcaster CBS showing the "wardrobe malfunction" lingered for years as hefty fines imposed by the Federal Communications Commission (FCC) continued to be appealed.

Media frames focused narrowly on Jackson's "breast-baring," as the BBC News (UK) and KMBC-TV Kansas City (U.S.) called it. The Australian Broadcasting Corporation talked of "exposure" and "moral outrage" while the sports network ESPN (U.S.) similarly described a breast "reveal" which sparked "mass outrage." When media began to complicate this basic frame of morally corrupt, provocative nudity, as CNN International did, they did so by asking whether a woman's "breast-baring" stunt for entertainment is protected by the First Amendment (obscenity, which nudity is defined as legally, is not protected). Notably, none of these media reports challenged underlying views of women's breasts as a marker of gender differences. This incident invited outrage and controversy without much thinking of the deeper, potentially problematic reason for why it did.

James Tankard (2003) observes that framing is not simply about what is presented; rather, it is also about what voices or perspectives are eliminated. One perspective that was not presented in the news coverage about Jackson's semi-nudity is how the female breast is understood in contrast to that of the male breast. Implicit in this controversy is the understanding that women's breasts are not to be "revealed" or "exposed;" instead, the female breast is to remain covered up. Had roles been reversed, if Jackson revealed one of Timberlake's breasts, it would have been a comedic moment. While such norms about gender are deeply engrained, they are maintained by media rather than questioned.

Tankard (2003) reminds us that framing reflects the "richness" of media's presentations and the "subtle differences that are possible when a specific topic is presented in different ways" (p. 96). Indeed, the different ways in which gender is communicated through media reveal a richness, even as the discourses also reflect a society's culturally-based conception of commonality and classification. Sarah Crymble (2009) details how magazine advertisements targeting women sell the notion of dualities in our identities. Dualities are blends of oppositions, a seeming resolution of a dualism. The **dualism** refers to two concepts, here pertaining to identity, that appear to exist in opposition to each other, as if mutually exclusive. In terms of gender, society often dichotomizes between nurture and nature, logic and emotion, as if these concepts were mutually exclusive. The **duality** combines oppositions, making them seem to work together. The concept of duality can, at first blush, appear progressive and inclusive of differences within a gender identity. To illustrate this notion of duality, there is the DeBeer diamond company's "right hand" ring advertising campaign: "Your left hand likes evenings at home. Your right hand loves a night out…" Similarly, a Calvin Klein fragrance advertisement for Contradiction, according to Crymble, is built around the notion of duality: "She is always/and never the same." One interpretation of

Figure 10.5 This Calvin Klein ad illustrates the notion of duality by giving the model characteristics that society often considers to be both masculine and feminine.
Source: Hennessy (Schieffelin & Co.). Vogue (October 1, 2000). Vol. 190, Issue 20, page 21.

these advertisements, and their messages, is that media are asking women to proudly embrace the multiplicity in their identities, and thereby not be confined by singular feminine categories. However, another interpretation is that these advertisements incite identity dissonance. They play on female anxieties and the tensions between societal standards and the expectations that women should be treated equally and given the opportunity of advancement. Is it more "positive" that women be all things to all people—professional by day, tigresses by night? Or, to quote the classic Enjoli perfume ad, "bring home the bacon" (work hard by day), and "fry it up in a pan" (be a housewife after a hard day's work)? Or does this sort of imagery suggest that, although women might be bankers and veterinarians by day (to quote a line of Bacardi rum advertisements), they are still just "bodies" to be looked at by men?

Men are not spared the dissonance either. Sometimes, they appear in dualities. Calvin Klein and other men's underwear adverts often feature men with traditional aspects of masculinity—a muscular build, chiseled features, short haircut—yet also with feminine characteristics of careful skin care, lack of body hair, and postures and gaze that seduce the camera (Figure 10.5). More often their gender performance of masculinity is even more restrictive and narrowly defined (in dualisms) than women. "Real" men are frequently depicted as hard, not soft. Stoic, not emotional. They are strong, resourceful, and independent (e.g., Rambo or any action hero depicted by Arnold Schwarzenegger) as opposed to dependent or communal, traits that have been represented as synonymous with weakness and a lack of masculinity. Men's power and effectiveness are often tied to their heterosexuality, as evidenced by "male-enhancement" advertisements for products such as Viagra and Enzyte, which link virility to heterosexual masculinity. As such, there are few media images of the kind of encompassing dualities targeting women. Consumers of media fare are led to believe that the presence of behaviors such as dramatic emotions, effeminate mannerisms, and fanciful dress must necessarily correspond to a non-masculine identity. Men who are believed to be situated outside of traditional masculinity are consequently understood to be inferior or abnormal. This understanding is asserted even when the man in question has not made such an identity claim for himself (Cobb & Coleman, 2010).

More, popular media have had a field day exploiting the notion that some men cannot find the courage to be gay, and thus move through society on the "down low." This notion of hiding one's "true" gay identity behind the cover of a relationship with a woman has been featured in popular literature, on television talkshows, and in entertainment media such as film and television. The concept of the "down low" implies that men do not have access to identity multiplicity, instead suggesting that they are either feminine or masculine, gay or straight, and these identities cannot be congruent or simultaneous. Additionally, in this view, the gay side of men's identity trumps and erases their interest in women—in short, they cannot embrace both men and women, or simultaneously be "masculine" (straight) and "feminine" (gay).

What do you think? In what ways do media reflect upon, reinforce, or challenge definitions of a society's gendered behaviors? Can you identify differing gender role norms across cultures? For example, how is masculinity framed in advertisements from around the globe?

Representational absences as an impediment to intercultural communication

As we consider the ways in which media can facilitate, or hinder, communication, we must also be mindful that barriers exist in more areas than how media represent cultures. Intercultural communication can encounter challenges due to the absence of key frames, information or cultural competences. For example, one form of representational noise is the frequent stereotypical depiction of Arab Muslims as extremists and terrorists in Western Europe and the United States. Such stereotypes have the effect of conventionalizing grossly oversimplified, if not troubling, concepts of a group and culture.

Another way to devalue individuals and groups is to exclude a people from representing experiences that would be viewed as mundane for others. In chapter 5, this was referred to as symbolic annihilation. For example, Muslim women, particularly those wearing *hajibs* (e.g., scarves or veils) are rarely presented as providing expert commentary on "Western" news programs (e.g., U.S., Canada, Germany, France, etc.) and are depicted as never having any choice in their attire. While there are places where covering the hair is required by law or familial and societal pressure, many Muslim women choose to wear it as an expression of modesty and piousness. This representational absence means that Muslim women are not only rendered "out of sight," but their ability to contribute to useful information and extend our knowledge is erased. The additional result is the subtle implication that Muslim women are passive and without agency, or the ability to have their own voices.

ON THE NET

Browse around Theory.org (http://www.theory.org.uk)—it has sources on various types of media and cultural analysis (feminist, postmodern, queer theory, and so on), theorist trading cards, and action figures. For example, check out this interesting video on Web 2.0 design versus traditional media as they pertain to social change: http://www.youtube.com/watch?v=MNqgXbII_o8. How might Web 2.0 change the way we understand culture? What impacts might this or the traditional Internet have on world cultures?

Beyond traditional media: How do new media and culture shape each other?

Today's social movements, in addition to the fact that they are often set to a funky, collectivity-inducing beat, are being organized at the speed of light, and across greater distances thanks to digital media—specifically email, the blogosphere, and social networking sites. At one time, in a section on new media, we might have addressed the Internet as well, but interactive media, as well as the Internet, give us an ability to communicate with, as well as assemble and coordinate masses across distance in a short amount of time. This was demonstrated vividly in Egypt's "Arab Spring" in early 2011, when young protesters organized demonstrations using email, cell phones, Facebook, Twitter, and SMS text messaging. They built up such large protests that the President was forced to resign after less than three weeks of people hitting the streets, making social media one of the contributing causes to the Arab Spring (Kahn, 2012).

Many point to the power of the Internet and specifically blogs and social networking sites like Facebook or MySpace to rally and unite people, rather quickly and in large numbers, in ways not seen or heard of before. As the Jena Six protests showed, this new media environment can result in social mobilization. Blogs, or websites that feature a log of posts, offer the chance for new voices to impact current events. According to technologies scholars Hargittai, Gallo, and Kane (2008), blogs can be often authored by one or more people, are typically published independently, that is, without any (editorial) oversight, and have the *potential* to reach multitudes. Blogs may be considered prime examples of the power of free speech and of the importance of contributing to the public sphere.

Blogs, social network sites, and Twitter have already been around for a while, but they are now gaining the interest of intercultural scholars. Robert Shuter (2012), in his article for *The Journal of Intercultural Communication Research*, introduces a new field of study that he calls "Intercultural New Media Studies" (p. 219). He notes the value of new media, especially interactive media, in specific areas of cultural research, such as the development of hybrid cultures where people from multiple cultures share the same network. We could expand that to consider how new media help people negotiate identities in diasporic cultures, such as when Saudi students travel from home to various cultures around the world and maintain notions of identity through Facebook, Twitter, and instant messaging (IM'ing).

Interactive and other new media have much to do with our lives and our culture. Just like the Internet, and previous electronic and other media before it, new media shape culture and culture shapes new media. In the words of Marshall McLuhan, who envisioned the Internet as early as 1964, "The personal and social consequences of any medium . . . result from the new scale that is introduced into our affaires . . . by any new technology" (McLuhan, 1964, p. 7). If we listen to the words of Marshall McLuhan and those who followed him, in theories first known as **technological determinism** and later **media ecology**, the channel a media uses, or the technology of a society, shape all the rest of what happens within that society. Joshua Meyrowitz (1994) discusses how electronic media return us to a similar state to when we lived in oral, tribal cultures, with elements of simultaneous action and reaction and the rise of sensory experience as a prime form of communicating. He argues how electronic media, from television on, blur our social identities and physical boundaries.

As it applies to cross-cultural and intercultural communication, Shuter (2012) contends, we use interactive and other new media to manage and negotiate our own identities and—for example, through online gaming—creating new hybrid communities that cross cultural boundaries as we create new "in-groups" for ourselves (I'm a "gamer." I'm a player of MMORPGs (Massively Multiplayer Online Role-Playing Games). I'm a "Wowhead" (heavy *World of Warcraft* player)). Interactive media can also serve as a channel for intercultural dialogue to reduce the sorts of conflicts we address in chapter 6. It can serve a role in adjusting to new cultures as we build networks with people from the new culture and help in our return home as we maintain more contact with the people back home that we ever could have done in the days of handwritten letters. Shuter demonstrates that these functions are not distinct, because even playing online games can help one in the adjustment process. Researchers can use online research to learn things about culture when face-to-face studies are harder to conduct. For example, one study found that Asian game players' avatars remained at a larger distance when interacting with other Asian avatars, but moved closer when interacting with European player avatars, suggesting spatial flexibility for Asians when interacting with a person from their own or other cultures (Hasler & Friedman, 2012).

New media and research in this area have direct implications also for civic and political engagement. For example, we can research Facebook and other interactive media to uncover prejudice and other ideologies. For example, one study presented in the *Journal of Intercultural Communication Research* discovered that Japanese women reported lower body satisfaction when viewing Facebook images followed with thin-promoting messages (Taniguchi & Lee, 2012). Yet another study revealed that, in all of seven nations studied, men's profile pictures showed more "facial prominence" than those of women, suggesting ideologies of masculine dominance in all cultures. Through media activism, users of Facebook and others got Facebook to shut down a page dedicated to people talking about and promoting date rape, arguing that, even if such postings were done in humor, they still promoted a climate where such assault is more likely to occur (Becker Stevens, 2011). Thus, a starting point in our use of new media, as with any media we produce or consume, is to be aware of the types of messages we are creating and the ideas that they contain that may disadvantage or disparage people in different groups or may promote certain ideas even without intention. But beyond that, we can also use media, new and old, to build civic engagement. For example, we can work with nonprofit agencies that work in different cultures to build pages and share information in ways that may support and speak to local cultures, even if those cultures tend to blend together into a more global community through new media (Waters & Lo, 2012; see also chapter 11). We can be engaged, as were those in the Arab Spring movement, to negotiate social change within our own cultures, as seen in the U.S. social network discussions and postings in light of 2013 Supreme Court rulings on gay marriage. And we can use social media to make connections with people from around the world for our own better understanding and, through this, for a more unified world.

Summary

In this chapter, we introduced how mediated communication can inform and impact our intercultural relationships. It is important to note that phenomena such as music becoming the pulse of a social movement, or media serving as agents complicating gender identity, are just the tip of the iceberg when it comes to media's role in our social world. There is much more to learn about the ways in which media can facilitate as well as challenge intercultural communication. It is worthwhile to question how advertisements, blogs, and even our gaming behaviors draw upon and maintain social norms, or how the invisibility or exclusion of groups from representations might have the effect of furthering ignorance or even creating new stereotypes. Because media often ignore certain groups, present them in restricted roles or presentations, or actually portray stereotypical images of them, the prevalence of some cultural communication can actually make us less familiar with our communities and issues, rather than more so. On the other hand, we have come to understand how digital technologies provide us with access to issues across vast distances, almost instantaneously, and serve as new centers for communities and springboards for social movements.

As we consider the socio-political impacts of media, it is also important to ask how we might become even better citizens in today's media environment. One way to do so is to become savvy media consumers. Not all media messages are created equally, and it is our responsibility to rely on credible, trustworthy sources of information before drawing conclusions about a people, place, or event. Similarly, we need not dismiss our favorite media sources outright. Instead, we should be keenly aware of the unique functions they serve. For example, the public service station C-Span's unedited coverage of a President Obama speech has a different goal and function than does CBS news anchor Katie Couric's coverage of the President's speech. Moreover, Couric's blog, Couric & Co. (CBS News, 2013), which talks about the anchor's preparations in covering the President's speech, and her reaction to it, has yet a different purpose. We should also be mindful of the usefulness of attending to dissenting perspectives, not just those sources of information that transmit the things or ideas that we favor. The result of such attention is a deepened understanding of how media shape the cultural environment in which we live.

Another way to improve our engagement as citizenry is to contribute to the public sphere with our own media messages. As we have discussed here, there are many ways to "have our say"—or introduce our cultural affinities to others—such as posting video diaries or blogging. But, we should not forget "old" media outlets, such as community access television or radio. Ideally, the media we create should prompt discussion, and even allow for feedback, thereby turning audiences of "receivers" into participatory "senders." These two moments combined—having one's say and being heard—are perhaps one of the most important keys to a civil society and democracy. As such, participating in intercultural communication to help enlighten, and learn from, those around us may be one of the most crucial elements of civic action we can take.

KEY TERMS

Lasswell's model of communication, 204
media dependency theory, 205
transmission view of media
   communication, 205
ritual view of media communication, 205
public sphere, 207

media frames, 212
gender, 214
dualism, 215
duality, 216
technological determinism/media
   ecology, 219

Discussion questions

1 Compare and contrast the transmission and ritual views of communication as these relate to a specific identity. For example, what would the transmission say about the representation of the elderly and its impact on audience? What would the ritual say about the elderly and media?

2 In what ways does your college or university encourage discourse of important issues? What are some of the media outlets that exist for both the college and for students to present their ideas openly, without restriction?

3 How do you feel that the media "frames" certain groups in comparison to the dominant group? What is your evidence? Do you feel that framing in some media (such as news, reality shows) differs in its social importance or likelihood to be believed than framing in other media, such as *The Simpsons* or online comics? Why or why not?

4 Take a close look at journalistic media in your nation as it relates to other national cultures, such as the reporting of crisis in other nations. What ideologies or assumptions do you feel that your news media support in relation to specific nations?

5 Popular music has played a central part in revolutions and protest around the world, but people in many nations where it is used question its effectiveness. What do you think the strengths and benefits are of trying to mobilize publics for action or change using popular music (e.g., Green Day, Rage Against the Machine, Nueva Canción)?

Action points

1 Analyze media of some form in your community, such as magazine covers in your local bookstore, the comics in your daily newspaper, or even the images or discussion of people of different religious, racial, sex/gender, sexuality, or other groups, in your favorite magazine. If your analysis reveals inequalities in representation (either in percentages based on your national population or in terms of breadth of roles) or stereotypical

images, send your analysis to the publishers, editors, or directors, or write a letter to the editor of your local paper with your findings.

2 Create a media message of your own—well argued and with evidence of your points— that supports some aspect of civic involvement, or social change. This might be a letter to an editor, a guest editorial, or a blog entry.

3 Compare two or more different media sources about the same issue or event (e.g., blogs of your favorite news source or pundit, sketches on faux-news shows such as *The Colbert Report* or *The Daily Show*, news editorial programs such as *The O'Reilly Factor*, or sources local to your own country. Try to choose sources that are quite different in focus (e.g., a letter to the editor versus a newscast). How do these differ in intended audience, in scope of coverage, in types of evidence provided for the points being made, and in the general form and function of the media? How might you treat each differently as you make your own decisions?

For more information

Columbia Journalism Review —*Who Owns What*: http://www.cjr.org/resources
Croteau, D.R., & Hoynes, W. (2002). *Media/Society: Industries, images, and audiences* (3rd ed.). Thousand Oaks, CA: Pine Forge Press.
Douglas, S. (2010). *Enlightened Sexism: The seductive message that feminism's work is done*. New York: Henry Holt.
Fairness & Accuracy in Reporting: http://fair.org
Fisherkeller, J. (2002). *Growing up with television: Everyday learning among young adolescents*. Philadelphia, PA: Temple University Press.
Jenkins, H. (2006). *Fans, bloggers, and gamers: Media consumers in a digital age*. New York: NYU Press.
Media Access Project (MAP): http://mediaaccess.org
Neal, M.A. (2002). *Soul babies: Black popular culture and the post-soul aesthetic*. New York: Routledge.
Potter, W.J. (2008). *Media literacy*. Thousand Oaks, CA: Sage.

References

Becker Stevens, A. (2011). Dear Facebook: Rape is no joke. *Ms.blog Magazine*, September 19. Accessed March 26, 2013, at http://msmagazine.com/blog/2011/09/19/dear-facebook-rape-is-no-joke/
Black, H.L. (1960). The Bill of Rights. *New York University Law Review*, 35, 865–881.
Calhoun, C. (1992). *Habermas and the public sphere*. Cambridge: Polity Press.
Carey, J. (1989). *Communication as culture: Essays on media and society*. London: Unwin Hyman.
CBS News (2013). Couric & Co. Accessed March 25, 2013, at http://www.cbsnews.com/sections/couricandco/main500803.shtml
Chattopadhyay, S. (2012). Framing 3/11 online: A comparative analysis of the news coverage of the 2012 Japan disaster by CNN.com and Asahi.com. *China Media Research*, 8(4), 50–61.

Cobb, J., & Means Coleman, R. (2010). Two snaps and a twist: Controlling images of gay Black Men on television. *African American Research Perspectives*, 13, 82–98.
Crymble, S. (2009). *Articulations of desire and the politics of contradiction: Magazine advertising, television fandom, and female gender identity dissonance*. Unpublished Dissertation, University of Michigan.
deFleur, M., & Ball-Rokeach, S. (1982). *Theories of mass communication* (4th ed.). New York: Longman.
Dori-Harcohen, G. (2012). The commercial and the public "Public Spheres": Two types of political talk-radio and their constructed publics. *Journal of Radio and Audio Media*, 19, 152–171.
Gamson, W.A., & Modigliani, A. (1989). Media discourse and public opinion on nuclear power:

A constructionist approach. *American Journal of Sociology, 95*, 1–37.

Habermas, J. (1989). *The structural transformation of the public sphere: An inquiry into a category of bourgeois society*. Cambridge, Mass: MIT Press.

Hargittai, E., Gallo, J., & Kane, M. (2008). Cross-ideological discussions among conservative and liberal bloggers. *Public Choice, 134*, 67–86.

Hasler, B.S., & Friedman, D. (2012). Sociocultural conventions in Avatar-mediated nonverbal communication: A cross-cultural analysis of virtual proxemics. *Journal of Intercultural Communication Research*, 238–259.

Kahn, A.A. (2012). The role of social media and modern technology in Arabs Spring. *Far East Journal of Psychology and Business 7*(4), 56–63.

Kurylo, A. (2012). Linsanity: The construction of (Asian) identity in an online New York Knicks basketball forum. *China Media Research, 8*(4), 15–28.

Lasswell, H. (1948/1967). *Power and personality*. New York: Viking.

Lee, K.C., & Baldwin, J.R. (2004). History of "speech communication" research: Models and messages. In J.R. Baldwin, S.D. Perry, & M.A. Moffitt (Eds.), *Communication theories for everyday life* (pp. 55–73). Boston: Allyn & Bacon.

Leonard, J. (1997). *Smoke and mirrors: Violence, television, and other American cultures*. New York: New Press.

McLuhan, M. (1964). *Understanding media: The extensions of man*. New York: McGraw-Hill.

McPhail, T.L. (2006). *Global communication: Theories, stakeholders, and trends* (2nd ed.). Malden, MA: Blackwell.

Meyrowitz, J. (1994). Medium theory. In D. Crowley & D. Mitchell (Eds.), *Communication theory today* (pp. 50–77). Cambridge, UK: Polity Press.

Procunier v. Martinez, 416 U.S. 396, 427 (1974).

Rith, S. (2009). Hun Sen decries reliance on foreign styles in the arts. *The Phnom Penh Post*, July 23. Accessed March 25, 2013, at http://www.phnompenhpost.com/index.php/2009072327340/National-news/hun-sendecries-reliance-on-foreign-styles-in-the-arts.html

Shuter, R. (2012). Intercultural new media studies: The next frontier in intercultural communication. *Journal of Intercultural Communication Research, 41*, 219–237.

Szemere, A. (1992). Bandits, heroes, the honest, and the misled: Exploring the politics of representation in the Hungarian Uprising of 1956. In L. Grossberg, C. Nelson, & P.A. Treichler (Eds.), *Cultural studies* (pp. 623–639). New York: Routledge.

Taniguchi, E., & Lee, H.E. (2012). Cross-cultural differences between Japanese and American female college students in the effects of witnessing fat talk on Facebook. *Journal of Intercultural Communication Research*, 260–278.

Tankard Jr., J.W. (2003) The empirical approach to the study of framing. In S.D. Reese, O.H. Gandy, & A.E. Grant (Eds.), *Framing public life: Perspectives on media and our understanding of the social world* (pp. 95–106). Mahwah, NJ: Lawrence Erlbaum Associates.

Tebbel, J.W. (1976). *The media in America*. New York: New American Library.

Tuchman, G. (1978). Introduction: The symbolic annihilation of women by the mass media. In Tuchman, G., Daniels, A.K., & Benét, J. (Eds.), *Hearth and home: Images of women in the mass media* (pp. 3–38). New York: Oxford University Press.

Waters, R.D., & Lo, K.D. (2012). Exploring the impact of culture in the social media sphere: A content analysis of nonprofit organizations' use of Facebook. *Journal of Intercultural Communication Research*, 297–319.

Contexts

Part four

The channels of messages that we discussed in part three are used in different contexts and present us with several issues. Rather than separate contexts and issues, we treat them together here, because issues arise within specific contexts. Globalization, for example, places message exchange within the "context" of global media and message flow, but presents "issues" of cultural change and preservation. In chapter 11, we address globalization. We note that much of globalization occurs as a result of global media flow; however, we also point out that such flows are not always equal for all parties involved and are, in fact, resisted by many in non-Western cultures, as they spread ideas and behaviors unequally, with greater flow from cultures with more powerful market economies and media structures.

Chapter 12 introduces the context of cultural adaptation. Many people travel abroad, so we should know the types of symptoms that accompany "culture shock." However, we note that cultural transition need not be a bad thing, as it also brings us personal growth. We present—and discount—the commonly used "U-curve" or stage model of acculturation that many universities use to guide their students, and present other ways to understand both going abroad and coming home. Much of what helps one adjust is also what makes one a competent communicator, and travel experience often makes one more interculturally competent, so we also address the idea of cultural competence in this chapter.

Another context in which we experience intercultural communication is relationships, so we address this in chapter 13. Specifically, we compare different views of how relationships might grow between people of different cultures and what issues might be present in such relationships, as well as different cultural patterns an intercultural couple might adopt.

Intercultural Communication for Everyday Life, First Edition. John R. Baldwin, Robin R. Means Coleman, Alberto González, and Suchitra Shenoy-Packer.
© 2014 John R. Baldwin, Robin R. Means Coleman, Alberto González, and Suchitra Shenoy-Packer.
Published 2014 by John Wiley & Sons Ltd.

Culture also impacts relationships in that in most cultures, certain types of relationships are stigmatized. Finally, a key element in most relationships is how partners resolve conflict. While conflict resolution occurs both in relationships and organizations, we treat it here, as it is integral to understanding family, friend, and romantic relationships as well. Finally, we introduce negotiation, as it is closely related to conflict.

Chapter 14 presents a context of communication central to our focus on political and civic engagement: political communication. We introduce the notion of politics and its connection to culture. Here you will read about important parts of our political process that shape the cultures in which we live—hopefully for the better—such as social movements and political leadership. We include examples of specific social movements, such as the Green Belt movement in Africa and the immigrant rights movement in the United States. There are also examples of types of leaders and specific political leaders who have sought to change culture and the world in positive ways.

Finally, chapter 15 presents the organizational context. Space keeps us from also including chapters on educational, health, or religious contexts, but we hope that readers will be able to extend some of what they read in this chapter to other types of organizational context. After reviewing the important role of work in our lives, we talk about how new technology and global connections are changing the culture of work around the world, with new types of workers, new relationships between workers and organizational leaders, and new approaches to organization. Where we addressed the impact of globalization on media in chapter 11, here we address the impact on local and international organizational cultures. Finally, tying this context back to what we present in chapter 4, we present a framework of how organizational attitudes and relationships can vary across cultures.

Chapter 11

Global media, global cultures: How do culture and globalization influence each other?[1]

Chapter objectives

After this chapter, you should be able to:

→ **Define and give examples of global media**

→ **Provide examples of media products that have crossed borders or have inspired cultural productions in another country**

→ **Outline some of the historical and technological influences in the history of global media**

→ **Evaluate the impact of globalization on notions of time and space**

→ **Describe what is driving globalization of the media and predictions about its long-term effects**

→ **Discuss positive and negative implications for global media in terms of local cultures**

Culture on the global media stage: How does the global flow of information impact culture?

Power and globalization: What drives the global media?

[1] This chapter was co-authored by William Lafi Youmans, Assistant Professor at George Washington University's School of Media and Public Affairs.

n 1984, the rap group World Class Wreckin' Cru released the 12-inch single *Surgery*. The single celebrated one of the core elements of rap music and hip hop culture—the DJ. It is the DJ who not only brings the music, but also puts it together to create unique blends, or mixes, of sounds and beats that are the hallmark of hip hop music. However, the group's song reminds us that the DJ is just one central part of rap music; the others are the technological tools upon which hip hop DJs are so reliant—headphones, mixing boards, speakers, and turntables.

POP CULTURE

Lyrics from World Class Wreckin' Cru highlight the global forces, even within a single culture, of blending cultural beliefs and discourse styles with technological tools—here, to craft hip hop music. Records. Mixer. Turntables. Speakers.

7 days a week, He's on call, to get the party people up off the wall.
You'll feel motivated… as He operates… cause party energy is what He generates.
He'll prescribe for you his potent elixir
—two turntables, speakers, and a mixer.

(*Surgery* by World Class Wreckin' Cru, 1984)

Rayvon Fouché, (2009; 2012) a technology scholar at the University of Illinois-Urbana Champaign, uses the example of the DJ and her/his technological resources to illustrate how the art form of rap music is the quintessential global intercultural phenomenon. Fouché reminds us that hip hop DJs rely upon turntable, speaker, and mixing board technologies such as those created by the Japanese electronics company Technics to develop "party energy." To put it more pointedly, hip hop culture's origins become much more complicated when we consider more broadly the sources of all that has contributed to the essence of hip hop. Prof. Fouché's work is guided by a research question that is useful to all of our thinking: What are the multiple, global intersections and relationships between cultural representations, racial identification, and technological design?

At the heart of this question, and what we are most concerned with in this chapter, is the notion that mediated communication knows no borders. Keeping with the hip hop example, we can imagine how diverse cultures have influenced the art form, but also how the art form has similarly informed cultures. For example, some have linked breakdancing to Chinese martial arts, while the popular American rap group, the Wu-Tang Clan, pay homage to Hong Kong Kung Fu films through their name and lyrics.

We can also talk about a host of other media that have gone global—from the films of Bollywood to the children's television show *Sesame Street*. **Global media** can be understood as sources of mass communication that involve the transmission of messages, formats, programming, or content across national boundaries. It is often a complex, trans-national network of different media systems. It still makes sense to understand global media, much as we do traditional communication, through a model of senders and receivers. Similarly, global media operate in patterns by which we can speak of **sending countries**, those where global media sources are based, and **receiving countries**, those that consume global media products based in other countries. While the growth of multinational corporations increasingly breaks down this distinction, it is still possible to generalize flow patterns of cultural and media products from certain countries or regions to others.

Global media need not have the purposeful goal of becoming a global phenomenon, even though content creators usually would like the largest audience possible. A media product, such as a television show or performer, created for one country could catch on elsewhere, and be translated or dubbed in different languages. For example, the popular British television show *Pop Idol* became *American Idol* in 2002. Shakira, who recorded her CDs in Spanish, was a well-known brunette performer in Latin America and Europe years before she became the blond singer of *Whenever, Wherever*, and *Hips Don't Lie*. Global media companies, those with production and distribution channels in different countries, may produce media with the idea and goal of sending it to multiple countries. This has economic benefits since it means gaining more revenues. In other instances, there is a concerted effort to circulate media to other countries and cultures in order to have some public or political impact. For example, the Children's Television Workshop, the producer of the U.S. children's television show *Sesame Street*, offered the series internationally to countries such as Bangladesh, Indonesia, Jordan, Kosovo, Northern Ireland, Palestine, Russia, and South Africa, with the hope of addressing conflict or empowering children to better their societies (Figure 11.1). Media content can move across borders and reach new audiences through many different means and with different goals. This chapter summarizes some of the mutual influences between culture and globalization, including positive and negative consequences for local cultures from globalization.

Figure 11.1 Characters from Pakistani Sesame Street are displayed in Lahore, Pakistan.
Source: KM Chaudary/AP/ Press Association Photos.

Culture on the global media stage: How does the global flow of information impact culture?

As the 2009 Hollywood blockbuster film *Avatar* drew in record box office sales worldwide, the Chinese government ordered its country's theaters to pull the movie's 2–D version to make way for the 2010 Chinese government-subsidized biopic *Confucius*, about the ancient Chinese philosopher, whose thinking has been deeply influential in China (LaFraniere, 2010). China, which has in place strict limits on the number of foreign movies that can be shown and how long they run, allowed the 3-D version to run (Figure 11.2). The reason for these limits was to protect China's film industry from losing market share to non-Chinese moviemakers.

Break it down

The major Hollywood studios make most of their money from global markets. Try to figure out the impact of U.S. films on foreign markets. Select a country outside of the U.S., and then identify the top four movies, based on box office sales, for that country. Identify who produced those movies by researching the film company and its affiliated media conglomerate, and make a note of which country it originates from. See the worksheet below for a model on how to approach this exercise. Note that Hollywood dominated the global media landscape in 1999. Based on your study, has anything changed since then? What are the implications for local cultures and international media flow, based on your findings?

COUNTRY:

Top 4 films	Production company	National origin
1.		
2.		
3.		
4.		

Bloggers and film critics in China speculated that it was not simply the rapid success of *Avatar* that alarmed officials. Some theorized that the plot too closely resembled the controversial government and corporate policies of forced removal, or the mass evictions of people to make room for new development. On an online forum in China, one viewer drew the connection:

They are very much alike. For instance, the conflict in the film also starts with land. When real estate developers want a piece of land, the local residents must move away; if they decline to leave, then real estate developers will resort to violent ways. (Han, 2010)

Figure 11.2 Chinese moviegoers donned 3-D glasses to watch *Avatar* in Hefei, in Anhui Province. Source: AFP/Getty Images.

Another joked that the Chinese demolition crews should sue James Cameron, who produced and directed *Avatar*, for pirating their actions.

One underlying message of *Avatar* is an environmental one. Cameron himself said at a news conference that he saw the movie "as a broader metaphor, not so intensely politicized as some would make it, but rather that's how we treat the natural world as well" (Itzkoff, 2010). Debates about the environment in general, as with globalization, mirror debates about global media. The environment is like global media in that what one country does impacts others. Pollution, for instance, does not stop at a country's borders. Increasingly, news, entertainment, and images have the same kind of fluidity. Transportation technologies have been a boon to media globalization. Reels of the latest film or boxes of a popular novel can be shipped by airplane to distant theaters or bookstores in a matter of days, or even hours. In the era of the Internet, this sort of border-crossing is instantaneous. As soon as someone in Tanzania updates her Facebook status, her friend in New Zealand can see the change. Communication technologies such as radio, satellite television and the Internet make it inexpensive for information and other media content to move through the world. Therefore, while governments may try to control media exposure—such as China's movie import limits or the American government's censorship of war images—there is no way to fully prevent media messages from circulating. More, information sources and media environments are increasingly impacted by this dynamic global connectivity.

Most often, global media is discussed within the context of **globalization**, the social, cultural, economic, and political integration of different parts of the world. Globalization is facilitated by the movement of goods, capital, ideas, and people among nations. Under this definition, globalization has been taking place for as long as humans have moved. However, current globalization processes are arguably more intense, given advances in transportation and communication technology (Giddens, 1990). Also important is the integration of the global economic system, which allows for a more rapid circulation of people, ideas, and resources.

Central to contemporary globalization—since the end of the Cold War in the late 1980s—is the economic engine of **capitalism**, an economic system based on exchange through markets and the private ownership of capital. Global media, though going back decades, emerged most prominently in its current form in the early 1990s, after capitalism expanded in the midst of the Cold War's end. The Cold War saw the world split into three ideological camps: the capitalist bloc, centered on the United States; the communist bloc, which emerged around the Soviet Union (Russia and surrounding countries); and the non-aligned countries, of which Egypt, India, and Indonesia were leaders. These divisions meant that no one economic system ruled the world. As a result, for a time, international media were constrained from having truly global reach. First, as countries in Eastern Europe, South America, Asia, and Africa allied themselves with one side of the Cold War or the other, countries tended to import only media from those countries. Also, because of the challenge of opposing countries' media, countries deliberately blocked media input from other countries. In fact, the primary global media crossing Cold War lines were state-run broadcasters that were founded to fight the Cold War through messages and reporting representing their sponsoring governments; stations such as Radio Free Europe (United States) and the British Broadcasting Corporation (BBC) were broadcasting across borders and ideological lines. With the end of the Cold War, economic integration and capitalist media prevailed, leading to a proliferation of private media crossing international lines.

Globalization is symbolized by the fact that an audience in China can enjoy *Avatar*, the most costly Hollywood movie up to that point. At the same time, a cinema audience in the United States, albeit probably a smaller one, watched the 2008 film *Red Cliff*, produced by Magnolia Pictures, which was then the most expensive Asian-produced film. The John Woo-directed Chinese epic film presented the legendary Battle of Red Cliffs during the end of the Han Dynasty. In the age of media globalization, expensive movies are often made with international audiences in mind. They must be marketed internationally, with the movie posters framed differently for different audiences.

Just because both movies could be seen in both places, it does not mean that globalization is an equal or mutual process. While *Avatar* made more than 540 million yuan ($80 million) in the Chinese box office, *Red Cliff* pulled in little over half-a-million dollars in the United States. This relates to one of the most important debates in global media: whether global media means stronger and more powerful countries and companies will come to dominate international media environments.

Many are concerned with what this means for the native cultures and national identities on the receiving end of global media. Some critics tend to see globalization as a homogenizing force. Others argue that globalization also includes fragmentation, which means that standardization is not truly possible; while another group of critics argue that cultural interactions and borrowings are natural in history (as we have seen with hip hop culture), and that more often cultures adapt concepts and tools from other cultures in unique, hybrid ways. The cultural implications for the growing spread of media globally are considerable.

The global media experience

Have you listened to a song by Jamaican-born singer Bob Marley, seen the American television show *The Office*, or viewed news reports from the Al-Jazeera network headquartered in Qatar? If so, you have been on the consuming end of global media. The global nature of the mediated communication we experience in our lives is often inescapable, and frequently, we do not even know how international the media product is that we witness. For example, the popular

American situation comedy, *The Office*, was developed from a British series of the same name. The British actors were replaced by American ones and the American show was set in Scranton, PA. The humor changed as well. It came to reflect cultural differences in comedy.

Perhaps you were one of the one hundred million people to watch Susan Boyle astound the audience with her vocals on the British version of the reality-based talent show American Idol. If so, you saw first-hand how media content can travel between countries with ease in various forms and in different avenues. In her first appearance on the program, she seemed so awkward and un-starlike, yet shocked the audience with her impressive singing. Susan Boyle was first seen by many in the United States in mid-2009 on YouTube, a video-hosting website that lets anyone upload their own clips. She was not introduced in the United States as she was in the UK, on a regular television channel. Many learned about this video clip from their peers—friends and families—through email, social networking sites (Orkut, hi5, Facebook, Twitter, etc.). As Boyle became an Internet sensation, local and national entertainment and news programs began to cover her worldwide popularity. Even more people, those who still gained their news through the traditional channels of communication, learned about her eventually. Her popularity shows that there are still national divisions in the still powerful systems of television networks. Additionally, online content can easily go **viral**—that is, spread rapidly at the person-to-person level. This can have the effect of bringing the media experiences in one nation to another nation, even if the traditional media, such as TV networks, are not fully integrated. In a more recent example, South Korean overnight superstar, Psy, sang *Gangnam Style*, a parody video about the materialism of an upscale Seoul, South Korea, neighborhood (Figure 11.3). The video went viral, with

Figure 11.3 South Korean pop star Psy, whose video, *Gangnam Style*, went viral, with 131 million YouTube views in its first 52 days, making it the fifth most viral video of all time.
Source: Charles Sykes/AP/Press Association Images.

131 million YouTube views in its first 52 days, making it the fifth most viral video of all time, and earning Psy a prominent place in the New York, U.S.A. massive New Years festivals (Webfluenz, 2012).

Satellite television: The progenitor of global media

While national television systems such as cable TV or traditional over-the-air, terrestrial broadcasters are not fully integrated internationally, the proliferation of satellite television has greatly expanded the reach of stations to hit regions. **Cable systems** are limited by the reach of the wires, which transmit the TV signals. **Over-the-air, or terrestrial broadcasting** involves signals transmitted through the air from land-based antenna and is limited in reach to a radius of relatively flat ground, based on the power of the antennas. While signals of this nature may cross borders if the receiver is close enough to the source of the signal, their limited reach does not make them a significant feature of the current global media context. **Satellite TV** requires a powerful uplinking antenna on earth, sending a signal to a communications satellite that is stationed in space. The satellite processes and reflects the signal to an area of the earth where homes with satellite dishes receive the signals. This reaches a generally greater percentage of the earth than does terrestrial broadcasting; also, satellite television can carry more channels than cable or terrestrial broadcasting. In many parts of the world, satellite dishes are ubiquitous, on the tops of homes and businesses everywhere.

Satellite television was called the "new media" before the Internet became widespread. Satellite TV grew to define new audiences and led to the growth of regional and transnational channels. It also significantly undermined the power of national governments to control their population's media diets. In many ways, the story of the global media can be said to begin with satellite television. Today, an increasing number of countries are sending satellites into space. However, as Thomas McPhail (2010) notes, only satellites at a specific height at the equator have maximum coverage; and the available locations for these satellites are already occupied by the industrialized (Western) powers that first had the technology and funds to put satellites there, leaving less desirable locations, with smaller signal spread, for newly developing nations.

Producers in one country will purchase successful programs produced in other countries and either dub their country's language over the original programs or include subtitles. One of the easiest television formats to **cross-over**, or adapt from one country to another, is animation. Dubbing new languages over animated moving mouths works better, it seems, and this correlates to the large number of cartoon adaptations. Comic books, by the same token, are frequently translated and republished for new national audiences. A leading producer of animated content is Japan. In 2003, animation, including *manga*, or comics, and *anime*, or cartoons, was a $26 billion industry for the country (Thussu, 2008). The avenues for cross-over can be varied as well. The television show *Mobile Suit Gundam Wing*, which first aired in Japan in 1995 to only moderate success, came to the United States through **fansubbed** videotapes—videos in which fans provided the subtitles. The show was then carried by the Cartoon Network, where it became very popular, to the extent that it was more popular in North America than in Japan. Other well-known Japanese shows that gained visibility in North America include *Dragon Ball Z* and *Pokémon*. The latter was a major franchise that included shows, video games, soundtracks, movie, toys, and a trading card game. Japan's influence on U.S. films has stirred controversy. When the U.S.-made 2012 film *The Hunger Games* was released, comparisons were made to the 2000

Japanese-made film *Battle Royale*. The plot of the Japanese film centered on a small group of teenagers selected by the government who must fight to the death until there is one winner. This closely resembles the plot of *The Hunger Games* novel (Collins, 2008) and film.

POP CULTURE

Are there international programs in your media diet? Remember that some programs that clearly have origins within a single national culture were born in other cultures and then modified and remade for local audiences. For example, U.S. American shows *American Idol* and *The Office* were adapted from the British shows, *Pop Idol* and *The Office*, respectively. Find out the backgrounds of your favorite programs. If they did not originate outside of your country, are they shown in other parts of the world? What do the changes in the program tell you about cultural values and notions of identity in your country?

Telenovelas are Spanish- and Portuguese-language serials that focus on the personal lives and dramas of small casts of individuals. They emphasize themes of personal betrayal, rocky and dramatic human relationships and morality—themes with universal appeal. These programs are deeply popular around the world, reaching a global audience of two billion people in every major region of the world. The biggest national producers are Argentina, Brazil, Colombia, Mexico and Venezuela. Each year, more than 12,000 hours of *telenovelas* are produced. Though these shows originally were created for particular national audiences, certain countries have made an effort to export the serials elsewhere. This has meant shedding markers of nationality, such as language. In other cases, producers have aimed for larger Latin American audiences by including characters of diverse national backgrounds. The exportation of *telenovelas* also shows that programs developed by countries outside of the industrialized global powers have widespread cultural appeal and also fit within the definition of global media. One of the most famous cross-over examples, *Yo Soy Betty, la Fea*, aired from 1999 to 2001 on Radio Cadena Nacional (RCN) in Colombia. This *telenovela* about an unattractive economist working for a highly successful fashion design company was so popular it led to international adaptations in 18 different countries, in several different languages. In the United States, for example, it became *Ugly Betty*. The show had strong popularity with over four million viewers through 2009 (Seidman, 2009) and winning dozens of ALMA, GLAAD, Emmy, and other awards (IMDd.com, n.d.). It was finally canceled in 2010 after four seasons. In each country, the show maintained elements of the original plot, yet added its own cultural flavor.

Magazines are another format that has seen rapid globalization. *Cosmopolitan* magazine, for example, went from a family magazine published locally in the United States in 1886 to a global young women's publication that has 59 national editions. The international audiences get the same recipe of news and tips on love, fashion, beauty, health, self-improvement, and entertainment, as well as a heavy assortment of advertisements for skin products, perfumes, make-up, and clothing lines. Although it was a feminist magazine for a brief time in the 1960s, its current form has been criticized by many for representing women stereotypically and advancing an unobtainable vision of beauty that adds to the social pressures already felt by young women. Its popularity in many parts of the world, where it adapts to local tastes, attests to the power of global media to realize unique forms tailored toward specific audiences while at the same time pushing some universal standards.

ON THE NET

Visit one of *Cosmopolitan* magazine's many national edition websites and review it for similarities and differences with the U.S. website (http://www.cosmopolitan.com/). For example, the Philippines website, http://www.cosmo.ph, uses some terminology and features celebrities unique to the island nation; however, it shows generally the same content as the American version. Consider how *Cosmopolitan* is globalizing standards of beauty. What are those standards? What does globalization of beauty standards mean in a larger context of women's role relationships, rights and equality?

Instantaneous cultural exchange: When time becomes timeless

The movement of goods, people, ideas, and messages across different lands is not new. History is full of large migrations, global trade, religious movements, and explorations. Just think about the global dimensions of religions. Buddha, for example, was born in modern-day Nepal, died in India, and is currently revered by followers throughout the world. Proselytizing, or the active effort to spread religions, has been in many ways a global communicative activity.

Historical empires, such as the Kush kingdom in northeastern Africa, used global communication networks of messengers to administer their territory and subject peoples. During different historical times, different modes of communication allowed people to send and receive information along wide distances. From human messengers carrying letters or memorized messages, to smoke or mirror reflection signals, to messenger pigeons, to wire and wireless telegraphy, global communication has always occurred. So, why is globalization treated as something entirely new?

While global movement may not be a purely modern phenomenon, globalization makes sense as a term when one considers the fundamental changes to space and time, and our subjective conceptualizations of them in this new era. In the past, before the 19th century telegraph wire, which allowed the long-distance transference of codes through a cable, it was impossible to send instant information along great distances. This means that it would take significant time and movement across great distance to communicate. **Space** refers to the physical distance between points, and **time** is the temporal or sequential distance—or how long it takes to do something. For much of human history, communication outside of the face-to-face setting involved significant constraints of great distances and the length of time it took to traverse those distances.

Globalization has created a highly integrated world where space and time no longer obstruct direct interaction. Manuel Castells (2000), a leading theorist of this new information age, proposed that we now experience "timeless time." He argues that space and time have been transformed, with timeless time superseding the clock time of the industrial era. New communication technologies, namely online networks, are fundamentally changing our sense of time and how it proceeds (Castells, 1997).

Networked communications allow for the simultaneous interaction between one person in France and another in Thailand, for example, and hyperlinks on websites and search engines mean we can achieve instant informational gratification—media content is accessible at our fingertips with very little wait. Processes and inquiries that took months in the past now take almost no time, changing how we understand the time needed to do things. This is enabled by a communications space so narrowed that we can say physical distances are simply less relevant between and within societies when it comes to media and communication.

One scholar, Marshall McLuhan (1964), predicted the rise of a "global village" due to international dependence on mass communication and the connectivity it promised. For McLuhan, technologies were "extensions" of the human body. For example, the car was an extension of our feet, clothing was an extension of our skin, and so on. Computer technologies were extensions of the human nervous system. In this vision, "across the ocean" was as far away as "around the corner" when it came to communication. From this, he argued the world would come together as a village, where peoples' consciousness and identities converge.

That such grand transformations of a world coming together as a village are not yet realized does not make the prediction completely inaccurate. A more defensible characterization would be that "the globalization of the media has enabled the creation of a thriving international market, which now encompasses the globe" (Thussu, 2008). The term "market" is useful for understanding global media because media's growth was a function of companies and individuals having greater access to more foreign markets for media fare after the end of the Cold War. What this means is that shows and formats developed in one part of the world are increasingly adapted or simply translated elsewhere. Also, the term market calls to mind a bustling place full of exchange, some equitable and some not. It is "thriving" because the change is rapid and the diffusion of creative programming is moving in new directions with a great degree of flux.

The inequality of global media flow

The analogy of market would not be complete without an understanding that the development of a global media is not happening on equal terms. It is rather unequal, based on an imbalance between wealthier nations and poorer ones. For each country, global media can mean something different. For many in more powerful nations—those nations that send media—global media are beneficial in terms of bringing more revenue. The tight market for media in the United States means that only the most competitive media products get into the country, or are received. Poorer countries tend to be *receivers* of media. As such, they face the threat of being bombarded with media imports. This makes it more difficult for local media to develop, as they will invariably cost more to produce than it would cost to buy cheap, imported programming. The lack of a robust media market also means that poorer countries do not get to assume the role of *senders* as often as powerful countries do. Media scholars in the early days of global media were especially concerned with the inequality of media flow. Media dependency theory, which arose in the 1970s, postulated global media as being developed and produced in richer **core countries**, and being exported to weaker **periphery countries** (McPhail, 2010). While many scholars no longer see this as a primary pattern, there are many still interested in the question of power in determining who provides and who consumes information.

The globalization of media, specifically certain media forms being exported into other countries, has raised concerns about the impact on local cultures. The concern is two-fold. The first concern is that some countries will cease trying to develop indigenous media because of the expense as well as because of the great availability of other, often Western, media forms. The television network MTV has encountered criticism for its international push. MTV Worldwide presents entertainment programming through more than

Figure 11.4 MTV Spring Break 2006 provides a vivid example of how youth from many cultures are presented in a way that shows extreme homogeneity, a homogeneity that supports beauty standards primarily from certain cultures.
Source: Everett/Photoshot.

three-dozen affiliates, from MTV Adria to MTV Hungary to MTV Ukraine. In some countries, locally produced entertainment has waned or is not even attempted while yielding to the MTV behemoth. We cannot quickly categorize such globalization as good or bad, as in most cases it both benefits and harms the nations that produce and those that consume global media (Mohammed, 2011). For example, with the help of MTV and its international reach, pop stars such as Michael Jackson became a household name in virtually every part of the world. Of course, the obvious downside is that the media machines that catapult a Michael Jackson to global stardom may be doing so at the expense of other (local) figures that do not have access to the same backing.

The second, interrelated concern is what new cultural tropes are introduced to, and even imposed upon, other cultures. A **cultural trope** here is like a literary formula or theme upon which media producers draw: media have certain formulas—types of shows, standard plot lines, typical characters. Returning to the MTV example, in 2006 MTV presented a spring break special in which the network simulcast scenes that featured college-aged partiers from Asia, Australia, Europe, and the U.S. The simulcast was presented by dividing the television screen into four blocks that presented scenes from various locations from each country or continent. The scenes are stark in their homogeneity. In each "block," young people are seen dancing to exactly the same songs in clubs, while doing the same dances, while attired in remarkably similar clothing (Figure 11.4). Cultural homogeneity, however, is not the only concern with such images. Rather, some of the countries MTV featured were selected because they are moneyed, technological powerhouses. The exclusion of other countries means that their cultures remain hidden from the MTV audience.

Another area of inequitable development is that of Internet accessibility. Differential rates of **Internet penetration** (the percentage of a given country that has Internet access) should be of concern, given its growing importance as a tool of global interconnectivity. The Internet may provide the best basis for a globalization that benefits receiving countries, since the Internet would let them organize and relate internally, mobilize their own identities, and seek out alternatives against outside unaccountable influences. However, the Internet is most available to the wealthiest and most industrialized countries. This raises questions about the reach of the information revolution and the prospects for a better future in a networked world.

Power and globalization: What drives the global media?

The narrative presented in this chapter so far mostly attributes global media's advances to technological innovations. However, we must be careful about making claims based on **technological determinism**, which ascribes communication developments and effects to technology and understates other factors, whether social, cultural, behavioral, or economic. Technology, after all, is used in different ways by different people, suggesting that technology cannot be the sole explanation.

Some scholars provide an alternative explanation, **cultural imperialism**. This perspective treats global media as a purveyor of certain cultural and political—usually Western— values, to the exclusion of others in the weaker countries of the world. This one-way transference of culture is enabled by global differences in power. In the imperialism perspective, global media networks, such as MTV and its regional and national variants, come to dominate and threaten cultural expressions and mores native to a receiving country. Global media, as part of a greater corporate industry, furthers values such as consumerism, and promotes escapism.

However, we could argue that the fundamental causes and trends in global media are not quite so simple. There are many cross-cutting examples and nuances. There are sites of resistance to power within global media; there are forms of expression that emerge to impact and change dominant global media. Also, the reasons for globalizing media can be multiple. We can see an example of this in Brazilian music, especially in the development of Brazilian rock music in the 1960s and 1970s. Some have argued that Brazilian popular music is never neutral, but is always either borrowing from or resisting foreign forms. *Tropicália*, a form developed largely by Caetano Veloso and Gilberto Gil in the late 1960s and early 1970s, does both. Whereas Popular Brazilian Music (MPB) strove deliberately to resist international forms to be truly Brazilian (while ironically still borrowing from other Latin and European forms of music), *Tropicália* embraced foreign forms but deliberately "cannibalized" them. That is, singers transformed foreign forms into a more Brazilian form, taking the best of the foreign forms and conquering the forms by adopting and adapting them (Chidester & Baldwin, 2013). Greg Wise's (2008) argument applies especially to Brazilian music, that adoption of foreign forms is as much an issue of cultural push from the core nations as it is cultural pull from peripheral nations where people, for different reasons, are drawn to core- nation media products.

As another example, the most affordable programming is reality TV shows, which are less expensive to produce. Purchasing them and adapting them requires some subtitling work, but that is all. For a new channel, where the dearth of audience research means an unreliable basis for charging advertisers, cheaper programs are the ideal and have been tested and proven as an attractive format for advertisers. Buying and airing them is an economic no-brainer. In this scenario, technology, the formation of a satellite channel, economics and the cultural power of reality TV-producing nations, all came into play.

What do you think? Marshall McLuhan (1964) argues that electronic media have brought us all together into a "global village." Do we live in a global village? In what ways have communications technology and specific media platforms, such as social networking websites (e.g., Facebook, Twitter), brought you closer to other parts of the world? Is a global citizenry truly possible? What would it look like? Can you name examples of cultural imperialism? What avenues of resistance are available despite them?

Global media from above and from below: Hip hop

It is useful to think of global media falling along a spectrum: on one end, global media from above refers to any programs and communications that are delivered from organizations, cultures, and countries that are richer and more powerful than the receiving audience. Global media from below, on the other end of the spectrum, refers to communications originating from people who are on par with the receiving audience. The intersection of international and local influences and meanings is called **interlocalization** (Szalvai, 2009). This section explores one example of interlocalization as a way to understand better the nature of global media.

Although rap music is often seen as a uniquely American musical form that spread around the world, it is important to be aware of its international origins and exportation. We have already learned about the international technological contributions to rap music. Still, there is even more to this story. According to *Can't Stop Won't Stop* by Jeff Chang (2005), the story of rap and hip hop culture begins in Jamaica, the Caribbean nation with a very strong musical tradition. He writes, "Reggae, it has often been said, is rap music's elder kin" (p. 23). While hip hop took shape in New York City, its earliest progenitors included young Jamaican immigrants. The central figure in Chang's story is DJ Kool Herc, or Clive Campbell (Figure 11.5). He immigrated with his family to the Bronx borough of New York City in 1967. He began DJing parties, and innovated the technique of continuously mixing two of the same albums to loop a break beat, a percussion-driven part of songs, to create one long beat. This drove audiences wild. Dancers began trying new styles, spinning on the ground and adapting moves from Hong Kong kung fu flicks. This gave way to breakdancing. Kool Herc and members of his crew also rhymed over the looped beats, which they called rapping. While the birth of a musical genre has many influences and personalities, and such a quick history is bound to leave much out, hip hop took off from the ground up.

Even before this new musical form spread throughout the United States by storm, it began to grow in its global reach. In the early 1980s, a French journalist and independent record label owner living in New York organized a tour of the earliest hip hop stars to Europe. Headlining the bill was the legendary Afrika Bambaataa, who appealed to pan-African sentiments in the efforts of his Zulu Nation organization, among other things. It also included the Soulsonic Force and the Rock Steady Crew, which included Puerto Rican dancers, and others. They demonstrated hip hop's four elements—rapping, dancing,

Rap music reflects very specific aspects of some Black U.S. cultures and of the history of young, urban Black males in the U.S. But it can also reflect the interconnectedness of the world, as seen in these lyrics by Keith Murray and Nas:

From interstate to tri-state to international
Mr. Keith Murray always keeps it classical
They had me up in England, mic stranglin
Jewels danglin while my single jingle jangling
Number one in my field, never defeated
Went to Sweden demonstrated malicious mic beatings
I was with my right hand man, Redman
When I did the Ichiban crane style in Japan
I transform like Dr. Bruce Banner
Stepped off the plane and blacked out up in Canada
                    (Keith Murray, *World Be Free*, 1996)

So I'm deadly now because of one reason, they listening
In Budapest, Japan, China, and Switzerland
                              (Nas, untitled, 2008)

Figure 11.5 DJ Kool Herc is called "The Father" for his foundational role in hip hop history.
Source: Johnny Nunez /Wire Image/Getty Images.

DJing and graffiti-writing—to small crowds in England and France. Hip hop was not part of the mainstream media experience internationally yet. However, its growth was visible.

Today hip hop is a fully globalized musical form. The biggest stars, such as Jay Z, Kanye West and Eminem are global figures who tour internationally and are played in radio stations worldwide. Since these artists work for and are managed by the largest music corporations in the world, they reflect the process of globalization from above. The hip hop movement, in this respect, is an interlocal phenomenon: it is driven by the interests of the economic elite, though its earlier days saw a more organic development, driven by the interests and needs of poor, urban youth. Hip hop is important because it complicates this below-above distinction and draws attention to the interactive possibilities between the global and the local. What is just as important is that now countries around the world, from Senegal to Poland to New Zealand, have their own native hip hop movements that take place in their unique national contexts. For example, Senegalese rappers are actively involved in trying to reform the country's political system. In Dakar, the West African country's capital, the DJ and rapper Xuman told the BBC in 2007 that "I wanted to make sure the album was released just before the elections. I'm hoping it will help people to see politicians with different eyes" (Ronsini, 2007). DJ Xuman's music levels charges against the government and calls on the youth to vote.

Diverse cultures have influenced the art form of hip hop; hip hop has also similarly impacted cultures and found new expressions in different global landscapes. This shows how multi-directional cultural flows between nations can be. Of course, as we have seen, global media is not without its critics, many of whom warn against the world's development under globalization.

What do you think? Hip hop artists can be found in China, Bangladesh (Bangla hip hop), Norway, and many other countries. In some ways, it may differ in each culture, but in other ways, hip hop retains some elements of the culture(s) from which it sprang. In what ways is hip hop a culture in and of itself? How is it affected by global media? How does it affect other cultures?

The challenges of global media flows

The rise of global media impacts national cultures in ways that are still unfolding and developing. Like globalization in general, this causes many a great deal of anxiety as the uncertainties of development under such influences seem to pile on. This inspires much wonderment and speculation about the world's communication direction. What does an increasingly globalized media mean for cultures and their unique characteristics, as well as their autonomy? Many in the developing world, especially, came to feel as though their native cultures were being bombarded by foreign media, spreading alien values, and that this bombardment would distort the youth of their countries. These concerns took shape in an international document called the *Convention on the Protection and Promotion of the Diversity of Cultural Expressions* (UNESCO, 2005), drafted by numerous countries through the General Conference of the United Nations Educational, Scientific and Cultural

Figure 11.6 A worker in Shanghai, China, removes a poster for *The Da Vinci Code* after Chinese censors ban the movie.
Source: Mark Ralston/AFP/Getty Images.

Organization in 2005. In it, they argued that "the processes of globalization . . . represent a challenge for cultural diversity, namely in view of risks of imbalances between rich and poor countries" (UNESCO, 2005). They fear that globalization threatens the fragile balance between influence and domination, that the cultural effects of global media are homogenizing—that is, getting rid of the differences between peoples. Proponents of this view argue that global media lead to **convergence**, the idea that we are becoming alike and consuming fewer sources.

Some governments of countries on the receiving end of global media try to assert their national power by regulating or censoring global media. As we have noted, some nations, such as China, put formal limits on the number of imported movies (Figure 11.6). Other countries focus on excluding particular content to prevent negative cultural influences. At times, these can be culturally neutral. Thailand, for example, banned smoking scenes on television. They cited this as an effort to prevent young people from gaining an interest in smoking. The government censored smoking in *The Simpsons* by blurring out representations of cigarette puffing by the show's characters. In other instances, censorship is a large-scale project. Saudi Arabia banned access to nearly 400,000 web pages, one of the most exhaustive Internet filterers in the world. The stated aim is "protecting citizens from offensive content and content [that] violates the principles of Islam and the social norms" (Bunt, 2009, p. 71).

Another source of concern for national governments is that global media, especially new media, can be used by political dissidents to put pressure on their governments and advocate for political change. Over the summer of 2009, protesters in Iran took to the streets against the re-election win of Mahmoud Ahmadinejad. As the government cracked down on the protests, often violently, reformers leaked photos on short reports to the world via Twitter, a social networking site that lets people broadcast short messages to followers. The government was trying to restrict access to certain websites as well as SMS text messaging, but did not stop Twitter. Users on Twitter re-sent the messages and images from Iran, eventually pushing mainstream media like CNN to devote more attention to the brutal government crackdown on dissenters. The killing of Neda Agha-Soltan, whose last moments were posted on YouTube, drew international outrage. Iran eventually caught on and tried to limit Internet access, as well as the ability of journalists to report on what was taking place.

Twitter, as with other social networking sites such as Facebook, is an interesting variation of global media in that it can be used locally, and can affirm non-global identities. Some refer to this as **glocalization**, a mix of "globalization" and "localization." This implies that a global platform can have localizing applications, meaning it can used to bring neighbors closer together. Twitter demonstrated most vividly its "glocal" nature during the shooting spree in Mumbai, India, in late 2008. As several gunmen roamed the city firing on anyone they saw, witnesses and those escaping sent text messages and tweets to update the locations of the shooters. Their localized reporting was communicated to others and thus became part of a way to survive the ongoing emergency. In less dramatic form, these sites allow people to meet up with other residents who live nearby, by offering geography-based Twitter lists. Craigslist, an international, virtual bulletin board for everything from jobs, to used products, rental listings and personals, has maintained separate pages for individual cities to promote the local. Glocalization is also seen in magazines or newspapers that publish region-specific editions. One could argue that *Cosmopolitan* magazines in different countries are an example of that, even though others may see these as an example of cultural imperialism.

Some scholars are concerned that online communication leads people to form web-based communities premised on rules of inclusion—networks of similar people who grow further detached from the diversity of the world. At an extreme level, this could lead to **divergence**, or the fragmentation of peoples into smaller identities and networks of association. This could happen without the localization element. If people used the Internet to interact and identify only with like-minded people internationally, to the exclusion of others, new media could be contributing to fragmentation based on whatever drew the like-minded people together. Some question what this would mean for national social fabric, especially if imagined communities shift from national bodies to trans-national affiliations.

In one extreme vision of global divergence, Benjamin Barber (1996) posited that the world faced a showdown between two social dynamics: McWorld versus Jihad. These terms represented on one hand the forces of corporate globalization, by which corporations gain political power, and on the other, an extreme embrace of traditional values, either traditionalism or religious fundamentalism. His idea was that the universalizing pressures of corporate power would ignite tribalism and other narrow reactions in response. Barber felt that neither of these visions was promising for democracy.

Against such a doomsday scenario, others have called into question the binary logic, or the thinking that the world must choose one or the other direction. To make such a prognosis requires a basic assumption that there are such things as pure, authentic cultures that have not been impacted by others. Only with this assumption does the fear of cultural intermingling make sense. Those taking this view advise us to take a step back and see the inherent **hybridity**, or mixed nature of cultures formed through histories of borrowing, copying, and mutual influencing. To understand the world's cultures as basically **syncretic**, or combinations of various systems of thought and influence, is to see the recently accelerated global movement of ideas, people, capital, and messages not as a necessary threat to cultures, but rather as an exciting stage in further hybridization. However, as we will note in chapter 12, such syncretism or hybridity is seldom neutral. Some groups always have more access to the means of creation, distribution, or access to media forms and contents than other groups, and thus can control at least to some degree the nature and rate of hybridization.

Finally, we should note that many of the channels that relate to globalization mentioned here, from video-sharing sites (like YouTube), to social networking sites (like Facebook, MSN, MySpace, or Twitter) to Internet chat, link the mediated forces of globalization to face-to-face communication. So far, most of the discussion of globalization has focused around media; future thinkers must also look to see how globalization informs folk culture, everyday lived experience, and face-to-face communication of individuals in their own cultures and as they interact interculturally. We will address specific aspects of globalization as it pertains to culture and business communication in chapter 15.

Summary

We have learned that media and technologies have a global impact. They support the circulation of all manners of cultural forms and communications from all parts of the globe. However, we have also learned that the mediated dissemination of cultures is not always equal. Rather, certain cultural stories, events, and messages get more (or less) attention than others. The result of such privileging is that only some cultures become more influential while others are rendered less powerful. One way to think about this unequal distribution of power is to consider who gets to tell their stories, and have those stories circulated, versus those whose stories are ignored or are told for them by others. To illustrate, in the fall of 2009, California-based TriStar pictures released the science fiction film *District 9* to North America and the UK. The film was directed by Neill Blomkamp, a South African, and produced by Peter Jackson, a New Zealander. In the blockbuster film, Nigerians are represented as hyper-violent gang members who deal in guns, exploit the less powerful, murder, and believe in superstition to the point that they engage in cannibalism in the hope of digesting the desired traits and powers of those they kill. In response, the Nigerian government banned the film from its country, dismayed by how they were stereotypically represented by others. The fear was that such representations would reflect poorly upon the people and cultures of Nigeria.

We have learned in this chapter to consider who is creating and circulating media messages, whose messages dominate, and the implications of messages created from inside a culture versus those created by those external to it—in short, what is globalized, and our intercultural exchanges, may be dramatically altered by who gets to participate in the global conversation. However, we also have learned that media globalization holds great promise and hope. There are predictions of a truly global village arising out of media's ability to help us conquer space and time. Perhaps the most optimistic view rests in notions of cultural hybridity. Holders of this view are interested in how new cultural forms emerge as a result of the coming together of different cultures. For them, globalization is not a simple top-down process, but one that results in complex and varied cultural outcomes, some good and some bad. The important thing to take away from this discussion is that we should not make sweeping generalizations about globalization. It may make more sense to think of what works and what does not work for cultures, and under what conditions communication between them is most effective.

KEY TERMS

global media, 228
sending countries, 228
receiving countries, 228
globalization, 231
capitalism, 232
viral, 233
cable systems, 234
over-the-air, or terrestrial
    broadcasting, 234
satellite TV, 234
cross-over, 234
fansubbed, 234
space, 236

time, 236
core countries, 237
periphery countries, 237
cultural trope, 238
Internet penetration, 238
technological determinism, 239
cultural imperialism, 239
interlocalization, 240
convergence, 243
glocalization, 244
divergence, 244
hybridity, 244
syncretic/syncretism, 244

Discussion questions

1 Discuss the effects of cultural imperialism. What would critics of cultural imperialism have to say about these? Also consider more favorable possible outcomes of this form of cultural engagement.

2 Consider where you think we are headed in this global media age. Is it toward cultural convergence or cultural divergence?

3 In what ways has technology served to facilitate intercultural communication across national borders?

4 Have your favorite bands or singers toured internationally? List which countries they performed in, to get a sense of where else they are also popular. You may be able to find fan websites based in those countries.

5 Think about the global media reviewed in this chapter and what you are exposed to in your life. Would you consider them forces of convergence, divergence, or something else?

Action points

1 Watch a foreign film. Given the enormous movie industries in places like India, Hong Kong and Europe, global cinema is becoming less and less American. Movies from those countries are rarely shown in the large movie theaters or on television, so going out of your way to track down movies from other countries could be a great learning experience. Ask yourself whether you liked the movie, and why.

2 Study your favorite name brand of clothing. See what you can find out about where and how it is produced. What global flows of management, production, transportation, and consumption characterize your brand? Compare it to other brands. Do some have better global records than others? What are some actions you could take in situations of economic inequality? Discuss in your class the strengths and limitations of such strategies as large-scale product boycotts.

3 In groups or pairs, with your instructor's supervision, conduct a small research project in which you either interview or survey people *within* a group (e.g., the motivations of members or the activities of the group) about how much media from other countries they consume. Discuss your findings with the class. What type of knowledge does your study give you? What are some types of knowledge or claims that you could *not* make from your study?

For more information

Boyd-Barrett, O., & Rantanen, T. (Eds.) (1998). *The globalization of news*. London: Sage.

Castells, M. (1996). *The rise of the network society*. New York: Blackwell.

Chalaby, J. (Ed.) (2005). *Transnational television worldwide: Towards a new media order*. London: I.B. Tauris.

Curtin, M. (2007). *Playing to the world's biggest audience: The globalization of Chinese film and television*. Berkeley, CA: University of California Press.

Hills, J. (2002). *The struggle for control of global communication*. Urbana: University of Illinois Press.

Kraidy, M. (2005). *Hybridity: Or the cultural logic of globalization*. Philadelphia: Temple.

Kraidy, M. (2009). *Reality television and Arab politics: Contention in public life*. Cambridge: Cambridge University Press, 2009.

Nye, J. (2004). *Power in the global information age: From realism to globalization*. London: Routledge.

Thussu, D. (2006). *Media on the move: Global flow and contra-flow*. London: Routledge.

Thussu, D. (2009). *International communication: A reader*. London: Routledge.

UNESCO (2005). *Convention on the protection and promotion of the diversity of cultural expressions*. http://unesdoc.unesco.org/images/0014/001429/142919e.pdf

References

Barber, B. (1996). *Jihad vs. McWorld: How globalism and tribalism are reshaping the world*. New York: Ballantine Books.

Bunt, G. (2009). *iMuslims: Rewiring the House of Islam*. Chapel Hill: UNC Press.

Castells, M. (1997). An introduction to the information age. *City*, 7, p. 6–16.

Castells, M. (2000). *End of millennium*. Oxford: Blackwell.

Chang, J. (2005). *Can't stop won't stop: A history of the hip hop generation*. (Intro DJ Cool Herc). New York: St. Martin's Press/Picador.

Chidester, P.J., & Baldwin, J.R. (2013). Shattering myths: Brazil's *Tropicália* movement. In L. Shaw (Ed.), *Song and social change in Latin America* (pp. 27–48). Lanham, MD: Lexington.

Collins, S. (2008). *The hunger games*. New York: Scholastic.

Fouché, R. (2009). Hip-hop and African American innovation. *The Lemelson Center for the Study of Invention and Innovation*. Accessed Aug 31, 2013, at http://invention.smithsonian.org/resources/online_articles_detail.aspx?id=543.

Fouché, R. (2012). Analog turns digital: Hip-hop, technology, and the maintenance of racial authenticity. In T. Pinch & K. Bijsterveld (Eds.), *The Oxford handbook of sound studies* (pp. 505–525). Oxford: Oxford University Press.

Giddens, A. (1990). *The consequences of modernity*. Stanford, CA: Stanford University Press.

Han, J. (2010). Avatar: A eulogy for China's "nail houses". *China View*, January 13. Accessed July 29, 2012, at http://news.xinhuanet.com/english/2010-01/13/content_12804107.htm

IMDb.com (n.d.). *Awards for "Ugly Betty"*. Accessed July 29, 2012, at http://www.imdb.com/title/tt0805669/awards

Itzkoff, D. (2010). You saw what in "Avatar"? Pass those glasses! *The New York Times*, January 20. Accessed July 29, 2012, at http://www.nytimes.com/2010/01/20/movies/20avatar.html

LaFraniere, S. (2010). China's zeal for "Avatar" crowds out "Confucius". *The New York Times*, 29 January. Accessed July 29, 2012, at http://www.nytimes.com/2010/01/30/business/global/30avatar.html?_r=1

McLuhan, M. (1964). *Understanding media: The extensions of man.* New York: McGraw-Hill.

McPhail, T. L. (2010). *Global communication: Theories, stakeholders, and trends* (3rd ed.). Chichester: Wiley-Blackwell.

Mohammed, S.D. (2011). *Communication and the globalization of culture: Beyond tradition and borders.* Lanham, MD: Lexington.

Seidman, R. (2009). TV ratings: Dollhouse returns quietly, Ugly Betty bounces back (33%). *TV by the Numbers*, December 5. Accessed July 29, 2012, at http://tvbythenumbers.zap2it.com/2009/12/05/tv-ratings-dollhousereturns-quietly-ugly-betty-bounces-back-33/35356/

Szalvai, E. (2009). Roma project: A case study set in Europe. In T.L. McPhail, (Ed.), *Development communication: Reframing the role of the media* (pp. 175–198). Malden, MA: Wiley-Blackwell.

Thussu, D.K. (2008). Globalization of the media. In Donsbach, W. (Ed.), *The international encyclopedia of communication.* Oxford: Blackwell.

UNESCO (2005). *Convention on the protection and promotion of the diversity of cultural expressions.* Accessed Jan 27, 2010, at http://unesdoc.unesco.org/images/0014/001495/149502e.pdf

Webfluenz (2012). *Gangnam style: The social media phenomenon*, September 11. Accessed April 15, 2013, at http://www.blog.webfluenz.com/2012/09/gangnam-style-the-social-media-phenomenon

Wise, G. (2008). *Cultural globalization: A user's guide.* Malden, MA: Blackwell.

Chapter 12

Adaptation and intercultural competence: How can I be effective in a new culture?

Chapter objectives

After this chapter, you should be able to:

→ Explain the notion of culture shock, its symptoms, and some basic causes

→ Compare the U-curve notion of adjustment, with alternative views for how adjustment happens

→ List at least three reasons why coming home from another culture may be difficult

→ Differentiate between psychological adjustment, behavioral adaptation, and assimilation

→ Define intercultural communication competence, and list three main areas that influence it

Cross-cultural adaptation: How can I better adjust to a new culture?

Rethinking acculturation: What happens when cultural groups live side by side?

Coming home: Will it be as easy as it sounds?

Intercultural communication competence: How can I get the job done... and still be liked?

Intercultural Communication for Everyday Life, First Edition. John R. Baldwin, Robin R. Means Coleman, Alberto González, and Suchitra Shenoy-Packer.
© 2014 John R. Baldwin, Robin R. Means Coleman, Alberto González, and Suchitra Shenoy-Packer.
Published 2014 by John Wiley & Sons Ltd.

erhaps you have traveled to another country or region during school holidays or as an exchange student. Maybe you visited a different culture within your own country, such as on a service project. In such cases, you may have experienced difficulty. However, authors who study cross-cultural transitions suggest that difficulties we feel during short-term trips differ from those felt by **sojourners**—those who travel abroad for a longer time, say one to five years, with intent to return home (Kim, 2005), or who move to another culture permanently (**immigrants**), perhaps involuntarily (**refugees**). Janet Bennett (1977) suggests that when there is a "loss of a familiar frame of reference"—whether that is a move to another area, the loss of a loved one, or a major job shift—there are both loss and change: "Culture shock bears a remarkable resemblance to tensions and anxieties we face whenever change threatens the stability of our lives" (p. 45).

Anyone who travels to another culture, within or outside of her or his nation of origin, goes through some form of transition. But transition experiences help to make us more complex and complete individuals, helping us to be better intercultural communicators. The purpose of this chapter is to introduce notions of cultural adjustment and competence, and to provide hints about how to recognize stress during transition and make the most of it.

Cross-cultural adaptation: How can I better adjust to a new culture?

People have different experiences when they travel abroad. If you are a university student, you know that the same is true of those who go through the transition of moving to a new university (Figure 12.1). But why do we have stress to begin with, and why do some people process it differently than others? In this chapter, we summarize the notion of cultural adjustment, look at its symptoms and some models to explain it, and explain some things

Figure 12.1 The number of international students traveling between cultures continues to increase, with 2.8 million college students leaving their territory or country of origin to study in 2007, according to UNESCO (van der Pol, 2009). Source: Michael Dwyer/Alamy.

that might impact it. This understanding, in turn, should help us find ways to deal with the stress of transition to a new culture.

Adjustment and culture shock: Defining the terms

On the surface, cross-cultural **adjustment** is a simple concept, referring to the process one goes through in adjusting to another culture (Kim, 2001). Young Yun Kim (2005) uses this term to encompass a variety of related terms, each with its own nuance—like "culture shock, acculturation, adjustment, assimilation, integration, and adaptation" (p. 376). The general idea of cross-cultural adjustment is one of "unlearning" one culture and learning another. As we grow up in our native cultures, we go through a process of **enculturation**, learning our own culture. **Acculturation** is the learning and adapting of some amount of the values, behaviors, and ways of thinking of the new culture (Kim, 2001); at the same time, we "unlearn" or lose some of our own culture, a process known as **deculturation**. **Assimilation** is when one adopts the behaviors and ways of thinking of a host culture.

What do you think? To what degree do you think someone has to "lose" her or his own culture in order to be effective in a new culture? Does your answer differ for a sojourner as opposed to an immigrant or refugee? How can or should groups negotiate their cultural uniqueness with their sense of identity and unity with the larger nation or culture?

These terms lead to new questions: Do we ever learn enough of the other culture to get by, but deliberately keep parts of our own culture? Can we learn the other culture and still feel miserable and depressed, as we feel we are not being true to ourselves? Or can we go about blissfully ignorant of the new culture, but be totally comfortable, even confident in our own arrogant belief that our own culture is better? Jeffrey Ady (1995) suggests that there are major problems in the study of cross-cultural adjustment, as researchers define and measure "adjustment" in different ways.

Whatever adjustment is, most scholars agree that people experience tension and discomfort when we lose the familiar cues we are used to in our environment (Hall, 1973). Kalvaro Oberg (1960) coined the term **culture shock** to refer to a sense of "anxiety that results from losing all of our familiar signs and symbols of social intercourse" (p. 177). People often see culture shock as an emotional response to the loss of one's own culture (Adler, 1975), often resulting in symptoms of disorientation, sadness or anger, grief, nostalgia, or even psychosomatic disorders. But how does this culture shock occur? Can we predict how we might experience it?

Models of cultural adjustment

The U-curve Based on a study of Norwegian Fulbright scholars, Sverre Lysgaard (1955) developed a well-known model of cultural adjustment, the **U-curve** of adjustment, which suggests that travelers go through stages (Lysgaard saw three, though many today speak of

Figure 12.2 Even though the U-curve model of adjustment seems to make sense, much modern research questions its accuracy.
Source: Liu & Lee, 2008, reproduced by permission of Emerald Group Publishing Ltd.

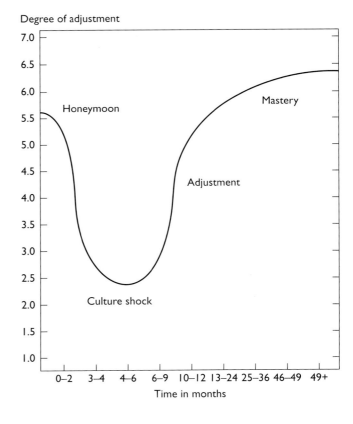

four, Figure 12.2). The first stage of euphoria, often called the **honeymoon stage**, is a time of happiness and excitement as one first arrives at a new culture. Everything is new, and even aspects that may not be as enjoyable are reframed in terms of the great experience of traveling to a new culture. The second stage, often called the **crisis stage**, represents a time of difficulty as one confronts ongoing cultural differences and loss of expected cues. At this stage, travelers often go through fight or flight (Dodd, 1998). With "fight," they lash out against the culture or act out, perhaps turning to alcohol, drugs, or other escape mechanisms, or complaining about the culture and making negative comparisons to their own supposedly superior culture. Others choose "flight," running away from the culture. Travelers might spend lots of time alone, get depressed, or spend time only with people from their own culture. A third possibility is for the traveler to "go native," to totally accept the new culture while rejecting the culture of origin.

The crisis stage is said to occur often between three and six months—so it is different from stress one might have about difficulties on a short-term trip. It comes from a longer-term lack of cues and disorientation, as the cultural frameworks of the traveler melt and reform. Most travelers work through this to the third stage, the **adjustment stage** or "flex" stage (Dodd, 1998) , which reflects a growing sense of understanding and being able to live and succeed in the new culture. Finally, one reaches a sense of balance, of full effectiveness. People often call this the **integration stage**, as the traveler has taken the new culture and made it a part of her or himself.

The model makes sense of the struggles many people feel during cultural transitions, and it reflects several truths about adaptation that we agree with. First, all travelers go through some sort of stress when moving to a new culture, whether around the world or from the country to the big city. Second, adjustment is often uncomfortable, leading to feelings of loss, anger, or powerlessness in the new culture. Third, the process of adjustment takes time. One should not expect quick results, and one should expect the long-term process of adjustment to be different than the momentary setbacks or negative experiences one might have on a tourist trip. The U-curve receives tremendous support, with many university travel programs, international consultants, and businesses training their travelers that these are the stages through which all travelers pass.

Unfortunately, it lacks in research support, and scholars today are proposing new models to make sense of adjustment. As early as a generation ago, scholars began to debunk the U-curve. Austin Church, in 1982, reviewing 150 articles on cultural adjustment, noted that "phase" or "stage" models like the U-curve had only limited support. While most travelers experience the symptoms, they might not experience the stages in order. Some might move forward and then back. And, although the process of adjustment does take time, it is difficult to predict *when* travelers might experience shock, as travelers work through the process at different speeds. In a later study, Daniel Kealey (1989) found that out of 277 technical advisors in 20 developing nations, only about 10% actually experienced adjustment in what one might call a "U-curve." In addition, many scholars have discussed a wide array of factors that lead to improved cross-cultural adjustment, such as previous travel experience, knowledge of the language, willingness to travel, flexibility, age (with children adjusting quicker than adults), and so on. The growing list of variables and the inadequacy of the U-curve have led authors to propose other models for adjustment. We will consider only two approaches here.

. . . .

ON THE NET

Look up online travel guides, such as GoAbroad.com's guide for traveler's to Spain (http://www.goabroad.info/Spain.html?gID=587), **or travel sites, such as StudentsAbroad.com** (http://studentsabroad.com/), **or the Worldwide Classroom** (http://www.worldwide.edu/index.html). **Consider college websites for international students, including that of your university).** **Go to** http://en.wikipedia.org/wiki/Culture_shock **at Wikipedia. Do any of these teach the U-curve as if it were fact? Do they provide any word on the evidence that challenges the U-curve? What might be the implications of teaching travelers that they will all go through these phases?**

. . . .

Kim's theory of cross-cultural adjustment Young Kim (2001), after years of research with many different populations, especially Korean immigrants to the United States, derived a theory of cross-cultural adjustment that builds upon our understanding of adjustment in several ways. Kim's (2005) most important addition to our understanding of adjustment, for our purposes, is that she sees adaptation as deeply related to communication. Certainly, there are psychological aspects of the traveler and structural aspects of the environment. But pressure to conform or host receptivity can only be conveyed through communication.

It is also through communication that the traveler either clings to her or his own cultural group or moves into the new culture. The traveler needs to become involved in face-to-face communication, such as spending time with host nationals and watching host-culture media (some media are better than others!). But, contrary to many writers, Kim suggests that ongoing communication with one's own group and media from one's own culture can also make adjustment easier, as long as that communication helps the traveler to build a bridge into the new culture.

Second, similar to previous approaches, her theory considers aspects of travelers that will help them to adjust, such as flexibility to change and strength of character (for example, the ability to deal with difficult situations). But Kim makes several extensions to the typical psychological approach. First, she looks beyond typical approaches that just try to predict adjustment with variables to see adjustment happening within a system. The traveler moves to a culture and adjusts within an environment, so Kim considers that it is not only aspects of the individual, but also of the environment, that impact adjustment. If a host culture is hostile to a group of sojourners (for example, with prejudice or stereotypes), that may work against adjustment. This is an important consideration: often, we assume adjustment is in the power of the traveler, but social and economic constraints, including low-paying jobs in the language of one's home culture, lack of opportunity, or prejudice from dominant culture, may get in the way of someone's adjustment. Pressure to conform could increase adjustment, if adjustment refers to one's ability to follow the rules of the culture. If one moves into a situation where there are many from the person's own group (high ethnic group strength), this, in turn, would slow down adjustment. The tension between these variables begins to suggest that there are different types of adjustment, as pressure to conform might increase assimilation but be psychologically stressful.

A third major contribution by Kim (2005) is that, unlike the notion of culture shock, Kim sees potential in cultural transition. Adjustment is like starting a rigorous exercise program. At first, you must break down muscles in order to rebuild them. In the same way, the traveler *must* go through stress in order to break down old ways of thinking. Adaptation leads to growth, making travelers stronger than before. Also, unlike the U-curve, Kim sees adaptation as an ongoing process in which travelers continue to face new challenges, each bringing more growth, following what Kim calls a **stress-adaptation-growth dynamic**. Adjustment is cyclical, with increased adaptation over time, but in a two-steps-forward-one-step-back, or a "draw-back-to-leap" pattern (Kim, 2005, p. 384; see Figure 12.3). Because stress can be useful for travelers' growth, we prefer to talk about "cultural adjustment" rather than "culture shock."

Figure 12.3 Kim (2005) feels that cultural adjustment does not follow a strict U-curve, but, instead, it is cyclical, as the traveler faces new stresses. Source: Reproduced from Kim & Ruben, 1988, p. 312, by permission of Sage Publications, Inc.

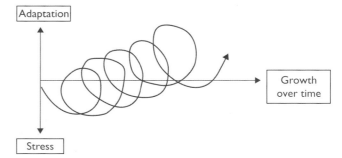

Break it down

A big part of sojourners' adjustment deals with host receptivity and the chances sojourners have to interact positively with people from the host culture. Pressure to conform may help newcomers assimilate to a new culture, but it might also make psychological adjustment more difficult.

What types of sojourners are there in your university, workplace, or community? Take a concrete step to show them your receptivity to them, to give them opportunities to interact with you, and to make their psychological adjustment easier. What can you do to be a positive part of their adjustment?

Different domains of adjustment Several writers now argue that we should not think of adjustment as a single thing, but that there might be different "domains" or areas of adjustment (Black *et al.*, 1991; Selmer & Fenner, 2009). These might be different areas of demand, such as work or school versus relationships, where someone could be performing well in school, but have poor relationships (Ady, 1995). One study found that, as international students spent more years in Japan and learned the language better, they could accomplish tasks better but had less fulfilling relationships with the Japanese (Tanaka *et al.*, 1994). Possibly, as language improves, Japanese hosts remove social support from travelers, who realize that they are still "outsiders" to the culture. Colleen Ward has done extensive work to outline two different types of adjustment: **psychological adjustment**, "associated with psychological well- being or emotional satisfaction," and **sociocultural adjustment**, which deals with one's ability to "fit in" and get tasks done within one's environment (Ward *et al.*, 1998, p. 279). The first dimension deals with stress and coping, and the second with learning the culture.

With this in mind, we offer more refined definitions: **Cross-cultural adjustment** deals with one's coping or psychological health when moving to a new culture (Kim, 2001; Ward, 2004). **Cross-cultural adaptation** refers to one's ability to negotiate the culture to accomplish tasks (shopping, etc.), to "fit in" by adapting some degree of aspects of the host culture (Ward, 2004, p. 186), possibly forming stable and functional relationships (Kim, 2001). Ward and her colleagues have done many studies on the two dimensions, noting that they are related to different things we encounter in a new culture. For example, a study of international aid workers in Nepal (Ward & Rana-Deuba, 1999) found that those who continued to identify with their home culture actually experienced less depression in Nepal, but those who identified more with the new culture had better sociocultural adaptation.

Writers continue to develop new understandings of adaptation. For example, Melissa Curtin (2010) discusses how previous literature mistakenly treats adaptation as a one-way process, with the traveler adapting to the culture; in fact, both parties adapt to each other, though in unequal power relationships. Other writers highlight problems in most communication theory that have implications for the theories here. In terms of Miike's

(2007) critique of Western theories (see chapter 1), these theories focus on the individual, independence, reason, and self-enhancement. Kim's theory talks about how adjustment aids individual development; and all the theories here focus on pragmatic adjustment (getting around) and psychological wellbeing of individuals. At the same time, Kim's theory considers aspects both of context (pressure to conform and the degree to which different contexts welcome specific groups of strangers) and of interconnectedness to others in the process of adaptation.

Rethinking acculturation: What happens when cultural groups live side by side?

In the Nepal study, the researchers (Ward & Rana-Deuba, 1999) relied heavily upon a conceptualization of acculturation provided by John Berry (2004). In this framework, while acculturation refers, most precisely, to one's acceptance of aspects of a culture and identification with that culture, Berry suggests that we should not think of this as straightforward adaptation. Rather, one can adopt different elements of the culture. In some cases, individuals can fully embrace and identify with both cultures (**integration, or biculturalism**); in other cases, they can deliberately resist the new culture and maintain elements their original culture. Or individuals can become **marginal**, where they end up identifying with neither the host nor the original culture, often ceasing to want any interaction. Acculturation is often measured by one's acceptance of the new culture's language, use of host culture literature, friendship networks, food choice, recreational activities, and so on.

Like Kim (2005), who suggests that sojourner adjustment is impacted by the host culture's acceptance of the traveler, Richard Bourhis and his colleagues (1997) suggest that we cannot think of the minority member's acculturation as based only on an individual's adjustment. We must also consider whether the people in the majority accept or expect integration of the minority group. The dominant culture has a part in the sojourner's approach by means of their attitudes toward strangers and minorities—to separate them intentionally or unintentionally (**segregation**), allow them to maintain both group and new/dominant culture identities (**multiculturalism**, often called **cultural pluralism**), expect them to lose their own cultural identity to become like the mainstream (**melting pot**, commonly called the assimilation model), or simply negate their existence, having no relations with them (**exclusion**) (Sam & Berry, 2010; see Figure 12.4).

In sum, recent researchers see cultural adaptation in a more complex way. Many immigrants *are* acculturating, but not to dominant culture. Susan Keefe and Amado Padilla (1987) for example, suggest that there are several different patterns of Latina/ Latino "acculturation," depending on the community to which Latinas/Latinos move upon arrival to the United States, the degree to which incoming migration continues, and the amount of kin and family one has when one arrives. In fact, they suggest, many Mexicans who move to the United States are not adjusting to mainstream American culture, but to a specific Mexican American culture, which is distinct in important ways from Mexican culture.

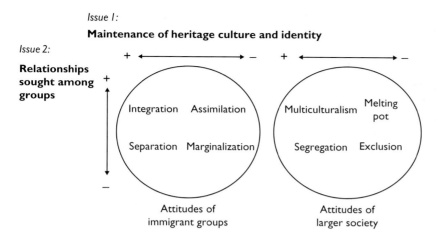

Issue 1:

Maintenance of heritage culture and identity

Issue 2:

Relationships sought among groups

Integration   Assimilation

Separation   Marginalization

Attitudes of
immigrant groups

Multiculturalism   Melting pot

Segregation   Exclusion

Attitudes of
larger society

Figure 12.4 John Berry suggests that people traveling to another culture or living in a dominant culture as minority members can highlight different identities. But the dominant culture also exerts pressure on the identity of the traveler.
Source: Reproduced from Sam & Berry, 2010, p. 477, by permission of Sage Publications, Inc.

Break it down

Refugees constitute a specific type of traveler. Often, refugees move to communities with people descended from the same culture (or with other refugee communities). Various Internet news sources number the total refugee population in the world between 10 and 35 million. Research a refugee group (the closer to your home, the better). What are the social conditions that created the refugee problem? What social issues, conditions, barriers, and benefits face the refugees in their new home? How might this relate to their adaptation to the new culture? Share the news with your friends or your class.

This relates the idea of cultural pluralism—the idea that members of co-cultural groups should embrace their own culture. Proponents of this view may not disagree with the notion of "unity" with a culture, but may feel that unity is not based on cultural homogeneity. In some cases, members of cultural groups actively resist identification with the dominant culture or embrace what we call **selective adaptation**—the acceptance of some elements of the dominant culture but not others. We see such adaptation among many (but certainly not all) Asian Indian Americans. Radha Hegde (1998) interviewed Asian Indian women about the different ways the women negotiated sex, race, and cultural identities. In some cases, their choices were related to stereotypes and racism they felt from the dominant culture; in other places, such as the preservation of Indianness in the home, it was to provide a cultural haven from the dominant culture. Indians within America might maintain their religion and festivals, form cricket clubs to play in the parks on Saturdays, and continue to wear traditional Indian clothes, even while acting very "American" in the workplace.

At the same time, Asian Indians may share cultural similarities with "PIOs" (Persons of Indian Origin) throughout the world, from Toronto to Trinidad, from Uganda to the United Arab Emirates. To this end, Rona Halualani and Jolanta Drzewiecka (2008), for example, discuss the notion of **diaspora**, when a group from a specific homeland is spread out across a wide geographic area, such as the Jewish diaspora. They discuss Hawaiian and Polish identities, noting, for example, that there is a way of talking about Polish identity that links Polish-descended peoples anywhere to "romanticized notions of primordial descent" (p. 60). These ways of talking and thinking (discourses), link Polish émigrés everywhere to a certain notion of Polishness that provides a "reassuring bedrock" that sustains them through difficult times and cultural and geographic changes (p. 60). As diasporic groups rub together against local cultures, each takes from the other in cultural blends that reflect **hybridity** (Drzewiecka & Halualani, 2002). However, such blends are always negotiated, with both sides having different types of power. In most cases, the dominant culture picks the terms in ways that benefit its own social structure and cultural privilege.

As we see, cultural adjustment—either through travel abroad or co-cultures living together within the same geographic space—is anything but simple. In some ways, one's individual acculturation, as well as the "assimilation" of a group within a community, is predictable. In other ways, it is negotiated through communication, always shifting and changing, and through power relations with dominant cultures. Our understanding of adaptation and acculturation can benefit from scientific, humanistic, and critical approaches we discuss in chapter 2.

Coming home: Will it be as easy as it sounds?

At the end of the Lord of the Rings trilogy by J.R.R. Tolkien (1955/1965), as Frodo returns home after destroying the Ring, he has a quiet chat with Gandalf, the wizard. "There is no real going back," he says. "Though I may come to the Shire, it will not be the same; for I will not be the same. I am wounded with knife, sting, and tooth, and with a long burden. Where shall I find rest?" (p. 268). Gandalf does not answer him. We would think that coming home from another culture should be easy. After all, we know our own culture, our friends, our family—don't we?

The return home to one's culture is often so difficult, someone created the term, **return culture shock**. Just as we believe that "cultural adjustment" is a better way to think of the transition process traveling abroad, we refer to the experience of returning home as **return cultural adjustment**. This refers to the process of adjusting to one's culture psychologically and behaviorally when returning home. Since the travelers likely know their way around, sociocultural adjustment may not be as difficult as the adjustment abroad, though people have to adapt behaviors and may, in fact, experience only partial "re-acculturation." It seems that psychological adjustment—including depression and overall wellbeing—may be the most important in returning home.

The process and nature of return cultural adjustment

John Gullahorn and Jeane Gullahorn (1963) extended the idea of the U-curve to include a new series of stages when one returns to a home culture. Just as the real stress of cultural transition (whether it happens in a "U" shape or not) occurs over a longer stay, we would

Figure 12.5 The W-curve. Many international employers and schools, such as the Munich Business School, provide travelers with some adaptation of the W-curve to explain what they might expect when they return home. Source: Image used courtesy of A. Uwaje.

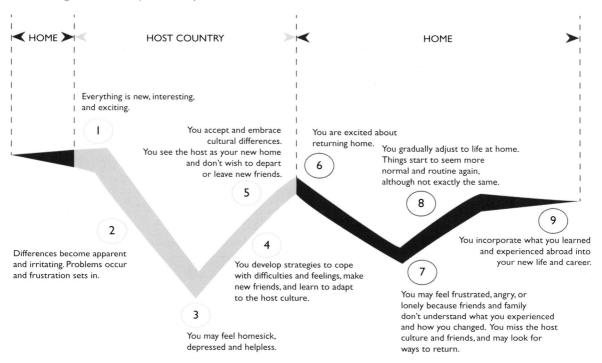

HOME ◄►◄   HOST COUNTRY   ►◄   HOME   ►

Everything is new, interesting, and exciting.

1

You accept and embrace cultural differences. You see the host as your new home and don't wish to depart or leave new friends.

5

You are excited about returning home.

6

You gradually adjust to life at home. Things start to seem more normal and routine again, although not exactly the same.

8

2

Differences become apparent and irritating. Problems occur and frustration sets in.

4

You develop strategies to cope with difficulties and feelings, make new friends, and learn to adapt to the host culture.

9

You incorporate what you learned and experienced abroad into your new life and career.

7

You may feel frustrated, angry, or lonely because friends and family don't understand what you experienced and how you changed. You miss the host culture and friends, and may look for ways to return.

3

You may feel homesick, depressed and helpless.

expect the stages of return adjustment also to only take place, or at least be amplified, after a longer stay. Still, one of your authors already felt some symptoms after a one-month trip to Chile and Argentina, immersed into the cultures by staying in host nationals' homes. Gullahorn and Gullahorn added a second "U" to the first, to make what they called the **W-curve** of return adjustment (Figure 12.5). The authors argue that returning sojourners may feel the same symptoms of "alienation, anomie, and rejection" that they may have felt traveling abroad (p. 33). The idea of the W-curve is that, as sojourners anticipate coming home, they are excited, looking forward to some of the things they missed, seeing people they love. It is like a new honeymoon stage of anticipation. After some time, the sojourner may feel a sense of loss or nostalgia for the foreign culture, sometimes even glamorizing in her or his mind the less enjoyable aspects of the travel abroad. Most people "adapt," coming through the process to reach a stage of functioning in the new culture.

Just as with cultural adjustment for those who live abroad, scholars have tried to understand why return adjustment is difficult. Gullahorn and Gullahorn, studying research grant recipients traveling who returned from abroad (1963), noted that older travelers handled the return home easily, mostly feeling a loss of status, while college-aged travelers felt "lost" when returning home, perhaps because their expectations or their values had changed. Also, those who traveled to more culturally distinct cultures (traveling from the United States to the Middle East, as opposed to northern Europe) had more difficulty returning home, noting that their sending institutions did not take advantage of the things that they had learned abroad. This early study reflects what later scholars have said as they have tried to determine some of the causes for difficulty in return adjustment:

→ *A change in ourselves and others*: Because we have been in close contact with another culture over a period of time, we often change. Clyde Austin (1987) suggests that value change is a main reason for difficulty in return adjustment. Shelley Smith (1998) suggests that both the travel abroad and the return home should be understood in terms of identity change. A woman from a culture where women are protected by men, but with less ostensible rights, might return home and feel frustrated at her lack of liberty (just as a woman from a culture where women are ostensibly liberated might return home from the other culture feeling a lack of protection).

→ *A change in relationships*: Not only are we changing, but so are the people we leave at home. Judith Martin (1986), for example, found that students who had studied abroad felt closer to their parents upon returning home than to their friends. Perhaps younger people, who are still in a time of development, are more susceptible to value change. When we leave our friends, it is like leaving a snapshot—we both remember what we were like at departure, but when we reunite, we are not the same. Our parents, however, may know us more deeply, so the relationships remain stable or even strengthen. The ease of online (e.g., video) and new (text messaging) communication may ease the impact of travel abroad on friendships.

→ *Unrealistic expectations and disillusionment*: It is a common understanding that having realistic (but overall positive) expectations helps our travel abroad. But often when we come home, we find ourselves ambivalent, even critical, of our home culture. Asako Uehara (1986) found that 40% of her U.S. participants who had engaged in international student exchange "had become aware that the United States is a big, affluent, and powerful country in the world;" 66% spoke objectively about the host culture, but seemed freer to criticize the United States.

→ *Lack of appreciation*: Many who travel abroad feel that when they return, people do not really want to know about their experiences. Even those who ask sometimes seem to tire after a few minutes of explanation. Often, employees who travel abroad grow frustrated with the narrow-mindedness (or lack of a broader cultural world view) of their colleagues (Harris & Moran, 1996), and many times companies do not seem to want to take advantage of new knowledge and ways of thinking that employees bring back. As a result, many employees leave the company that sent them abroad within a year of returning home.

One of our students, Kyle, came back to the United States from a semester in Ireland. At one point, he got in an argument with his family, because he claimed that, based on its consumption of a large portion of the world's energy resources and slowness to adopt recycling, the United States was wasteful. His family claimed adamantly that the United States is not a wasteful culture. His father said, "If you liked it so much in Ireland, why don't you just go back?". Kyle tried to show his pictures to his family, and a relative told him, "You don't need to bring those out. No one really wants to see them." While this might be an extreme case, in many cases, travelers have a hard time fitting back in, especially if returning from a large metropolitan area abroad to a small town culture in their own country.

Break it down

Returning sojourners often face the problem that people really don't want to just sit and listen to them. If you know someone who has traveled and lived abroad recently, invite the person out for a cup of tea/coffee, a soda, or a meal. Ask to look at her or his pictures. Sit. Listen. Ask questions.

Making the going and coming home easier

Several authors outline success strategies for easing the transition when one travels abroad. Philip Harris and Robert Moran (1996), for example, suggest cultural preparation, learning about communication in the new culture, interacting with host nationals as much as possible, being open-minded and even adventurous, being patient, having realistic expectations, and framing the experience as a challenge. Shelley Smith (2002) adds that we should try to suspend judgment on things that are unfamiliar to us, accept the need to retreat from time to time to embrace our emotions, and be willing to talk to people in our host culture about misunderstandings. Kim's (2005) theory, which we described earlier, suggests the use of host media that familiarize us with the culture as well as using interaction and media with people from our own group to serve as a bridge. We add to these the need to consider not only the needs of the traveler, but also those of partners and children, as research has found that a spouse's expectations of a sojourn as well as the spouse's adaptation once there, are related to important aspects of the adjustment of expatriate managers (Black & Stephens, 1989).

While many companies and universities today now provide training for students and employees traveling abroad, it is much less common for them to provide training on the return home. As noted, return-home adjustment varies from person to person. While most may adjust to coming home easily enough, some may seek counseling to deal with depression or related issues. Unfortunately, returned sojourners are often reluctant to seek counseling (Gaw, 2000). Judith Martin and Teresa Harrell (2004) list things that sojourners can do prior even to leaving for another culture, while they are there, in preparation for the return home, and once they get home. One of these strategies, no doubt made much easier with Internet chat and video capabilities, is to maintain contact with the home culture so one knows what is happening with the culture and in the lives of loved ones while away. Finally, sojourners can often seek to become "mediating persons"—bridges to help those in their home cultures either understand different cultures or prepare to travel themselves (Wilson, 1985).

ON THE NET

Vagabondish.com, "The Travelzine for Today's Vagabond" hosts a long list of people's stories about returning home and facing culture shock. Read some of these at http://www.vagabondish.com/how-to-survive-reverse-culture-shock/. **If you have traveled to another culture (or even returned home after a year at school), did you experience stress? Write your own story! What would you suggest to travelers to ease their transition back home?**

Again, these points echo the experience of one of our ex-students, Chérise, who upon returning to smalltown midwest culture, could not cope with the local mindset. We recommended she travel to a big city and meet other former travelers and international people. She now works with children in a multi-ethnic, multinational school, travels widely and is very satisfied negotiating both her own culture and other cultures. At first, she took what Bradford "J" Hall (2005) calls an **alienated approach** to returning abroad, missing her culture abroad, being bitter and critical about her home culture, as opposed to a **resocialized approach** taken by some who quickly shed their abroad culture and re-adopt their home culture. Now Chérise has moved to a **proactive approach** that sees the good (but is not afraid to address the bad) in both her home and former host cultures.

Intercultural communication competence: How can I get the job done…and still be liked?

Much of this book could be about being a competent communicator when traveling to or working with people from other cultures. But as we will see, "intercultural communication competence" has come to have some very specific meanings in the area of intercultural communication. Second, in some ways, it is closely related to adaptation, as one often gains competence through traveling to and adapting to one or more different cultures.

Understanding intercultural competence

On the surface, we might think that intercultural competence is a fairly simple concept—is one communicating clearly or effectively in another culture? In fact (as perhaps academics are prone to complicate everything!), it is a complicated concept and is related to communication effectiveness. For years, researchers struggled to sort out the dimensions and definitions of these terms. Hiroko Abe and Richard Wiseman (1983) isolated five aspects of "effectiveness:" The ability (1) to communicate interpersonally, (2) to adjust to different cultures, (3) to deal with different societal systems, (4) to establish interpersonal relationships, and (5) to understand others" (p. 63). In a later study, Wiseman and some colleagues (1989) measured "competence" in terms of one's culture-specific understanding, culture-general understanding, and positive feeling for the other culture, finding that things such as ethnocentrism, level of knowledge about the culture, and perceived social distance from the other culture influenced these three aspects. Brian Spitzberg (1994) lists dozens of different skills and attitudes that had been linked with intercultural competence and effectiveness. The list includes things such as charisma, flexibility, empathy, non-ethnocentrism, personality strength, optimism, self-efficacy, and ability to facilitate communication.

Brian Spitzberg and William Cupach's (1984) book, *Interpersonal Communication Competence*, has framed much of the discussion of competence since. First, the authors drew a clear line between effectiveness and competence. **Communication effectiveness** refers specifically to one's ability to accomplish tasks—that is, the "achievement of interaction goals" (p. 102). But **communication competence** is to be effective while also being appropriate to the rules of the situation (**communication appropriateness**), including preserving relationships, maintaining face or decorum, abiding by contextual rules, and so on. We have all known speakers who "get the job done" (effectiveness), such as persuading people in a small group setting, but who leave a trail of hurt feelings and anger. We also know those who follow all the rules of social communication (appropriateness), but cannot clinch a sales deal, get a date, or whatever their communicative goal is. To be competent, then, one must be both effective and appropriate. The second major contribution of this work was to conceptualize the vast array of aspects of competence and effectiveness into three main categories: knowledge, motivation, and skills.

Spitzberg (1994) provides a model of **intercultural communication competence** based on these notions. He sees some aspects of competence present within the knowledge, motivation, and skills of the communicator (such as valuing the communication of others—a motivation, knowledge of "how to communicate well" (p. 351) or of task-specific details, or the skills of knowing how to gain knowledge of the other culture), of the episode (for example, whether or not communicators meet each others' expectations), and of the relationship (for example, whether the communicators find mutual attraction or build trust with each other). Many intercultural communication scholars, even if they do not adopt Spitzberg's model, now frame competence in terms of appropriateness and effectiveness. Guo-Ming Chen and William Starosta (2008) start with this definition of competence and then break competence down into several types, including social competence, linguistic competence, communicative competence, and relational competence.

This area of intercultural research continues to grow, with a many-chaptered handbook dedicated to intercultural competence published in 2009 (Deardorff). More recent researchers have proposed newer models. Guo-Ming Chen and William Starosta's (2008) model includes three dimensions, similar to knowledge, motivation, and skills. The affective dimension, intercultural sensitivity, focuses on emotions and feelings, including a respect for cultural difference. The cognitive/knowledge dimension, intercultural sensitivity, deals with awareness of difference; and the behavioral/skill dimension pertains to task accomplishment in intercultural situations. And Lily Arasaratnam's (2006) approach includes "empathy, motivation, attitude towards other cultures, experience, and listening (interaction involvement)" (p. 94).

Peter Adler (1977) coined a classic term that relates to intercultural competence: the "multicultural man," or, as we shall call it, the **multicultural person**. This new type of person is someone who can serve as a catalyst for dialogue between cultures. She or he is able to move easily between different cultures, like a surfer going between waves. In a sense, the person ceases to belong fully to any culture, but instead "lives on the boundary" (p. 26). The person is marginal, never fully belonging to one culture or the other, fitting into any culture, but outside of all of them (Bennett, 1993). This relates to a notion that Young Yun Kim and Brent Ruben (1988) introduce in their theory of intercultural transformation. They define **intercultural transformation** as a process people go through in which they learn new ways of thinking, feeling, and behaving beyond the "limits of their original culture" (p. 306). They argue that individuals who have a wide range of intercultural experiences, including travel (even adjustment to multiple cultures over time), develop a new repertoire of ways to think, act, and feel. They develop a "broadened and deepened understanding of the human condition and cultural differences that are larger than any one cultural perspective" (p. 314). The notions of the multicultural person and intercultural transformation, then, link to cultural and return adjustment, because they suggest that as we travel and return (and travel and return, and travel and return), we actually become more complete, broad-minded, and effective individuals even within our own cultures.

Beyond the multicultural person: Intergroup effectiveness

Of course, like notions of adjustment and acculturation, the ideas of the multicultural person and intercultural communicator competence are more complicated than they first seem, in two ways. First, many scholars who have researched the notion of intercultural competence have explained it as an idea that should apply across cultures. That is, if a manager, Rachel, has the particular sets of knowledge and skills that would make her effective in one culture, then she should be effective in any culture. Of course, researchers do not believe that any one person would be high on every single one of the many variables that relate to competence, but the more of them Rachel scores higher on, the more effective she should be, whether she goes to Trinidad, Thailand, or Tunisia. Future research, however, might consider whether certain variables are more important depending on the culture or the mission. It might be that, while some traits will help Rachel wherever she goes, if she is outgoing and energetic, she might fare well in Tegucigalpa; but if she has more of a reserved character, that might suit her in Taipei. And structural and cultural factors apart from Rachel's disposition may influence whether she is successful in Tehran or Toledo.

What do you think? Intercultural communicator competence is an important consideration for companies sending employees on international assignments, both in terms of employee selection for cross-cultural positions and in employee training. Consider some of the variables in this section. Which do you think might be trainable, and how might you go about training on these variables? Imagine you are selecting an employee for a specific location and position: will the "benchmark" standards work, or is there also something to be said for matching employee character to the position?

As we noted earlier in some cases, the environment might be particularly important to whether one is competent or can even become a "multicultural person." Lise Sparrow (2008) analyzed interviews with and essays of a variety of women who should be and wanted to be "multicultural." Contrary to the literature on the multicultural person, which suggests that one can achieve a sense of positive marginality between cultures, being accepted in any culture, Sparrow found that "women, in particular, . . . in spite of their commitments to intercultural communication, spoke consistently of their identities in relation to contexts of being excluded or included on the basis of their race, religion, ethnicity, and gender" (p. 250). The women, who had come to the United States from countries such as Zaire, Viet Nam, and India, reported being abused or denied privileges both in their own countries and in the United States. Some confronted prejudice and barriers of status and privilege. In sum, Sparrow notes, the notion of the "multicultural person" is not as simple as it seems. Sparrow points out that, rather than marginality between cultures, women and other travelers often need to find their own sense of rootedness, a sense of relationship, of home, to help them sustain difficulties they face in their new environments. This highlights not only the role of the environment in determining our effectiveness, but also the possibility that being "multicultural," in the sense of being fluid and without a cultural reference, might also leave us with a sense of void in our identity, which may not always be healthy.

Summary

In this chapter, we summarized issues relating to adjustment, both going abroad and returning home. We considered the U- and W-curves, which suggest that when people travel to another culture for a longer period of time, they go through stages of psychological stress and adjustment. We also considered newer approaches to adjustment, which suggest that perhaps adjustment is cyclical, or that one might be adjusted in one area of life, but not in another, and that these may increase or decrease. Regardless, we have argued that the stress of adjustment, including the stress of coming home, is not necessarily a bad thing. It can lead to a great sense of personal growth, as we take a broader view of the world and of the human condition, and as we learn new ways of doing things. Adjustment to other cultures is related in some ways to the notion of intercultural communication competence, when one is able to accomplish tasks in another culture while also acting in appropriate ways. Some feel that, as we gain more and more intercultural experiences, we might become adept at surfing between cultures seamlessly, feeling tied to none, and adapting to the culture in which we find ourselves.

Traveling to other cultures shows us new ways to think, feel, and act, and this helps to uncover how much of what we do in our everyday lives is a choice. Once we have adjusted to another culture, we now have more choices, and we can adopt our own cultural views of success, beauty, friendship, and so on, or we can create new models based on the cultures to which we have traveled. At the same time, as hopeful as we are in the benefits of travel abroad, we realize that our effectiveness and adaptation to other culture exist in the context of how that culture treats us. Racism, xenophobia, stereotypes, unequal opportunities (see chapter 6) may keep us from becoming truly effective. Unfortunately, often when cultural situations work against the success of the stranger, the people in the culture blame the stranger for not succeeding, rather than recognizing the culture's own role in the difficulty.

KEY TERMS

sojourner, 250
immigrant, 250
refugee, 250
adjustment, 251
enculturation, 251
acculturation, 251
deculturation, 251
assimilation, 251
culture shock, 251
U-curve, 251
honeymoon stage, 252
crisis stage, 252
adjustment stage, 252
integration stage, 252
stress-adaptation-growth dynamic, 254
psychological adjustment, 255

sociocultural adjustment/cross-cultural adaptation, 255
integration/biculturalism, 256
marginality, 256
segregation, 256
multiculturalism/cultural pluralism, 256
melting pot approach, 256
exclusion, 256
selective adaptation, 257
diaspora, 258
hybridity, 258
return culture shock/return cultural adjustment, 258
W-curve, 259
alienated approach, 262
resocialized approach, 262

Discussion questions

1 Discuss with other students your own experiences moving in and out of cultures, even if that is from your home culture to the culture of your university. In what ways are domestic moves (within a country) and foreign moves similar and different?

2 If you have traveled to another culture, what are some things that made you more or less effective or helped you to adapt or not adapt? These might be aspects of yourself or the situation. What skills would you like to work on in yourself to make you a more effective intercultural communicator?

3 If you are in a class, break up into groups? Imagine a job cultural assignment to a specific culture: which of you would you send and why?

4 Do you think that the same things would make one effective in a cross-cultural situation (like moving from France to South Africa), as in an intergroup situation (say, interracial communication)? What skills, attitudes, or emotions might become more important in one situation or another?

5 Do some research on a major refugee group in your country. What are the social and economic conditions of the group? How might those impact the group's adjustment?

Action points

1 Your school likely has an international student program or a program to teach students the language of your country. Contact these programs to see if there is an "international friend" aspect to them. Make a commitment to start spending a bit of time each week with a student, to get to know them and learn about her or his culture.

2 As we have seen in this chapter, part of one's adjustment to a new culture is based on the acceptance and support the new culture provides the traveler. See if your community has a second-language or citizenship program to provide assistance to immigrants to your community. Get involved in giving language or citizenship lessons, or academic tutoring to immigrants in your community.

3 If there is an immigrant group in your community, find out about local festivals or holiday seasons (such as Chinese New Year, Ramadan, or Diwali). Attend a festival, or even several, from the same group. See what you can learn about that cultural group that would add to your own understanding and experience of the world. (Note: a single experience will not make you an expert or multi-cultural person! But it will start you on the process of cultural learning.)

For more information

Deardorff, D.K. (Ed.). (2009). *The Sage handbook of intercultural competence*. Thousand Oaks, CA: Sage.

Paige, R.M. (Ed.). *Education for the intercultural experience* (2nd ed.). Yarmouth, ME: Intercultural Press.

Sam, D.L, & Berry, J.W. (Eds.). (2006). *The Cambridge handbook of acculturation psychology*. Cambridge, UK: Cambridge University Press.

Storti, C. (2001). *The art of coming home*. Yarmouth, ME: Intercultural Press.

References

Abe, H., & Wiseman, R.L. (1983). A cross-cultural confirmation of the dimensions of intercultural effectiveness. *International Journal of Intercultural Communication, 7*, 5367.

Adler, P.S. (1975). The transitional experience: An alternative view of culture shock. *Journal of Humanistic Psychology, 15*(4), 13–23.

Adler, P.S. (1977). Beyond cultural identity: Reflections on cultural and multicultural man. In R.W. Brislin (Ed.), *Culture learning: Concepts, application, and research* (pp. 24–41). Honolulu, HI: University of Hawaii Press.

Ady, J.C. (1995). Toward a differential demand model of sojourner adjustment. In R. Wiseman (Ed.), *Intercultural communication theory* (pp. 92–114). Thousand Oaks: Sage.

Arasaratnam, L.A. (2006). Further testing of a new model of intercultural communication competence. *Communication Research Reports, 23*, 93–99.

Austin, C. (Ed.). (1987). *Readings in cross-cultural re-entry*. Abilene, TX: ACU Press.

Bennett, J. (1977). Transition shock: Putting culture shock in perspective. *International Journal of Intercultural Relations, 4*, 45–52.

Bennett, M. (1993). Towards ethnorelativism: A developmental model of intercultural sensitivity. In R.M. Paige (Ed.), *Education for the intercultural experience*. Yarmouth, ME: Intercultural Press.

Berry, J.W. (2004). Fundamental psychological processes in intercultural relations. In D. Landis, J.M. Bennett, & M.J. Bennett (Eds.), *Handbook of intercultural training* (3rd ed., pp. 166–184). Thousand Oaks, CA: Sage.

Black, J.S., Mendenhall, M., & Oddou, G. (1991). Toward a comprehensive model of international adjustment. An integration of multiple theoretical perspectives. *Academy of Management Review, 16*, 291–317.

Black, J.S., & Stephens, G.K. (1989). The influence of the spouse on American expatriate adjustment and intent to stay in Pacific Rim overseas assignments. *Journal of Management, 15*, 529–544. doi:10.1177/014920638901500403

Bourhis, R., Moïse, L.C., Perreault, S., & Senécal, S. (1997). Towards an interactive acculturation model: A social psychological approach. *International Journal of Psychology, 32*, 369–386.

Chen, G.-M., & Starosta, W.J. (2008). Intercultural communication competence: A synthesis. In M.K. Asante, Y. Miike, & J. Yin (Eds.), *The global intercultural communication reader* (pp. 215–237). New York: Routledge.

Church, A. (1982). Sojourner adjustment. *Psychological Bulletin, 91*, 540–575.

Curtin, M. (2010). Coculturation: Toward a critical theoretical framework of cultural adjustment. In T.K. Nakayama & R.T. Halualani (Eds.), *The handbook of critical intercultural communication* (pp. 270–285). Malden, MA: Wiley-Blackwell.

Deardorff, D.K. (Ed.). (2009). *The Sage handbook of intercultural competence*. Thousand Oaks, CA: Sage.

Dodd, C.H. (1998). *Dynamics of Intercultural communication* (5th ed.). Boston, MA: McGraw-Hill.

Drzewiecka, J.A., & Halualani, R.T. (2002). The structural-cultural dialectic of diasporic politics. *Communication Theory, 12*, 340–366. DOI: 10.1111/j.1468-2885.2002.tb00273.x

Gaw, K.F. (2000). Reverse culture shock in students returning from overseas. *International Journal of Intercultural Relations, 24*, 83–104.

Gullahorn, J.T., & Gullahorn, J.E. (1963). An extension of the U-curve hypothesis. *Journal of Social Issues, 19*(3), 33–47.

Hall, B.J. (2005). *Among Cultures: The challenge of communication*. Belmont, CA: Wadsworth.

Hall, E.T. (1973). *The Silent Language*. New York: Anchor.

Halualani, R.T., & Drzewiecka, J.A. (2008). Deploying "descent": The politics of diasporic belonging and intercultural communication. In L.A. Flores, M.P. Orbe, & B.J. Allen (Eds.), *Intercultural Communication in a Transnational World* (pp. 59–90). Thousand Oaks, CA: Sage.

Harris, P.R., & Moran, R.T. (1996). *Managing Cultural Differences: Leadership strategies for a new world of business*. Houston: Gulf.

Hegde, R.S. (1998). Swinging the trapeze: The negotiation of identity among Asian Indian immigrant women in the United States. In D.V. Tanno & A. González (Eds.), *Communication and Identity across Cultures* (pp. 34–55). Thousand Oaks, CA: Sage.

Kealey, D.J. (1989). A study of cross-cultural effectiveness: Theoretical issues, practical applications. *International Journal of Intercultural Relations, 13*, 387–428.

Keefe, S.E., & Padilla, A.M. (1987). *Chicano Ethnicity*. Albuquerque: University of New Mexico Press.

Kim, Y.Y. (2001). *Becoming Intercultural: An integrative theory of communication and cross-cultural adaptation*. Thousand Oaks, CA: Sage.

Kim, Y.Y. (2005). Adapting to a new culture: An integrative communication theory. In W.B. Gudykunst (Ed.), *Theorizing about Intercultural Communication* (pp. 375–400). Thousand Oaks, CA: Sage.

Kim, Y.Y., & Ruben, B.D. (1988). Intercultural transformation: A systems theory. In Y.Y. Kim & W.B. Gudykunst (Eds.), *Theories in Intercultural Communication* (pp. 299–321). Newbury Park, CA: Sage.

Liu, C.-S., & Lee, H.W. (2008). A proposed model of expatriates in multinational organizations. *Cross-Cultural Management, 15*, 176–193. DOI: 10.1108/13527600810870615.

Lysgaard, S. (1955). Adjustment in a foreign society: Norwegian Fulbright grantees visiting the United States. *International Social Sciences Bulletin, 7*, 45–58.

Martin, J.N. (1986). Patterns of communication in three types of reentry relationships. *Western Journal of Speech Communication, 50*, 183–199.

Martin, J.N., & Harrell, T. (2004). Intercultural reentry of students and professionals: Theory and practice. In D. Landis, J.M. Bennett, & M.J. Bennett (Eds.), *Handbook of Intercultural Training* (3rd ed., pp. 309–336). Thousand Oaks, CA: Sage.

Miike, Y. (2007). An Asiacentric reflection on Eurocentric bias in communication theory. *Communication Monographs, 74*, 272–278.

Oberg, K. (1960). Culture shock: Adjustment to new culture environments. *Practical Anthropology, 7*, 170–179.

Sam, D.L., & Berry, J.W. (2010). Acculturation: When individuals and groups of different cultural backgrounds meet. *Perspectives on psychological science, 4*, 472–481. DOI:10.1177/1745691610373075.

Selmer, J., & Fenner, C.R., Jr. (2009). Spillover effects between work and non-work adjustment among public sector expatriates. *Personnel Review, 38*, 366–379. DOI:10.1108/00483480910956328.

Smith, S. (1998). Identity and intercultural communication competence in reentry. In J.N. Martin, T.K. Nakayama, & L.A. Flores (Eds.), *Readings in Cultural Contexts* (pp. 304–314). Mountain View, CA: Mayfield.

Smith, S.L. (2002). The cycle of cross-cultural adaptation and reentry. In J.N. Martin, T.K. Nakayama, & L.A. Flores (Eds.), *Readings in Intercultural Communication: Experiences and contexts* (2nd ed., pp. 246–259). Boston: McGraw-Hill.

Sparrow, L.M. (2008). Beyond multicultural man: Complexities of identity. In M.K. Asante, Y. Miike, & J. Yin (Eds.), *The Global Intercultural Communication Reader* (pp. 239–261). New York: Routledge.

Spitzberg, B.M. (1994). A model of intercultural communication competence. In L.A. Samovar & R.E. Porter (Eds.), *Intercultural Communication: A reader* (7th ed., pp. 347–359). Belmont, CA: Wadsworth.

Spitzberg, B.M., & Cupach, W.R. (1984). *Interpersonal Communication Competence*. Beverly Hills, CA: Sage.

Tanaka, T., Takai, J., Kohyama, T., & Fujihara, T. (1994). Adjustment patterns of international students in Japan. *International Journal of Intercultural Relations, 18*, 55–75.

Tolkien, J.R.R. (1955/1965). *The Return of the King*. Boston: Houghton Mifflin.

Uehara, A. (1986). The nature of American student reentry adjustment and perception of the sojourn experience. *International Journal of Intercultural Relations, 10*, 415–438.

van der Pol, H. (July, 2009). *New trends in international student mobility*. UNESCO Institute for Statistics.

Ward, C. (2004). Psychological theories of cultural contact and their implications for Intercultural Training and Interventions. In D. Landis, J.M. Bennett, & M.J. Bennett (Eds.), *Handbook of Intercultural training* (3rd ed., pp. 185–216). Thousand Oaks, CA: Sage.

Ward, C., Okura, Y., Kennedy, A., & Kojima, T. (1998). The U-curve on trial: A longitudinal study of psychological and sociocultural adjustment during cross-cultural transition. *International Journal of Intercultural Relations, 22*, 277–291.

Ward, C., & Rana-Deuba, A. (1999). Acculturation and adaptation revisited. *Journal of Cross-Cultural Psychology, 30*, 422–442.

Wilson, A. (1985). Returned exchange students. *International Journal of Intercultural Relations, 9*, 285–304.

Wiseman, R.L., Hammer, M.R., & Nishida, H. (1989). Predictors of intercultural communication competence. *International Journal of Intercultural Relations, 13*, 349–370.

Chapter 13

Relationships and conflict: How can I have better cross-cultural relationships?

Chapter objectives

After this chapter, you should be able to:

→ Describe several approaches to what makes relationships grow more intimate

→ Outline five patterns of possible integration of cultural difference in a relationship

→ Summarize five stages of conflict

→ Illustrate the behaviors associated with five different conflict styles and discuss how personal and cultural factors may lead someone to prefer one style over another

→ Discuss some of the issues someone would need to be aware of in intercultural negotiation

Culture and communication in relationship: How do intercultural relationships grow and thrive?

Relational and organizational conflict: How can I make intercultural conflict more productive?

Intercultural Communication for Everyday Life, First Edition. John R. Baldwin, Robin R. Means Coleman, Alberto González, and Suchitra Shenoy-Packer.
© 2014 John R. Baldwin, Robin R. Means Coleman, Alberto González, and Suchitra Shenoy-Packer.
Published 2014 by John Wiley & Sons Ltd.

ynthia Malone (2011), Honolulu "Intercultural Relationships Examiner" reporter for Examiner.com, describes several well-known intercultural couples in Hollywood—fashion model Iman, from Somalia, and British singer David Bowie; Beverly Hills restaurateur (from Austria) Wolfgang Puck and Ethiopian fashion designer Gelia Assefa. The reporter talks of how Puck and Assefa celebrate "two cultures that blend together a perfect mix of fashion and food." Iman describes her relationship with Bowie: "It was nerve-wracking at the beginning, the first five minutes, but we got on famously and have been together ever since." We know there are many famous and even wealthy international couples, such as the highest-paid celebrity couple, according to *Forbes* online magazine, Brazilian fashion model Gisele Bündchen and NFL quarterback, Tom Brady (Antunes, 2011; Figure 13.1).

The article gives evidence that intercultural relationships are an area growing in interest around the world. In the United States, David Crary, AP Reporter, states that "besides superstardom, Barack Obama, Tiger Woods and Derek Jeter have another common bond: Each is the child of an interracial marriage" (2007). Sharon Lee and Barry Edmondson (2005), summarizing U.S. Census data over several years, note that interracial marriages constituted less than 1% of all marriages in 1970 but over 5% in 2000. Sources vary on this figure, but some say that as many as one in seven (about 14%) of new marriages are interracial (CBS News, 2010). Among Latinos, 25% marry across ethnic lines; and the number of U.S. American children growing up in a multiracial family has risen from 900,000 in 1970 to over three million in 2000. **Miscegenation**—the marrying of individuals across ethnic or racial lines—is growing around the world. The numbers would be even stronger if we considered all forms of **intermarriage**, marriage between people of perceived outgroups regardless of the grounds—religious, cultural, racial, and so on.

At the same time, what the news article that begins this chapter hides is the complexity of intermarriage. As Malone (2011) describes, online news articles often frame intergroup relationships as a harmonious blending of food and fashion, perhaps after a brief period of struggle, perhaps by necessity of the online reader's expectations for upbeat news. But

Figure 13.1 Brazilian fashion model Gisele Bündchen and NFL quarterback Tom Brady are one example of a famous intercultural couple.
Source: Elise Amendola/AP/Press Association Images.

Chapter 13   Relationships and conflict: How can I have better cross-cultural relationships?

271

all couples' relationships have some difficulties, and issues of cultural difference, racial difference, or social stigma may impact this. This chapter will explore culture and relationships, including conflict, and will end with the extension of our understanding of conflict and negotiation to workplace relationships.

What do you think? Before you continue reading, think about possible differences between types of "inter" relationships. Jot down your answers or discuss with your classmates: What issues might be the same or different in an interethnic or interracial marriage as opposed to one that is interreligious or crosses social class lines? Will issues be different in a marriage or civil union relationship than in dating? How about between dating and friendship? What are some tips you might give for people in different types of relationship?

Culture and communication in relationship: How do intercultural relationships grow and thrive?

A **relationship** is a connection between two or more individuals in which they have both rights and responsibilities toward each other beyond what would be expected in interaction with strangers. As authors describe friendships, dating relationships, and marriage, they look at different things. Sociologists look at how demographic, class, and other variables influence mate selection and the likelihood for **exogamy** (marrying outside of one's perceived group). Some consider the long-term social impact of intercultural marriage or intergroup friendship on levels of tolerance within a society. Psychologists might analyze relational and psychological processes within an intercultural relationship, such as the emotional satisfaction. Linguists might be interested in how children learn language when the parents are from different language groups. Communication scholars have focused on various aspects, but especially on message exchange in the process of relational development.

What partners bring with them into relationships

Partners bring a variety of experiences and differences, many of them cultural, into a relationship (Figure 13.2). Dugan Romano (2008), a cross-cultural psychologist, giving examples of specific relationships between people in many different cultural combinations, describes many differences in things such as cultural values, food and drink, attitudes toward sex, relationship with friends and extended family, handling of finances, approaches to illness, and ethnocentrism.

Cultural values   Cultural **values**, such as those described in the frameworks in chapter 4, often impact relationships. A partner from a collectivist culture might feel much more responsibility in terms of time and financial support to extended family. A resident of Canada

Figure 13.2 People in intercultural friendships, romances, and work relationships bring cultural and personal differences and similarities to the relationship. What are some concrete things they could do to recognize and solve such differences? Source: Kymri Wilt/Danita Delimont/Alamy.

who is from the Philippines might feel an obligation to ensure that nieces and nephews obtain a good education, something that does not make as much sense in the mainstream North American understanding of the **nuclear family** (spouses and children). Different commitments to extended family, workplace, or community might impact romantic or marriage relationships, as partners debate how much time to spend with extended networks or how much of the household income should go to these networks. Related to the notion of relation to family is the extent of involvement of the extended family in relationships. In any romantic or marriage relationship, partners' families can try to influence the relationship in unwanted ways. Some researchers of intercultural marriage say that the impact of extended family is especially likely to be felt once a couple has children and the grandparents try to guide the parents in the "right" (i.e., their culturally understood) way of raising children.

Definitions and expectations for the relationship   Of course, much of our discussion earlier assumes that the partners have the same definition of what the relationship should be. Especially in today's changing terrain of romantic relationships, with

What do you think? Carley Dodd and John Baldwin (2002) highlight many elements that mark positive family cultures, like supportive communication, cohesion, adaptable family rules, and communication receptivity, noting how these might be experienced in culturally different ways. Describe the specific values and communication rules in the family in which you grew up. These are usually not stated openly—they are the patterns people follow, sometimes healthy and sometimes not. In what ways do you see yourself repeating these rules—or deliberately going against them—in your current relationships?

friends with benefits or **booty call** relationships becoming an item of discussion in some Western cultures, it is important for romantic partners or potential spouses to know what are the expectations of the other in terms of the relationship itself. Does romance or marriage imply sexual fidelity? Do the two become "one flesh" in marriage, or are they expected, to a large degree, to maintain their distinctness?

Such questions also apply to friendships. Cross-cultural travelers soon realize that the rules and expectations of friendship change from culture to culture. Just because we can translate the word "friend" to some other language does not mean we know what friendship means in that culture. Scholarship among U.S. Americans shows there are different cultural expectations among groups within the same country. Mary Jane Collier (1991), doing open-ended questionnaire research among Latino, African, and White Americans, found that the Latinos saw a friend as someone with whom you could be emotionally open, Whites, as someone with whom you could "be yourself," and African Americans, as someone who would also be there to help with life's practical and material problems.

Motives Partners in both friendship and romantic relationship can also differ in the motives that they bring to the relationship. We like to think that we grow more intimate with someone simply because we like her or him. But we might seek an intergroup friend because we want to feel more tolerant or because we deliberately want to raise our awareness about another group. Some early writers cite negative reasons for interracial marriage—getting even with one's parents, getting even with the dominant culture, or raising one's status (Char, 1977). Movies like Spike Lee's 1991 *Jungle Fever* suggest sexual curiosity as a reason for interethnic romance. However, a study in Texas (U.S.), draws the not-so-shocking conclusion that the main reason people reported dating people outside of their ethnic group is because they like each other, with motives of sexual interest, personal gain, or showing oneself unprejudiced much lower in importance (Lampe, 1981). The most common reasons for not dating across ethnic lines were lack of opportunity (due to informal segregation of neighborhoods and schools) and opposition from parents.

We must, at the same time, consider societal regulations and norms for the relationship as an important input factor to a relationship. These become especially relevant for marriages marked by some aspect of diversity, either between partners or in relation to the dominant culture; and this influence is different enough from what is usually considered by psychologists and communication scholars that we will deal with it separately below, under a discussion of "stigmatized relationships."

How do intercultural relationships work?

Relational development All of us meet a variety of people every day, in our classes, at our workplace, at get-togethers, even on public transportation. We usually ignore the host of people that cross our paths. But some strangers become acquaintances and eventually close friends, lovers, or long-time partners. As we consider what draws us closer to one person than to another, we realize that these principles apply both to romantic relationships and friendships, to work- and other types of relationships. Romantic relationships pose different issues, because often we move toward living with another person in a long-term, even lifelong relationship. Different researchers provide different explanations as to why relationships—for people of the same or different cultures—grow closer.

Perhaps the simplest notion of what draws relational partners together is **propinquity**, or physical closeness between people. We are more likely to form relationships with those with whom we work, or study, or who live in the same apartment building—or, by extension, in our most frequently visited chatrooms or Twitter feeds—rather than someone who is distant (physical or virtually). Of course, we have contact with a great many people who are physically or electronically "close," but we do not form relationships with them, so something besides living close must make the relationships grow. In the multicultural world we describe in chapter 1, it is more and more likely that we will find ourselves in close contact with people culturally different from us, either in our physical or cyber world.

Some scholars suggest simply: the more similar we are to people, the more we will grow to like them. This **similarity-attraction hypothesis** (Byrne, 1971) explains that people are more likely to date or marry within their own groups, though there are also other explanations such as ethnocentrism, prejudice, and family pressure (see chapter 6). One interesting study finds that it is not so much demographic (racial, age, social class) similarity that draws people together, but similarity in values, hobbies, and beliefs (Hammer, 1986).

Others suggest that what drives relationships toward intimacy is **self-disclosure**, defined as revealing things about oneself to someone else, specifically things the other would not normally be known by the other and about which there is at least some risk of sharing. **Social penetration theory** explains this perspective (Altman & Taylor, 1973): The more we self-disclose, the closer we will grow. Self-disclosure varies in the intimacy of detail that we share (**depth** of self-disclosure) and the number of topic areas (**breadth** of self-disclosure). While some topics seem more superficial, such as hobbies or tastes in music, and others deeper, like political philosophy, we can share any topic with varying levels of depth. For example, Sebastian could share superficially that he is a Christian Democrat or he could discuss deeply how his self-esteem is related to his inability to play sports.

The theory has at least three implications for intercultural communication. First, culture influences what we share about and how we share about different topics. One study found that students from collectivist cultures in a U.S. Pacific university had a greater difference in depth of self-disclosure—but not breadth—between face-to-face and Internet relationships than students from individualistic cultures (Tokunaga, 2009). Second, in most cases, people self-disclose differently with those they perceive to be in their in-groups rather than out-groups, with the latter influenced by cultural norms and levels of prejudice. Finally, intercultural communication researchers often assume that, in deeper relationships (and thus, deeper levels of self-disclosure), issues of ethnic, age, class, and other diversity become much less important.

Uncertainty reduction theory (Berger & Calabrese, 1975) suggests that the better we can predict and explain the behaviors of another person, the more relationships will grow.

We are more likely to try to reduce uncertainty under certain conditions, such as if the other person can reward or punish us, if we will have future interaction, or if the person acts in some way that we do not expect. The last situation seems especially important in cases where partners are culturally different. The theory accounts for a variety of aspects of perception and communication related to reduced uncertainty, such as sharing communication, perceiving similarity, having nonverbal warmth, or having the same networks of friend. In the 1980s, William Gudykunst extended uncertainty reduction to cross-cultural situations (Berger & Gudykunst, 1991), noting, for example, that in some high-context cultures (Japan), people seek different information—more about background and context—to understand others than people in low-context, individualistic cultures (the U.S.A). He later added the notion of **anxiety**—feelings of uneasiness, tension, or apprehension that occur in intercultural interactions. Gudykunst (2005) suggests that uncertainty and anxiety are both necessary for the growth of intercultural relationships, as they keep us interested in interactions; but if either is too high, we might want to exit the relationship. It is not the presence of these things in our relationships, but our ability to manage them that is important.

Relational maintenance   The approaches discussed before sometimes take an all-or-nothing approach: the more self-disclosure, the more predictability, and so on, the more the relationship will grow. A different perspective suggests that there are different tensions, or **dialectics**, within relationships. These tensions are unique in that both ends of each tension are always present, both contradicting and completing each other (Baxter & Montgomery, 1996). For example, in any relationship, one needs a balance of boundaries around information *and* sharing, of time with the partner (friend, romantic partner, spouse) *and* time with others, of predictability *and* novelty. Partners change from day to day and differ from each other. You might need more time together with your best friend right now, but she might be having a tough day and need a little space. And the tensions exist within individuals, between partners, and between the relationship and its surrounding relational contexts (should we spend more time with others outside the relationship or "just the two of us?").

It is not so much the presence of the tensions that determine outcomes in relationships, but how the partners work to resolve them. Research is only recently applying the idea of dialectics to relationships across cultures. For example, one study focusing on South Koreans on the social networking site, Cyworld, extends the dialectics to include a tension between "interpersonal

Break it down

Through your college or on your own (through a website like http://ppi.searchy.net/), find a conversation partner or an Internet pen-pal from another culture. Try to get to know the person. If it's an Internet pal, of course, keep in mind rules for safe chatting! While you might not become friends, what might be some things that would make your conversation relationship turn to "friendship?" How might such friendships impact your own view of the world—and how might your culture impact your view of friendship? What kind of impact, if any, might it have on your involvement in social action?

relations" and "self-relation," and notes how Cyworld allows development of cyberrelationships that become important to the collective Korean notion of *jeong* (togetherness and interdependence), while also allowing users to negotiate other tensions, like openness-closedness, through specific site channels that allow for more emotional communication (Kim & Yun, 2007).

The notion of dialectical tensions makes good sense if we consider a set of patterns of resolving cultural differences that Wen-Shing Tseng proposed in 1977. Tseng suggested that partners from different cultures tend to use one of several strategies for resolving cultural differences. To illustrate these, let us consider the case of Lea, a Belgian woman married to Massoud, an Iranian. They might simply adopt the cultural pattern of one of the partners. In this pattern, Lea might adopt Iranian ways, convert to Islam, and so on. Tseng suggests that in most cases, the wife adjusts to the culture of the husband. Or the couple might enact Belgian culture for a while, and then Iranian culture for a while, perhaps depending on the culture in which they live. A third approach would be to combine elements of both cultures. Thus, the couple might practice Islam, even if they live in Belgium, enacting more Western gender roles. Or the couple could adopt a "third culture"—a new set of patterns that is neither Iranian nor Belgian. The dialectical approach, however, suggests that the cultures of origin will sometimes move more toward one culture or more toward the other, but will always exist in tension.

The earlier example brings another relevant issue to play in intercultural relationships, and one that scholars have not given much attention to: interpersonal power. Beulah Rohrlich (1988) argues that one of the key areas to think about in intercultural romance and marriage is the issue of power. Who gets to make the decisions about which cultural standards, religion, and so on, the couple should adopt? Power is complicated by many factors—the location of residence, the influence of extended family, the language used in the home, the support of friends. Each partner would have "interpersonal" bases of power, such as who is more outgoing and dynamic. But research shows that in most cultures, men are granted more social power than women in many aspects. Even if partners in intercultural marriage or romance decide to grant the male a higher degree of decision-making and family-culture-guiding power, we would argue that they should be aware of this decision and make it mutually and deliberately.

Unique cultural relationship patterns

If we want to travel to another culture or understand relationships with people from other cultures, we also need to understand culture-specific views about relationship; in many cases, cultures have unique relational patterns. Here, we give examples of two specific cultural patterns. Even if your partner or friend is not from one of these cultures, you might find some commonalities to these themes as you discuss or develop relationships with that person.

Confucian relationships and kuan-hsi
Writers have described how East Asian relationships are often different from Western relationships. June Ock Yum (1988) outlines several aspects. She begins by outlining some of the main elements of Confucian relationships. Confucianism, itself, an Eastern philosophy based on the writings of Confucius (551—479 B.C.E.) framed relationships in terms of **propriety**—the proper behavior for the proper relationships and situational context. Confucius focused on five key relationships: ruler-subject, father-son, husband-wife, older brother-younger brother, and elders-juniors. There are clear societal expectations for how people in each role should behave in relation

Figure 13.3 June Ock Yum (1988) describes both communication and relationships between U.S. cultures and those influenced by Confucianism. Here we see a comparison of relationship patterns. Which pattern do relationships in your culture resemble most?

East Asian Orientations	North American Orientations
Particularistic: Different ways of interacting based on type of relationship (different status, etc.)	**Universalistic**: The same patterns are more likely across relationships, e.g. even of different status
Long-term and asymmetrical reciprocity: It is good for people to owe others, as it builds connections	**Short-term and symmetrical reciprocity**: It is good not to owe anyone anything, as it maintains independence
Sharp distinctions between in- and out-groups: You would likely treat people considerably different in your in-group.	**Less distinction between in- and out-groups**: You would be more likely to treat people similarly whether or not they were in your "in-group"
Informal intermediaries: You might use go-betweens in conflict, to arrange things, to build connections, and these might overlap with several relationships	**Contractual intermediaries**: You might have an intermediary only for a specific function (like a lawyer, a real-estate agent), but only for a short-term and not across functions.
More overlap of personal and public relations: For example, people in authority contexts (church, organization) often serving several relational functions. ("diffuse," See Ch. 4)	**More separation of personal and public relations**: People tend to relate to others in terms of a specific position— boss, friend, etc. ("specific")

to the other. This leads to key notions, discussed by Yum, such as the notion of **reciprocity**, in which each partner in the relationship gives, but also receives, and **selflessness**, in which each considers the needs of the other. As it comes to relationships, Yum notes that in relationships influenced by Confucian philosophy, specifically, Korean, Chinese, and Japanese: (1) We would expect reciprocity to be uneven, with the more powerful partner giving more to the relationship, especially materially. (2) Public and private relationships would overlap (See Figure 13.3). At the same time, while there are similarities across these three cultures, we must keep in mind that there are differences between and within them.

To highlight the notion of reciprocity, let us consider the Chinese notion of *kuan-hsi*—a Chinese notion of connectedness to others. The person who develops more *kuan-hsi* has more societal leverage—for example, connections with people in official positions in businesses or the governments that help people find jobs or work through the bureaucracy of the system (Chang & Holt, 1991). In the system of *kuan-hsi*, someone always owes someone something—a favor, a connection, and so on. This unequal balance, according to Yum (1988), helps maintain interpersonal connections in relationships, as opposed the Western (e.g., U.S. American) notion of short-term and symmetrical reciprocity. In the U.S. American approach, people like to "keep the slate clean." For example, if you buy me lunch this week, I'd better buy you lunch next week (or better yet, we will split the bill, each paying for our own). As long as no one owes the other anything, we maintain a sense of independence from each other, even in our relationships. There are cultural variations of the *kuan-hsi* development of interpersonal resources, though each is perhaps unique in how one builds and uses connection and influence. In Spanish-speaking countries, it is called *palanca* (leverage); in Brazil, the *jeito brasileiro* (the "Brazilian way"). It is *blat* in Russia and *wasta* in Saudi Arabia. In the United States, it is called *clout*, but may also be *nepotism*. Although it is desired and sought after in many countries, it has a negative connotation in the United States.

POP CULTURE

Around the world, famous couples or friends cross boundaries of nation, class, or race: Diana, Princess of Wales (UK) and her boyfriend Dodi Al Fayed (Egypt); close friends Tom Cruise (Church of Scientology) and Ben Stiller (son of Jewish and Irish Catholic parents); Michael Jackson (U.S. Black American) and Elizabeth Taylor (U.S. White American). One such couple was famous soccer player, Pelé, a Black Brazilian, who married White Brazilian model and actress Xuxa (Figure 13.4). Even though they were married only for a few years in the 1980s, their relationship remains famous within and outside of Brazil today. Can you think of any famous intercultural, interreligious, or interracial friends or couples? See what you can find out about them.

Figure 13.4 Pelé (do Nascimento), Brazilian soccer player, with wife Xuxa (Meneghel), model and actress, in a 1980s *Sports Illustrated* photo. What difficulties might an interracial couple, even a famous one, face in Brazil? How about in your country? How might fame make the relationship easier or harder?
Source: Luis Alberto/AP/Press Association Images.

Hierarchia and *confianza* in Colombia   Kristine Fitch (1998), after living for more than a year in Colombia, describes many aspects of Colombian culture, such as when one might use "*Usted*" or "*tú*" (it's not as simple as introductory Spanish classes make it sound!). Fitch (1994) introduces two foundations of Colombian social relationship: *confianza*, which is interpersonal trust or connectedness; and *hierarquía*, or social status difference. These guide the careful negotiating of requesting in work situations across status lines. Finally, Fitch (2002) describes an interesting relational ritual that she calls *salsipuede* ("leave if you can"). As one tries to leave a social gathering, like an evening party, the host or other partygoers must pull the person back into the party—"No—it's early. You can't leave yet!" Later, the person might try again, but there is still resistance. An hour after the first attempt, the person might leave gracefully. One cannot leave quickly without being seen as rude or perhaps harming relationships.

Societal power and intercultural and intergroup relationships

We have considered two approaches to relationship—a scientific approach that seeks to predict different aspects of relationships between people within, across, or between cultures, and an interpretive view that seeks to understand relationship practices specific to different cultures. But increasingly, scholars are also noting how societal power impinges on relationships. This may come in the form of stereotyping and attributions, in opposition to relationships, or, as noted before, in the way social power (such as privileging men in story-telling or adopting the husband's culture) plays out in relationships.

Attributions and stereotypes   Many people expect intergroup relationships, especially romance and marriage, to fail, which might work against these relationships as the people in them fulfill the expectations of those around them. In one study, people involved in intercultural marriage in Hawaii tended to blame their marital difficulties on "external" factors, such as language difference, cultural differences, and family interference, while those in same-culture marriage assigned the problems to personal differences, such as how to raise children, or spend time with friends. In fact, in all relationships, both individual *and* cultural factors may influence the relationship. It might protect our relationships to blame problems on the parents, on societal disapproval, and so on (the **Romeo and Juliet effect**, Graham *et al.*, 1985), but it might also keep us from seeing problems that are, in fact, individual to the partners involved, and not based on family, language, or culture.

Perhaps, as some argue (e.g., Gudykunst & Kim, 2003), ethnicity and other group identities become less important as relationships develop. But evidence suggests this is not always true. We might **refence** to let a group member from a group we do not like into our circle of relationships—that is, even though we develop a relationship with someone of another group, we consider that person to be different from the rest of the group ("You're not like other X's I know," Allport, 1954/1979). In this way, we still maintain stereotypes or prejudice even though we have a close relationship with someone of the other group. In an extensive study of 21 African American–European American couples in the U.S., Paul Rosenblatt and his colleagues (1995) found that, while race is not commonly a point of conflict in such couples, in times of stress, some partners resorted to calling partners racial epithets. This suggests that in societies divided by racial, caste, religious, or other differences, the ideas of society that are all around us can still sneak into our intimate relationships, even if we are usually appreciative of difference.

Opposition to relationships   Sometimes relationships between people of different groups are a target of **stigma** in a culture—that is, they are socially unacceptable, even to the point of being shamed or disgraced. For example, in some countries, like Brazil, miscegenation (racial/ethnic intermarriage) was encouraged, while in others, like the United States, it was taboo, even illegal in many states until 1967; some groups still oppose interracial marriage today—in 2011, a Kentucky, U.S. church banned interracial couples from being members (Ng, 2001). As late as 2009, many high school prom dances in Georgia were still segregated, sometimes making it impossible for friends to attend together (Doyle, 2009). Rosenblatt *et al.* (1995) note that one aspect of communication in interracial couples in the United States is the minority partner "educating" the White partner about racism, something the White partner is often not yet aware of. Interracial and interclass friendships are sometimes challenged when political issues or the need to help someone from the marginalized group arises. In some cases, societal opposition is so great as to forbid the relationship. Such opposition might also apply to the relationships of people of a particular group, especially gays and lesbians. Jacquie Taylor (2002) tells how she and her same-sex partner had to create new rituals to validate their relationship both for themselves and for their daughter. Homophobia and heterosexism (chapter 6) can become important in these relationships. While partners bring unique and cultural aspects to relationships, appreciation or non-acceptance by friends, family, and the larger environment may be a more prominent issue.

ON THE NET

Do an Internet search to find out the types of diverse relationship that exist in your nation or state. Look up news articles, Internet blogs, and so on, to see what types of acceptance these relationships receive in your area. What issues might they face in terms of housing, integration into social circles, and so on? What might you do, personally, to encourage a more respectful life for such couples, without, at the same time, making them just another "civic project" or "something interesting to look at?"

Relational and organizational conflict: How can I make intercultural conflict more productive?

Cross-cultural approaches to conflict resolution

One of the processes that characterizes most deep relationships at some point is conflict. The research on cross-cultural differences in conflict has looked at everything from brothers and sisters to romantic partners to workplace conflicts, often with the issues in the conflicts being the same. Managers, particularly those in human resources, spend hours resolving disputes, confrontations, and disagreements between warring colleagues. In small doses, conflict may even be healthy for relational development (though this conclusion may reflect our Western mindset as authors!). With regard to intercultural conflict, Stella Ting-Toomey and John Oetzel (2001) explain that conflict emerges when groups of people from different cultural communities who are involved in interdependent communicative objectives experience an emotional frustration caused by the perceived incompatibility of desired goals. Ting-Toomey (2003) defines **conflict** as the "perceived and/or actual incompatibility of values, expectations, processes, or outcomes between two or more parties from different cultures over substantive and/or relational issues" (p. 373).

Researchers outline five stages of conflict (Pondy, 1967). **Latent conflict** occurs when there is competition for resources that exceed their availability, when one side wants to exert control over what the other party considers to be their activity or under their control, and when two parties who must cooperate to attain a common goal are unable to reach a consensus. In **perceived conflict**, disagreeing parties become aware of tension toward each other and experience frustration. Because this type of conflict is often caused as a result of a misunderstanding of the other's true position, open communication may resolve the conflict. **Felt conflict** occurs when parties personalize their issues and involve egos in assessing individual and institutional motives. This stage may occur as a result of constant organizational demands that cause anxiety within an individual, leading the individual to vent her or his frustrations and work pressures in the form of displaced anger. In **manifest conflict**, conflict gets exhibited through open physical aggression, verbal expressions, dysfunctional organizational behaviors like sabotage, riots, mistreatment of the hierarchy, and so on. These behaviors may not necessarily be intended to hurt or frustrate others but may end up producing those outcomes. Therefore, manifest conflict refers to "behavior which, in the mind of the actor, frustrates the goals of at least some of the other participants. In other words, a member of the organization is said to engage in conflictful behavior if he consciously, but not necessarily deliberately, blocks another member's goal achievement" (p. 304). Finally, **conflict aftermath** results from an evaluation of outcomes as being productive or unproductive at each stage.

Importantly, culture may impact the different stages of conflict. Thomas Kochman (1981), for example, describes Black and White styles of conflict in the United States, such as different interpretations of allegations. African Americans use more emotional vocal dynamics (Johnson, 2002) and may raise their voices in a discussion, possibly leading White communicators to "feel" a conflict when the African American sees it only as a discussion (Kochman, 1981). In addition, as African Americans are more likely to live "in time," using time for the means of relationship and understanding, and Whites are more likely to live "on time," adhering to a clock-schedule, a White person may start to leave a conflict to get to another appointment, while the African American feels that the two should continue the discussion until the conflict is resolved, regardless of other appointments.

Depending on how individuals balance the incompatibility of goals and feel the desire to serve individuals' needs and goals versus the needs and goals of others involved in the conflict, there are five conflict management orientations typically described in this literature (e.g., Rahim, 2002, Ting-Toomey, 2005). **Avoiding (or withdrawing)** occurs when individuals prefer simply not to confront the other party, such as someone who has offended them, perhaps because of fear of the consequences resulting from a direct confrontation of the issue. Avoiding issues may work in the short term, but it is not productive for long-term organizational relationships. This style may be useful, however, when less is at stake, when the issue is trivial, when the issue can be managed with other (indirect) approaches, when you have no chance of winning, or sometimes just to let the offending party cool down and regain perspective.

Accommodating (yielding)—giving in to the demands of the other party—often requires the sacrifice of personal goals for the resolution of conflict and maintaining of a harmonious organizational relationship. Such sacrifices take the form of appeasement, abandoning one's principles for the greater good of the relationship in that context, and not minding one's own personal discomfort at the going-along-to-get-along mindset. This style can be used successfully when you find yourself in the wrong, when the issue of conflict is not as personally significant to you as it may be to the other party, to enable the building of social credit (or grace points) for you to be capitalized on at a later date, and when harmony, peaceful coexistence and collaboration is more important than individual success.

Competing (or dominating) is often considered a win-lose situation, because it works on the assumption that for one party to succeed, the other necessarily has to lose or fail. It is a style characterized by aggressive behaviors, overt disagreement, and extreme assertiveness, to the discomfort of the other party. A competing style can seriously damage relationships, put the parties into an attack–counterattack mode, and leave them angered, disrespected, and humiliated, with no intentions of seeking a cooperative solution. But if time is of the essence and a quick decision needs to be made, or when unpopular actions need to be implemented, or there is a threat of competitors taking advantage of your accommodating or collaborating efforts, this style may be the best and only option to exercise.

A **collaborating (or integrating)** approach—a win-win situation—works best when parties are committed to working together and resolving conflicts. This style encourages disgruntled parties to engage in dialog and work together to develop mutually beneficial solutions. Instead of avoiding or treating conflict as a contest, this approach accepts conflict as typical to organizational working lives. Brainstorming and developing creative solutions together gets all parties equally vested in the outcomes, thereby improving the quality of collaborative efforts. However, arriving at a consensual and mutually acceptable solution is often challenging, emotionally exhausting, and time-consuming.

Compromising (or conceding), a middle-range approach, is more aggressive than avoiding or accommodating but less involved than competing. In this approach, parties seek a solution collaboratively, usually with both parties gaining some objectives but not all of them. Although each party gains something in this approach, some see it as a lose-lose situation, because in order for conflicting parties to compromise and reach an agreement, they both have to give up something. A compromise is often triggered by self-interest, since parties act in ways that are most beneficial to themselves. This style may be used most effectively when parties are committed to mutually exclusive goals and when the temporary resolution of the dispute is more important than a long-term permanent solution.

Conflict negotiation skills are a huge asset to an international manager, along with third-party alternatives to dispute resolution like mediation and arbitration. The trick is to know which strategies to use and when. Stella Ting-Toomey (2005) developed a theory that predicts how different people from different cultures might negotiate conflict on the five styles mentioned. Her theory revolves around the notion of **face**, specifically, **positive face** and **negative face** (see chapter 7). She argues that people in collectivistic cultures are more likely to be concerned with positive face, and those from individualistic cultures, with negative face. Collectivists are more likely to be concerned with the face of the other person, and, thus, focused on the process of the communication, while the individualist will more likely focus on their own face and needs. Because conflict inherently challenges both negative face (as we try to persuade others) and positive face (as we challenge the competence of their ideas), Ting-Toomey predicts that collectivists will prefer to avoid or yield in conflict (Figure 13.5). This probably holds true especially in work or public contexts, and when the costs involved in the conflict are less. Individualists will be more likely than collectivists to seek dominating strategies. And, since collaboration requires both parties to address conflict squarely, this is also the approach that individualists are more likely to prefer. Ting-Toomey also incorporates power distance and self-construal (see chapter 4) into her theory.

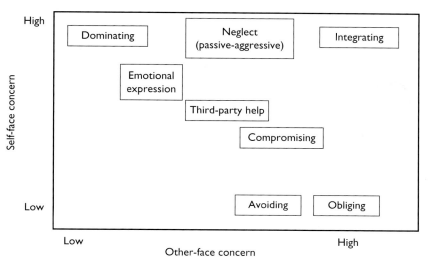

Figure 13.5 Stella Ting-Toomey (2005) predicts that collectivists will be more likely to avoid, withdraw, or compromise in conflict when possible. What influences the approach that you take? What factors besides culture may be at work? Source: Reproduced from Ting-Toomey & Oetzel, 2002, p. 160, by permission of Sage Publications, Inc.

Ting-Toomey and others have done many studies that support the main predictions of her theory. For example, John Oetzel and his colleagues (2003) did a survey study of Mexicans, Japanese, Germans, and U.S. Americans. They found that across cultures, student participants used more respect and sharing feelings with parents than with siblings, and less pretending and aggression. Participants in countries higher in individualism and lower in power distance did use some dominating and collaborating strategies more than those in collectivistic and low power-distance cultures; and collectivists used more avoiding. At the same time, German participants used more self-face concern than U.S. Americans (two more independent cultures), and Japanese participants expressed feelings more than those from Mexico.

International negotiation

Fatehi (2008) declares that the most difficult and important task for international managers is negotiation. This process requires the careful consideration of another party's needs and goals before making a mutually agreeable decision. What makes international negotiations challenging are the sheer number of laws, regulations, business practices, and standards of operations, not to mention the cultural differences that add layers of complexity to the process. **Negotiation** is "a special form of social interaction or decision-making that (a) involves more than one party; (b) who hold potentially conflicting interests, as well as common interests or interdependence to motivate each to remain within the relationship or complete the exchange; and (c) requires a reciprocal exchange of information" (Schmidt & Conaway, cited in Schmidt *et al.*, 2007, p. 221). Negotiation involves three aspects: the negotiation process; the parties in the negotiation; and the final outcome or agreement that emerges from the negotiation (Fatehi, 2008). In addition to these components, there are aspects of negotiating that need to be remembered, such as: each party's expected outcomes; the negotiating team make-up and motivation; physical factors such as site, space, operational procedures and use of time; and style of communicating and negotiating (Beamer & Varner, 2008).

Wallace Schmidt and his colleagues (2007) summarize a three-phase intercultural conflict negotiation model. In the **background phase**, parties undertake essential planning for the negotiation session. This includes analyzing one's own position in the process and carefully planning one's communicating language. Each party should gather and organize pertinent information regarding the situation, keeping in mind all the involved people, their varied interests, available options, and criteria such as market value, expert opinion, customs, laws, industry practices, and others (Fatehi, 2008). In addition to identifying one's own interests, priorities, goals, and strategies, one must also understand the mindset, personality attributes, perceptions, cultural values, norms, beliefs, and expectations of the other negotiating party. Even as one collects cultural information about the other party, one should also be mindful of the dangers of cultural stereotyping and cultural profiling (Schmidt *et al.*, 2007).

In the **process phase**, the actual negotiation, collaborative engagement or competition occurs between the parties. Parties communicate back and forth within their intercultural context and shape the reality of the ongoing negotiation with the unique characteristics they bring to the table. According to Schmidt *et al.* (2007), two specific negotiating styles emerge during this phase: a **distributive, or positional negotiation**, which involves competitively pushing for one's own goals and agenda with little regard to the other party; and **integrative, or principled negotiation** that uses collaborative strategies and considers the needs and expectations of the other party to develop mutually satisfying ends. Principled negotiation (PN) advocates negotiating on merits. PN "provides parties to a negotiation with a method of focusing on basic interests and mutually advantageous solutions" (Fatehi, 2008, p. 200). PN values other members' perspectives, and negotiators—having gained trust and credibility—work to share information reciprocally and improve their mutual situations. The last stage, the **outcome phase**, is the culmination of all events and communication that comprised the conflict negotiation process. The process itself and the outcomes are evaluated to see whether expectations were surpassed or fell short of predetermined goals. This phase determines the nature of future interactions and whether or not there is potential for more business partnerships.

Of course, an international/intercultural negotiation is never an event, it is always a process, and that process can be a really long and time-consuming one. In addition to negotiations, *mediation* and *arbitration* are two other methods used in conflict reconciliation. **Mediators** are neutral third parties that try to resolve disputes with reason and compromise instead of more aggressive measures. They have no power to impose a decision upon the disputing parties but work collaboratively with the two parties to arrive at a third-party mediated, mutually acceptable solution. Mediation by a third party is particularly helpful if the two conflicting parties have reached a stalemate or voluntarily agreed to have a third party intervene (Schmidt *et al.*, 2007). Ann Nevelle Miller (2012/2009) notes how the use of mediators of various sorts is an essential part of Sub-Saharan African culture, not only in the workplace, but also in interpersonal and dating relationships. Arbitration is yet another dispute resolution alternative that conflicting parties can opt for. **Arbitrators** are neutral, objective, third parties that can resolve a conflict based on the facts of the conflict situation presented to them. Unlike mediators, arbitrators are permitted to impose a binding decision on the parties in conflict (Schmidt *et al.*, 2007).

Even with all the information gathered from the earlier discussion, if individuals do not behave in culturally intelligent and sensitive ways, no negotiation will be successful. Culture influences not only the style of negotiating but also what groups consider important within the context. Fatehi (2008) explains that collectivistic cultures have larger number of members in their negotiating teams, while individualistic cultures may have just one person. A negotiating team's make-up may be based on how a culture values the age and seniority of a member, a member's expertise, and members' decision-making authority and status within the organizational hierarchy or even in that society. Knowledge of the opposite negotiating team's characteristics will help the home team navigate the conflict.

When holding negotiations internationally, it is also important to learn about nuances unique to the other culture that may differ from one's own, such as how the culture uses time. Negotiators from the United States, for example, are not known for being patient and may use direct and indirect ways to push their negotiating party into a resolution, while the Japanese consider taking time to make a decision is a sign of maturity and wisdom (Beamer & Varner, 2008). Emotions are of extreme importance during the communicating and managing of conflict. People in high-context and low-context cultures may emote differently with different objectives and toward different ends. Whether to display emotions and what kind of emotions to display are culturally motivated and interpreted. Cultural differences also exist between deal-focused (DF) and relationship-focused (RF) negotiating groups. Fatehi (2008) argues that the majority of the world's cultures are RF, and believe in dealing with people they trust, such as their friends and family members. When doing business with strangers, people from such cultures first try to develop relationships with their new negotiating or business partners to get to know them better and build trust. The DF types believe in wasting no time in seemingly pointless small talk or extended chats about what they consider irrelevant or frivolous topics. The sooner a deal gets done, the better.

In forging international business relationships through successful negotiations, it is imperative that the two parties be mindful of each other's cultural norms and values. The proper way of greeting someone from a foreign culture, the acceptance of humor in professional settings, the politeness of making eye contact, perceptions of silence, expectations for personal space, appropriateness of body language and gestures, the role of religion in social and professional interaction, and so on, are all issues to consider before venturing into negotiations with a different cultural group. Individuals and groups who are culturally sensitive, flexible in communicating and negotiating styles, and considerate of differences will gain the richest of experiences from international negotiation opportunities.

Summary

We began our look at relating culturally by considering different types of relationships where culture and difference are involved. We saw that people bring into relationships different motives, relational definitions, and values. Through processes such as learning about similarities, learning to predict and understand the other's behavior, self-disclosure, and resolving relational tensions, our relationships grow, as we continue to work out individual and cultural differences. Each culture also has unique aspects and nuances of relationship patterns. As we travel to other nations and have relationships with people from other cultures within our own, we must also be aware of the role of structural power and ideologies. For example, do we only accept friends if they become like our culture expects them to be?

One type of relational pattern is conflict. Our discussion presents different types of conflict strategy and approach, as well as issues present in negotiation as these relate to work relationships. However, as one study cited earlier (Oetzel *et al.*, 2003) notes, the strategies also have application for relationships with our parents, siblings, friends, and lovers.

Understanding relationships and conflict is useful in terms of civic engagement. First, we can work together within our relationships to both become and help others become socially aware within our friendship circles. Working together in socially relevant action also builds bonds of friendship, as we share "fellowship" in a task of making the world a better place. And forming friendships and romance across cultural and national lines helps to bring harmony and appreciation of other cultures to the world as a whole. Finally, in intercultural personal and work relationships, we are bound to have conflict. Understanding the ways that other groups perceive and practice conflict will keep us from imposing our own expectations on them. And, perhaps through better relationships and conflict, we can build synergy with others, rather than working on our own toward social involvement and change.

KEY TERMS

miscegenation, 270
intermarriage, 270
relationship, 271
exogamy, 271
values, 271
nuclear family, 272
friends with benefits, 273
booty call, 273
propinquity, 274
similarity-attraction hypothesis, 274
self-disclosure, 274
social penetration theory, 274
depth, 274
breadth, 274
uncertainty reduction theory, 274
anxiety, 275
dialectics/dialectical tension, 275
propriety, 276
reciprocity, 277
selflessness, 277
kuan-hsi, 277
Romeo and Juliet effect, 279
refence, 279

stigma, 280
conflict, 281
latent conflict, 281
perceived conflict, 281
felt conflict, 281
manifest conflict, 281
conflict aftermath, 281
avoiding (or withdrawing), 281
accommodating (or yielding), 281
competing (or dominating), 282
collaborating (or integrating), 282
compromising (or conceding), 282
face, 282
positive face, 282
negative face, 282
negotiation, 283
background phase, 284
process phase, 284
distributive, or positional negotiation, 284
integrative, or principled negotiation, 284
outcome phase, 284
mediator, 284
arbitrator, 284

Discussion questions

1 In groups, come up with strategies for success or coping in intercultural friendships, romance, workplace relationships, or families. The Internet has many sources that might help you come up with a list. What would you add from your own experience?

2 How do you feel that people in your culture perceive intergroup unions (romance, marriage)? Which intergroup unions do you feel are more accepted, and why? (For example, are interreligious, intercaste or interclass unions more accepted than others? Are some racial/ethnic combinations more accepted than others?)

3 For one week, keep a journal of friends you talk to through social network sites, noting how long, how often, and how deeply you talk. After the week, compare networks with other students. How "diverse" is your network? What are some advantages of diverse relationship networks?

4 We saw in this chapter that inter*cultural* relationships (e.g., Norwegian–Belarussian) might face different issues than inter*group* relationships (e.g., Black–White). We discussed conflict between people of different national cultures. What issues might you have to consider, in addition, if you wanted to discuss interethnic, interracial, or interreligious conflict?

5 Find a cross-cultural simulation game regarding conflict or negotiation, such as The Emperor's Pot (Batchelder, 1996). In such games, people are often assigned to different cultures. After the game, discuss your feelings and aspects of negotiation you experienced during the exercise.

Action points

1 Find another person in your church, organization, or school, who is different from you. You may not become friends, but commit to meeting every one or two weeks. Try to really listen and understand about the person's life, and share your life with them.

2 Watch the news to find out about some of the political and social conflicts in your area. In what way is culture, or group identity, or politics involved in the conflict? Give a report on the conflict in class. How might information you learned in this chapter help people in the situation negotiate conflict?

3 Join a social advocacy group for a cause in which you believe. Do some deeper research on the varieties of strategy that people can use to address conflict (e.g., Ting-Toomey & Oetzel, 2001). Discuss with members of your organization the usefulness of different strategies for conflict and negotiation in different settings.

For more information

Avruch, K. (2000). *Culture and conflict resolution*. Washington, DC: United States Institute of Peace.

Broome, B. (2005). *building Bridges across the Green Line: A guide to intercultural communication in Cyprus*. United Nations Office of Project Services (UNOPS).

Gudykunst, W.B., Ting-Toomey, S., & Nishida T. (Eds.). (1996). *Communication in personal relationships across cultures*. Thousand Oaks: Sage.

Kriesberg, L. (2006). *Constructive conflicts: From escalation to resolution*. Lanham, MD: Rowman & Littlefield Publishers.

Romano, D. (2008). *Intercultural marriage: Promises and pitfalls* (3rd ed.). Boston: Intercultural Press.

Zakaria, N., Amelinckx, A., & Wilemon, D. (2004). Working together apart? Building a knowledge-sharing culture for global virtual teams. *Creativity and innovation Management, 13*, 15–29.

References

Allport, G.W. (1954/1979). *The nature of prejudice.* Reading, MA: Addison-Wesley.

Altman, I., & Taylor, D. (1973). *Social penetration.* New York: Holt, Rinehard, and Winston.

Antunes, A. (2011). "The world's highest paid celebrity couples." *Forbes*, August 19. Accessed Jan 24, 2013, at http://www.forbes.com/sites/andersonantunes/2011/08/19/the-worlds-highest-paid-celebrity-couples/

Batchelder, D. (1996). The emperor's pot. In H.N. Seelye (Ed.), *Experiential activities for intercultural learning* (pp. 85–99). Yarmouth, ME: Intercultural Press.

Baxter, L.A., & Montgomery, B.M. (1996). *Relating: Dialogues and dialectics.* New York: Guilford.

Beamer, L., & Varner, I. (2008). *Intercultural communication in the global workplace.* Boston: McGraw-Hill Irwin.

Berger, C.R., & Calabrese, R. (1975). Some explorations in initial interaction and beyond. *Human Communication Research, 1*, 99–112.

Berger, C.R., & Gudykunst, W.B. (1991). Uncertainty and communication. In B. Dervin & M.J. Voigt (Eds.), *Progress in communication sciences* (Vol. 10, pp. 21–60). Norwood, NJ: Ablex.

Byrne, D. (1971). *The attraction paradigm.* New York: Academic Press.

CBS News. (2010). *Study: 1 in 7 new U.S. marriages is interracial*, June 4. Accessed Dec 9, 2011, at http://www.cbsnews.com/stories/2010/06/04/national/main6547886.shtml

Chang, H.-C., & Holt, R. (1991). More than relationship: Chinese interaction and the principle of *kuan-hsi. Communication Quarterly, 3*, 251–271.

Char, W.F. (1977). Motivations for intercultural marriage. In W.S. Tseng, J.F. McDermott, & T.W. Maretzki (Eds.), *Adjustment in intercultural marriage* (pp. 33–40). Honolulu: The University Press of Hawaii.

Collier, M.J. (1991). Conflict competence within African-, Mexican-, and Anglo-American friendships. In S. Ting-Toomey & F. Korzenny (Eds.), *Cross-cultural interpersonal communication* (pp. 132–154). Newbury Park: Sage.

Crary, D. (2007). Interracial marriages surge across U.S. *USA Today*, April 12. Accessed Dec 9, 2011, at http://www.usatoday.com/news/health/2007-04-12-interracial-marriage_N.htm

Dodd, C.H., & Baldwin, J.R. (2002). The role of family and macrocultures in intercultural relationships. In J.N. Martin, T.K. Nakayama, & L.A. Flores (Eds.), *Readings in intercultural communication: Experiences and contexts* (pp. 279–288). Boston: McGraw Hill.

Doyle, L. (2009). Segregated high school proms divide Georgia's students. *The Telegraph*, June 21. Accessed Feb 3, 2012, at http://www.telegraph.co.uk/news/worldnews/northamerica/usa/5586617/Segregated-high-school-proms-divide-Georgias-students.html

Fatehi, K. (2008). International management and the cultural context. In K. Fatehi (Ed.), *Managing internationally: Succeeding in a culturally diverse world.* (pp. 124–149). Thousand Oaks, CA: Sage.

Fitch, K.L. (1994). A cross-cultural study of directive sequences and some implications for compliance-gaining research. *Communication Monographs, 61*, 185–209.

Fitch, K.L. (1998). *Speaking relationally: Culture, communication, and interpersonal connection.* New York: Guilford.

Fitch, K.L. (2002). A ritual for attempting leave-taking in Colombia. In J.M. Martin, T.K. Nakayama, & L.A. Flores (Eds.), *Readings in intercultural communication: Experiences and contexts* (2nd ed., pp. 149–155). Boston: McGraw-Hill.

Graham, M.A., Moeai, J., & Shizuru, L.S. (1985). Intercultural marriages: An interreligous perspective. *International Journal of Intercultural Relations, 9*, 427–434.

Gudykunst, W.B. (2005). An anxiety/uncertainty management (AUM) theory of effective communication. In W.B. Gudykunst (Ed.), *Theorizing about intercultural communication* (pp. 281–322). Thousand Oaks: Sage.

Gudykunst, W.B., & Kim, Y.Y. (2003). *Communicating with strangers: An approach to intercultural communication* (4th ed.). Boston: McGraw Hill.

Hammer, M.R. (1986). The influence of ethnic and attitude similarity on initial social penetration. In Y.Y. Kim (Ed.), *Interethnic communication: Current research* (pp. 225–237). Newbury Park: Sage.

Johnson, F. (2002). *Speaking culturally: Language diversity in the United States.* Thousand Oaks, CA: Sage.

Kim, K.-H., & Yun, H. (2007). *Cying* for me, *cying* for us: Relational dialectics in a Korean social networking site. *Journal of Computer Mediated Communication, 18*, 298–318. doi:10.1111/j.1083-6101.2007.00397.x

Kochman, T. (1981). *Black and White Styles in conflict.* Chicago: University of Chicago Press.

Lampe, P.E. (1981). Interethnic dating: Reasons for and against. *International Journal of Intercultural Relations, 6*, 115–126.

Lee, S.M., & Edmondson, B. (2005). New marriages, new families: U.S. racial and Hispanic intermarriage.

Population Bulletin, 60(2). Accessed Dec 9, 2011, at http://www.prb.org/pdf05/60.2New Marriages.pdf

Malone, C. (2011). Celebrity intercultural relationships. *Examiner.com*, April 7. Accessed Dec 9, 2011, at http://www.examiner.com/intercultural-relationships-in-honolulu/celebrity-intercultural-relationships

Miller, A.N. (2012/2009). When face-to-face won't work: Use of informal intermediaries to communicate interpersonally in Sub-Saharan Africa. In L.A. Samovar, R. Porter, & E. McDaniels (Eds.) *Intercultural communication: A reader (*13th ed., pp. 179–189*)*. Belmont, CA: Wadsworth.

Ng, D. (2001). Kentucky church bans interracial couples. *ABC World News*, December 1. Accessed Feb 2, 2012, at http://abcnews.go.com/US/kentucky-church-bans-interracial-couples/story?id=15065204

Oetzel, J., Ting-Toomey, S., Chew-Sanchez, M.I., Harris, R., Wilcox, R., & Stumpf, S. (2003). Face and facework in conflicts with parents and siblings: A cross-cultural comparison of Germans, Japanese, Mexicans, and U.S. Americans. *The Journal of Family Communication, 3*(3), 67–93.

Pondy, L.R. (1967). Organizational conflict: Concepts and models. *Administrative Science Quarterly, 12*, 296–320.

Rahim, M.A. (2002). Toward a theory of managing organizational conflict. *The International Journal of Conflict Management, 13*, 206–235.

Rohrlich, B.F. (1988). Dual-culture marriage and communication. *International Journal of Intercultural Relations, 12*, 35–44. doi:10.1016/0147-1767(88) 90005-3

Romano, D. (2008). *Intercultural marriage: Promises & pitfalls* (3rd ed.). Boston: Intercultural Press.

Rosenblatt, P.C., Karis, T.A., & Powell, R.D. (1995). *Multiracial Couples: Black and White voices.* Thousand Oaks: Sage.

Schmidt, W.V., Conaway, R.N., Easton, S.S., & Wardrope, W.J. (2007). *Communicating globally: Intercultural communication and international business.* Thousand Oaks, CA: Sage.

Taylor, J. (2002). Performing commitment. In J.M. Martin, T.K. Nakayama, & L.A. Flores (Eds.), *Readings in intercultural communication: Experiences and contexts* (2nd ed., pp. 310–318). Boston: McGraw-Hill.

Ting-Toomey, S. (2003). Managing intercultural conflicts effectively. In L.A. Samovar & R.E. Porter (Eds.), *Intercultural communication: A reader* (10th ed.) (pp. 373–384). Belmont, CA: Wadsworth/Thomson Learning.

Ting-Toomey, S. (2005). The matrix of face: An updated face-negotiated theory. In W.B. Gudykunst (Ed.), *Theorizing intercultural communication* (pp. 71–92). Thousand Oaks: Sage.

Ting-Toomey, S., & Oetzel, J. (2001). *Managing intercultural conflict effectively.* Thousand Oaks, CA: Sage.

Ting-Toomey, S., & Oetzel, J.G. (2002). Cross-cultural face concerns and conflict styles: Current status and future directions. In W.B. Gudykunst & B. Mody (Eds.), *Handbook of intercultural communication* (2nd ed., pp. 143–163). Thousand Oaks: Sage.

Tokunaga, R.S. (2009). High-speed Internet access to the other: The influence of cultural orientations on self-disclosures in offline and online relationships. *Journal of Intercultural Communication Research, 38*(3), 133–147.

Tseng, W.S. (1977). Adjustment in intercultural marriage. In W. S. Tseng, J. F. McDermott, & T. W. Matetzki (Eds.), *Adjustment in intercultural marriage* (pp. 93–103). Honolulu: The University Press of Hawaii.

Yum, J.O. (1988). The impact of Confucianism on interpersonal relationships and communication Patterns in East Asia. *Communication Monographs, 55*, 374–388.

Chapter 14

The political context: How can we use communication to shape politics and culture?

Chapter objectives

After this chapter, you should be able to:

→ **Understand and explain politics as cultural communication**

→ **Explain how politics and culture are interrelated**

→ **Identify examples of culture-based social movements**

→ **Understand the politics of immigration**

→ **Understand values for intercultural political leadership**

Politics, culture, and communication: How do politics relate to culture?

Making change happen: What are some examples of successful social movements?

Intercultural political leadership: What strategies can we use to bring about change?

Intercultural Communication for Everyday Life, First Edition. John R. Baldwin, Robin R. Means Coleman, Alberto González, and Suchitra Shenoy-Packer.
© 2014 John R. Baldwin, Robin R. Means Coleman, Alberto González, and Suchitra Shenoy-Packer.
Published 2014 by John Wiley & Sons Ltd.

n April 2011, music icon Bob Dylan played a concert in Beijing. In a career that began in the early 1960s, this was his first concert performance in China. Chinese officials reviewed and approved the song list and made sure that it did not include well-known songs of political protest such as *The Times They Are A-Changin'* and *Blowin' In The Wind*. Dylan did not perform these songs, which had fueled political activism across nations and decades. His decisions to perform in China and agree to a setlist review left some wondering if Dylan had decided to "give up the fight" in exchange for a payday (Whitehead, 2011).

Though Dylan performed songs that were approved by the government censors, the performance was still charged with political significance. Dylan began his concert with a song from *Slow Train Coming*, an album of Christian devotion. *Gonna Change My Way Of Thinking* tells the audience that they should adopt "a different set of rules" and "stop being influenced by fools". Dylan sang this song in a country where Christians worship secretly in "underground churches" and risk arrest by the police if discovered (Mattingly, 2011). While Dylan's songs may not have seemed political to the Chinese censors, his message was highly subversive in a climate of religious repression.

Dylan's concert allows several observations about politics, communication, and culture. First, political messages can be embedded in all kinds of expression—songs, speeches, paintings and graphic art, novels and essays, clothing, and so on. Political messages can occur almost anywhere at any time. Second, political messages are created and delivered in a cultural context. The songs banned by the Chinese officials were written by Dylan during the 1960s. These songs were used to support the peace movement and the civil rights movement within the United States during the 1960s and 1970s. In other words, the songs were associated with questioning and opposing government authority (what the Chinese officials wanted to avoid). Additionally, Dylan's concert occurred at a time when China's international influence was increasing—along with international criticism of human rights abuses. This concert was an experiment that tested the balance between state control and openness to Western popular culture. Third, political expression is open to interpretation. The Chinese officials believed that Dylan's "protest" songs might incite the listeners to rebel—but would listeners even understand the English lyrics and references to events in the United States?

POP CULTURE

Popular music is used in many cultures for political means, either to support the current government or ideologies, or to protest. In Chile, for example, *nueva canción* (new song) singers in the 1970s sang songs of farm reform and social justice—and hundreds were killed by Pinochet's right-wing government in the stadium-turned-jail in Santiago.

With classmates, come up with a list of groups or singers in your culture who sing messages that are either mildly or overtly political. How effective do you feel their messages are, and why?

In 2011, Dylan turned 70 years old and he is notorious for his raspy voice. If listeners did understand the lyrics, would they react to them in the same way as a 1960s U.S. American college student? The Chinese officials were taking no chances, but it was ironic that the Western press interpreted Dylan's concert differently. The West read more political significance in the fact that Dylan allowed his set to be reviewed and approved than in his actual song selection. Fourth, political expression often carries profound importance to governments and citizens alike. The Chinese attempted to protect national policy and cultural values by removing songs that might lead listeners to question authority. At the same time, Western journalists protected the value of free speech and free artistic creativity as they condemned Dylan's apparent submission to state control. Sometimes, a concert isn't simply a concert.

This chapter explores the nature of political communication and its implications for intercultural relations and civic engagement. We define political communication and explore two particular political domains that are especially relevant to intercultural relations. We also examine the nature of political leadership in international and diverse contexts and provide a leadership model that responds to the ever-increasing demands for dialogue and understanding.

Politics, culture, and communication: How do politics relate to culture?

Like culture, "politics" has many definitions. Most broadly defined, **politics** refers to the identification and public negotiation of competing interests. Like culture, politics presumes the creation and public sharing of meaning. Typically, we place politics in the realm of government. In democratic systems, politicians campaign for office and, if elected, politicians make laws, oversee the mechanisms of the state (agencies, services, taxation, etc.), negotiate legislation with opposition parties, and campaign for re-election. Civic engagement in the realm of government means knowing and following how government works, paying attention to political debates, and volunteering in efforts to help pass or defeat proposed legislation. In a single-party state like China, civic engagement means knowing the laws enacted by the central government and acting consistently with those laws. It means going to the website of the local party leaders and reading their posts. Above all, being engaged means acting virtuously to render assistance to others in need and to uphold order in the community.

In democratic systems, **communicative engagement** means participating in civic dialogue and making full use of expressive opportunities to influence deliberative democracy. Ideally, our participation has the potential to "convert society into a great community" (McKinney et al., 2005, p. 7). The person who practices communicative engagement seeks out opportunities to be heard on issues and is a critical reader and viewer of political messages.

There is another meaning to "politics." We will call this **politics 2.0**. Politics 2.0 refers to how social structures and institutions work to maintain their authority. This is what is called the "politics of consensus and consent" (Deetz, 1990, p. 46). For example, the competitive and selective qualities of U.S. sports teams "mirror the values and beliefs of the dominant culture" (Miller, 1999, p. 189). The doctrine of American exceptionalism plays out in athletic competition from high school to the professional conferences. Teams become synonymous with regional and national ideals, making team support an act of patriotism. Questioning a team name, for example, would be treasonous. Imagine, then, the challenged faced by Native American activists who protested the 1995 Baseball World

Series between the Atlanta Braves and the Cleveland Indians. The protesters' claims that both teams demean Native American heritages with a logo (Cleveland's Chief Wahoo) and fans' actions (the Braves fans' "tomahawk chop") could not be seriously considered because baseball is "American as apple pie" and "America's pastime." In addition, the Native Americans "lost" the competition for the U.S. West, and as outsiders (the losers) had limited legitimacy (Miller, 1999, p. 191). Unlike repressive regimes that resort to violence to subdue the opposition, team owners and sports organizations do not need to limit protest. By linking baseball teams to such powerful influences as Manifest Destiny and American Exceptionalism, the teams protect their revenue stream against critical review by the already formed consensus of the public.

Like white positionality in the U.S. (Whiteness, chapter 9), politics 2.0 encompasses everyday actions that we regard as "natural" and "normal" that actually function to protect and advance the goals of dominant interests. When we renew a driver's license or pay taxes, we perform our consent to be permitted to drive and to have our income returned to the state or local government. When we use the term "American" when we really mean "a U.S. citizen," or when we do not think of someone from Bolivia or Paraguay as "American," we uphold the notion that the U.S. is the true and only America and that everyone else in the Americas (North, Central, and South) does not have a claim to that name. Terms such as "gender politics," "identity politics," or "politics of the everyday," usually are directed to pointing out how we enact our consensus on these topics or how we attempt to disrupt consensus.

POP CULTURE

What are some of your own practices—ways of talking, joking, dressing, shopping—that support current ways of thinking and political systems? For example, perhaps you find yourself "competing" with others of your age to mark your status. In some cultures, that is done through purchasing new material goods or technology. Or perhaps the use of technology itself supports a particular set of values. The values may be useful for you, as long as you are aware that you are following them, and not doing so blindly. What are some ways you can resist these ways of thinking and acting, if you should choose to do so?

Returning to the notion of communicative engagement, and combining this notion with our second sense of politics, we can now see that participating in democracy is highly variable and problematic. Do people living in urban neighborhoods have the same opportunity to travel to a voting station on election day? Does a person who has been unemployed or on a low income have the same opportunity as an affluent person to write an opinion letter to the local newspaper or to donate to a political candidate? Critical communicative engagement reflects upon the presence of dominant interests in our everyday practices and invents possibilities for disrupting practices that maintain inequity or hide exploitative interests. In intercultural contexts, we should attempt to identify "what conventional practices must be altered or expanded to allow for the discourse of the Other to be heard—and not only heard, but heeded" (McKerrow, 2000, p. 43). The next section illustrates these polar notions of politics by examining intercultural social movements.

Making change happen: What are some examples of successful social movements?

Quite often, intercultural communication is central to accomplishing political resistance and critique. Wide-scale, organized activism to advance social and political criticism and change is called a **social movement** (Stewart *et al.*, 2007). While some movements may be "revivalist" and seek to reassert "an idealized past" (such as the Tea Party movement in the United States), many are "innovative" movements that seek to assert and implement new values and perspectives (p. 14). Innovative movements are most relevant to the formation of new intercultural relations.

Social movements are outside of established social institutions. Hence, one characteristic of social movements is that they are "uninstitutionalized collectivities." Social movements have belief systems that leaders and members can express with some conviction. Social movements define and pursue a moral good that leaders and members believe will make conditions better for people. Social movement messages are directed outward—to non-members (to gain new members or to gain support for change). Messages are also directed inward—to members (to maintain support and to mobilize members for action in support of goals). Finally, a movement has some sort of organization in order to maintain itself and mark progress toward its stated goals (Stewart *et al.*, 2007, pp. 7–16).

While an understanding of social movements is important to placing a speech or text in a political and cultural context, another exciting concept also is available. As we learned in chapter 9, **vernacular discourse** refers to locally produced meanings. It is "discourse operating within local communities" (Ono & Sloop, 1995, p. 20). Vernacular discourse is in the realm of politics 2.0 and allows us to examine the politics of the local. Critical focus is upon marginalized communities and their interaction with the dominant interests because vernacular discourse "makes visible power relations among subjects" (Calafell & Delgado, 2004, p. 6). Since local meanings many times function persuasively to mediate relationships between marginalized and dominant communities, we also use the term **vernacular rhetoric**. This section examines the vernacular rhetoric of two innovative social movements that seek to address intercultural inequity.

The Green Belt Movement

Upon her death in the fall of 2011, Wangari Maathai may not have been a household name in the United States, but she was a world famous activist known to millions. President Obama issued a statement that praised her work. The Green Belt Movement, he said, "stands as a testament to the power of grassroots organizing, proof that one person's simple idea—that a community should come together to plant trees—can make a difference, first in one village, then in one nation, and now across Africa" (The White House, 2011).

The Green Belt Movement (GBM; http://www.greenbeltmovement.org) began in Kenya in the 1970s. Maathai's goal was to empower the women of Kenya to protect the rural environment against degradation and misuse, by planting trees. The trees would provide windbreaks for schools and neighborhoods, prevent soil erosion, provide firewood for cooking and allow a harvest of fresh fruit. Just as important, local women would learn new practices for planting and caring for the trees, and they would establish a new relationship with their local governments—a relationship based on mutual respect and equality (Maathai, 2004). In learning these new practices, the women would be critically engaged with their local government (Figure 14.1).

Figure 14.1 Professor Wangari Maathai, founder and advocate of the Green Belt Movement in Africa, stands up to hired security guards in the Karura Forest, Nairobi, Kenya, in April 1999. Source: Simon Maina/AFP/ Getty Images.

The GBM existed outside of official government programs and at times challenged the government. When the Kenyan government planned to replace Nairobi's central park with a building complex of offices and retail shops, Maathai objected, and filed a lawsuit to stop the development. The government threatened to outlaw the group, and banished the organization to Maathai's home. The heavy-handed reaction by the government drew international support for Maathai and the building complex was abandoned (Bretton, 1998, p. 15).

Rhetorical communication was critical to the GBM. Maathai and her staff conducted workshops with the local women, which consisted of days of dialogue. The workshops led the women to reset their relationships to the land, their husbands, their government, and the future. Human rights advocate Frances Moore Lappé interviewed Maathai and asked about the persuasive power of the workshops. Maathai stated,

"Now that can take two days discussing, and that's when the personal transformation takes place. That's when people realize, yes, they may have been misled, but they have brains and they also can think. That's when we make a break, and from then on we are dealing with a different kind of person—very motivated, self-conscious, willing to make decisions, willing to go back to their communities and make a difference"

(Lappé & Lappé, 2002, p. 186).

Eventually, Maathai mobilized more than 60,000 women to plant 20 million trees.

The basis of persuasion for the GBM is evident in the use of vernacular terms and knowledge. The slogan for the GBM was, "Save the Land Harambee." *Harambee* is the Swahili word that means "all pull together," and this word became the national slogan with Kenya's first president, Jomo Kenyatta (Maathai, 2004, p. 20). Maathai adapted the term to create an environmental mission and created a slogan that was recognized across the hundreds of communities in Kenya where the GBM recruited new members.

In addition to vernacular terms, vernacular knowledge also was valued by the GBM. When the foresters tried to teach the women about planting, they often used scientific terms and described complex procedures for planting. Again demonstrating independence from existing institutions, the GBM eventually substituted the methods of the foresters with the methods developed by the women's ancestors. The women shared planting knowledge throughout their communities and became very innovative and resourceful. The foresters judged the women's methods unprofessional, but the GBM called the women "foresters without diplomas" (Maathai, 2004, p. 28).

The GBM lies at the intersection of three global movements—women's empowerment, peace, and environmental. Maathai resisted patriarchy by providing a means for women to gain autonomy and change conditions in their communities. Maathai also considered violence and war as conflicts over resources. To improve the resources for all meant reduced conflict. Finally, creating a "greener" Africa allowed the continent to heal from decades of poor land use. The GBM clearly articulated its moral struggle against the forces of repression and exclusion. The GBM employed vernacular discourse and knowledge to gain members and to demonstrate a contrast to Western-educated politicians and foresters.

In 2004, Maathai was awarded the Nobel Prize for Peace. She continued to work for international awareness for women's agency and the environment. The GBM now has a goal to "Plant for the Planet" by extending its reach to additional countries. The GBM has enlarged its scope and become much more sophisticated. How the GBM will survive with the loss of its founder and charismatic leader remains to be seen, but the broader social movements in support of women, peace, and the environment continue.

What do you think? In this section, we are addressing leaders who have taken political action on issues specific to their regions and nations. In other regions, issues have included childcare, affordable medicine, censorship, joblessness, and human trafficking. What are some pressing issues in your own area that need the action—that of strong political leaders as well as that of everyday citizens—to bring about change?

The immigrant rights movement

Among the most contentious issues confronting our global communities are struggles surrounding immigration and citizenship. Who enters a country, by what method, for how long and for what purpose, is a serious preoccupation in many parts of the world. It is serious because immigration ultimately involves questions of belonging and who becomes "one of us." Who belongs and who does not is political because the path to citizenship and entry into a community highlight particular interests of the community. The interests might include workforce demands, special relationships and agreements with other nations, humanitarian response to a crisis, or notions of national identity and pride. In this section, we will explore how these interests come into play in the U.S. immigrant rights movements.

Immigration is the entry into a country by a citizen of another country who then desires to remain in the country. A person (like a tourist) who enters a country with no intention of remaining is a non-immigrant (Chen, 2012, p. 264). Many of the conflicts around the world involve immigrants rather than non-immigrants. **Diaspora** refers to the movement of populations from one part of the world to another (chapters 3, 12). This movement can be sudden or it can occur over time. **Diasporic citizen** refers to a person who is a member of a group that has moved or been displaced. For example, in the 1940s and 1950s, thousands of people from mainland China and Taiwan immigrated to Central America seeking work. This created the Chinese diaspora in Panama (Siu, 2005). By nationality, the second- and third-generation descendents are Panamanian, but they remain diasporic citizens as they mediate the Chinese customs and values of their heritage with the equally meaningful Latino customs and values in Panama. Like the immigrant, "being diasporic means experiencing both identification with and displacement from both 'home' sites at once" (Siu, 2005, p. 11).

The common notion is that immigrant persons are legal or illegal. But it is not that simple. Like most identities, immigrant identities are contingent; that is, they are formed and understood in relation to a culture's values and history of immigration. Discourses on immigration and immigrant identities are shaped within "particular systems of inequality and domination" (Drzewiecka & Steyn, 2012, p. 2). While much of the debate on U.S. immigration policy falls into the realm of politics, the debate also is framed by politics 2.0!

Particularly after the attacks on the United States on September 11, 2001, there has been increasing attention on the U.S.-Mexican border. The calls to "secure our border" are now common in political discourse in the United States. But this discourse is also directed at people, namely the immigrants and migrant workers who are affected by new laws. In their study of the political rhetoric surrounding the passage of Proposition 187, the 1994 California law that withheld education and other benefits to undocumented persons, Ono and Sloop (2002) discovered that immigrants were depicted as human capital, criminal, immoral, and diseased (pp. 29–35), reminding us of the importance of cultural metaphors (chapter 9). By 2007, the Congressional effort to reform national immigration policy failed and by the end of the decade the perception was that "behind every social ill lurks a brown-skinned illegal immigrant" (Powers, 2007, p. 13A).

As anti-immigrant rhetoric intensified, an oppositional social movement gained new strength (Figure 14.2). Its purpose was to create a counter-narrative that would frame the

Figure 14.2 Protesters create a counter-narrative in support of immigrants. Source: Emmanuel Dunand/ AFP/Getty Images.

plight of the immigrants as a humanitarian issue. From March through May, 2006, demonstrations involving hundreds of thousands were held in Dallas, Texas, Chicago, Illinois, Los Angeles, California, and Phoenix, Arizona. Disparate groups from labor unions to the Catholic Church supported the demonstrations (Pineda & Sowards, 2007). In many California cities, students walked out of classes and waved signs that read, "We are not criminals!" (Campo-Flores, 2006, p. 32). Farmers in agricultural states supported the movement, claiming that food supplies were jeopardized from the lack of farmworkers. Activists like Enrique Morones acted locally. He founded Border Angels, a nonprofit organization that honored with white crosses those who had perished crossing the border, and volunteers assisted immigrants by placing water bottles in desert areas.

The movement organizers were able to reach across cultures to gain support from non-Latino immigrants. They studied the strategies of the anti-immigrant coalitions by following Valocchi's (2010) view that, knowing "how the dominant society frames an issue, then activists can use that knowledge in their own framing strategies" (p. 13). They drew upon the immigrant history of the United States to place the actions of those coming to the United States in a more favorable light. They also claimed the role of patriots, by waving the U.S. flag along with the flags of other nations (Pineda & Sowards, 2007). The struggle over immigration policy and the humanitarian status of immigrants is unresolved.

As the Green Belt Movement and the immigration rights movement suggest, the effectiveness of a movement depends to a great extent on forming intercultural coalitions. The next section describes the leadership required to work across cultures.

Intercultural political leadership: What strategies can we use to bring about change?

From a communication perspective, **leadership** can be defined as a process of influencing a group of individuals to achieve a common goal (Northous, 2013). Leadership occurs in a social context, and when members of a team are from differing cultural groups, there is the opportunity for intercultural interaction. Leadership, whether we are considering politics or politics 2.0, is a political act. Achieving a "common goal" implies broader interests. If you are leading a "dance marathon" in your community to raise funds for children ill with an incurable disease, what does this really mean? In the realm of politics 2.0, we might ask a few questions. Why are these funds necessary in the first place? Is it because not enough research is being conducted on this disease by corporate or government medical centers? Is it because the disease cannot be treated in a way that generates profit for pharmaceutical companies? Is it because adults can lobby government officials to direct research funds for adult diseases and children cannot? This section explores political intercultural leadership and the implications for our future interactions with others.

Majora Carter and the Bronx River Alliance

There are at least three unique elements to the leadership agenda of a co-cultural leader: two-pronged attention; dispelling negative stereotypes; and proof of self (Alire, 2001). Two-pronged attention is the awareness of the leader to the group as a whole and to other co-cultural group members. Dispelling negative stereotypes refers to the need for the leader to be aware of and counter any negative associations to the leader's race, nationality, or ethnicity that followers might bring to the situation. This is a task that a leader from the dominant culture will not need to address. The third element is proof of self; again, the leader from the dominant culture does not need to constantly maintain credibility to the followers. The co-cultural leader must be aware that some followers may continue to question the leader's decision-making. The leader must be mindful to reinforce credibility throughout the duration of the project (Alire, 2001).

Majora Carter (Figure 14.3) is an example of a co-cultural leader who performs a strong and successful leadership agenda. Carter was born in the South Bronx of New York City. She attended a science magnet school, and received degrees from Wesleyan University and New York University. She began her career in 1998 at The Point Community Development Corporation, where she served as associate director. During this time, the City of New York decided to build a waste treatment plant along the Bronx River, near where Carter lived. She successfully prevented the city from building the waste plant and instead founded Sustainable South Bronx, a nonprofit organization whose goal was to transform the neglected portion of the Bronx River into a multi-purpose green space, with bicycle and walking trails, new landscaping, and programs for healthy eating. In 2005, Carter was the recipient of a MacArthur Foundation "genius" grant, a $250,000 "no-strings attached" award in support of her work on improving the environment (MacArthur Fellows Program, 2005).

Carter performed critical communicative engagement. She argued that if pollution affected affluent citizens as much as it does people of color living in urban areas, there would be more of a demand to explore "green energy" (Holloway, 2008). She viewed what

Figure 14.3 Majora Carter successfully led a coalition of local organizations to reverse the decision to build a waste treatment plant in her South Bronx neighborhood.
Source: James Leynse/Corbis.

was happening to the South Bronx River in the context of social and economic inequalities. In her speeches and programs, she dispelled stereotypes listeners may have had about her African American heritage by stressing how her working-class family settled in the Bronx and pursued the "American Dream" with a passion. She also emphasized her education and her commitment for those who might question her credibility.

Majora Carter was able to build a coalition of dozens of Bronx organizations to work to improve an area that was becoming toxic from neglect. Her "proof of self" as an African American woman allowed her to gain followers, and attract donors and support on the New York City Council. The next section discusses a style of leadership that many would conclude is even more demanding.

Break it down

In the preface to this book, we cited findings that the Millennial Generation vote less than older citizens, though may be more likely to take actions to challenge elite ideas and listen to others. At the same time, 18- to 25-year-olds volunteer less than those younger and older than them. What are possible reasons for these trends? What concrete strategies can you think of to increase civic action among the 20- to 25-year-old group? Specifically, what are some steps to develop more leaders like those in this section?

Servant leadership and TOMS shoes

Leadership focuses on the achievement of group goals but we recognize that leaders accomplish individual goals as well. On the reality television show, *The Apprentice*, a contestant may be given the task of leading a team to develop the best marketing for a product. Each member of the team wants the team to succeed, but there is little doubt that the leader ultimately wants the others to hear Donald Trump say, "You're fired!". But what if the approach was different? What if the leader's goals were exactly the same as the followers? What if the leader's goal was to serve the interests of the followers only? This approach to leadership is known as **servant leadership**.

In his book, *The Case for Servant Leadership* (2008), Kent Keith summarized the key ideas of Robert K. Greenleaf, who originated the concept of the servant leader in the 1970s. Servant leaders "are motivated to make life better for others, not just themselves" (p. 10). They do not covet power; they empower others. Such leaders are humble and caring; they are good at building good relationships with others, and they are willing to learn from and be led by others. Cesar Chavez is mentioned in chapter 9 as an extraordinary speaker who drew on Euro-American and Mexican influences to unionize migrant farmworkers in California. He dedicated his life to improving the working and living conditions of the farm workers. Yet he lived modestly. He spoke simply, yet directly and sincerely. He truly measured his success by the amount of improvement in the lives of the farmworkers. He and Dolores Huerta, the co-founders of the United Farm Workers, are examples of modern-era servant leaders (Sowards, 2012). Wangari Maathai, mentioned earlier in this chapter, is another example of a person who was dedicated to advancing the interests of women and their families, quite often at the expense of her own wellbeing.

In cultures that prize competition and individualism, the notion of being in a servant-like relationship to others is difficult to imagine. It is difficult to imagine this relationship within our home culture, let alone across cultures! Although meeting the expectations of servant leader is rare (and is often a subjective judgment), we can identify individuals who are selflessly reaching across cultures. One example is Blake Mycoskie and TOMS.

By 2006, Blake Mycoskie was ready for a vacation; at the age of 29, he had already started four businesses and had been a contestant with his sister on television's *The Amazing Race*. He chose to vacation in Argentina where, as he stated, "My main mission was to lose myself in its culture" (Mycoskie, 2011, p. 4). He discovered that many Argentine children could not afford to buy shoes. This meant they could not go to school, and he saw that they were often sick due to infections picked up from walking barefoot. At the same time, Mycoskie noticed that many who could afford shoes wore a distinctive canvas shoe called an *alpargata* (p. 4). Mycoskie's insight was to sell a redesigned version of the *alpargata* and use the profits to supply shoes to children in need (Figure 14.4). TOMS means "tomorrow's shoes," which, for Mycoskie, "is about a promise—a better tomorrow" (p. 6). It is estimated that sales of TOMS in four years have generated one million pairs of shoes in over 40 countries (Oloffson, 2010). In the fashion of a genuine servant leader, Mycoskie stated that "giving may be the best investment you'll ever make" (p. 20).

There are several elements to Mycoskie's narrative that are instructive for servant leaders in intercultural contexts:

1 Mycoskie was empathetic to the conditions of others, even if he did not share those conditions.

2 He entered the new environment with curiosity and acceptance.

3 He drew from his environment to create an innovative solution to an important problem.

4 He was motivated by a desire to serve.

Figure 14.4 Blake Mycoskie began the One for One Movement. Every pair of shoes purchased is matched with a pair donated to children in need. Source: Michael Kovac/Wire Image/Getty Images.

It is also worth noting that Mycoskie was not particularly seeking to begin an enterprise whose purpose was to benefit others at no cost to them. After all, he originally went to Argentina as a tourist to take a break from his for-profit ventures. Mycoskie's story reminds us that, no matter what our disposition, we can become servant leaders if we are receptive to the experiences of others, and if we are able to change our priorities and put the needs of others first.

What do you think? Oprah Winfrey has been honored for her philanthropic work. Millions of television viewers and magazine readers are informed and inspired by her views and actions, including establishing a leadership academy for girls in South Africa. At the same time, Winfrey has amassed great personal wealth. *Forbes* estimated in 2011 that Winfrey was worth $2.7 billion (O'Connor, 2011). Does Oprah qualify as a servant leader?

Summary

This chapter has described two notions of politics. One notion considers electoral politics and our civic obligation to be knowledgeable and to participate in democratic processes. This is political engagement. The second notion considers how dominant interests gain our consent as citizens by infusing our daily activities and practices with normalcy and nationalistic pride. This second notion—politics 2.0—leads to critical communicative engagement. Politics 2.0 asks us to understand co-cultures in relation to one another. What meaning and identities are privileged, and which are invisible? Who benefits from the invisibility or marginalization of certain co-cultures?

Living and acting with critical awareness is never an easy task. The reality for many of us is that, whether we live in a democracy or a single-party state, we support our political institutions; we accept the broad legal frameworks that constrain our actions and we understand the utility of annual rituals like filing income taxes. At the same time, we have the capacity to critique and judge. We know—and so do our governments—that we have the capacity to resist. We might be driven by a sense of justice, or we might consider the welfare of those closest to us in our community, or perhaps we are driven by personal dissatisfaction. Resistance may come in different forms: founding a new political party, engaging public protest as at Tiananmen Square in Beijing, China, in 1989, or at Tahrir Square in Cairo, Egypt, in 2011, defecting to another nation, or taking up arms against the state. Our relationships to our nations and cultures can be complicated and contradictory, and often we create a balance between loyalty and dissent. Exploring the two levels of politics described in this chapter allows us to be knowing actors in our communities.

This chapter also presented social movements as opportunities for intercultural interaction. The Green Belt Movement and the immigrant rights movement were successful because Wangari Maathai and immigrant rights activists were able to adopt vernacular (or local) meanings as they created their messages.

Finally, this chapter explored leadership as a political endeavor. Majora Carter worked against an entrenched attitude that held that the South Bronx was devoid of value. Her public messages display the three elements for leaders who are people of color: two-pronged attention, dispel negative stereotypes and reinforce "proof of self," or credibility. Blake Mycoskie was seen as a servant leader; that is, an individual who placed the interests of the children of Argentina (and other countries) before his own. Cesar Chavez and Wangari Maathai, other examples of servant leaders, might well have subscribed to Mycoskie's motto: "Giving is what fuels us. Giving is our future."

KEY TERMS

politics, 292
communicative engagement, 292
politics 2.0, 292
social movement, 294
vernacular discourse, 294
vernacular rhetoric, 294

immigration, 296
diaspora, 296
diasporic citizen, 297
leadership, 298
servant leadership, 300

Discussion questions

1 How do you participate in local and national politics? Are you as engaged as you would like? How is your participation guided by formal and informal rules?

2 Do you believe that you have more or fewer opportunities for political engagement than others?

3 What would motivate you to join a social movement? What risks would you take to advocate a cause you believed in?

4 What companies have adopted Mycoskie's "one for one" business model? Is this model effective? Are you more or less likely to purchase a product (even if you have to pay a little more) if it benefits children in other parts of the world?

5 Do you believe that you could lead a diverse group to accomplish a common goal?

6 Do you believe you could be a servant leader?

Action points

1 Conduct a Google search for Green Belt Movement and use Google Maps to examine the terrain of Kenya and surrounding countries. What environmental issues does your community face?

2 Using census data and other demographic information, determine the number of immigrants living in your community. Determine where they come from and what drew them to your community. What is the relationship between your community and immigrant populations? Welcoming? Hostile? Mixed?

3 Develop a timeline of activities relating to the Occupy Wall Street movement. How did this movement combine elements of politics and politics 2.0?

4 See Majora Carter on YouTube at: http://blog.ted.com/2006/06/27/majora_carter_o/ What are her most current projects? What can you apply from her activism in helping your community?

For more information

Flores, L.A. (2003). Constructing rhetorical borders: Peons, illegal aliens, and competing narratives of immigration. *Critical Studies in Media Communication, 20*, 362–387.

Griffin, R.A., & Calafell, B.M. (2011). Control, discipline and punish: Black masculinity and (in) visible whiteness in the NBA. In M.G. Lacy & K.A. Ono, (Eds.), *Critical rhetorics of race* (pp. 117–136). New York, NY: NYU Press.

Holling, M.A., & Calafell, B.M. (2011). *Latina/o discourses in vernacular spaces: Somos de una voz?* Lanham, MA: Lexington Books.

Negrine, R. (2008). *The transformation of political communication: Continuities and changes in media and politics.* Houndmills: Palgrave.

Ngugi, T.W. (1986) *Decolonising the mind: The politics of language in African language.* Oxford: James Curry Ltd.

Stevens, S.M., & Malesh, P. (2009). *Active voices: Composing a rhetoric of social movements.* Albany, NY: SUNY Press.

References

Alire, C.A. (2001). Diversity and leadership: The color of leadership. *Journal of Library Administration, 32*, 95–109.

Bretton, M.J. (1998). *Women pioneers for the environment.* Boston, MA: Northeastern University Press.

Calafell, B.M., & Delgado, F.P. (2004). Reading Latina/o images: Interrogating *Americanos. Critical Studies in Media Communication, 21*, 1–21.

Campo-Flores, A. (2006). Immigration. *Newsweek,* April 10, pp. 30–38.

Chen, H. (2012). Temporally legal: My traveling across borders of im/migration. In A. González, M. Houston, & V. Chen (Eds.), *Our voices: Essays in culture, ethnicity, and communication,* (5th ed., pp. 263–269). New York, NY: Oxford University Press.

Deetz, S. (1990). Representation of interest and the new communication technologies: Issues in democracy and policy. In M.J. Medhurst, A. González, & T.R. Peterson (Eds.), *Communication and the culture of technology* (pp. 43–62). Pullman, WA: Washington University Press.

Drzewiecka, J.A., & Steyn, M. (2012). Racial immigrant incorporation: Material-symbolic articulation of identities. *Journal of International and Intercultural Communication, 5*, 1–19.

Holloway, M. (2008). The green power broker. *New York Times,* December 12. Accessed Aug 21, 2011, at http://www.nytimes.com/2008/12/14/nyregion/thecity/14majo.html?_r=1&ref=majoracarter

Keith, K.M. (2008). *The case for servant leadership.* Westfield, IN: The Greenleaf Center for Servant Leadership.

Lappé, F.M., & Lappé, A. (2002). *Hope's edge: The next diet for a small planet.* New York: Jeremy P. Tarcher/Putnam.

Maathai, W. (2004). *The Green Belt Movement: Sharing the approach and experience.* New York: Lantern Books.

MacArthur Fellows Program. (2005). *Majora Carter, Urban revitalization strategist,* Sept 1, Accessed August 21, 2011, at http://www.macfound.org/fellows/753/

Mattingly, T. (2011). *Terry Mattingly on Religion: Dylan does his thing in China.* Accessed Jan 15, 2012, at http://www.tmatt.net/2011/04/18/dylan-does-his-dylan-thing-in-china/

McKerrow, R.E. (2000). Opening the future: Postmodern rhetoric in a multicultural world. In A. González and D.V. Tanno (Eds.), *Rhetoric in Intercultural Contexts* (pp. 41–46). Thousand Oaks, CA: Sage.

McKinney, M.S., Kaid, L.L., Bystrom, D.G., & Carlin, D.B. (2005). The role of communication in civic engagement. In M.S. McKinney, L.L. Kaid, D.G. Bystrom, & D.B. Carlin (Eds.), *Communicating politics: Engaging the public in democratic life* (pp. 3–26). New York, NY: Peter Lang.

Miller, J.B. (1999). "Indians", "Braves", and "Redskins": A performative struggle for control of an image. *Quarterly Journal of Speech, 85*, 188–202.

Mycoskie, B. (2011). *Start something that matters.* Random House, New York, NY.

Northouse, P. (2013). *Leadership: Theory and practice* (6th ed.). Thousand Oaks: CA: Sage.

O'Connor, C. (2011). Forbes 400: Meet America's richest women (and not just Oprah and Meg). *Forbes,* September 22. Accessed July 7, 2012, at http://www.forbes.com/sites/clareoconnor/2011/09/22/forbes-400-meet-americas-richest-women-and-not-just-oprah-and-meg/

Oloffson, K. (2010). In Toms' shoes: Start-ups copy "one for one" model. *The Wall Street Journal,* September 30.

Accessed Aug 10, 2012, at http://online.wsj.com/article/SB10001424052748704116004575522251507063936.html

Ono, K.A., & Sloop, J.M. (1995). The critique of vernacular discourse. *Communication Monographs, 62*, 19–46.

Ono, K.A., & Sloop, J.M. (2002). *Shifting borders: Rhetoric, immigration, and California's Proposition 187*. Philadelphia, PA: Temple University Press.

Pineda, R.D., & Sowards, S.K. (2007). Flag waving as visual argument: 2006 immigration demonstrations and cultural citizenship. *Argumentation and Advocacy, 43*, 164–174.

Powers, K.A. (2007). Immigrants become targets for all of society's ills. *USA Today*, August 29, p. 13A.

Siu, L.C.D. (2005). *Memories of a future home: Diasporic citizenship of Chinese in Panama*. Stanford: Stanford University Press.

Sowards, S.K. (2012). Rhetorical functions of letter writing: Dialogic collaboration, affirmation and catharsis in Dolores Huerta's letters. *Communication Quarterly, 60*, 295–315.

Stewart, C.J., Smith, C.A., & Denton, R.E., Jr. (2007). *Persuasion and social movements* (5th ed.). Long Grove, IL: Waveland.

Valocchi, S. (2010). *Social movements and activism in the USA*. New York: Routledge.

Whitehead, J.W. (2011). Bob Dylan's Asia tour: Has freedom lost its voice? *Huffington Post*, April 11. Accessed Jan 15, 2012, at http://www.huffingtonpost.com/john-w-whitehead/bob-dylan-asia-tour-has-freedom-voice_b_847445.html

(The) White House (2011). *Statement by the President on the passing of Wangary Maathai*. Accessed Mar 30, 2012, at http://www.whitehouse.gov/the-press-office/2011/09/26/statement-president-passing-wangari-maathai

Chapter 15

Intercultural communication in international organizational contexts:
How does culture shape business, and how is business culture changing?

Chapter objectives

By the end of this chapter, you should be able to:

→ Describe specific changes in the global corporate workplace and worker as a result of new technology and information

→ Discuss the strengths and limitations of globalization on world cultures

→ Outline specific dimensions of cultural difference that may impact organizational communication

→ Compare the divergent and convergent views of business in a globalizing world

→ Provide examples of specific organizations and individuals who use organizational communication for civic or political engagement

A new contract: How are technology and information changing the culture of work and workplaces?

Cultural variability: How does culture shape the organization?

A new world: What is the impact of globalization on business?

Corporate responsibility: How can my company make a difference?

Intercultural Communication for Everyday Life, First Edition. John R. Baldwin, Robin R. Means Coleman, Alberto González, and Suchitra Shenoy-Packer.
© 2014 John R. Baldwin, Robin R. Means Coleman, Alberto González, and Suchitra Shenoy-Packer.
Published 2014 by John Wiley & Sons Ltd.

ave you ever wondered what it is about work that makes everyone from country music stars to creators of reality shows sit up and make public commentary? In *That's How Country Boys Roll*, Billy Currington describes their inspiring work ethic as, "They work, work, work, all week till the job gets done;" in *Shiftwork*, Kenny Chesney explains the rigor and matter-of-factness of a blue collar worker's shift work: "He's hot, sweat drops, 'round the clock, door never locks, noise never stops, not all day, work seven to three, three to eleven, eleven to seven. Shift work, tough work." Gretchen Wilson, another country music star expresses the sentiments of overworked and underappreciated mothers everywhere when she declares in *Full Time Job*:

> I'm a mother, I'm a lover,
> A chef, a referee,
> I'm a doctor and a chauffeur, seven days a week…
> It's the hardest gig I've known; I work my fingers to the bone.
> Yea, the dishes and the diapers never stop…
> I know this may come as a shock…
> But this here's a full time job.

In the United States, it is not uncommon to get defined by one's occupational engagement. It is socially acceptable and appropriate to ask a person what she or he does for a living. It is possible that the reason people ask and answer this question in some cultures is to establish their social standing and connections. Presumably, this kind of class-status evaluation is common to the United States. Is it the same in your culture or co-culture? What is the value of work in your culture?

Organizational communication is a discipline within communication studies that focuses specifically on organizing behaviors across contexts. More commonly, this discipline explores the nuances of communication in organizations. Katherine Miller (2011) defines organizations as comprising five critical elements: the existence of a *social collective*, which occurs when a group of people *work together* to *fulfill organizational and individual goals*, by *coordinating activities*, within *varied levels and nuances of organizational structure*, while simultaneously being *embedded within an environment of other organizations*. Communication is the glue that binds all the different organizational processes, systems, procedures, applications, interactions, and other shared realities together.

The discipline of organizational communication has traditionally been U.S.-centered. In recent years, the scope of this discipline has traversed across cultures such as Brazil (Marchiori & Oliveira, 2009) and Germany (e.g., Theis-Berglmair, 2013). In this chapter, we focus on intercultural/cross-cultural organizational communication, and draw on the literature from globalized workplaces that necessitate diversity and demand inclusivity. We will first, following a discussion of the changing nature of workplaces, explore the different approaches and orientations to intercultural communication in organizations; and second, explain the twin concepts of convergence and divergence, and provide a typology of organizations and related international involvement.

A new contract: How are technology and information changing the culture of work and workplaces?

If you pick up any book with labor and occupations as its subject matter, academic or otherwise, at least in the United States, what the book most actively provides today is an argument for how the nature of our work, along with our workplaces, is in a state of flux. As most cultures gradually transitioned from agrarian societies to the industrial age, slowly but steadily work engagement moved from agriculture-intensive farm work to manufacturing work that engaged the worker's physical self. Gradually, the industrial age gave way to the information era—the one in which we live today. Around the world, businesses and individuals are impacted by growing technology and information (Figure 15.1). Consequently, work has shifted from physical to intellectual.

New workers, new contracts

Today, **knowledge workers** or those with the "best access to information … involved in the transfer, reprocessing, or transmittal of information" (Eisenberg *et al.*, 2010, p. 20) are coveted for their expertise and technology based know-how. The implicit **psychological contract** between an employer and employee, defined in terms of an understanding of mutual obligations and expectations (Herriot & Pemberton, 1996) is getting renegotiated. The **old social contract** guaranteed lifetime job security and a reasonable pension if you only showed your commitment to your work and employer, put in a hard day's labor, and showed good behavior. Under the terms of the **new social contract**, the nature of employee-employer relationship is getting rewritten. No longer can the employer guarantee job security; and the employee no longer wishes to get tied

Figure 15.1 Shanghai's Apple store opened at Pudong in 2010. The store was immediately too small, leading to the opening of a new store at Huaihai Road, which was also not big enough. Apple is talking about opening two new stores. Source: STR/epa/Corbis.

down to any one employer, either. Allegiances for one's own continual professional development and growth are replacing fleeting organizational loyalties and commitment. Furthermore, skills once considered germane to competency and professional growth are becoming obsolete as newer workplace demands take over. For example, according to a recent article in *The Economist* (2011), Japanese firms now court recruits who have amassed educational and professional experiences in foreign countries in order to stay competitive in a global economy.

Shifting alliances may be excused if one considers that perhaps the catalyst for this phenomenon is the changing nature of work itself. In the U.S., as part-time, contingent, contract, and micro work, along with telecommuting, flex-time, and job sharing become popular, individuals may merely be adjusting to those changes by developing and self-managing their careers. When Yahoo's CEO, Marissa Mayer, banned employees from the privilege of working from home, analysts wondered if the move would be bad for workers' morale, since popular trends promote **telecommuting** or working remotely, usually from one's home, with the help of technology. One *Forbes* reporter even wondered if Mayer's new rule, which is imposed with the intention of increasing productivity, reflects management bias, and takes us back into the "stone age" (Goudreau, 2013).

Mayer's move may be the exception rather than the rule; most indicators suggest contemporary knowledge-work based careers will be employee driven. Different nuances characterize today's careers by focusing on two types specifically (Inkson, 2007): **boundaryless careers** occur when "individuals move between organizations with increasing frequency" (p. 9); **portfolio careers** occur when "the individual, rather than pursuing a single, full-time job, balances a portfolio of different and changing opportunities" (p. 9). As early as 1976, Douglas T. Hall, in his book *Careers in Organizations*, explained how individuals who take charge of their own careers channel the mythological figure, Proteus, who was able to change his shape seamlessly to suit a situation. **Protean careers** are managed by the individual, not the organization.

Workplaces are changing to keep up with the new generation of workers. Perhaps one of the bigger changes has been in the number of organizations subscribing to virtual work and incorporating telecommuting opportunities for their workers. Mediated by technology, working virtually or telecommuting enables workers to work from distant locations, perhaps even from home where a better balance of work and life may be achieved. A **virtual organization is** defined as an organization whose members are geographically distributed across time and space such that they work at different times in different locations and use computer technologies to coordinate work activities.

Organizations that used to conform typically to the framework of brick-and-mortar physical structures are reaching beyond the scope of traditional boundaries and going where the employees and markets are, even around the world.

Globalization and corporate and local cultures

Going global and branching out into new foreign markets has almost become a cross-industry norm in today's competitive business environment. By having employees working in different parts of the world, and across time zones, computer-mediated technologies allow for work to continually occur 24/7, defying both time and space constraints. Communication scholar Cynthia Stohl (2001) explains that **globalization** is the "interconnected nature of the global economy, the interpenetration of global and domestic organizations, and communication technologies that blur temporal and spatial boundaries" (p. 325). We treat this topic as it relates to media and culture more in chapter 11, but here we discuss its implication specifically for corporate cultures.

Globalization is no longer just a buzzword, as it was until a just a few decades ago. It is our reality today. In many supermarkets you will find vegetables, fruits, and other products from different parts of the world. In U.S. stores, we frequently see everything from mangoes to candy to asparagus to coffee that come from countries like India, Belgium, Peru, and Nicaragua respectively. What a truly global eating experience (if you suspend judgment on global footprint and method of growing)! Clothes that we shop for at retailers like Gap, Mango, Zara, or H&M are often manufactured in the developing world at extremely low costs but sold to consumers at highly marked-up prices. No wonder some stores can afford to have "80% off" sales – they are still making money even with those deep discounts!

. . . .

ON THE NET

For a more detailed and critical view of how globalization affects our global community, please watch the video, *The Corporation* freely available on the Internet with a reasonable request for donation for the creators and designers of the documentary (http://thecorporation.com/). Watch some segments (or all 23 chapters on YouTube) and read the section below. What do you think are some strengths and advantages of globalization, for both global and local businesses and cultures?

. . . .

Much has been written, said, and analyzed about globalization and its effects. While the more apparent changes brought about by globalization—such as the influx of foreign-made products into domestic markets, ease of travel, forging of cross-cultural business partnerships, and others—get written about frequently, one must wonder about what goes on behind this face of globalization. Have you ever wondered who the folks behind these changes are, or what might be the circumstances under which they may have to work to please an ever-increasing and ever-demanding global clientele?

In his documentary, *The Other Side of Outsourcing*, New York Times reporter Thomas Friedman traveled to Bangalore, India, to witness first-hand how globalization was occurring behind the scenes and how it was affecting the everyday people who make the lives in developed economies more comfortable and even possible. Communication scholars Mahuya Pal and Patrice Buzzanell (2008) examined the processes at a call center operation in Kolkata, India, and their implications for the employees. They found that call center employees actively negotiated and invoked strategic identities for themselves, even as they were involved in a cultural tug-and-pull, being Indian by day and assuming Western (U.S. American) names and identities by night when answering calls from customers (Figure 15.2).

Leslie T. Chang's (2008) book, *Factory Girls: From Village to City in a Changing China*, gives us a rare insight into the working conditions and migrant lives of young girls, mostly teenagers and young adults, who work extremely long hours for paltry wages and under

Figure 15.2 Employees in call centers, such as this one in Bangalore, India, have to actively negotiate their identities as they interact daily with customers across national and cultural borders.
Source: Sherwin Crasto/Reuters/Corbis.

very harsh conditions in Dongguan, an industrial city in Southern China. Another documentary, *The Corporation* (see "On the Net," earlier), provides us with a unique lens with which to view apparel we buy because proceeds from the sale are said to benefit some deserving organization. Makers of the documentary investigate a popular celebrity's brand of clothing sold under the impression that a portion of the sale is being donated to a children's organization. They conduct similar investigations at sweatshops in Honduras, the Dominican Republic, and other parts of the developing world, and showcase the ugly face of global exploitation by large corporations.

Regardless of the many critical lenses with which one can view globalization, one has to admit that to run a corporation successfully at the global level, you need more than just good pricing strategies. Wallace Schmidt and his colleagues (2007) argue that hiring the right kind of people is critical to global success: "Global managers must be accommodating to the tapestry of cultures and sensibilities that are tied to success in a variety of countries. They must be able to mediate between disparate factions and manage a complexity of human issues" (p. 7). They further declare that the growth (and success) of an organization in a foreign land depends unequivocally on effective communication. However, what makes communication effective will vary between cultures.

Cultural variability: How does culture shape the organization?

There are as many definitions of culture as people you ask (see chapter 3). Our culture provides a framework within which to understand ourselves and those around us—a "software of the mind" (Hofstede & Hofstede, 2005). Having read this textbook so far, you already have a fairly good understanding about culture. We all generally and intuitively know what culture means and represents for us, at least connotatively. But what about an organization's culture? For organizational scholar Edgar Schein (1992), **organizational culture** refers to "those elements of a group or organization that are most stable and least malleable" (p. 5). More formally, he defines the culture of a group (and an organization) as:

> A pattern of shared basic assumptions that the group learned as it solved its problems of external adaptation and internal integration, that has worked well enough to be considered valid and, therefore, to be taught to new members as the correct way to perceive, think, and feel in relation to those problems. (p. 12)

Organizational and cultural scholars have contributed significantly to our understanding of how cultures differ (see chapter 4). In the following pages, we apply cultural dimensions specifically to the workplace. Readers can also draw implications to other professional contexts such as the classroom, the health context, the legal system, the church organization, and so on.

Trompenaars and Hampden-Turner's cultural orientations

Universalism-particularism   Trompenaars and Hampden-Turner (1998) apply Talcott Parsons' (1951) pattern variables specifically to cultures. First, people in **universalist cultures** are more likely to believe that what is right or good can be clearly defined and applied. They may adhere to specific standards governing norms of behaviors (rules) and codes of conduct, and strongly believe that these rules and codes can be applied universally. **Particularist cultures**, meanwhile, tend to pay greater attention to relational obligations and contexts. They value the nature of relationship they share, whether it is with a co-worker or friend, and evaluate a situation based on the strength of that relationship, as well as on the relative status of participants. In organizational contexts, a universalist considers a deal a deal, and a trustworthy person is one who honors and keeps his or her word. Particularists understand that reality is relative and that legal contracts may often need to be modified, because of which they place their trust on those individuals who honor changing circumstances.

Individualism-communitarianism   Similar to individualism-collectivism, whether cultures are individualist or communitarian depends on the extent to which people in those cultures tend to consider themselves as part of a collective or community of people, or focus primarily on the "I" value and encourage freedom of thought and expression, and take responsibility for their own actions. In terms of conducting business, individualists authorize individual decision-making, and may conduct business alone. Organizations from individualistic cultures provide individual performance assessments and incentives and actively seek out higher performers or champions for special rewards. In communitarian organizations, decisions are made in groups under the assumption of joint responsibility, surrounded by persons with high status intervening and contributing to those

Figure 15.3 The business-card exchange in Japanese culture is an important aspect of one's "face," and how it is exchanged demonstrates importance of respect and status. Source: Hideki Yoshihara/Alfo Foto Agency/Alamy.

discussions. In such organizations, more attention is given to teamwork and cohesiveness, along with the continual building of lasting relationships with business partners and co-workers. The Japanese business-card exchange reflects these first two dimensions: the length and timing of the bow reflects relative status (particularism), but the importance of image or "face" represented by the card represents pride in one's company (communitarianism; Figure 15.3).

Neutral-affective The differences experienced by affective and neutral cultures have to do with the nature of their interactions and desire toward exhibiting or separating emotions. People in neutral cultures tend to refrain from visibly showing their inner emotions. Trompenaars and Hampden-Turner (1998) caution, "The amount of emotion we show is a matter of convention" (p. 70) and therefore warn individuals about over-interpreting differences in emotional presentations. Affective cultures are more openly emotive and often rely on nonverbal communication presented by laughing, smiling, and frowning to get across their points and thoughts. In the workplace, those with a tendency toward emotional neutrality may be motivated to dismiss as unprofessional, expressions of extreme joy or grief. Affective cultural representatives easily reveal their thoughts and feelings, both verbally and nonverbally. This enthusiasm or readiness to communicate should not be taken for agreement of a negotiated contract or decision, warn Trompenaars and Hampden-Turner. Likewise, just because those from neutral cultures mask their emotions, appear in control of their facial expressions, or lack emotional variety does not mean that they are disinterested or bored.

Specific-diffusive This difference between cultures refers to the "degree to which we engage others in specific areas of life and single levels of personality, or diffusively in multiple areas of our lives and at several levels of personality at the same time" (Trompenaars & Hampden-Turner, 1998, p. 83). For example, in a specific culture such as the United States, a manager may be the boss in the workplace, someone who directs and supervises others' behaviors; but if the manager was outside of the context of work, let's say at a rock-climbing event organized for the purposes of teambuilding, she or he may defer to the subordinate employee who has more experience or expertise in this activity. In other words, just because the manager is the boss at work does not mean that that title applies in all contexts. On the other hand, in a diffusive culture such as Mexico, the boss is always the boss under any circumstances, and will be deferred to on all respects regardless of whether she or he has expertise or skills in that particular nature or not. Clearly, cultures vary in how much meaning-making is derived from the context implicitly versus explicit verbalization of the same.

In business transactions, as in their personal lives, people from specific cultures are often direct, precise, purposeful, and transparent in their communication. As a result, shared knowledge of any given context is typically unambiguous and obvious, like in the case of low-context cultures. In diffusive cultures, unlike specific cultures where private spaces are highly valued and harder to enter into without the other's permission, private spaces are large and diffusive allowing for one person to be admitted into various facets of an individual's life. In other words, once trust is established, a co-worker will also be a friend for life, participating in all your life, family, and other personal events. There is often blurring or blending of work and life spaces. The focus is on relationships and organizational members as a whole. Employee turnover and mobility are low, emerging from loyalty to one's organization, rather than being based on skills or credentials. Communication is often indirect, evasive yet tactful, not completely transparent, and circular in style, with high value on the context for meaning-making. Relationship building, studying the history, background connections, and cultural norms of business partners, along with allowing for sometimes seemingly "purposeless" meetings to occur, all demand patience from people from specific cultures, just as those from specific cultures may frustrate those from diffusive cultures with their compartmentalization and lack of personal loyalty in the workplace.

Achievement-ascription Whether one considers her or his success a result of individual attainment or a consequence of birth or kinship is what differentiates achievement and ascription status. In some societies, certain individuals are accorded higher levels of respect and attention because of what they have accomplished on their own merit. Individuals are considered responsible for their own lives and expected to be ambitious go-getters who create their own success, akin to members of a *doing* culture. In others, respect and attention are ascribed to you because of who you are as a result of your family background, age, gender, class, education, and so on. Individuals are expected to give in to often pre-destined paths of other/external-created realities and be in harmony with their environment, like in *being* cultures (Kluckhohn & Strodtbeck, 1961; see chapter 4). In organizational situations, people in achievement-oriented cultures tend to show respect for superiors based on the quality and effectiveness of their knowledge and expertise, titles are used sparingly and only if absolutely required, and typical work groups are made up of people of varying gender and age. Ascription-oriented cultures often use titles extensively to establish status and seniority. Respect for superiors who are usually older, well-qualified males, is unquestioned and gauged as a measure of one's commitment and loyalty to the organization. In Figure 15.4, we compare Trompenaars and Hampden Turner with Hofstede.

So far, we have examined some critical cultural elements that differ across cultures. It is important to remember that these dimensions are not meant to be absolute divisions between cultures. To the contrary, the purpose of this discussion on the elements of cultural difference is to provide a roadmap for thought and adaptation for when we encounter people from cultures different from ours in organizational settings. It is also important

Figure 15.4 Trompenaars and Hampden Turner (1998) and Hofstede and Hofsede (2005) list different cultural dimensions that will impact organizational communication, policy, and structure.

Trompenaars and Hampden-Turner's Cultural Differences	Hofstede's Cultural Dimensions
Universalist-Particularist	Individualism-Collectivism
Individualism-Communitarianism	Power Distance
Neutral-Affective	Masculinity-Femininity
Specific-Diffusive	Uncertainty Avoidance
Achievement-Ascription	Long-Short Term Orientation

to note that the relevance of these dimensions is not confined to interaction between people from different international settings; they also apply to interactions with people from our own cultures who identify with different co-cultures. Not surprisingly, many countries, such as Canada and India, abound in internal cultural diversity and complexity. For example, in India alone, with a population of over 1.2 billion people, one can find people from various religious backgrounds, tribes, and ethnicities, speaking hundreds of different languages (not dialects, but languages with their own grammar, structure, script, and literature) and thousands of different dialects living within the boundaries of one nation. Fatehi (2008) refers to this "dissimilarity and diversity among cultural components" (p. 134) as **cultural heterogeneity**.

What do you think? Termed as China's "Me Generation," and a consequence of the world's most populated nation's one-child policy instituted in the early 1980s, the current Chinese generation is coming of age at a time when world businesses and manufacturers are courting China for its huge, lucrative consumer base. This generation, often considered as suffering from the "Little Emperor Syndrome" due to the lavish attention and extravagant resources parents provide their only offspring, has been called a "spoiled generation that highly values materialism and self-realization" (Yi *et al.*, 2010, p. 601).

Similar trends have been reported in other parts of the world as well. To understand the current generation of workers in the United States, CBS News' 60 Minutes news magazine provides an interesting perspective of the "Millennial Generation" (CBS News, 2008). A study in Canada and the United States (Trzesniewski & Donnellan, 2010) concluded that while today's youth are more cynical and less trusting of institutions than previous generations, with regard to "egotism, self-enhancement, individualism, self-esteem, locus of control, hopelessness, happiness, life satisfaction, loneliness, antisocial behavior, time spent working or watching television, political activity, the importance of religion, and the importance of social status" (p. 58), there was very little meaningful difference between a generation from 30 years ago.

How is the current generation of young men and women characterized in your culture? Do you think, as some reports suggest, that today's generation is made up of entitled, narcissistic, self-absorbed, and self-obsessed praise seekers worldwide?

Orientation toward time

Diversity between and within cultures can also be examined in how different groups approach time. One's relationship with time is often an indication of her or his cultural socialization, and we present different time orientations in chapter 8. The dimensions discussed there—past-present-future, monochromic-polychronic, and formal-informal time—will certainly structure organizational life and communication (see chapter 8). Trompenaars and Hampden-Turner's (1998) explication of time in sequential-synchronized cultures gives us an additional time orientation with which to make sense of organizations around the world.

Sequential-synchronic People in some cultures tend to view time as a limited commodity and therefore use proverbs such as 'time is money," and phrases such as "managing time," "saving time," "having a good time," and "wasting time." Sequential or monochronic cultures approach time as a series of sequential acts and events where one carefully follows the other, in order. Synchronic or polychronic cultures on the other hand, think nothing of multitasking and doing several things simultaneously (Hall, 1983). Each approach is efficient in its own way. Successfully completing one task before turning your attention to the next keeps us focused and organized. Meanwhile, doing a number of activities parallel to each other may enable us to get more things accomplished in a given period. People who do more than one thing at a time may get infuriated, insulted, or impatient with people handling one task at a time, while those who engage in multiple actions at the same time may inadvertently anger or insult those who prefer doing only one thing at time.

The ideas discussed in sequential-synchronic time orientations are connected to the idea of linear-active, multi-active, and reactive cultures (Lewis, 2006). In cultures that use linear-active time, people do one act in sequence, strictly follow their planned schedules and time-tables, are punctual, mind their own business, work specific hours, like fixed agendas, respect formality, avoid interrupting, are reluctant to accept favors, and stick to plans and facts. Multi-active cultures view time synchronously, believe in the abundance of time, are usually extroverted and talkative, are not hesitant to ask personal questions of others, are people oriented, frequently interrupt conversations, are not always punctual, seek and fulfill favors easily, use open body language, and are comfortable with last-minute changes of plans and unpredictable schedules. To these orientations, Richard Lewis (2006) also adds cultures that use time reactively or people who listen before they leap. For example, instructors in different cultures (with education being a type of organization) favor different styles. In the U.S. American style, impulsivity is often valued, with instructors using class time to facilitate discussion in order to arrive at knowledge. Students are encouraged to speak up, even if they are not sure of the answer, reflecting an **impulsive culture** (Lieberman, 1991).

Reflective-impulsive On the other hand, students from other cultures, such as those in East Asia, if they speak in class at all (based on different status perceptions of teacher/student relationship) will only speak when they are positive of the answer, exemplifying a **reflective**, or "listen-before-you-leap" culture. Students from such cultures may often have difficulty if they travel to the United States for education, where a portion of one's class grade might even be based on (impulsive-style) participation. In organizational settings, such as business meetings, people from reactive cultures rarely interrupt as they concentrate on what the speaker is saying. Unlike linear and multi-active cultures where the mode of communication is a dialogue, according to Lewis (2006), those in reactive cultures prefer the "monologue-pause-reflection-monologue" mode (p. 35). These individuals are often introverted, respectful of fellow communicators, and easily able to see the big picture. They react to the others' timetable, consider statements as promises, use subtle body language, and believe in saving and giving face.

***

What do you think? *Der Spiegel*, a major German newspaper, reports that, as prostitution is legal in Germany, companies often provide opportunities for sex as an incentive for deserving employees in the business world (Jüttner, 2011). Even though, culturally, Germans consider paying for sex a taboo topic, the practice of arranging for these meetings as a reward for employees is apparently quite common. The article reports how a Hamburg-based insurance company treated its best employees to a corporate prostitution party at a bathhouse in Budapest. Sex workers were given color-coded bands to represent the different services they would provide to the executives depending on their status within the hierarchy.

This episode has created a lot of controversy within German business circles, with most people arguing against sex as an incentive, even though some argue that after a certain level, employees and customers will no longer be happy with ordinary pay raises and bonuses. Sex-based incentives, apart from raising many layered ethical dilemmas, also discriminate against female executives, as one person interviewed for the piece explained. Given that the benefactors of such "rewards" `are those operating in the corporate hierarchical boy's club, the incentive is not particularly attractive for women, she says.

What do you think? If a country generally accepts sex favors and prostitution as legitimate in the business context, should we (or the businesses we work for or support) accept such practices if we work in those cultures? What other sorts of business practice can you think of where different cultures might perceive different behaviors as ethically acceptable? (See chapter 2 for a discussion of ethics.)

A new world: What is the impact of globalization on business?

As businesses become global and develop fields of operation outside their home countries, individuals at the forefront of these changes, such as global business managers, expatriate employees who travel overseas to manage or guide their organization's foreign operations, workers of an organization who work for a foreign corporation, clients, and other stakeholders, all need to develop **cultural synergy**. In other words, individuals and organizations, alike, need to become culturally aware and competent in cross-cultural communication situations. Another important skill to learn is that of **cultural intelligence**, defined as "an outsider's seemingly natural ability to interpret someone's unfamiliar and ambiguous gestures the way that person's compatriots would" (Earley & Mosakowski, 2004, p. 140). Whether cultural intelligence is a skill or can be learned may be up for debate, but a culturally competent person is able to "tease out of a person's or group's behavior those features that would be true of all people and all groups, those peculiar to this person or this group, and those that are neither universal nor idiosyncratic" (p. 140; see chapter 12). A culturally competent person is able to grasp, identify, and understand the cultural nuances, values, attitudes, and behaviors that a person embodies and is thereby able to make more informed cross-cultural communication choices based on her or his understanding of those cultural subtleties. This level of intelligence is especially important when organizations set their sights on growing businesses worldwide. Organizations can no longer afford to stay culturally neutral.

Convergent and divergent hypotheses of business in a globalizing world

Stohl (2001) argues that multinational corporations are at the "intersection of diverse communicative, cultural, and social practices" today (p. 325). In her extensive scholarship on globalization and organizational communication, she highlights two research trends that characterize how organizations react to globalization, cultural diversity, and global competitiveness: convergence and divergence. In the following discussion, we use organizational and corporate culture interchangeably.

The **convergence** hypothesis suggests that as a result of a set of imperatives embedded in today's globalizing business economy and communication technologies, more and more organizations follow similar structures and operational patterns across markets and foreign nations. Specific features of a global environment, such as international trade agreements, new technologies, market deregulations, and others, necessitate a minimization of differences to develop similarity in organizational structural adaptation. Communication under this hypothesis is seen as a "conduit for the acquisition of resources, capital, information, and expertise, and structure is seen as a complex web of relationships designed to meet the survival needs of an organization" (Stohl, 2001, p. 325). The convergence perspective acknowledges that there is cultural variability between organizations, among nations and its people, but these forces of diversity are insignificant when compared to the need for global organizational survivability and alignment with the same and interdependent economic and technological structures.

The **divergence** perspective focuses on cultural differences and the relative meanings individuals, cultures, and organizations associate with global forces that bring about changes in their respective environments. This perspective is represented in all the cultural dimensions discussed in the previous sections of this chapter. As we have already examined, different cultures approach organizational functioning differently depending on their cognitions, values, and orientations toward time, nature, community, and action, among others. Global managers and organizations wanting to successfully operate in foreign countries under this perspective must be mindful of national and corporate cultural differences, the role of communication in business interactions, everyday practices, and the coexistence of internal co-cultural, ethnic, religious, and ideological differences that make up a culture. Unlike the convergence perspective that drives toward similar actions and assumes that such similarity of actions, messages, and processes enhance global competitiveness, cooperation, and collaboration, the divergence perspective focuses on "human interpretation and experience of the world as meaningful and intersubjectively constructed" (Stohl, 2001, p. 326); that is, people in each culture create their "world" through communication, leading to a continued need for awareness of cultural difference.

Types of organization

There are several descriptors for global business that people often use interchangeably: global, multinational, international, and so on. How an organization is classified, however, depends on its strategic position, organizational structures, corporate mission and ambition, and other management processes and practices. In this section, we will discuss monolithic, multinational or plural, multicultural, international, global, and transnational organizations.

Monolithic organizations

Monolithic organizations are highly homogenous, identify with one country and consist of one dominant cultural group. There is a strong emphasis on assimilation, and new members outside of the dominant culture are expected to assimilate into the organization's way of doing things. Outsiders or those from a cultural minority may often struggle with strong prejudices native members have of them and face discrimination. Almost all organizations prior to their involvement in foreign business are monolithic and represent their own cultures abroad. They believe that home-culture norms, attitudes, values, and behaviors are the best, and consider home-country nationals more intelligent and trustworthy than foreign partners, turning them into ethnocentric corporations. In some cases, this may even lead to attempts to exclude workers not from the dominant culture of the organizational employees or management

Multinational/plural organizations

Multinational, or plural organizations typically identify with one nationality but do business in several countries. Host country personnel are in charge of all major organizational decisions and strategies, and even when multinational operations are established, they are expected to follow host country organizations' preferences. Plural organizations believe that local (foreign) nationals who are responsible for day-to-day operations in the host country know what is best for them and that, as long as they continue making a profit for the home country organization, they may be left alone. The top managers in plural organizations often have an ethnocentric perspective on management and consider their own way of doing things as the best. A multinational organization or corporation (MNC) allows for partial structural integration of host-country personnel into informal networks, potentially leading to reduced prejudice and discrimination. However, it is still considerably challenging for those outside the home country, who may not strongly subscribe to the prevailing cultural norms of the MNC, to climb the upper echelons of corporate hierarchy. These kinds of organization are also called polycentric organizations.

Multicultural organizations

Multinational and **multicultural organizations** are both culturally heterogeneous, with the big difference being the latter's valuing of cultural diversity. Multicultural organizations identify with one country, and there is recognition of internal co-cultural diversity within the organization and its national boundaries. These organizations are characterized by full structural and informal integration of cultural minorities, an absence of prejudice and discrimination, and minimal intergroup conflict. This kind of organization provides functional cross-cultural and diversity management training and workshops, as employees collectively work toward inclusivity and integration.

International organizations **International organizations** identify with two or more countries, with each country's personnel following their own distinct cultural attributes. The home or parent company is collaborative in transferring and facilitating the adapting of the home organization's knowledge or expertise to foreign markets. At the same time, both units work synergistically by sharing common functions across regions. An international orientation is extremely important to these organizations, and they work interdependently with regional (foreign) headquarters to develop local corporate strategies and plans with local research and development, product innovation, capital expenditure, executive selection and training, among others. These organizations are also known as *regiocentric*.

> **What do you think?** Most likely, either your school or workplace has local (e.g., ethnic, sex, age, sexual orientation, physical ability), and national diversity. What aspects of diversity do you see within your organization (business, religious institution team, family, school, etc.)? Does your organization actively encourage diverse perspectives as well as identities? In what ways does your organization respect, promote, ignore, or marginalize diversity? What are behaviors that you, yourself, engage in to support or marginalize diversity?

Global organizations **Global organizations** identify with the global system. They treat the entire world as an integrated and highly interdependent whole. The focus of the entire organization is on developing and growing world markets with local objectives. One's affiliation with her or his organization becomes more important than nationality. Global organizations operate as stateless corporations in establishing universal standards with required local modifications. Subsidiaries across foreign markets work in unison to meet worldwide consumer demands and allocate resources. Operating virtually borderless, the organizations extend good ideas and strategies across foreign operations; they overcome political barriers with good intentions; they practice corporate citizenship and responsibility; and they exchange financial, technological, and human assets. These organizations are also known as *geocentric*.

Transnational organizations **Transnational organizations** recognize that no one approach to global competitiveness represents the final truth and that each method has its own merit (Bartlett & Ghoshal, 2002). Therefore, transnational corporations make selective decisions regarding costs, assets, and resources allocations, efficiency and innovation processes, and flow of products, people, and information. Transnational corporations develop flexible responsiveness to changing customer tastes, technologies, and regulations by building "systematic differentiation of roles and responsibilities into different parts of its organization" (p. 71). They also empower the local (foreign) subsidiary to play the key role in its national operations. Finally, they encourage managers to develop shared vision and individual commitment toward a worldwide learning and sharing of knowledge.

National/corporate cultures

It is not a stretch of our imagination to think that most corporate cultures represent the national cultures from which dominant or parent organizations emerge. The leadership of an organization has tremendous influence on how cultures are executed and performed. However, corporate culture itself develops from a mutually shared but implicit understanding among the majority of the people regarding their assumptions about reality, truth, time, and space, about human nature, activity, and relationships (Schein, 1992). Likewise, Trompenaars and Hampden-Turner (1998) argue that there are three aspects of organizational structure that determine corporate culture: the relationship between employees and their organization; the hierarchical system that identifies supervisors from subordinates; and the general views of employees about the organization's destiny, mission, and objectives, and their roles in all of this (1998). Providing a two-dimensional perspective on corporate cultures based on equality-hierarchy and person-task orientation, Trompenaars and Hampden-Turner (1998) identified four types of corporate culture: family, Eiffel Tower, guided missile, and incubator.

Family A **family** metaphor for corporate culture implies a traditional head of the household, or "father" figure at the top of the organizational hierarchy. This kind of culture is personal, with face-to-face relationships, while also remaining power-oriented and perhaps even authoritative. The organizational leader is considered to be in a position of power, given great authority but expected to care for employees like his or her children and act in their best interest. Despite the nature of power embedded within this position, this power is looked upon as intimate, well-meaning, and non-threatening. Employees desire the leader's approval and this approval, when achieved, is considered a reward in itself. Workers in such organizations work collaboratively like most family members and toward the collective good of the organization or family unit. While there is a definite pressure to perform, this pressure is moral and social rather than financial or legal.

Eiffel Tower Given its strictly vertical and unidirectional structure, the **Eiffel Tower** metaphor for corporate cultures represents a bureaucratic division of labor with clearly prescribed roles and functions for individual workers. Successful planning and implementing of corporate strategy and vision depends on all personnel playing their designated roles and responsibilities. The boss in this kind of a corporate culture just happens to be a person, because essentially this person is a role that could potentially be played as easily by someone else. Unlike a supposed benevolent family-like hierarchy in the family-style corporate culture, the different levels of hierarchy in an Eiffel Tower culture are clearly defined, and roles, duties, and responsibilities are unequivocally conveyed to you. Because one's power and authority come from the role one plays within the organization, they do not extend beyond that specific corporate environment. Individual workers are valued for their contributions to corporate goals, but personal relationships are avoided in such cultures, to maintain objective judgment and avoid favoritism.

Guided missile These corporate cultures work on egalitarian principles but remain impersonal and task-oriented, like the Eiffel Tower-based organizational structures. **Guided missile** organizations are task-oriented, focus on the end goal, and assign responsibilities to teams or project groups with different levels and kinds of expertise. These kinds of groups tend to be temporary, and relationships dissipate with the conclusion of the project at hand. Members within these cultures are not affectionate or loyal to each other or their groups. As groups dissolve, members will join other groups to work on new projects. Changes happen frequently and are easily accepted. Motivations are generally intrinsic and because a number of differently specialized individuals work together on a temporary basis, these cultures tend to be individualistic and performance based.

Incubator **Incubator** cultures believe in individual fulfillment and satisfaction from work. They allow individuals to indulge their natural creative selves and provide multiple opportunities for self-expression. The logic of such cultures is to enable a break from mundane work routines and monotony. Incubator cultures are personal as well as egalitarian. Individuals perform crucial roles as they complete innovative projects and services. These organizations are typically entrepreneurial, and individuals working here are not constrained by organizational loyalties; rather, employees continue to stay with the organization based on an emotional commitment to the nature of their work and its potential reach and scope. As with the guided missile, motivation is intrinsic, and individuals may easily put in 70–80 hours a week because they enjoy what they do and do not consider it work.

You will notice that in all of the previous discussion, we have refrained from using the names of specific countries as examples of the different cultural elements. We do so on purpose, to avoid placing national cultures into mental boxes and to prevent stereotyping of individuals just because they are from a specific country. It is easy to read these cultural dimensions and then associate an individual we know from a particular culture with those characteristics. Not only is there difference within cultures, such as by age group (see the "What do you think" text box on China's "Me Generation" earlier in this chapter, to see how China illustrates this example), but even organizations within any given culture might adopt one style or another.

What do you think? Many authors (e.g., Keyton, 2005) describe how each organization has its own "culture." Think about an organization to which you belong (company, team, family, school department, etc.). Which of the metaphors best illustrates your organization's structure? Describe the ways people communicate. For example, what do people call the boss, and how open is communication? Are co-workers cooperative or suspicious of each other? What type of ceremonies or celebrations does your organization have? What are public or informal, private stories people tell about founders, co-workers, and so on? What do these say about the values, self-image, and assumptions of your organization?

Corporate responsibility: How can my company make a difference?

Case studies of corporate social responsibility

In today's fast paced, money-grabbing, success-hungry, highly competitive global business environment, how much should organizations worry about being socially responsible? The question is itself meaningless since organizations can no longer afford to remain silent spectators to the many concerns that abound in society. **Corporate social responsibility** refers to the obligatory services and practices organizations should provide to their global communities as a gesture of symbiotic gratitude.

→ Corporate watchdogs consistently rank Timberland Company among the top socially responsible companies. Adhering strictly to their "Code of Conduct," Timberland cultivates leaders and programs that work ceaselessly to reduce environmental impact by developing grassroots community-based service projects, green initiatives including reducing the carbon imprint of their products, community engagement, and incorporating sustainable practices.

→ The Body Shop is another organization that gets high marks for acting in socially responsible ways. By creating a sustainable supply chain strategy and actively engaging in community-driven projects, this organization works to fulfill its corporate mission and values.

→ Terracycle, a green company, is determined to "outsmart waste." It essentially collects (and people are asked to send in their waste) previously considered non-recyclable or hard-to-recycle waste materials and converts them into reusable products. In an organizational culture that represents how this organization actually lives its brands, the inside of its workplace carries a logo of the company made from repurposed drink pouches, with office walls and ceilings decorated with old lamps, movie reels, conference room tables with old bowling alley lanes and doors, handbags made from candy wrappers, office dividers made from plastic bottles, and desks separated by vinyl records, among other creative and innovative reuse of previously used items.

Break it down

Investigate the corporate policy of one of the global companies discussed in this section (Timberland: http://community.timberland.com; The Body Shop: http://www.thebodyshop-usa.com/; Terracycle: http://www.terracycle.net/; you will find a pictorial tour of Terracycle's 99% recycled office at http://www.businessinsider.com/terracycle-office-tour-2011-8). As you think about your college career and the organizational life that will follow, make a list of socially responsible values that you think should guide you as you work for or manage a company. Imagine (and write down) some concrete things you might be able to do, even as an entry-level worker, as you enter your professional life.

Intercultural organizing and communication for civic engagement

In recent years, organizational communication scholars have encouraged activities that take their work from theory to social change and civic engagement. On one hand, employees can organize against unfair organizational policies, as demonstrators in China did to protest

Apple, Inc. policies they claimed included child labor and 24-hour workdays (Moore, 2012, see Figure 15.5). On the other hand, there is also the rise of an entire type of organization directed at civic engagement. Organizational scholar Laurie Lewis (2005) observes that the rise of the civil society sector, which is also known as the nonprofit sector or the third sector, is a global phenomenon. Engaging in our communities, local or international, while remaining mindful of cultural nuances, can lead to personally enriching experiences for the scholar-practitioner, and mutually benefit collaboration partners, and the collective social worlds we cohabit. By communicating ideas, engaging in dialogue, encouraging multiple perspectives, examining tensions that may paradoxically inspire communication (Ganesh & Zoller, 2012), and fostering collaborative networks and relationships, as students and scholars of intercultural organizational communication, we are empowered to serve our global communities. At the same time, as mindful communicators, we need to develop other-centered capacities capable of cultural intelligence and sensitivity.

One organizational scholar who has experienced the emotions of an international intercultural collaboration first hand is Alexandra G. Murphy, professor of Communication Studies at DePaul University in Chicago, USA. Since 2005, Murphy has had an ongoing partnership with one of Kenya's largest religious non-governmental organizations. Based on a model of capacity-building and volunteerism, and in collaboration with her Kenyan partners' goals, Murphy's work with this organization includes designing, implementing, and evaluating their school- and family-based HIV/AIDS education curriculum that reaches over 400,000 children and 1500 families. In an introspective narration of her experiences, she recalls how the partnership called for a subtle "dance between identity, power, and

Figure 15.5 Demonstrators outside an Apple store in Hong Kong protest about the poor working conditions of employees of Taiwan's Foxconn, which manufactures Apple products.
Source: Philippe Lopez/AFP/Getty Images.

collaboration" (Murphy & Dixon, 2012) between U.S. and Kenyan partners, due to the culture- and religion-specific offenses that the latter perceived. Murphy observed that despite a positive U.S.–Kenya relationship, the former is often considered a culturally imperialistic power whose political and economic intentions were not always trusted by the locals.

International intercultural civic engagement activities for social change necessarily include concerns over issues of power, identity, voice, and communication (Murphy, 2012). Because U.S. funds provide the resources for the partnership, the desire for a successful outcome of collaborative efforts creates dialectics of social discourse and political appropriateness, and dilemmatic norms of culturally sensitive education and information dissemination protocols. Culturally motivated to using direct communication to problem-solving, the U.S. partners had to learn to adapt to the Kenyan partners' style of using strategic counter-spaces and a form of silent communication to exert indirect power, while the Kenyans had to learn to understand U.S. styles of communicating in order to make the partnership work. Murphy recommends that in international intercultural social engagement activities, partners reassess communicative acts of exclusion, silence, and agenda-setting in the context of power relations. This engagement includes a self-awareness, on the part of the people involved, of their own positions and advantages in the collaboration, as well as cultural values they might be imposing on the other.

Summary

In this chapter, we defined organizational communication and considered how organizations are evolving in the face of new technology and information, cultural difference, and globalization. In examining the changing nature of work, we discussed virtual organizations and the increasing need for cultural variability, cultural synergy, and cultural intelligence. We then presented Trompenaars and Hampden-Turner's descriptions of cultural differences that mark organizations. We also focused on the two trends that Stohl believes are reactions to globalization: convergence and divergence. Finally, we presented typologies of organizations in terms of how they blend different cultures and how they construct their own corporate cultures. We closed by considering ways that organizations can engage the community for social good, giving case studies of both organizations and individuals who are making a difference. The important point to remember is that intercultural communication is especially important for success in international organizational contexts. Communication is essential to organizing, and organizing without communication is simply non-existent.

KEY TERMS

organizational communication, 307
knowledge workers, 308
psychological contract, 308
old social contract, 308
new social contract, 308
telecommuting, 309
boundaryless careers, 309

portfolio careers, 309
Protean careers, 309
virtual organizations, 309
globalization, 309
organizational culture, 312
universalist cultures, 312
particularist cultures, 312

Discussion questions

1 How would you apply the definition of organizational communication used in this chapter to understanding the role of communication in organizations in your own culture?

2 Are the concepts of the old and new social contract applicable in your culture? How are forms of employment in your culture similar to or different from the discussion here?

3 Stohl's definition of convergence and divergence, while commonly used in discussions surrounding communication and globalization in organizations, may be considered as limiting to the scope of organizational ambitions. What are your thoughts on these two concepts? How would you apply these concepts to global/multinational organizations? Will you be able to identify whether an organization is following the convergence or divergence model, depending on your knowledge of an organization's mission statement, advertising and marketing campaigns, and services or products offered?

4 This chapter highlights the differences between cultures. What are our similarities? There are about seven billion of us cohabiting this Earth today. What are the common pan-cultural concerns and issues that affect us collectively and as world citizens?

Action points

1 Define globalization as you understand it. What is the history of globalization in your culture? How does this phenomenon affect your life, personally and professionally? Now pick a foreign country of your choice and research how globalization started affecting that country. For example, one of our authors who grew up in India in the 1990s watching the only national television channel, Doordarshan, associates globalization with the sudden influx of tens of international cable channels on Indian television.

2 Pretend you are considering developing a business in a foreign country. First, pick a country with which you want to do business. Then, read and research online, the different business/professional etiquettes that might challenge your own cultural values and mannerisms. Brainstorm ideas on how to approach business dealings in this new culture. For example, for businesses to develop and grow successfully in many parts of Latin America, one needs to establish a strong network of connections with

decision-makers. Business cannot be rushed and you really need to get to know your potential future business collaborates on a personal basis first; only when a comfortable level of trust and friendship is established may the business topic be raised. If you are not from Latin America, these practices may seem unprofessional or time-consuming. However, these are accepted as a normal part of doing business in this part of the world.

3 How does your culture define diversity? In the U.S., diversity is collectively understood as differences in race, gender, sexual orientation, social class, national origin, religious affiliations, and (dis)ability status. How do the diverse workgroups in your culture work together in an organization? What are the tensions and issues that are most important to an inclusive organizational culture in your country?

For more information

Bardhan, N., & Weaver, C.K. (Eds.). (2011). *Public relations in global cultural contexts*. New York: Routledge.

McIlrath, L., Lyons, A., & Munck, R. (Eds.). (2012). *Higher education and civic engagement: comparative perspectives*. New York: Palgrave-Macmillan.

Moran, R.T., Harris, P.R., & Moran, S. V. (2011). *Managing Cultural Differences: Global leadership strategies for cross-cultural business success* (8th ed.). Burlington, MA: Butterfield-Heinemann.

Varner, I., & Beamer, L. (2011). *Intercultural Communication in the Global Workplace* (5th ed.). New York: McGraw-Hill.

Wiseman, R.L., & Shuter, R. (Eds.). (1994). *Communicating in Multinational Organizations*. Thousand Oaks, CA: Sage.

References

Bartlett, C.A., & Ghoshal, S. (2002). *Managing across Borders: The transnational solution*. Boston, MA: Harvard Business School Press.

Chang, L.T. (2008). *Factory girls: From village to city in a changing China*. New York: Spiegel & Grau.

CBS News (2008). The "millennials" are coming. *60 Minutes*, May 23. Accessed Aug 29, 2013, at http://www.cbsnews.com/stories/2007/11/08/60minutes/main3475200.shtml

Economist. (2011). Hello world: Japanese firms are waking up to the merits of hiring globe-trotting recruits, August 27. Accessed Nov 11, 2011, at http://www.economist.com/node/21526941

Eisenberg, E., Goodall, H.L., & Trethewey, A. (2009). *Organizational communication: Balancing creativity and constraint* (6th ed.). New York: Bedford/St. Martin's.

Earley, C.P., & Mosakowski, E. (2004). Cultural intelligence. *Harvard Business Review*, October, 139–146.

Fatehi, K. (2008). *Managing internationally: Succeeding in a culturally diverse world*. Thousand Oaks, CA: Sage.

Ganesh, S., & Zoller, H. (2012). Dialogue, activism, and democratic social change. *Communication Theory*, 22, 66–91.

Goudreau, J. (2013). Back to the stone age? New Yahoo CEO Marissa Mayer bans working from home. *Forbes*, 25 February. Accessed Aug 29, 2013, at http://www.forbes.com/sites/jennagoudreau/2013/02/25/back-to-the-stone-age-new-yahoo-ceo-marissa-mayer-bans-working-from-home/

Hall, D.L. (1976). *Careers in organizations*. Santa Monica, CA: Goodyear.

Hall, E.T. (1983). *The dance of life: The other dimension of time*. New York: Anchor.

Herriot, P., & Pemberton, C. (1996). Contracting careers. *Human Relations*, 49, 759–790.

Hofstede, G., & Hofstede, G. J. (2005). *Culture and organizations: Software of the mind – intercultural cooperation and its importance for survival*. New York: McGraw-Hill.

Inkson, K. (2007). *Understanding careers: The metaphors of working lives*. Thousand Oaks, CA: Sage.

Jüttner, J. (2011). German prostitutes speak out: "Corporate sex parties are commonplace". *Spiegel*

Online, May 25. Accessed April 15, 2013, at http://www.spiegel.de/international/business/german-prostitutes-speak-out-corporate-sex-parties-are-commonplace-a-764830.html

Keyton, J. (2005). *Communication and organizational Culture*. Thousand Oaks, CA: Sage.

Kluckhohn, F.R., & Strodtbeck, F.L. (1961). *Variations in value orientations*. Evanston, IL: Peterson and Company.

Lewis, L. (2005). The civil society sector: A review of critical issues and research agenda for organizational communication scholars. *Management Communication Quarterly, 19*, 238–67.

Lewis, R.D. (2006). *When cultures collide: Leading across cultures*. Boston: Nicholas Brealey.

Lieberman, D. (1991). Ethnocentrism and problem-solving. In L.A. Samovar & R.E. Porter (Eds.). *intercultural communication: A reader* (6th ed., pp. 229–234). Belmont, California: Wadsworth.

Marchiori, M., & Oliveira, I.L. (2009). Perspectives, challenges, and future directions for organizational research in Brazil. *Management Communication Quarterly, 22*, 671–676.

Miller, K. (2011). *Organizational communication: Approaches and processes* (6th ed.). Belmont, CA: Wadsworth.

Moore, M. (2012). Apple 'attacking problems' at its factories in China. *The Telegraph*, January 27. Accessed Sep 2, 2013, at http://www.telegraph.co.uk/technology/apple/9043924/Apple-attacking-problems-at-its-factories-in-China.html

Murphy, A.G. (2012). Discursive frictions: Power, identity, and culture in an international working partnership. *Journal of International and Intercultural Communication*, iFirst Article, 1–20.

Murphy, A.G., & Dixon, M.A. (2012). Discourse, identity, and power in international nonprofit collaborations. *Management Communication Quarterly, 26*, 166–172.

Pal, M., & Buzzanell, P. (2008). The Indian call center experience: A case study in changing discourses of identity, identification, and career in a global context. *Journal of Business Communication, 45*, 31–60.

Parsons, T. (1951). *The social system*. Glencoe, IL: Free Press.

Schein, E. (1992). *Organizational culture and leadership*. San Francisco, CA: Jossey-Bass.

Schmidt, W.V., Conaway, R.N., Easton, S.S., & Wardrope, W.J. (2007). *Communicating globally: Intercultural communication and international business*. Thousand Oaks, CA: Sage.

Stohl, C. (2001). Globalizing organizational communication. In F.M. Jablin & L.L. Putnam (Eds.), *The new handbook of organizational communication: Advances in theory, research, and methods* (pp. 323–378). Thousand Oaks, CA: Sage.

Theis-Berglmair, A.M. (2013). Why organizational communication has not gained a foothold in German-speaking communication studies – Until now: An historical outline. *Management Communication Quarterly*, Online First. doi:10.1177/0893318912470078

Trompenaars, F., & Hampden-Turner, C. (1998). *Riding the waves of culture: Understanding cultural diversity in global business*. New York: McGraw Hill.

Trzesniewski, K.H., & Donnellan, M.B. (2010). Rethinking "Generation Me": A study of cohort effects from 1976–2006. *Perspectives in Psychological Science, 5*, 58–75.

Yi, X., Ribbens, B., & Morgan, C.N. (2010). Generational differences in China: Career implications. *Career Development International, 15*, 601–620.

Conclusion

Readers come to a book like this with different reasons and from different backgrounds. Some are students, others business professionals; readers come from around the world or represent diverse cultural backgrounds from within a nation. You might have opened this book with many cultural experiences on your life record, or you might be someone who thinks they have never had a true "intercultural" interaction. Some may have been looking for practical work solutions, and others for ways to integrate culture into social change and civic engagement. Many readers are already involved in civic and political engagement, and others have not yet found or made the opportunity for such engagement.

We see several themes that run through this book. The first is that we all have choice to respond to our surroundings, yet not all choices are equal. Each of us is constrained by birth, age, ability, location, family, and so on. Thus, we live a life between choice and constraint. We feel that cultural knowledge gives us more choice over our actions: we realize how much of what we do is cultural, so have more choices to go against the norm, if we choose to do so, or to go with the norm, but embracing the beauty of culture, rather than passively floating through life, "culturally" speaking.

We framed the book largely in terms of civic and political engagement, because we feel that civic life is important for citizens, regardless of where you live. There are many reasons to be involved in our communities and world. Our goal has not been to persuade you any particular direction regarding political issues, though we would be naïve or deceptive if we told you that we do not have our own perspectives. We hope that you find the book helpful for engaging civically in the world around you.

At the same time, we live in a material world, with school, job, and relationships. So, although we wanted to focus on social action, we also hope you learned more about relationships, consumption and production of media, the global workplace, cross-cultural adjustment and competence, and other practical issues. So, we sought to make the book practical both professionally and civically.

There is a lot to learn about culture. Message production and consumption is complex, with language and nonverbal elements interacting to accomplish many tasks, from expressing feelings to giving directions. We have focused on some specific contexts and aspects of using language, such as rhetoric. And increasingly, we cannot separate our use of language and nonverbal behavior from our understanding of media messages and social media, so we have included discussion of those here as well. Messages—mediated and face-to-face—are impacted by many things: the messages we receive as we are growing up, educational contexts, and, increasingly, the global flow of media.

However, we have highlighted that media and face-to-face messages can be best understood if we look to underlying ideas upon which they are built. These underlying ideas from

Intercultural Communication for Everyday Life, First Edition. John R. Baldwin, Robin R. Means Coleman, Alberto González, and Suchitra Shenoy-Packer.
© 2014 John R. Baldwin, Robin R. Means Coleman, Alberto González, and Suchitra Shenoy-Packer.
Published 2014 by John Wiley & Sons Ltd.

one perspective might be things such as cultural values and the beliefs and norms that intersect with those values. We have introduced (and evaluated) several frameworks of such values; but if you travel abroad or work with people of a specific group or culture, the information here should serve only as a springboard into your own investigation of specific cultures. We all continue to learn all our lives about differences and similarities that unite us. From a different perspective, our face-to-face and mediated communication are also built upon underlying systems of ideas—"ideologies". And in every society, these sets of ideas struggle together, as groups seek prestige and power to define terms. We hope that awareness of the existence of these ideas and how they are maintained, negotiated, and at times manipulated will make you a more responsible user and producer of messages.

Finally, we hope that throughout this book you have found the delight in understanding others and ourselves that has driven us, as authors, to investigate the rich areas of culture and communication. We welcome your insights and thoughts on the book, as we continue to build each other up and sharpen each other for the task of making this a more harmonious and equitable world for all.

Glossary

Accommodating (yielding): A conflict approach in which one party gives in to the requests or demands of the other

Acculturation: The process of learning another culture, and one's sense of identification with that culture—in part or whole—either through moving to live in that culture or through two cultures living side-by-side in the same geographical space

Adjustment: Broadly defined, the process one goes through changing one's behavior and adapting psychologically in transition to another culture

Adjustment stage: The third stage of the U-curve, in which travelers feel a growing sense of understanding and being able to live and succeed in the new culture

Agency: The degree of choice we are aware of having in a particular situation

Alienated approach: An approach to returning home from another culture in which the traveler becomes overly critical or bitter about the home culture

Altruism: The notion of doing good for someone, even a stranger

Anxiety: Feelings of uneasiness, tension, or apprehension that occur in intercultural interactions

Appreciation: The attitude and action of not only accepting a group's behaviors, but also seeing the good in them, even adopting them, and actively including the individuals of a group

Arbitrator: A neutral, objective, third party who can resolve a conflict based on the facts of the conflict situation presented to her or him

Argot: Language used by those in a particular underclass, often to differentiate themselves from a dominant culture (e.g., prostitutes, prisoners)

Arms-length racism: A form of racism in which we might be friendly toward people of other races, but want to keep them at a distance, such as not having them as neighbors, friends, or romantic partners

Assimilation: Giving up one's own culture to adopt another; that is, accepting both behaviors and underlying ways of thinking

Asylum seeker: Someone who is seeking legal protection from the new state, rather than simply moving there because of conditions of strife

Attitude: A disposition to relate to things, actions, or people in certain ways

Attribution: A process by which we give meanings to our own behavior and the behavior of others

Avoiding (withdrawing): A conflict approach in which individuals prefer to simply avoid confrontation with the offender or may be afraid of consequences resulting from a direct confrontation of the issue

Axiology: A set of assumptions about the role of values in research

Backchanneling: Verbal and paralanguage cues used to indicate we are listening to another communicator

Background phase: The initial phase of negotiation, in which parties assess their position, consider what they know of the other parties, and plan out their communication language

Basso's hypothesis: A hypothesis by anthropologist Keith Basso, upon observing use of silence among the Apache, that people may use silence to respond to situations of uncertainty

Behavior valence: In expectancy violation theory, the positive or negative evaluation we give to a behavior that violates our expectancies

Belief: An assumption that someone has about the nature of something; a cognition (thought) about the connection between two or more concepts

Belief system: A set of interrelated beliefs, including values, world view, norms, and mores of a culture

Booty call: A relationship form in which two partners hold no expectation of relational intimacy or fidelity, but when one contacts the other for sex, the second person complies

Boundaryless careers: The notion of individuals moving between organizations with increasing frequency

Breadth: In social penetration theory, the number of topic areas about which we self-disclose

Intercultural Communication for Everyday Life, First Edition. John R. Baldwin, Robin R. Means Coleman, Alberto González, and Suchitra Shenoy-Packer.
© 2014 John R. Baldwin, Robin R. Means Coleman, Alberto González, and Suchitra Shenoy-Packer.
Published 2014 by John Wiley & Sons Ltd.

Cable systems: Communication systems that are limited by the reach of the wires, which transmit the TV signals

Capitalism: An economic system based on exchange through markets and the private ownership of capital

Categorical imperative: An ethical approach in which there is a clear right or wrong, regardless of culture or circumstance, based on logic

Categorization: The mental process of grouping things, attributes, behaviors, and people into like clusters

Channel: The medium through which a message travels from an information source to a destination

Chronemics: The conceptualization and use of time

Civic engagement: Involvement in the community, regardless of politics

Classification: How we understand things and people in terms of categories

Co-cultural communication: Communication between people of different groups within a larger, dominant culture

Co-cultural group: A group or culture that exists within the same space as other groups or cultures, sharing some aspects of a dominant culture

Code: A set of related sounds/images that represent an idea

Code-switching: Changing linguistic forms of speech, whether between registers, between elaborated or restricted codes, or between languages

Collaborating (integrating): A conflict approach in which parties seek to maximize their own rewards while also facilitating the meeting of the goals of the other party

Color blindness: A strategy for reducing prejudice in which people attempt to ignore "race" or ethnicity in social interaction

Communication: The process of creating and sending symbolic behavior and the interpretation of behavior between people

Communication accommodation theory: A theory that seeks to predict how people might adjust their communication in certain situations, the various factors that lead to such changes, and the outcomes of different types of changes

Communication appropriateness: Following rules of a context or relationship in communication

Communication competence: A combination by which a communicator is both effective and competent

Communication effectiveness: The ability to accomplish our desired tasks through communication

Communication for social change/developmental communication: Communicative efforts to bring more development to other communities

Communication system: The set of signs and symbols we use to transfer ideas, emotions, or impressions to others

Communicative engagement: Participating in civic dialogue and being fully aware and expressive in public deliberation

Communicator reward valence: In expectancy violation theory, the perceived reward or punishment that we think we can receive from a person who violates our expectancies

Competing (dominating): A "zero-sum" conflict approach in which one party is concerned primarily with meeting their own goals, seeking to win the conflict regardless of cost to the other party

Compromising (conceding): A conflict approach in which each party makes concessions, giving up some goals to achieve others

Conflict: A difference in values, processes, expectations, or results—real or perceived, and related to interpersonal relations or decision-making content—between two people or groups

Conflict aftermath: The outcome of an evaluation of outcomes as being productive or unproductive at each stage

Confucian work dynamism: A cultural orientation based in Confucian philosophy that values respect for tradition, thrift, persistence, and personal steadiness—that is, a long-term pragmatism

Connotation: The set of feelings an individual associates with a particular word

Constitutive approach: A view of social reality that suggests that we create social reality through communication, rather than culture, sex, and race merely predicting how we communicate

Contact cultures (high- and low-contact cultures): Cultures that differ in the degree to which members tend to seek more sensory input during face-to-face interaction through various nonverbal channels

Contact hypothesis: A theoretical statement that suggests that the more time people from groups that do not like each other spend with each other, the better group relations will become

Convergence (1): The process of changing our behavior to be more like that of the person with whom we are speaking

Convergence (2): A hypothesis that suggests that as a result of a set of imperatives embedded in today's globalizing business economy and communication technologies, more and more organizations follow similar structures and operational patterns across markets and foreign nations

Conversational episode (CE) or communication ritual: A portion of a conversation that has a distinct beginning and ending

Core countries: Wealthier nations that drive economic and media growth in the world

Corporate social responsibility: The obligatory services and practices organizations should provide to their global communities as a gesture of symbiotic gratitude

Crisis stage: The second stage of the U-curve, in which travelers go through a period of stress, often feeling a need to complain or withdraw, with symptoms of stress, fatigue, powerlessness, depression, or even psychosomatic sickness

Critical: An approach to research with assumptions that social inequalities and injustice exist and that research and theory should seek to address these

Cross-cultural communication: Research that involves comparative studies between cultures

Cross-over: Adaptation of media products from one country to another

Cultural communication: The study or practice of communication in a single culture

Cultural heterogeneity: Dissimilarity and diversity among cultural components

Cultural imperialism: The view that global media are the purveyors of certain cultural and political—usually Western—values to the exclusion of others in the weaker countries of the world

Cultural intelligence: An outsider's seemingly natural ability to interpret someone's unfamiliar and ambiguous gestures the way that person's compatriots would

Cultural myth: A narrative that is popularly told to teach preferred ways of behaving

Cultural relativism: An approach to ethics and social research that states that we should not make moral or ethical judgments upon other cultures and that each culture should determine for itself what is right

Cultural synergy: The nature of relationships and networks that can develop between individuals and organizations, when people become culturally aware and competent in cross-cultural communication situations

Cultural trope: A literary formula upon which media producers draw, in which media have certain formulas—types of shows, standard plot lines, typical characters, etc.

Cultural values: Values held by the majority of members of a given culture

Culture: The way of life of a group of people, including symbols, values, behaviors, artifacts, and other shared aspects, which continually evolves as people share messages; and is the result of struggle between different groups who share different perspectives, interests, and power relationships

Culture shock/cultural adjustment: A sense of anxiety experienced in a new culture, usually over a longer period of time, as a result of losing a sense of the expected social cues one has in one's own culture

Deculturation: The process of unlearning one's own culture when one lives for an extended period of time in a different culture

Denotation: The relatively objective dictionary-type definition of a word

Depth: In social penetration theory, the intimacy of detail that we self-disclose

Developmental communication/communication for social change: Communicative efforts to bring more development to other communities

Dialectic: For Aristotle, the rigorous methods for testing competing claims used by scientists and other experts

Dialectics/dialectical tension: A tension between opposing "poles" or aspects of a relationship in which both ends of each tension are always present, both contradicting and completing each other

Dialogic ethic: An ethical approach in which we converse directly with people of other cultures before affirming ethical stances that involve those people

Diaspora: Where the people of one geographic area and group spread out across many different cultures

Diasporic citizen: A person who is a member of a population that has moved or been displaced

Differentiated and undifferentiated codes: Language codes characterized by more (or less) levels of difference between speech registers, depending on the person with whom we are speaking

Diffusion: The spread of artifacts, behaviors, and ideas across a group or culture or between groups or cultures

Directive: In speech acts theory, speech used to influence the behavior of another person

Discourse (1): There are two competing definitions. A type of language usage for a particular situation (e.g., courtroom discourse, interview discourse)

Discourse (2): The way that a notion is described in terms of other ideas in society (e.g., the discourse of beauty)

Discursive elements of language: Elements of language use linked to a broader pattern of meaning

Display rules: Cultural rules about the display of emotion, indicating when, to whom, in what context, and how much we should show certain emotions

Distributive, or positional negotiation: Negotiation that involves competitively pushing for our own goals and agenda with little regard to the other party

Divergence (1): When we highlight our own communication style when talking with people from other groups to mark it as different from our communication

Divergence (2): The fragmentation of peoples into smaller identities and networks of association, focusing on individual, organizational, and cultural meanings and differences in response to forces of globalization

Division: The different beliefs and ways of interacting that potentially lead to intercultural conflict

Dualism: A supposed opposition of two concepts or characteristics, for example as they pertain to identities, in which the terms contradict each other

Duality: A combining of two oppositions in discourse (imagery or words) in which the two oppositions seem to work together

Efficacy, self-efficacy: A belief that we can accomplish a task to which we set ourselves

Eiffel Tower: A metaphor for corporate cultures that represents a bureaucratic division of labor with clearly prescribed roles and functions for individual workers

Elaborated code: A way of speaking in which people spell out the details of meaning in the words in a way that those outside of the group can understand them

Emblem: A gesture that has an explicit verbal translation that is known among most members of a group

Emic approach: An approach to researching culture in which researchers seek to set aside their own understandings and understand a culture's meanings or behaviors from the perspective of the culture

Enculturation: The process of learning one's own culture

Epistemology: A set of assumptions about knowledge and what counts as data

Ethical egoism: An ethical approach in which we make choices based simply on what seems good or beneficial to us, without regard for others

Ethics: How we judge the rightness or wrongness of our interactions with others

Ethnic cleansing: The attempt to remove a population by murder or forced deportation from a country or area of a country

Ethnicity: A sense of shared history and geographical ancestry, usually along with other markers, such as culture, language, or religion

Ethnocentrism: A perception in which people see their group as the center of everything, possibly superior to others, using their group or culture as a reference to judge other groups

Ethnography of communication: A method of research and writing that involves detailed observing, usually involving interaction with people, to understand the lives of a group of people

Ethnophaulism: A racial slur, or name for another group

Etic approach: An approach to researching culture in which researchers start with a framework or theory developed outside of cultures and apply it to cultures, for example to compare cultures on some dimension

Exacting style: A communication style in which speakers give information as necessary

Exaggerated style: A communication style in which speakers use language not so much to describe reality precisely, but to embellish upon it (e.g., exaggeration, metaphor)

Exclusion: A response in which a dominant cultural group simply negates the existence of an immigrant or minority group, having no relations with them

Exogamy: Marrying outside of one's perceived group, as opposed to *endogamy*, marrying within one's group

Expectancies: Expectations for nonverbal and verbal behavior based on our culture, our personal preferences, and our knowledge of the other communicator

Face: The image that people want others to have of them in interaction

Family: A metaphor for corporate culture that implies a traditional head of the household, or "father" figure at the top of the organizational hierarchy

Fansubbed: Translated subtitles on video content that are generated by fans rather than the producers

Faux pas: A mistake we make in our own or another culture; a breach of etiquette that brings embarrassment to self or others

Feedback: Some sort of verbal or nonverbal response, to the sender

Felt conflict: When the parties in conflict personalize their issues and involve egos in the assessing of their individual motives, and those of the institutions and others

Formal time: A time reference to a specific time on the clock

Friends with benefits: A relationship form in which two partners agree that they are just friends, but they occasionally have sexual interaction

Fundamental attribution error: An error of perception in which we overestimate the role of personal characteristics in someone else's behavior and do not place as much weight on context

Gender: Cultural and social expectations based on biological sex

Global media: Sources of mass communications that involve the transmission of messages, formats, programming or content across national boundaries

Global organizations: Organizations that treat the entire world as an integrated and highly interdependent whole

Globalization: The interconnected nature of the global economy, the interpenetration of global and domestic organizations, and communication technologies that blur temporal and spatial boundaries; the social, cultural, economic, and political integration of different parts of the world, facilitated by the movement of goods, capital, ideas, and people between nations

Glocalization: A mix of "globalization" and "localization," meaning the interaction of global and local processes, products and influences

Golden mean: An ethical approach in which people avoid extreme positions, or choose the middle road in making ethical choices

Guided missile: A metaphor that represents organizations that are task-oriented, focus on the end goal, and assign responsibilities to teams or project groups with different levels and kinds of expertise

Guilt: A negative emotion that entails personal responsibility for a wrong committed

Guilt culture: A culture in which people are more likely to be motivated by a sense of remorse when they behave badly, based on a sense of personal responsibility

Haptics: Nonverbal behavior involving touch

Hate crime: An act of open discrimination, vandalism, physical or sexual abuse, or other harmful behavior (including "flaming" behaviors on Internet video and news sites) that is based on group belonging

Hegemony: Some form or level of control over another group, such as political, cultural, or economic power; how the powerful keep their power in a society, largely by making their (dominant) ideologies seem commonsense, taken-for-granted and not worthy of questioning

Heterosexism: A system of images, policies, and collective thought that privileges heterosexual relationships and marginalizes or disenfranchises those in homosexual relationships

High-context cultures: Cultures in which meaning is more often implicit, that is, inside of the communicators, because they know what to expect based on the circumstance and on role and status relationships

High culture: The activities and expressions that represented what people believed to be moral and intellectual refinement (opera, theater, museums)

Homophobia: An irrational fear of someone who is lesbian or gay

Honeymoon stage: The first stage of the U-curve, in which travelers feel a time of happiness and excitement as they first arrive at a new culture

Humanistic: A perspective to research that assumes that humans are unique from other aspects of the natural world, such as through their cognitive abilities, ability to make choice, or symbolic nature

Humanistic principle: An ethical approach that states that we should treat others well and not do anyone harm

Hybridity (1): The blending of cultural elements from two or more cultures, such as when a portion of a diasporic group moves to a single region and cultures influence each other; the blend is usually favored or directed by the group with more power

Hybridity (2): The view that cultures are inherently mixed, and not pure, because they are formed through histories of borrowing, copying, and mutual influencing

Hyperexplanation: A form of convergence Whites often use with Blacks or members of other minority groups (U.S.), including repetition, grammar and word choice simplification

Identification: When communicators connect their perspective to that of another; the opposite of division

Identity politics: The practice of laying claim to an identity in order to help ourselves integrate into our communities and fit into parts of our social world; how groups with these identities vie for various types of power—social status, economic power, the power to define social norms, and so on

Ideology: A system of meanings and assumptions that each of us holds to assist us in making sense of the social world as well as our role and function in that world

Immediacy: Verbal and nonverbal behaviors that show warmth, liking, and affiliation

Immigrant: Someone who travels to another culture, with intent to stay permanently

Immigration: The entry into a country by a citizen of another country, who then desires to remain in that country

Impulsive culture: A culture in which thinking while speaking, or learning through communicating, is encouraged; thus students may speak up, even if they are not sure of the answer

Incubator: Organizational cultures that believe in individual fulfillment and satisfaction from work

Individualism/collectivism (I/C): A culture's orientation toward the self in relation to others; the degree to which a culture values individual (or nuclear family) goals and belonging, or adherence to the needs and goals of larger in-groups

Individuation: When we see a person as an individual, rather than simply as a member of a group

Informal time: Time references that refer to more vague expressions of time than formal time, such as "after a while," "later," and so on

In-groups: Those groups to which we see ourselves belonging

Instrumental and affective styles: Whether communication is more goal-directed (instrumental) or emotional and expressive (affective)

Instrumental values: Those characteristics, traits, or "modes of conduct" that people in a culture hold to be important for reaching societal goals

Integration/biculturalism: An approach to acculturation in which travelers or minority members, rather than unlearning their culture, become able to negotiate well both culture of origin and dominant culture

Integration stage: The final stage of the U-curve, in which a traveler reaches a more or less stable identity, taking on the new culture as her or his own

Integrative, or principled negotiation: Negotiation that uses collaborative strategies and consciously considers the needs and expectations of the other party to develop mutually satisfying ends

Intercultural communication: Communication between people of two different cultures in which cultural differences are large enough to impact the production or consumption of messages

Intercultural communication competence: A communicator's ability in another culture both to reach task completion and to do so while also following the appropriate rules of the situation

Intercultural rhetoric: attempts at gaining cooperation in which at least two cultural rhetorical traditions meet

Intercultural transformation: A process in which, through adapting to new culture(s), communicators gain new ways to think, act, and feel beyond our culture of origin

Intergroup communication: Communication in which perception of the other person as a group member becomes important, regardless of real cultural differences

Interlocalization: The mutually influencing interaction between international and local interests and meanings

Intermarriage: Marriage between people of perceived out-groups regardless of the grounds—religious, cultural, racial, and so on

International communication: Often interchangeable with intercultural communication; sometimes refers specifically to national media systems and the role of culture in shaping those systems

International organizations: Organizations that identify with two or more countries, with each country personnel following their own distinct cultural attributes

Internet penetration: The percentage of a given country that has Internet access

Interpretive: A perspective to research in which researchers provide a holistic interpretation of a behavior or text in its context, often admitting that it is the researcher's interpretation, rather than assuming it as a fact

Intolerance: Any thought, behavior, policy, or social structure that treats people unequally based on group terms

Intrapersonal communication: When one articulates messages to him- or herself, even within the mind

Invention: When someone within a culture derives or creates a new artifact, behavioral practice, or idea

Jargon: A vocabulary used by people within a specific profession or area (such as rugby players or mine workers)

Kinesics: Body movement, including gestures, stance, gait (how we walk), posture, and facial expressions of emotion

Knowledge workers: Those individuals with the best access to information and who are involved in the transfer, reprocessing, or transmittal of information

Kuan-hsi: An aspect of Chinese relationships that refers to the use of and developing of relationships as a social resource—similar to *wasta, palanque, blat, clout,* and the *jeito brasileiro*

Language: A system of verbal, nonverbal, and visual symbols that a group pieces together to share meaning

Lasswell's model of communication: A question posed by Harold Lasswell to guide media communication research: "Who, says what, in which channel, to whom, with what effect?"

Latent conflict: Perceived and/or actual incompatibility of values, expectations, processes, or outcomes between two or more parties from different cultures over substantive and/or relational issues

Law: A norm or rule that has been codified—that is, made formal by a government, with punishments established for violation

Leadership: a process of influencing a group of individuals to achieve a common goal

Low-context cultures: Cultures that place more meaning in the "explicit code;" that is, in the words themselves

Low/popular culture: The everyday activities and expressions of people

Maintenance: When we make no changes in behavior when speaking with other individuals or people in other groups

Manifest conflict: When conflict gets exhibited through open physical aggression, verbal expressions, dysfunctional organizational behaviors like sabotage, riots, mistreatment of the hierarchy, and so on

Marginality: A state in which sojourners or minority members end up not identifying with either the new or original culture, often ceasing to want any interaction

Masculinity/femininity: A cultural orientation that describes how the culture orients toward rules of men and women, including how rigid or flexible gender roles are and whether the culture is more direct and goal oriented or relational and face-saving

Media dependency theory: A theory that proposes that people's reliance on media is impacted by and impacts their social networks, the power of media in society, and social structural aspects, such as the complexity of society

Media frames: A concept that describes how media suggest the issues and controversies surrounding the story

Mediator: A neutral third party that tries to resolve disputes with reason and compromise instead of more aggressive measures

Melting pot approach: A response in which a dominant cultural group expects an immigrant or minority group to lose its own cultural identity to become like the dominant culture

Message: A set of symbols—words, sounds, or images—placed together to represent some meaning

Meta-ethic: An overarching guideline of behavior toward other people, which either can or should be applied to people in all cultures

Metaphor: A verbal expression in which an item that is well known is associated with another item that is less well known

Metaphorical archetype: A metaphor deeply embedded in cultural use and highly persuasive in public discourse

Microaggressions: Everyday expressions of intolerance that people of non-dominant racial, sex, gender orientation, and other groups must live with, which are often too subtle to even notice, but which become part of the fabric of one's life

Miscegenation: The marrying of individuals across racial or ethnic lines

Monochronic cultures: Cultures in which people tend to do one task at a time

Monolithic organizations: Highly homogenous organizations that identify with one country and consist of one dominant cultural group

Morality: How someone judges a behavior is right or wrong, good or bad

More: A very strong norm, with negative social results for violating it

Multicultural organizations: Organizations that identify with one country and there is recognition of internal

co-cultural diversity within the organization and its national boundaries

Multicultural person: A person who, through multiple cultural experiences, is able to negotiate various cultures easily, living between or beyond cultures

Multiculturalism/cultural pluralism: A response in which a dominant cultural group allows an immigrant or minority group to maintain both group and new/dominant culture identities

Multinational/plural organizations: Organizations that typically identify with one nationality but do business in several countries

Mutual intelligibility: The common meanings and interests people share in order to understand each other, necessary for identification

Nationalism: A pride in and/or loyalty to our own nation

Negative face: A desire to be seen as autonomous or independent of others

Negotiation: A form of decision-making that involves multiple parties with competing interests, yet with a reason to work those interests out together through exchanging information

New social contract: A new informal contract between employee and employer that breaks with old understandings and expectations of the ties of an employee to an organization

Noise: Physical or psychological interference that keeps the receiver from receiving the message as sent

Norm: An expectation for behavior with a moral component

Nuclear family: A family composed of the parents (father and mother) and their children

Objective culture: The artifacts that a culture produces

Oculesics: A culture's use of eye behavior, particularly gaze

Old social contract: The implicit contract between an employer and employee that ensured lifetime job security and a reasonable pension, in return for which the employee showed commitment to their work and employer, put in a hard day's labor, and showed good behavior

Ontology: A set of assumptions about the nature of reality

Organizational communication: A group of people working together to fulfill organizational and individual goals, by coordinating activities, within varied levels and nuances of organizational structure, while simultaneously being embedded within an environment of other organizations

Organizational culture: A pattern of shared basic assumptions a group learns as it solves its problems of external adaptation and internal integration

Orientalism: An ideology in the West (i.e., White, Judeo-Christian Europe and its former colonies) by which the Orient (especially Asia and the Middle East) becomes a mirror image of what is inferior and alien to the West

Othering: Excluding and rendering other people, based on some identity that they hold, as inferior or alien

Outcome phase: The last phase of negotiation, the culmination of all the events and communicative behaviors that comprised the conflict negotiation process

Out-groups: Groups with which we do not associate or cooperate

Overaccommodate: Converging too much or in ineffective ways

Over-the-air, or terrestrial broadcasting: A system of telecommunications by which signals are transmitted through the air from land-based antenna

Paradigms: A way of seeing or making sense of the world

Paralanguage/paralinguistics: Characteristics of voice and vocalization that are neither verbal nor strictly nonverbal, including rate of speech, volume, intonation, pronunciation, tone of voice, sighs, laughter, grunts

Particularist cultures: Cultures where people give greater attention to relational obligations and contexts and believe in truth as being relative

Patriarchy: A system of male-based power, in which men have authority or dominance (formal and/or informal) over women

Peace principle: An ethical approach that treats the human spirit as the basis for a universal ethics

Perceived conflict: When disagreeing parties become aware of their mutual tension toward each other and experience frustration

Periphery countries: Economically weaker nations that tend to import more products and media than they export, and that often produce primary goods that are used for manufacturing in and distribution by wealthier nations

Personal identity: Our concepts of ourselves as unique individuals; for example, personal characteristics, likes and dislikes

Political correctness: An attempt to change communication through terminology and references

Political engagement: Involvement that includes participation in the political system

Politics: The identification and public negotiation of competing interest

Politics 2.0: How social structures and institutions work to maintain their authority; how these structures gain

our consensus on their legitimacy, and how they gain our consent to control how we live

Polychronic cultures: Cultures in which people may prefer to do multiple tasks at the same time

Portfolio careers: Job records that balance a portfolio of different and changing opportunities instead of a single, full-time job

Positive face: A desire to be seen as competent or included/liked by others

Postcolonialism: A field of study that looks worldwide at problems created by colonization, seeking to bring awareness to these problems and provide empowerment to those harmed by colonial relations

Power: The level of control over another's thoughts, feelings, or behavior

Power distance: A cultural orientation that describes the degree to which social inequality is accepted in a culture, especially if those in the lower status groups accept that inequality as just and natural

Pragmatics: The aspect of language that deals with how we accomplish tasks with language, such as the ways we might make a request in different contexts

Prejudice: An attitude in which we seek to avoid someone or are hostile toward that person because of the attitudes we hold toward the person's group

Proactive approach: An approach to returning home from another culture in which the traveler sees the good and bad in both the host and home culture, taking in her or his identity portions of both

Process: As it refers to communication, the ongoing creation, sending, receiving, and interpretation of a message, often including feedback provided to the sender and the role of the message in the ongoing relationship or social system

Process phase: When the actual negotiation, collaborative engagement, or competition occurs between the parties

Propinquity: Physical closeness between people, and by contrast, virtual closeness, that implies increased contact

Propriety: Engaging in the proper behavior for the proper relationships or situation; saying what is right in different social and relational contexts, as well as saving and giving face

Prosody: The vocalic shaping of utterances, including pitch, volume, tempo, tone, and rhythm

Protean careers: Careers that are managed by the individual, not the organization

Proxemics: The use of interpersonal distance behavior, including territoriality

Psychological adjustment: One of two dimensions of adjustment, referring to one's psychological wellbeing or emotional satisfaction (often measured by looking at travelers' level of depression)

Psychological contract: The implicit contract between an employer and employee defined in terms of an understanding of mutual obligations and expectations

Public sphere: Amorphous (formless) communities where discourse is exchanged, to advance democratic, public participation in the contribution and circulation of ideas

Race: Supposed biological differences between groups, but influenced by social and political considerations

Racism: An action (or thought or communicative behavior) toward another person based on the person's perceived racial belonging, possibly with societal power held by the group of the perpetrator

Rape myth: A set of beliefs that justify men's sexual dominance, especially in terms of unwanted sexual contact with women

Reality: The actual object we perceive in our environment (as it relates to language)

Receiver: A device or instrument through which a destination source decodes or interprets a signal received from an information source

Receiving countries: Countries that consume global media products produced in other countries

Reciprocity: A practice of giving and receiving from others—can include material things, such as gifts, or information, such as in self-disclosure

Redlining: A practice in which banks avoid giving mortgages to people wanting to purchase in certain neighborhoods or to people of different ethnic or racial groups

Redneck racism: A form of racism in which one clearly feels one's group is (racially) superior to other groups; often expressed in clear statements of superiority, racial slurs, and so on

Refence: Allow someone from another group into one's circle of friends or relations, but see that person as an exception to the general feelings or stereotypes one has of that person's group

Reference: The thought image in our mind that either perception of reality or attention to a symbol brings about

Reference groups: Groups that we value and look to for guidance

Reflective culture: A culture in which speaking should reflect careful thought and clear knowledge of an answer

Refugee: Someone who travels outside of her or his country either by force or because of violence, oppression, or threat to freedom or life in one's own land, often based on reasons of group belonging (e.g., race, sex, ethnicity, political affiliation, tribal group)

Register: A form of speaking within a language that includes level of formality and word choice

Relationship: A connection between two or more individuals in which they have both rights and responsibilities toward each other beyond what would be expected in interaction with strangers

Remediation: Doing something concrete to make up to the injured party for a wrong or embarrassment

Resocialized approach: An approach to returning home from another culture in which the traveler sheds the foreign culture and adopts totally to the culture of origin

Restricted code: A way of speaking or "code" used by people who know each other well, including grammar, word choice (such as jargon or argot), and so on

Return culture shock/return cultural adjustment: The process of going through a period of stress when one returns home from a stay in another culture

Rhetoric/rhetorical action: Inducing cooperation through the use of symbols and meanings; for Aristotle, a practical art that seeks to discover the appropriate means for persuading an audience

Rhetorical communication: A message that is planned and adapted to an audience or multiple audiences

Rhetorical tradition: The historical and social influences and ethnic practices that inform a speaker's message

Ritual view of media communication: A view that includes transmission but adds the notion of our understanding of the way our world is portrayed and confirmed in media

Romeo and Juliet effect: When a couple feels it must be stronger due to societal or family pressure (that is, blaming problems on family and society)

Rule: A prescription or cultural belief about which behaviors are appropriate in certain situations

Sapir-Whorf hypothesis: The "linguistic relativity" view of language, which states that the language of a culture dictates the very way that people within that culture can think

Satellite TV: A system of telecommunications whereby a powerful uplinking antenna on earth sends a signal to a communications satellite that is stationed in space

Scientific: A perspective to research that assumes that the social world is predictable, based on internal and external causes, and that systematic research should seek to uncover those causes

Scripts: Cultural rules regarding expected behavior that include expectations of who does what (actors, roles), and any expected sequence of actions in a communication routine

Secondary baby talk: A form of convergence younger people sometimes use with older people, including higher pitch, simpler grammar, use of "we," and so on

Secular culture: A culture in which life problems and solutions are seen in terms of science and human ideas

Segregation: A response in which a dominant cultural group intentionally or unintentionally separates immigrant or minority groups into their own communities

Selective adaptation: A pattern by which an immigrant or minority group chooses some aspects of the dominant culture to adopt, but clearly maintains other aspects of the original culture

Selective attention: The idea that we only pay attention to certain things, often impacted by what we hold to be important, as well as our negative or positive expectations

Selective perception: A mental process through which biases shape how we interpret the stimuli in our environment

Selective recall: A mental process through which we only remember certain things that conform to our expectations or biases

Self-construal: A psychological notion of how strongly we see ourselves independent from others or connected to others

Self-disclosure: revealing things about ourselves to someone else, specifically things that would not normally be known by the other and about which there is at least some risk of sharing

Selflessness: A consideration of the needs of the other

Self-serving (or egocentric) attribution bias: An error of perception in which we give meanings to the behaviors of others and ourselves that protect our self-concept

Semantics: The area of language study that refers to word meanings and lexical choice (the number or type of words available to describe something)

Semiotics: A cross-disciplinary approach that looks at how meaning is conveyed through "signs"

Sending countries: Those nations where global media sources are based and products created

Servant leadership: A style of leadership that places the needs of the followers first

Sexism: A system of ideas, images, laws, beliefs, and practices that work against women in the favor of patriarchy

Shame: In cross-cultural communication research, a negative reflection upon one's group experienced as a result of one's behavior

Shame culture: A culture in which people are motivated more by a sense of social obligation, and are more likely to act in a way to protect the honor or "face" of their group

Sign: The combination of the signified and the signifier and the relationship between them

Sign systems: When different codes are placed together in a text to give meaning

Signified: An object or idea that is represented by a sound or image; part of a "sign"

Signifier: The sound or image that represents a concept or thing; part of a "sign"

Similarity-attraction hypothesis: A research proposition that the more similar we are to people, the more we will grow to like them

Social capital: A concept referring to investment in community, including social organization, trust, networks, a sense of citizenship, and norms

Social construction: The notion that concepts, such as race, gender, or our identities, are created through communication in the context of our social world, histories, and relationships

Social drama: A conflict that arises when a community norm or rule is violated

Social identity: Our self-perception in terms of roles (e.g., student/teacher), relationships (e.g., enemy, brother/sister, lover), or groups to which we belong (e.g., religious, racial, national)

Social movement: Wide-scale, organized activism to accomplish social change

Social penetration theory: A theory of relationship growth that suggests that self-disclosure is what causes people to grow closer together

Social system: A set of individuals, groups, and institutions within a society often working toward a specific function, and the relationships between them

Sociocultural adjustment/cross-cultural adaptation: One of two dimensions of adjustment, referring to one's sense of fitting in and ability to negotiate the culture (such as accomplishing tasks)

Sojourner: Someone who travels to another culture for a longer term, but with intent to return home

Solidarity (relational distance): The degree of familiarity and/or intimacy we have with another person

Space: The physical distance between points

Speaking with: Being an ally to a community; advocating the interests of a community along with its members

Speech acts theory: A perspective that looks at the types of actions people accomplish with speech

Speech code: The system of symbols, meanings, assumptions, and norms for communication adopted by a group of people

Speech codes theory: A theory of communication that considers the uniqueness of the speech codes in each community

Speech community: A group of people that shares a common speech code

Spirit(ual) (or sacred) culture: A culture in which there is more of a sense of presence of the spiritual or divine in everyday life

Stereotype: An oversimplified, often unvarying attribute assigned to a group or to a person because that person is a member of a group

Stigma: A lack of social acceptability of a group or person, sometimes to the point of shame or disgrace

Stress-adaptation-growth dynamic: An approach to cross-cultural adjustment that suggests that adjustment is cyclical: one feels stress from the new culture, but adapts to that stress, leading to new ways to act, think, and feel

Subjective culture: The thought elements of a culture, such as values, beliefs, attitudes, norms, and world view that are shared by a group of people

Subtle racism/prejudice: An intolerance that one still holds toward another person because of the group to which the person belongs, but that is expressed in difficult-to-notice ways

Succinct style: A communication style in which speakers use understatement or silence, giving less detail in a situation than the other styles

Sweatshops: Factories, often in developing nations where there is inexpensive labor

Symbol: A sound or visual representation of the reality

Symbolic: A characteristic of communication that describes how images, words, sounds, or nonverbal behaviors serve to represent something else

Symbolic annihilation of race: When groups and cultures are underrepresented or represented in troublesome manners, such as trivialization or condemnation, especially in media

Symbolic ethnicity: When people represent their ethnicity through signs or symbols, even if they have mostly assimilated to a dominant culture

Symbolic racism: A set of ideas expressing negative feeling toward minority members in a culture, which are embedded in other symbols or behind political attitudes

Syncretic/syncretism: The state of combined systems of thought and influence; an admixture of different ways of being

Taboo: A norm so strong that cultural members may not even talk about it

Technological determinism/media ecology: A theory that proposes that the media or technology we use shape all the rest of social life and culture, and that understates other factors, whether social, cultural, behavioral, or economic

Telecommuting: Working remotely, usually from one's home, with the help of technology

Terminal values: The end-states or desired outcomes of action for individuals

Territoriality: How a person or group perceives of and marks territory

Time: The temporal or sequential distance between points or events

Tolerance: The application of the same moral principles and rules, caring and empathy, and feeling of connection to human beings of other perceived groups

Transactional: A characteristic of communication that describes the way in which both partners produce and consume the messages of the other; that is, it is the give-and-take between two or more people in message exchange

Transmission view of media communication: A view of media in which media are believed to impart, send, give, or *transmit* information from sender(s) to receiver(s), through a fairly linear process

Transmitter: A device or instrument, including media or human voice and body, that we use to transfer symbols to represent some meaning

Transnational organizations: Organizations that recognize that no one approach to global competitiveness represents the final truth and that each method has its own merit

U-curve: A model of adjustment where one arrives in a new culture excited and well-adjusted, goes through a period of crisis, and then adjusts to the new culture

Ultimate attribution error: An error in perception that blends fundamental and self-serving attribution biases in which we give different meanings to the failures and successes of others than to ourselves

Uncertainty avoidance: A cultural orientation that describes the degree to which a culture accepts or dislikes uncertain and ambiguous situations; its orientation to clarity of structure

Uncertainty reduction theory: A theory of relationship growth that states that the better we can predict and explain the behaviors of another person, the more relationships will grow

Universal values: A set of values that some research suggests exist in all cultures to some degree

Universalist cultures: Cultures where people believe in unequivocal definitions and the universal application of right or wrong, and other moral behaviors

Utilitarianism: An ethical approach based on what is practical by determining the greatest benefit for the greatest number of people

Value: An idea or priority that a person (or culture) holds to be important and that serves as a guide for behavior

Vernacular discourse: Local meanings produced by marginalized communities that (1) affirm community membership and (2) critique power relations with the dominant culture

Vernacular rhetoric: The persuasive use of vernacular discourse

Voluntarism: The notion of giving our own time to a charitable organization

Viral: The rapid spread of media products, such as videos, at the person-to-person level to the point of mass distribution

Virtual organizations: Geographically distributed organizations whose members communicate and coordinate their work through the medium of information technology

W-curve: A curve describing a process adjustment, both sojourning abroad and coming home

World view: A set of assumptions or cognitions about things such as the purpose of humans, the nature of deity, the relative position of humans to nature and the rest of the cosmos

Xenophobia: A fear of things different; here, specifically, a fear of groups besides our own

Index

Intercultural Communication for Everyday Life, First Edition. John R. Baldwin, Robin R. Means Coleman, Alberto González,
and Suchitra Shenoy-Packer.
© 2014 John R. Baldwin, Robin R. Means Coleman, Alberto González, and Suchitra Shenoy-Packer.
Published 2014 by John Wiley & Sons Ltd.